Trends in Social Work
1874-1956

A HISTORY BASED ON THE PROCEEDINGS OF
THE NATIONAL CONFERENCE OF SOCIAL WORK

Trends in
SOCIAL WORK
1874-1956

A HISTORY BASED ON
THE PROCEEDINGS OF THE
NATIONAL CONFERENCE
OF SOCIAL WORK

By FRANK J. BRUNO
WITH CHAPTERS BY
LOUIS TOWLEY

COLUMBIA UNIVERSITY PRESS
NEW YORK · 1957

To

HOWARD R. KNIGHT

JUNE 23, 1889–OCTOBER 7, 1947

Farsighted leader; admirable administrator;
inspiring fellow worker; loyal friend

IN LOVING MEMORY OF A
CHERISHED ASSOCIATION

FOREWORD

WHAT HAS COME to be called social work dates back a long way. The expression in practical ways of the common human impulse to help another in distress was bound sooner or later to take organized form; and it did so markedly in this country during the last hundred years or more. One measure, in numerical terms alone, is the fact that approximately half the present annual expenditures of a majority of our states is devoted to the various services performed under the boards of welfare, health, corrections, and care of the insane; and fully half of the personnel of the states' employment is on these pay rolls. Including the large numbers in nongovernmental agencies, the total number of persons engaged in these and similar services in this country now almost certainly runs above one hundred thousand. Along with organized religion and education, social work has taken its place as a major concern of the local community, state, and nation.

The third quarter of the nineteenth century saw the beginnings of organized work in this field on a national scale. Then it was that national bodies interested in prison reform, public health, and the application of science to human relations were formed. In the same period the National Conference of Social Work came into being. It included in its scope dependency, mental disease, delinquency, and problems of health; as time went on it widened its interests to include the whole field of the public and private social services. That was a period when population was growing rapidly in the United States, people were moving westward; a developing industrial economy was drawing multitudes of workers to congested population centers; a period when ideas, social theories, and convictions were changing rapidly, and when technical knowledge and the exploitation of the natural resources of the nation speedily advanced.

The needs of the country, as seen by the small but capable group of pioneering social work leaders of that day—devoted men with a strong sense of public service—placed new and larger responsibilities upon social work and other efforts to promote the common welfare. They heard the summons for more efficient operation and a greater return in human values for the energies and resources expended. The time had come when problems could no longer be faced by one locality alone; the outlook, as one leader put it, must transcend the narrow boundaries of a state. The times called for a national clearinghouse of ideas and experience; a national medium for the exchange of opinion; a national forum in which to debate and appraise differing theories, policies, and practice; a platform from which could be presented fresh information on social problems and methods of dealing with them as the frontiers of knowledge were moved forward.

The record shows the purpose to have been diligently pursued. Over the years public administrators, leading thinkers in many fields, social philosophers, moralists, and practical and experienced workers responsible for day-to-day results differed, debated, discussed, and presented their factual and other conclusions on many issues. Among them were questions such as these: the right of the state to remove a child from his family because of poverty; the appropriateness of classifications of the poor as "worthy" or "unworthy"; the merits of the cottage system of housing insane patients; removal of children from almshouses; removal of the insane from almshouses; best methods of caring for epileptics; the practical value of reformation versus punishment in protecting society from crime; the usefulness and workability of indeterminate sentence and of parole; the relative merits of advisory or supervisory boards as against boards of control or administration; abolition of physical restraint of the insane; the possibility of training the feebleminded; institutional care of children as contrasted with foster home placement; the advisability of instituting special courts to try children's cases; relief as a basic right to those who are poor through no fault of their own; the place of recreation in a welfare program; the inportance of prevention of poverty, disease and delinquency as against, or in addition to, correction; the need of training on a professional level for social work; the community's stake in eliminating child labor; the community's stake in the prevention of unemployment and industrial accidents, and in the elimination of unhealthful working conditions; methods of diagnosing individual and family social disabilities; the desirability of cash relief; the social survey as a method of discovering and analyzing community problems and interpreting needs to the public; effective dissemination of information on personal hygiene and other phases of individual well-being; the importance of more reliable statistics and statistical methods in dealing with social ills and in administering social agencies; the place of research in advancing the social welfare. Literally hundreds of problems deeply concerned these men and women as they came together annually for the lengthy Conference sessions and later polished their contributions for the printed record.

Thus a new national agency took form. It grew from a handful of public charity officials to a body of 7,000 members, who came to the annual meetings to confer over what, in large measure, they were learning by doing. Some of their experience got into the Conference *Proceedings*, and some of it was stored away in the minds of workers of the period. It is an important part of our social heritage today.

One may say with some confidence, therefore, that this account of the Conference, which winnows out, records, and interprets this evolution in thought and attitudes, is an important segment in the total history of the United States. Much has been written on the development of our political institutions, our economic and industrial progress; our social history lags behind. Until it is more fully set forth, the significant lessons we may learn for our own sake and the peculiar contributions of America to world developments cannot be fully understood or appraised. Toward a more adequate chronicle of one significant aspect of our nation's social experience this reflection of the National Conference of Social Work is an important contribution.

The Conference has been fortunate in the choice of its historian. Mr. Bruno has not only been painstaking in detailed study of the documentary material of the organization, in search for outside data which would illuminate the record, and in pursuit of individuals who could supplement his findings; he has also brought to his task many years of personal experience as practitioner in social work and as teacher and head of one of our leading social work professional schools, his own rich knowledge of contemporary thought and social movements, and a rare ability to interpret Conference events against their changing national and world background. His timely labors have put the Conference greatly in his debt. The Conference, in undertaking this history, and Mr. Bruno in carrying it through, have in turn rendered invaluable service to future students of social work, to students of American history, and, we believe, to the public welfare.

SHELBY M. HARRISON

New York, New York   *Former General Director*
December 30, 1947   *Russell Sage Foundation*

FOREWORD TO THE SECOND EDITION

*I*T IS APPROPRIATE and timely that this significant chronological and historical record of social welfare be brought up to date. The 83d Annual Forum, held in St. Louis in May, 1956, marked the end of the National Conference of Social Work—after forty years we changed our name to the National Conference on Social Welfare.

The basic reason for the change was that "social welfare" is now considered to be a broader term than "social work" and as such constitutes a more accurate description of the subjects which are included in the Annual Forum programs and the many individuals who attend annual forums and who are not career social workers. The Conference membership in a sense reaffirmed our real and historic purpose to provide a free and open critical discussion and examination of basic issues and problems in social work and related fields. The magic words "National Conference" which have become so much a part of the social work vocabulary are unchanged. The initials and the symbol will remain the same.

And so, the year 1956 may be considered a bench mark in our history. An understanding of the past and an awareness of social work's position in the march of events are essential as a basis for charting our future. Karl de Schweinitz made an eloquent plea for the contribution of history to a stronger profession at the 1956 Annual Meeting of the Council on Social Work Education. "Speaking for the contribution of history," he said, "in this movement toward synthesis, I hope that social work will increasingly cultivate the long view and that, acting as a social force, it will help to incorporate perspective as a characteristic of our culture." The National Conference will continue as it has in the past to relate the social work profession to the social welfare field and to build on the knowledge of the past so that we can go forward.

The National Conference is fortunate that Louis Towley was available to continue the history written by the late Frank Bruno. Mr. Towley worked closely with Mr. Bruno in the compilation and writing of the original volume. His keen appreciation of historical events and their role in creating social issues and problems equips him admirably as our historian.

JOE R. HOFFER
Executive Secretary
National Conference
on Social Welfare

Columbus, Ohio
February, 1957

PREFACE

*I*N THE winter of 1945–46, the Executive Committee of the National Conference of Social Work, as part of its plan for the seventy-fifth meeting in the spring of 1948, authorized the publication of a volume recounting the development of the Conference. The assignment was accepted by the author on February 1, 1946, with instructions to have the manuscript ready by the fall of 1947, and to limit its size to not much more than three hundred pages.

There is no bibliography on which the book is based, except the *Proceedings* of the Conference. Reference to them is made in the body of the text in two ways: by the date alone, in parentheses, and also with the name of the speaker, the word *"Proceedings,"* and a date, e.g. (Edith Abbott, *Proceedings,* 1940). For influences outside the Conference and for contemporary thought and movement, the author was guided by his own knowledge. Where sources other than the *Proceedings* are drawn upon, acknowledgment is made by a footnote.

The Executive Committee left the author entirely free as to method and content. It placed the Editorial Committee of the Conference at his service as an advisory committee, and at two meetings, in the spring and summer of 1947, the committee offered itself freely and helpfully in discussing the plans and organization of the publication, and the sources of information to supplement the *Proceedings.*

In reconciling the puzzle presented by chronological data that should be organized topically, the device was adopted of dividing the seventy-odd years into three periods: the first ending with the twenty-fifth Conference in 1898; the second ending with the fiftieth Conference in 1923; and the third extending from 1924 to 1946. In each period those topics are included which seemed to be prominent in the minds of the Conference members; but no effort was made to follow any particular topic into the next period, or through all three of them.

No one could possibly be more aware than the author of the limitations of the book. The choice of material, the decision on what to emphasize and, especially, what to omit were his own. In this choice the author was not restricted, either by the action of the Executive Committee or by that of the advisory committee. The limit on the size of the book was an over-all controlling factor. Even if the limit had been much less drastic, a choice would still have had to be made. It is a situation inherent in all historical writings: the volume of source material is far greater than the writer can use, and his book becomes a reflection of his interest by which he selects those data which build up his thesis.

The author has relied heavily on such biographical sources as the *Dictionary of American Biography;* the *Dictionary of National Biography;* the *Encyclopedia of the Social Sciences; Who's Who in America;* and *Who Was Who in America,* and he wishes to express his appreciation for the exact data they contain. He also wishes to thank the Maryland Historical Society and the Wisconsin Historical Society for their prompt and valuable replies to his inquiries. To the many friends among social workers whom he has consulted he makes this grateful acknowledgment of their wholehearted responses to his inquiries. Especially does he recall with pleasure his consultations with the Boston and New York groups held in the summer of 1946, and with Howard R. Knight, the General

Secretary of the Conference, for the gracious way in which he transmitted the instructions of the Executive Committee and constantly held himself in readiness to be of service.

Most of all, I am indebted to Louis Towley, of the staff of the George Warren Brown School of Social Work, at Washington University, who read the manuscript of the entire book as it was prepared and made invaluable suggestions. If its structure is clear and its meaning plain, much of the credit for the result belongs to him.

It has been my good fortune to spend the two summers during the preparation of the book at the State College of Washington, Pullman, Washington, and at Colorado College, Colorado Springs, Colorado, which placed their well-stocked libraries at my disposal. Especially gracious have been the librarian of Colorado College, Louise F. Kampf, and her efficient staff.

FRANK J. BRUNO

Colorado Springs, Colorado
November 25, 1947

CONTENTS

Third Period · 1924–1946

Fourth Period · 1946–1956

First Period · 1874-1898

A FINE TIME of the year is chosen, when days are long, skies are bright, the earth smiles and all nature rejoices; a city or town is taken by turns, of ancient name or modern opulence, where buildings are spacious and hospitality hearty. The novelty of place and circumstance, the excitement of change, or the refreshment of well known faces, the majesty of rank or of genius, the amiable charities of men both pleased with themselves and with each other; the elevated spirits, the circulation of thought, the curiosity; the morning sections, the outdoor exercise, the well furnished, well earned board, the not ungraceful hilarity, the evening circle; the brilliant lectures, the discussions, or collisions, or guesses of great men one with another, the narratives of scientific processes, of hopes, disappointments, conflicts and successes, the splendid eulogistic orations; these and like constituents of the annual celebration, are considered to do something real and substantial for the advance of knowledge which can be done in no other way. CARDINAL JOHN HENRY NEWMAN, "WHAT IS A UNIVERSITY."

I · BEGINNINGS

*O*N MAY 20, 1874, representatives from the State Board of Charities of Massachusetts, Connecticut, New York, and Wisconsin met in New York and organized the Conference of Boards of Public Charities. Invitations to the meeting were sent jointly by the Section on Social Economy of the American Social Science Association and the Massachusetts State Board of Charities.

It was only the short space of eleven years since Massachusetts had created the first board in the country to supervise the administration of the state's charitable, medical, and penal institutions; but the device was so patently useful that by the spring of 1874 eight additional states had set up such bodies and were invited to the meeting to consider the proposal to establish some sort of clearinghouse of ideas and experiences between state boards. In addition to the four states represented at the initial meeting, Rhode Island, Pennsylvania, Michigan, and Kansas acknowledged the proposal and expressed their approval; one, the Illinois board, did not reply.

The New York meeting of 1874 was not the first at which representatives of state boards had met for consultation on their common problems. Frederick H. Wines, secretary of the Illinois board, and Andrew E. Elmore, president of the Wisconsin board, spent several days together in February, 1872, visiting institutions in Wisconsin, and were so impressed with the significance of their mutual discussions that they decided to invite the boards in the upper Mississippi Valley to meet together in

May of that year. Representatives from Wisconsin, Illinois, and Michigan held a two-day session in Chicago at that time. They were so pleased with the venture that they repeated it a year later in Milwaukee on April 15, 1873, representatives from the same three state boards attending. These meetings attracted national attention, and the American Social Science Association embraced the idea and enlarged it to include all the boards of both charity and health in the United States. Subsequent to 1874 boards of health were not invited. There was then in existence a national agency through which public health officials could exchange information: the American Public Health Association, organized in 1872. Some loss probably resulted from the separation of these two closely related fields, although the programs of the National Conference throughout the years usually included subjects in the field of health, and doubtless the programs of the national health organization contained many subjects of social import. Another earlier project, which overlapped the field of the National Conference, was the National Prison Association, organized in 1870. Relations with it were closer than with the American Public Health Association, since several members and officials of the National Conference served in similar capacity for the National Prison Association, which in later years became the American Prison Association.

The American Social Science Association, organized in 1865, was directly modeled after the National Association for the Promotion of Social Science of Great Britain, organized in 1857, and it functioned through four departments, education, health, finance, and jurisprudence, to which a fifth was added in the fall of 1873, social economy. Both the English and the American associations were embodiments of the conviction that the application of science to the problems in human relations would result in new discoveries and improvements in the field of social relationships. The area of social science was defined as "whatever concerns mankind in their social rather than in their individual relations [and] shades off easily and imperceptibly into metaphysics on one side, philanthropy on another, and political economy on a third." It is significant that its method was defined as the statistical interpretation of findings and their application to the entire social situation, and the purpose of social science is to promote human welfare. In one of the earliest statements of purpose of the Association are these words: "to develop the study of social science—to increase public wealth and to insure its proper distribution—[and] the diffusion of those principles which make the strength and dignity of nations." [1]

The Association contained in its membership a liberal sprinkling of the intellectual leaders of the Northern and North Central states of the Union, with the largest number in or about Boston and New York. Samuel Eliot was one of its presidents, as was also George William Curtis, the father of civil service in the United States. The Association was no stranger to conferences, for although outside its own meetings it had called none under its own auspices, yet its members were actively associated with them, and its *Journal* reports many. Enoch C. Wines, secretary of the New York Prison Association, was instrumental in creating the National Prison Association, probably on the initiation of the American Social Science Association, and in calling the First International Penitentiary Congress, which met in London in 1872. The Association's interests overlapped a wide section of the field later covered by the National Conference, such as immigration; [2] compulsory school attendance and child labor; the injury to the insane and to children involved in their retention in almshouses; the reform in penal philosophy being put into practice by Zebulon Reed

[1] American Social Science Association, *Transactions*, July, 1866, p. 13.
[2] In 1871 the Association published a handbook for the guidance of immigrants.

Brockway, then in Detroit; together with many references regarding the opportunities of state boards of charities and the handicaps under which they worked.

During its first session, held under the auspices of the Association, the Conference of State Boards invited other organizations and persons to sit with it and to take part in its discussions. Charles Loring Brace, of the New York Children's Aid Society, was a member of the Association and either sat in the deliberations of the Conference or was represented. Similarly, the New York State Charities Aid was invited and seemed to be a regular attendant as well as having a part in the program. Up to 1878, however, these representatives from other than Association members were not numerous, the meetings of the Conference tending to take on the nature of a section of a scientific association rather than a conference of professional practitioners consulting on their common interests, reporting current ventures, and establishing a common basis of ideas and philosophy. The Wisconsin delegation felt that this was a mistake, that it would be more helpful, if not more dignified, to meet as an independent body; and so, in 1877, Wisconsin announced that it would not send a delegation to the next year's meeting if the Conference were still a function of the Association. Consequently, the 1878 Conference was held without Wisconsin, and at that meeting it was voted to separate from the parent body. The meeting of 1879, therefore, marks the date of the first independent sessions of the Conference, and the name was changed from Conference of State Boards (or Conference of Charities) to the National Conference of Charities and Correction, a name which it bore for nearly forty years, or until it was changed, in 1917, to the National Conference of Social Work to conform to the philosophy of the times.

The declaration of independence from the Social Science Association was not particularly opposed by the members either of the Association or of the Conference, even though there was some overlapping of membership between the two bodies. It quickly resulted in a more vigorous Conference, with an expanded clientele and broader program. Whereas the Conference of 1878 was attended by only twenty-five persons who were not members of state boards, by 1880 the number had grown to over 125, most of whom were representatives of public institutions or agencies and delegates of private bodies.

The charity organization movement, appearing in this country in 1877, at once took an important place with the state boards in the personnel and programs of the Conference, maintaining a position both in numbers and in importance that caused some of the earlier promoters of the Conference to raise the question whether the original idea of the Conference was not being smothered and, possibly, should be rescued by a secession of the state boards.

The Conference changed its direction on its separation from the Social Science Association. It gradually ceased being a body interested in scientific inquiry primarily, and shifted its major emphasis to administration and methods of practice, giving only secondary consideration to scientific procedure under the general title of "prevention." This was both regrettable and inevitable. Its leaders were challenged by the insistence of their day-by-day problems: the numbers of insane were increasing at an alarming rate; children were being brought up in almshouses; the mentally deficient were an increasing menace to the well-being of society; dependency was placing an ever increasing burden on taxpayers, and efforts to treat it were apparently waging a losing battle. These were the matters on which its members had to give an account to their constituents, as well as to the legislatures of their states. They were pressing exigencies which could not wait long for an answer. Then, too, the field of practice and the field of science are selective of their own personnel, and rarely do the two interests combine in the same person. This was illustrated over and over again in the sessions of the Conference throughout its history; one set of papers—a minority—deal with theory, need for research, for examination of the nature of the problems under consideration, and presentations of possible theories or methods not yet used. Such appeals were listened to respectfully, but, for the most part, were not followed up until, at a later Conference, someone else repeated the same appeal, with about the same result. No, the delegates wanted to know and discussed tirelessly such subjects as: Is it better to care for dependent children in institutions or foster homes, and why? How can the growing number of insane be handled? How can pauperism be prevented? And what to do about it all? Now of course, the practitioner has a theory on which he is working; but this is usually a "tacit assumption" and does not often come into the area of debate or criticism; rather is it held without questioning. This dichotomy between theory and practice is not unique to the area under discussion. Practically all vocations and professions suffer from it; but it was peculiarly dangerous here because social theory was as yet tentative, needing the constant corrective of criticism and experimentation, whereas "tacit assumptions" usually lag behind the best current theory and are not easily amenable to change. The adoption of the new name, National Conference of Social Work, in 1917 recaptured the inclusive area of interest in human relations envisaged by the American Social Science Association, but the direction of the Conference remained unchanged.

The necessarily close attention given by the Conference to methods was not without gain, for untrammeled by the control of theory its members were free to experiment with means by which the job could be done, and so laid the foundation for the art of helping. This attention to method or, as it came to be

called, "technique," received reinforcement in the Conference
of 1915 when Dr. Abraham Flexner denied that social work
was a profession because, he claimed, it did not possess a distinct and educationally transmissible technique. Whatever the
merits of such a contention, practitioners were constantly compelled to develop method from the very first in order to secure
public approval, and it is not strange that, being under a constant fire of criticism in their day-by-day job, they should discuss its endless variety when they came to share their experiences with their peers.

2 · THE FOUNDING FATHERS

FOUR MEN, Franklin B. Sanborn, Frederick H. Wines, Andrew E. Elmore, and William P. Letchworth, were early credited with responsibilities for setting the pattern of the first meetings of the National Conference, and while there were general, scientific, and economic philosophies stimulating the thinking and action of the times, which may not safely be ignored, some knowledge of these men—and a few others—will throw light upon its beginnings.

Franklin B. Sanborn (1831–1917), born in New Hampshire, a descendant of forebears who came to America in the flood of Puritan migration in 1640, was a typical New England intellectual, "determined, democratic, liberty loving, positive, pugnacious," with a quick and caustic wit. After leaving Harvard, he moved to Concord to be near Emerson, spending the rest of his life in that home of distinctly American intellectualism. A transcendentalist, he showed the independence of judgment of that group, combined with a sturdy ethical conviction in human affairs. His lives of Thoreau, Bronson Alcott, and Emerson and his description of the Concord School furnish some of the best records of the personalities and philosophy of that brilliant group of American literary philosophers.

Becoming acquainted with John Brown, he served as secretary of the Massachusetts Free Soil Association. When John Brown told him of his plan to seize Harpers Ferry, Sanborn, reluctant to stand apart from action, even when he thought it ill advised, joined the movement. In the troubled times that followed the collapse of John Brown's project, Sanborn was summoned to appear before a Senate committee; rather than face the inquiry, he fled to Canada. On his return he was arrested on a writ issued to a representative of the Senate, but immediately released on habeas corpus; the Federal officer was chased out of town by a *posse comitatus,* and the next day the supreme court of the state ordered Sanborn's discharge. To the end of his life—and he lived to 1917—he was considered a subversive thinker by his conservative contemporaries.

As a member of the editorial staff of the Springfield *Republican,* 1868–1914, the outstanding liberal daily in the country, he had full opportunity to exercise his gift of writing and to express his deep convictions on the liberal movements of his generation.

When the Massachusetts State Board of Charities was created in 1863, Sanborn was persuaded to take the position of secretary (or executive) by its chairman, his friend Samuel Gridley Howe. He became its chairman in 1874, serving for two years, and in 1879 was appointed by the board to be State Inspector of Charities, in which capacity he promoted the use of homes for children, both delinquent and dependent, recruiting a body of local volunteers, mostly women, to serve as visitors. In addition, he initiated the use of foster homes for the chronic, harmless insane, patterned after homes in Scotland, Belgium, and France which he had seen in operation. The use of private homes for the insane aroused considerable opposition and criticism, which assumed such proportions that he was forced out of office. The system, however, was not abandoned, although its scope was considerably curtailed. His retirement from this project probably delayed by half a century the adoption of the parole system for mental patients, which has had even to the present only one good demonstration, that in New

York State, under Governor Herbert H. Lehman in the fourth decade of this century.

Sanborn served as the first secretary of the Conference of State Boards of Charities and was the editor of the first five volumes of its *Proceedings*. In 1881 he was elected its eighth president and up to 1910 continued to be the most regular attendant at, and consistent contributor to, its sessions. His papers are models of precise and forceful English; some are results of wide investigation, showing a firm, scholarly grasp of subject matter and a logical organization of findings and with more echo of the classics than is now often heard in Conference papers. They remain classics of their kind. More concerned with the theoretical aspects of social questions than were his co-workers, Sanborn showed an independence of judgment that at times caused him to differ with most of them, which difference he expressed without defensiveness or apology.

Although they differed widely, Elmore of Wisconsin and Sanborn of Massachusetts apparently had deep appreciation of each other's merits, for Elmore in introducing Sanborn for a short report said (1888), "Perhaps, all I need to say is that he is a Boston notion—and taking all in all we shall never see his like again."

Frederick H. Wines (1838–1912) was also born of early American colonial stock, his ancestors arriving from Wales about 1635 and settling in and around Charlestown, Massachusetts. He can hardly be understood apart from his father, Enoch C. Wines (1806–79), who was ordained as a Congregational minister in 1849 and who undertook several pastoral and educational projects unsuccessfully. When the elder Wines became secretary of the New York Prison Association in 1862 he found himself. Under his leadership, Richard L. Dugdale made his classical study of the Jukes family; he warmly backed Zebulon Reed Brockway's progressive administration at Elmira Reformatory; he promoted the first International Penitentiary Congress in London and was president of the second that met in Stockholm in 1878. He is said to have died as the result of overwork in its behalf. He wrote two of the earliest American books on the social services: *Report on the Prisons and Reformatories of the United States and Canada* (1867), which contained his findings from visits to every prison and reformatory in the Northern states and Canada; and *The State of Prisons and of Child Saving Institutions in the Civilized World* (1880), published posthumously, and apparently based on data gathered in connection with his work on the two international congresses.

His son, Frederick H. Wines, was graduated at the head of his class from Washington and Jefferson College in 1857, but bad eyesight and the Civil War delayed the completion of his theological education until 1865. He served a church in Springfield, Illinois, until 1869, when he was appointed the first secretary of the state board of Illinois; in that capacity he served continuously until 1898, with the exception of the four years (1892–96) of the administration of Governor John P. Altgeld, who as a reforming Democrat could not tolerate a conservative Republican in that important position. (In 1896 Wines served as editor for the Republican National Committee.) Twice he collaborated with the director of the United States Census, as special adviser on the defective and delinquent classes for the tenth census (1880), and in charge of the census on crime, pauperism, and benevolences in the United States for the eleventh census. He collaborated (1897–98) with John Koren in writing *The Liquor Problem in Its Legislative Aspects* for the Committee of Fifty on the Liquor Problem. After his retirement from the Illinois board and his work with the Census Bureau, Wines served as secretary of the New Jersey State Charities Aid Association in 1902–04.

His secretaryship of the Illinois board covered a longer period than that of any other state secretary in the country. His intellectual ability and social heritage fitted him admirably for a task that called for an unusual combination of qualities: enough flexibility to make concessions; an objective firmly held over the years; ability to impress people, including the legislature, with his sincerity and competence; and, like Sanborn, enormous capacity for intellectual labor combined with some facility in expression. While he made no claim to be the originator of the idea which blossomed into the National Conference, both he and Sanborn crediting Elmore with that honor, Wines certainly saw clearly that the problems with which a state board was struggling could not be faced by any one state alone. In his first report to the Governor, in 1869, after reporting on conferences he had called of superintendents of hospitals for the insane and the county commissioners of public charity, he went on to say,

the board has a very high appreciation of the necessity and possibility of making a national system of State boards . . . [as] a thoroughly effective means of interstate communication and exchange. . . . The immediate aim and results of any State Board are local—but its outlook must transcend the narrow boundaries of a state.

Lacking the philosophical or literary ability of Sanborn, Wines was broadly interested in his own special field, and not without creative imagination, although apparently he was not endowed with a sense of humor. He served as secretary of the National Prison Association from 1887 to 1889; he was one of those who worked to separate the National Conference from the American Social Science Association, and in 1883 he became its tenth president, at which time he made known his ideas of what the Conference should be and warned of the danger which menaced it through the accretion of agencies that threatened to smother its original purpose as a clearinghouse of state boards. Wines even raised the question of whether state boards might not have to secede from the Conference in order to preserve the function for which it was created; for, he said, if any other body or bodies, such as organized charities, should succeed in dominating the Conference, it would have lost its original purpose and have become something else. He was one of the organizers of the International Congress of Charities and Correction which met in Chicago in 1893, and on the death of former President Rutherford B. Hayes, vice president of the Congress, he took over the task of its administration. In Illinois he is remembered for the creation of the cottage system of housing insane patients at Kankakee, solving by that method some of the difficult problems presented by the need for differential treatment of patients, by their classification, and by the growth of the institution.

In contrast to Sanborn, his interests were concentrated in the field of social welfare; and especially in its public aspects, in which he had deep confidence although that phase of welfare activity was then subjected to widespread criticism. Without specific educational or other preparation for his vocation, unless association with his father had provided him with its fundamentals, Wines became the first American professional social worker. He learned from actual experience, but he did learn. His leadership in Illinois was unquestioned for nearly a third of a century, a leadership he won by wise, patient, and thoroughgoing workmanship. He called himself, when asked what he did, a "statistician," but he was fundamentally a pioneering practitioner in the public social services on the level of state administration. It might well have been with Wines in mind that the president of the Illinois state board, George S. Robinson, a lawyer, said at the Conference of 1881, "The care of the unfortunate is really a profession; it might almost rank with the learned professions, so great and varied is the information on all subjects required for its highest development." This is the first use of the word "professional" in referring to the practice of social welfare.

From the printed record of papers, especially of Conference discussions, Wines leaves the impression that his was a gifted, well-disciplined mind which perhaps did not "suffer fools gladly." The early Conferences were tight little oligarchies, directed by a few men identified with state boards who invited and tolerated others from the wider area of the social services, but did not draw them into their councils. It was an aristocracy, of sorts, and Wines seems to have been the dominating character. However, one who saw him when he was secretary of the New Jersey State Charities Aid Association describes him as courteous and patient, and quite free from the need to impress himself upon his listener.

Andrew E. Elmore (1841–1906), of Wisconsin, was president of the State Board on the occasion of Wines's visit to Madison, Wisconsin, in 1872, and a member of the board in 1874 when the organizing meeting of the National Conference was held in New York, but he did not attend that meeting. He is credited both by Wines and by Sanborn with first suggesting the organization of a national association of state boards. In the Conference of 1882 Elmore delivered an interesting recital of the events leading up to its organization; but his outstanding contribution was as chairman of its Committee on Resolutions, where his ready wit and his belief in the value of preserving the open forum character of the Conference enabled him to ward off the various efforts to introduce resolutions or controversial subjects, and yet keep everybody happy. He was a defender of the Wisconsin system of raising the standard of county care for the chronically insane, in which debate the Wisconsin delegation stood alone, with only Sanborn of Massachusetts coming vigorously to their defense. Elmore was the one who gave notice to the Conference at its second meeting in 1875 that Wisconsin would not continue to send delegates if the Conference remained a section—a side show, as he said—of the American Social Science Association. This was the schism that led finally to the separate organization of the National Conference in 1879.

Elmore represented the lay membership of the Conference, with an interest first created by his membership on a state board; and from that point of vantage he saw the national implications of a state's activity. He looked upon himself as representing the West—even the far West—in the councils of the Conference, assuming that there would be differences of opinion between the older and more settled East and the younger and growing West. Nevertheless, Wisconsin never wavered in its loyalty to the National Conference, remaining steadily true to the original faith in the value of such a medium for exchange of opinion, even when Wisconsin's opinion varied sharply from that of the majority of the members of the Conference. This loyalty to the Conference was equally true of Elmore's fellow members on the board, Hiram H. Giles, who became its chairman, and Professor Albert O. Wright.

Those who knew him said that Elmore was a man of broad vision. To improve the abhorrent conditions he found in Wisconsin, he sent members of the staff of the Wisconsin board to the New England states and even to Europe to survey their institutions and their different methods. He had many plans for reforming state institutions; he was deeply interested in the possibility of creating a national conference that would give the nine state boards that existed in 1872 a chance to exchange ideas and discuss common and special problems. According to a later statement by Sanborn, Wisconsin owed the excellency of its public welfare institutions to Elmore's leadership, as Massachusetts owed its development to the vision and organizing ability of Samuel Gridley Howe.

William Pryor Letchworth (1823–1910), like Elmore of Wisconsin, was a layman who, after retiring from business in Buffalo, New York, at the age of fifty, devoted his life to charitable services. Letchworth was a Quaker by birth; his ancestors, who had emigrated to America in the mid-seventeenth century, apparently transmitted to him unspoiled the Quakers' devotion to service, fidelity to the inner voice of conscience, and avoidance of all ostentation. His fellow officers and members of the National Conference treated him with a respect touching on reverence. He was a man of kindly sympathy and simple habits.

Letchworth was appointed a member of the New York state board in 1873, remaining on it until 1896, serving as vice president from 1874 to 1878, and president from 1878 to 1888. Three major interests absorbed his energies during his nearly a quarter of a century with the New York board: the removal of children from the almshouses and securing for them suitable and well-supervised placement in homes and institutions; learning the best possible way to handle the care of the insane; and, toward the end of his years of service, securing proper and specialized care for those afflicted with epilepsy. At the 1875 sessions of the Conference, Letchworth gave expression to his earliest interest by reading a paper by Mary Carpenter, of Bristol, England, written on the basis of her visits to almshouses, prisons, and jails, where she saw the plight of children held in those destructive environments. He then proposed a resolution recommending that state legislatures pass laws that would remove children from almshouses and make provision for their suitable care under conditions as nearly like family life as possible.

In pursuit of his interest in the care of the insane, Letchworth visited institutions in Great Britain, as did also Wines and Sanborn at later dates, where he found that Europe had advanced quite beyond America, both in an understanding of insanity and in methods for its care. On completing this study he wrote *The Insane in Foreign Countries* (1889). Eleven years later, when his interests were centered on the care of the epileptic, Letchworth brought out his second book, *The Care and Treatment of the Epileptic* (1900). He urged the segregation of epileptics from the insane as well as from the feeble-minded.

He was elected president of the Conference in 1884, and served in almost every capacity during his long association with it. He was also the first president of the New York State Conference of Charities and Corrections (1900). Although not a graduate of a college, Letchworth had the real student's capacity, as many of the papers that he presented at the Conference and his two books demonstrate. In 1893 New York University bestowed on him the honorary degree of LL.D., "for distinguished service to the State."

Although they were not so intimately connected with the National Conference as were Sanborn, Wines, Elmore, and Letchworth, the stories of three other men belong here so that we may have a more adequate picture of its first membership.

Theodore Roosevelt (1831–78), father of the President of the United States of the same name, was a descendant of a Dutch settler who came to New Amsterdam in 1649. A successful businessman, Theodore Roosevelt left his mark on the city and state of New York although he died before his forty-seventh birthday. In addition to his membership on the first New York State Board of Charities, and on the first board of the State Charities Aid Association of New York, he was one of the organizers of the Metropolitan Museum of Art, of the Museum of Natural History, and of the Union League Club, all of which still occupy a place of prominence in the cultural life of the metropolis. He also aided in the organization of the Sanitary Commission, which served the Northern armies in the Civil War in much the same way that the Red Cross has functioned in modern wars, and he was its representative in New York. Roosevelt suggested to Congress a policy of soldiers' allotments for their families that was similar to that adopted in the first and second World War. He stayed in Washington for three months, much to the dismay of Congress, until the bill authorizing such a plan became a law. He was offered an appointment as Collector of the Port of New York by President Hayes, but the nomination was defeated in the Senate by the influence of the Tweed machine. Williams College granted him the degree of LL.D.

The late President, Theodore Roosevelt, held his father in great reverence and credited him with furnishing a strong moral influence on his life. George William Curtis said of him that "he had the convictions of a reformer, with courtesy, courage and omnipresent tact of a gentleman. He was neither spoiled by good fortune, nor soured by zeal and his death, therefore, diminishes the active moral force of the community."

John V. L. Pruyn (1811–77) was president of the New York state board of which Roosevelt and Letchworth were members and which served as the host of the first Conference in 1874. He had recommended the organization of a state board to the Governor of the state, and became its president on its creation, holding that position until his death. In many ways his life paralleled Roosevelt's and Letchworth's, for he too spent much of his latter years in civic, educational, and philanthropic activities. He too was a descendant of early settlers, his Dutch ancestors having settled in Albany by 1665. A lawyer by profession, he laid the legal foundation for the consolidation of many of the small railroad lines in New York State that now comprise the New York Central System; he was elected to the state senate in 1861 and to Congress in 1863 and again in 1867. A stanch, old-fashioned Democrat, in Congress Pruyn worked for freeing the slaves and healing the wounds of the Civil War.

As state senator he promoted the erection of the State Capitol at Albany, much of whose splendor was due to his work on the Capitol Commission, from which he resigned in 1870 when the Tweed gang gained control and made of it a fruitful source of political plunder. Quite early in his career, in 1844, he was appointed a regent of the University of the State of New York and in 1862 became its chancellor, a post he retained to his death.

The name of Glenn runs throughout the entire period covered by the Conference: John Glenn of Baltimore; John M. Glenn, his nephew; and Mrs. John M. (Mary Wilcox) Glenn.

John Glenn (1829–96) was the son of a judge of the Federal District Court. Due to impaired eyesight, which resulted in blindness in his last years, he abandoned the study of law and became a successful real estate operator. His interest in the less fortunate led him to become identified with the Maryland School for the Blind, the Friendly Inn Association, the Provident Band, and the Charity Organization Society of his native city. President Daniel C. Gilman, of Johns Hopkins University, said of him, "it is no exaggeration to say that the Charity Organization Society of Baltimore today is very largely a monument to John Glenn."

John M. Glenn (1858–   ) is an attorney. Among other civic activities he served as a member of the Board of Supervisors of the City Charities of his native Baltimore from 1888 to 1907, when he was appointed director of the newly established Russell Sage Foundation of New York City. He served in that capacity until 1931. Glenn is a member of the Social Service Commission and of the Executive Committee of the Federal Council of Churches; but he will be best remembered for his kindly advisory services to all sorts of national agencies and to an endless number of persons engaged in the social services. He was president of the Conference in 1901. He has been a faithful member of the Conference; but rarely has he appeared before it in a formal manner, and he is the only president who did not feel called upon to deliver a presidential message.

Mrs. John M. (Mary Wilcox) Glenn (1869–1940), also of Baltimore, was secretary of the Henry Watson Children's Aid Society from 1897 to 1901 and of the Charity Organization Society from 1900 to 1901. After her removal to New York with her husband, she became a member of the board of the Charity Organization Society (later the Community Service Society); chairman of the Home Service Section of the New York and Bronx chapters of the American Red Cross during the first World War; president of the National Council of the Church Mission of Help, 1919–37, and of the Family Welfare Association of America, 1920–37. Mrs. Glenn was president of the National Conference in 1915, the only woman president whose husband had also served the Conference in that capacity. A devout member of the Protestant Episcopal Church, her contributions as a member of various committees and as a frequent speaker were suffused with deep religious feeling and a rugged faith in the democratic way of life.

Letchworth, Roosevelt, Pruyn, and the three Glenns represented a class early drawn into the orbit of public welfare. There were many others like them in different parts of the country. They combined a high intellectual capacity and the practical wisdom of the market place with a passion for social justice that made them public servants of rare quality; a combination and a result that have not been often duplicated since that first decade of the Conference's life.

Quite different from these pioneers of the National Conference was Zebulon Reed Brockway (1827–1920) whose name is synonymous with prison reform. He spoke before the Conference only four times in his extraordinarily long lifetime; he was not an officer of the Conference or its president at any time, and his speeches do not seem particularly significant as one reads them now. He did serve as president of the National Prison Association in 1897–98, and as honorary president of the International Prison Association in 1902. His biographer, describing his various and unsuccessful ventures in the business world, quotes a friend of Brockway as saying that "he will never become forehanded, for he has not the money getting instinct."

His road to his famous post at Elmira, New York, was a long and checkered one. In 1848 he was clerk in the Weathersfield (Connecticut) prison; in 1851, deputy to the warden at the Albany County Penitentiary; in 1853, superintendent of the Albany Almshouse; the next year, superintendent of the County Penitentiary at Rochester, New York; seven years later he was in charge of the House of Correction at Detroit. Then followed an interval of four years in business in which he showed his unfitness for meeting the demands of a competitive society; finally, in 1876, he took charge of the newly erected Elmira Reformatory. It would be interesting to know by what means the New York board, and specifically Pruyn, Roosevelt, or Letchworth, found Brockway or decided that this middle-aged man who had tried many projects with no particular success was the man to put in charge of this new venture in treating adult first offenders.

Toward the end of his twenty-four-year stay at Elmira, the state board preferred charges against Brockway on the basis of his cruel treatment of the prisoners under him, and recommended his dismissal. The Governor refused to follow the recommendation of the board and appointed a special committee, which exonerated Brockway. He remained for six more years as warden at Elmira, or until 1900, when he had reached his seventy-third year. Five years later he was elected mayor of Elmira and served for two years.

Brockway was not the originator of the idea of reform in place of punishment as the only treatment of the delinquent, but he was the first to have written into the statutes the indeterminate sentence and parole. While at first depending upon emotional appeals, he abandoned that method. Influenced by the contemporary philosophy of the European school of criminology, his method involved the education of the whole man, his capacity, his habits, and his tastes, by a rational procedure whose central idea was "the ennobling influences of established industrial efficiency."

Although Brockway did not often appear before the Conference in person, his name occurred many times in papers and in discussions, and the Elmira Reformatory became the symbol of the best example then existing of the incorporation of the principles of advanced penology, not only in this country, but also internationally.

3 · THE WORLD IN WHICH THE CONFERENCE WAS BORN

*T*HE THIRD quarter of the nineteenth century marked a phase in the transition of ethical philosophy, from the mysticism of medieval theory to a more scientific explanation of human behavior and motives. In a short space of time Buckle had written his history of *Civilization in England,* using the method of statistical correlation between economic data and social change to establish his thesis that historical direction could be understood by discovering the fluctuating factors occurring in the economic situation of an age. The social philosophy of Auguste Comte was made available to the English-speaking world by the translation of Harriet Martineau, developing the same theory of the possibility of discovering the causes of social change, on a wider front than Buckle had explored. In that same ten years (1850–60) Darwin's *Origin of Species* was published, concerned not primarily with social questions, but establishing on an enduring foundation the theory of the unity of living matter, that all changes occur in understandable ways and in response to causes that can be discovered. This theory of evolution was immediately seized upon by his contemporaries Huxley and Spencer to apply to social phenomena, with the result that Darwin's theory of evolution was the catalyst that broke up the old form of ethical philosophy as well as the more popular ideas of the dynamics of human behavior.

It is not to be assumed that these theories received instant or general acceptance. Of course, they did not. The "monkey trial" in Tennessee of only yesterday demonstrated that there is even yet a determined intellectual and assumed ethical opposition to its theory, and for the general public it is a good subject for a jest. The point is that the theory greatly reinforced the basis of intellectual liberalism, saving it from the charge of sentimentalism and wishful thinking. There is not much direct evidence that its implications were discussed by leaders of the Conference. Sanborn dealt with them at length in his papers before the Social Science Association, with which he remained in an official capacity through the rest of the century. The Rev. Oscar C. McCulloch, president of the Indiana Board of Charities and later of the National Conference (1891), was vitally interested in their connotations and is said to have spent much of his available time in discussing Spencer and the later writers, such as Henry Drummond and John Fiske, who were attempting to reconcile biological evolution with our ethical heritage.

It is significant, however, that most of the leaders of the Conference accepted the implications of a scientific approach to social problems. They acted on the tacit assumption that human ills—sickness, insanity, crime, poverty—could be subjected to study and methods of treatment, and that a theory for prevention could be formulated as well; that they were not the results of "sin" or of fate, to be borne with such patience as their victims could muster, or that they existed to give opportunity for the exercise of the charity of their fellow men. This attitude raised these problems out of the realm of mysticism into that of science. Of course, there were exceptions among the Conference members to this generalization; but not among the first few great leaders of the Conference.

As a result of the adoption of the scientific attitude, Conference speakers and programs looked forward toward progress, not backward toward a golden age. They believed in the future; that it was possible, by patient, careful study and experimentation to create a society much better than the one they lived in. They thought of this improvement, for the most part, in negative terms: elimination of sickness, crime, mental ills, and pauperism. They were not thinking particularly of the creation of a sounder social structure that might slough off such ills. This limitation of imagination probably was the cause of the disillusionment characteristic of liberal thought at the turn of the century. But that was still twenty or thirty years off. The stimulus of hope given by the new social science spurred early workers to a degree of application and zeal that has not since been duplicated.

Coming more closely to the task in hand in the English-speaking world, the attitude toward poverty was that of the reformers of the English Poor Law of 1834: that the plight of the poor was evidence of moral weakness to be eradicated by severe administration of relief. It is significant that the first committees of the Conference, its papers, and its declared purposes spoke of the elimination of pauperism, not of poverty. It was the weakness of the victims of destitution that called for study, for treatment, and even for cure, and not much attention was paid to those situations, external to the dependent, which might throw some light upon the reasons for their dependence. There were hints from time to time that moral factors might not be solely responsible for the existence of need, especially in the dependency of children and widowhood. But they remained a minority, and not an influential minority, throughout the nineteenth century.

In regard to other social ills, there were less definite obsessions. Mary Carpenter's work in England in substituting reformation for punishment was generally accepted by the Conference considerably in advance of its acceptance in practice, which even today receives little more than lip service in many institutions for juvenile delinquents. Brockway's work at Elmira in applying the same principle, plus parole, to the young adult offender was defended. The experiment at Mattrey, France, where juvenile offenders were cared for by what was there called the "family system," and in this country the "cottage system," was early advocated and gradually introduced. Men like Sanborn, Wines, and Letchworth, studying at first hand European methods with mentally ill patients, reported their findings without opposition in the Conference itself, although the adoption of a scientifically valid method of care for such patients has been blocked by many factors outside the power of the Conference to master.

In practically all the scope of the Conference's interest—poverty, crime, insanity, and sickness—contemporary society was exploring with considerable freedom the ways and means whereby the challenge of these ills could be understood, except in poverty. There, practically alone, the fixed idea—or obsession—blocked an untrammeled search for the roots of its widespread occurrence. There may have been some remnant of the caste system in such an attitude, a system that divided society into two groups, workers, or the poor, and the leisure class, with the parallel idea that the worker, who was the potential dependent, was only held to diligent labor by fear of poverty. Even Josephine Shaw Lowell, one of the wisest leaders in American philanthropic effort, said at the National Conference as late as 1890:

No human being will work to provide the means of living for himself, if he can get a living in any other manner agreeable to himself; . . . that the community cannot afford to tempt its members who are able to work for a living to give up working for a living by offering to provide a living otherwise . . . and the way to [avoid] this, is to provide [relief for the able-bodied] under strict rules inside an institution.

This is almost precisely parallel with what the essayist Bernard de Mandeville said in *The Fable of the Bees* over a century earlier (1714): "The Poor should be kept strictly to work; and [that it was] prudence to relieve their wants, but folly to cure them."

By 1870 the office of the overseer of the poor, or its equivalent, was in charge of public outdoor and indoor relief in local political units; the almshouse in some form served as the catchall for the community's outcasts; hospitals for mental diseases were gradually assuming responsibility for the custodial care of the insane; and, of course, local jails and state institutions had been established for delinquents with some promise of the coming separation into special institutions for women and children. In the private agency field there had been an increasing number of institutions for children, both dependent and delinquent; the New York Children's Aid Society had been sending children to homes with families in the Mid-Western states for the previous twenty years; and associations for improving the condition of the poor (provident associations, relief and aid societies) had been established in almost all the larger urban centers in the United States. Through the years there has been experimentation with personnel. At first the workers were entirely volunteers; then the agencies employed small paid staffs supplemented by large numbers of volunteers. Then came the period of a wholly paid staff, composed primarily of men; within recent years the social agencies have, for the most part, employed women, since they have found them to be more "reliable" (nothing is said about their being cheaper). There had been, by 1870, a few experiments in the social services, mostly in methods for the education of the blind, the deaf, and the mentally deficient.

Chronologically, the Conference was organized within a decade of the Civil War, and within the year after the beginning of one of the three great depressions [1] suffered by modern

[1] 1837; 1873; and 1929.

industrial nations. The meetings of the Conference took little notice of these events. No great Civil War figures ever became identified with the Conference. General Roeliff Brinkerhoff was in the quartermaster service, and while he was an influential leader in the Conference and in the National Prison Association, his military experience bore no relationship to his civic interests. The depression of 1873 is not mentioned in the 1874 papers, and in 1875 it appears only as an episode that is rapidly passing away.

Outside the recently created state boards of charity, the Conference seemed not to be particularly interested in the general field of charity. It was only as new agencies appeared in the field, such as the social settlements and the charity organization movement, that the Conference gradually broadened its scope and shared its management with others than representatives of state boards, as well as included in its programs the presentation of topics other than those engaging the immediate interest of members of state boards.

*P*ROBABLY as good a statement as any explaining the reasons for the establishment of state boards is the message from Governor Richard J. Oglesby, of Illinois, to the legislature of that state in January, 1869, based upon the findings of a joint legislative committee of the House and Senate:

It has been earnestly represented to me, in view of the separate organizations of our various charitable institutions under separate Boards of Management; the large number of inmates attending each and the constant demand for more room and accommodations for the large numbers necessarily excluded from the benefits of each; together with the important question of the means to be raised by taxation for the support and enlargement of the present or the construction of additional asylums; and to consider new questions arising out of experience as to the best modes of treatment and improvement of the various classes of patients and inmates of our several benevolent institutions, that our present system ought to be thoroughly and carefully reviewed and revised and the whole subject in its various bearings, placed in the hands of a Board, to be created, with full powers to investigate and report on all these questions, to be styled The Board of Public Charities.

The above quotation gives the situation—in subdued colors —that confronted the states in the seventh decade of the century. From time to time, in response to a petition or as the result of a special investigation, each state authorized the creation of an institution to care for a specific need: usually a hospital for mental patients, or a state prison, but occasionally other institutions, such as a school for the feeble-minded or, as in Massachusetts, an almshouse for the state's poor. Each of these institutions was administered by a board of managers ordinarily consisting of prominent local citizens. Usually appointed by the governor, the members of the board were at times chosen on a partisan basis. These boards were responsible only to the governor and, indirectly, to the state legislature from which each institution received its annual or biennial appropriation. Each institution was a law unto itself. A good administration would be accidental and unnoticed; a bad administration would escape criticism unless a public scandal were created. Each institution had to compete before the legislature with all the other institutions in the state for appropriations. Its board might be highly partisan in politics, and the personnel of the institution dependent for employment upon the political party in power.

So good a student of the development of public welfare in this country as Edith Abbott believes that this prostitution of the services of the state institutions to the whims of partisan politics was the chief reason for the creation of state boards. Such were some of the "deplorable conditions" found by Elmore in Wisconsin, and corrected by the Wisconsin state board. Letchworth in 1882 related two incidents in New York State that led to the creating of the New York board. A woman of some social standing voluntarily committed herself to the almshouse at Albany; when she left, she reported the shocking conditions she had found, only to be told to mind her own business. Appeals to higher authorities in the city brought the retort that a woman of her position might be better occupied than interfering with the duties of a public official. Later, a man badly hurt was refused admission to Bellevue Hospital in New York and later died uncared for, because the hospital admitting officer had left for the day. Appeals to city officials brought approximately the same response that had been given to the complaint in Albany. Word of this incident came to the ears of John V. L. Pruyn, who took it up with New York's governor, Reuben E. Fenton, and the result was the establishment of the state board.

It is to be noted that the Governor's message to the Illinois legislature called for a board with power to investigate and report; that is, it was to have only a supervisory function, very much as the English Board of Poor Law Commissioners established a central supervisory authority over the local parish overseers of the poor by the reform of 1834. Possibly the intention was to pattern the Illinois board after this governmental device for bringing about some uniformity in the local administration of public welfare and for increasing its efficiency. However, no uniform pattern was followed in the various states. Rhode Island, from the first, set up an administrative board, abolishing separate boards for each institution. Some states, such as Massachusetts, New York, and Pennsylvania, had pre-existing state authorities with limited functions, such as control of immigration, and these administrative functions were taken over by the new boards whose major responsibility was supervision. Nor was there unanimity of opinion, even in the early days, as to the wisdom of this circumscribed function. Sanborn, in his second annual report to the Massachusetts board (1865), said that because "the Board [is] not clothed with power—[it therefore could not] make desirable changes in the administration of several institutions. It could not substitute a single headed system for the present many headed one." Later (1882), in discussing the limited executive functions of the Massachusetts board, such as control of immigration, administration of the state Poor Fund, and "the recently added administration of public health laws controlling contagious diseases," he commented favorably on the effectiveness of such centralized authority, contrasting it with the ineffectiveness of control by supervision.

The conflict between the defenders of an advisory board and

the champions of an administrative one furnished the first debate to engage the energies of the National Conference. Certain representatives, notably those from Massachusetts, New York, and Pennsylvania, were taken slightly aback at the debate; for, as they said, their boards had some administrative functions, and since the states were assuming new duties in the field of public service, these new tasks tended to be added to the functions of the state boards rather than to be given to new executive bodies set up for their administration. However, Wines of Illinois was an outstanding proponent of the supervisory function of the board, to be quickly joined by A. G. Byers and General Brinkerhoff of the Ohio board, by Hastings H. Hart of the Minnesota board, and by Rev. Oscar C. McCulloch and Amos W. Butler of the Indiana board. So long as Rhode Island remained the only state with a board directly administering all charitable and penal institutions of the state, the debate remained mild, for Rhode Island was of the opinion that the success of a plan that worked in such a small state, where all the institutions were grouped in one place, could scarcely be a demonstration of the best plan for larger states with widely scattered institutions. During this period there was no clear-cut opinion expressed by anyone to the effect that centralized administration is desirable in itself.

Oddly enough, one of the excellent descriptions of the advantages of a supervisory board, in contrast with the administrative type, was given by George I. Chace, chairman of the Rhode Island Board of Charities and Corrections, in 1882. He felt that such a board had, with all its limitations, unfettered opportunity to visit state institutions; to report its findings to the governor, the legislature, and the public; to equip itself with the best knowledge available on the occurrence and method of treatment of the defective, delinquent, and dependent, serving as a guide to public opinion and legislative action; to call conferences for discussion of pertinent subject matter; and to advise institutions on qualifications of personnel. Chace maintained that the supervisory board should make itself an authority in its field. Boards of trustees would come to rely upon such expert guidance. Having no authority, the board must practice the art of public relations, especially in its dealings with the legislature and with trustees of the different institutions. It could conduct continuous investigations into the best methods practiced anywhere. As an interesting footnote to this list of theoretical advantages, a few items from Sanborn's second annual report discussed what the Massachusetts Board had done or was doing in that year (1865): (1) revision of the prison system of the state on lines laid down by French and Irish penologists; (2) extension of the reformatory system for educating neglected and vicious children; (3) appointment of a visiting agent for the supervision of dependent and delinquent children placed in families; (4) definition of the policy on keeping children in the almshouses of the state; (5) studying the means of lessening pauperism, with legislation to be proposed after but not before the investigation. Of these five diverse actions, only the third is administrative and exhibits the wide scope of activities that an imaginative leader may undertake with solely supervisory authority.

In 1881 Wisconsin established its Board of Control, centralizing management of all institutions in it, with the Board of Charities and Reform retaining its supervisory function; in 1885 Kansas organized its Board of Trustees of Charitable Institutions, vested with the same administrative authority. In 1891 Wisconsin abolished its supervisory board, leaving the Board of Control solely responsible for administration and supervision. These changes caused debates in the Conference between proponents of the advantage of the supervisory board, on the one side, and of the administrative, on the other, to take

on a vigor they had not previously shown. The defenders of
the new group, usually led by the delegates from Wisconsin,
pointed out the great savings of money effected by a centralized
administration. In criticism of the supervisory system, it was
pointed out, as Sanborn did back in 1865, that there were many
obvious reforms in methods and changes in the administration
of the individual institutions that a supervisory board could not
make directly, and therefore it would be under the necessity of
using the cumbersome and uncertain technique of persuasion
to effect the improvement. The principal arguments in favor
of the boards of control were budgetary: a unified account to
the legislature; control over the expenditures of the different
institutions; and allocation of budgetary allowances on the basis
of competent study of needs and their relation to the total
amount made available by the legislature. In passing, it should
be pointed out that the Illinois board had secured a budgetary
supervision amounting to control, and its submission to the legislature as a unit even under its limited supervisory powers.

The defenders of the supervisory function pointed out that
it was not necessary to have administrative control in order to
secure economy and efficiency. Citing the progress made by
Illinois and Massachusetts, they held that there was much to be
gained by retaining the separate boards of trustees for each
institution since that process identified a considerable group of
citizens, widely scattered over the state, with the state's interest in welfare. They maintained too that exercise of the supervisory function alone on the part of the board left each
institution free to experiment with different methods, whose
value could then be judged by the supervising body. A new
member of the Indiana state board, who was originally a believer in control rather than in a supervisory authority, came to
the conclusion (1891) that changes in the field of public welfare occur but slowly and only in harmony with popular con-

sent, and he announced his conversion to the supervisory function by the statement that "public opinion is harder to declare unconstitutional than a statute."

The defenders of the supervisory function, however, shifted their argument to the thesis that administration is unsuited to the task originally laid down for state boards, that is, to investigate causes, to initiate new methods in harmony with changing conditions, and to act as the watchdog of the actual administration of the public welfare agencies; that the board would necessarily be so engrossed with the day-by-day job of administering the large number of projects under its care that it would not have the time to give to these more fundamental tasks of a state board; and that an administrative agency by its very nature cannot at one and the same time be responsible for, and a critic of, its own performances. Wisconsin attempted to answer this last point by keeping in existence its Board of Charity and Reform for nearly ten years after the state's Board of Control had been organized, but finally abolished it in 1891. Minnesota, which adopted the control form of organization in 1899, created a Board of Visitors with wide investigational powers. However, when one public board investigates another on the same governmental level, intolerable situations are created.

In fact, the authors of the state boards of charities were seeking something quite different from what was desired by the initiators of boards of control. The former were created, for the most part, in states which had already established their charitable agencies and whose operations had been generally accepted. At any rate, it was more practical to establish a general supervisory agency to influence their gradual improvement than to destroy them and to begin all over again. The movement for the board of control started in the more recently settled West, where civic-minded leaders were conscious of the many mistakes made by the older states and determined to start with as clean a slate as possible. The West, in general the Mississippi River being the dividing line, adopted the method of control, while the states east of that line retained the older supervisory boards to the end of the century.

As these two systems are reviewed, it is clear that each one had the excellencies claimed for it, and each showed the weaknesses pointed out by its critics. The boards of control were certainly more efficient and more economical; they were among the first governmental agencies to make a successful stand against the corroding effect of the spoils system upon public administration, but this success was purchased at the price of progress in the art of helping.

One of the most brilliant chapters in American public welfare was written by the men who were big enough to exercise successfully the function of supervision. New means of tackling problems; coördination of effort; a careful, at times an almost inspired guidance of institutions in the choice of their personnel marked their leadership in the last two decades of the century as unique in the history of the country's struggle to master the subtle problems of dealing wisely and justly with its dependent wards. Undoubtedly, it required an unusual quality of leadership in membership and in its executive for a board to be successful in its vaguely defined supervisory function. Only those with vision, broad enough to be captured by the worthwhileness of the task and strong enough to outlast delay and frustration, would make a success of the board. Some states discovered such men in Hastings H. Hart, Frederick H. Wines, Amos W. Butler, A. G. Byers, General Roeliff Brinkerhoff, and Franklin B. Sanborn. It is not to be supposed that there were no more of them; but there were few boards wise enough—or lucky enough —to choose them. And the selection of lesser men spelled the collapse of the whole project. In the first part of the twentieth century several states abolished their boards as useless cogs in the machinery of public welfare, because of failure in leadership.

The typical state board of charities consisted of a number of citizens appointed by the governor and serving without salary, some boards including the governor himself and some excluding him, and with responsibility to choose a secretary (or executive) and to determine policies. This structure indicates the importance of the board's choice of secretary. Usually, the members of the board served for three, five, or seven years, in overlapping terms, whereas the secretary was appointed to an indefinite tenure. Such a device was set up to divorce the administration of public welfare from the influence of partisan politics. Governor Altgeld's displacement of Wines in Illinois is only one of many instances in which such protection was unavailing. On the whole, however, the device was sufficiently successful to have justified its adoption. When the state board of control was introduced, the unpaid board was eliminated, and a full-time, paid board of three or five was substituted with the board itself having administrative functions. The existence of this multiple-headed executive board violated all sound principles of administrative structure. It resulted, in general, in a sort of negative excellency: honesty, relative freedom from political influence, economical management, but a stalemate in the positive virtues of courage, imaginative invention, and the choice of outstanding personnel. The spur for these developments was often found in sources outside the boards of control, and even of the public services, such as the state conferences of charities and correction, which by 1897 were being held in eleven states and the District of Columbia. In the region where the state boards of control were established, the North Central Mississippi Valley, each state except Iowa and the Dakotas had held a conference by 1897.

The task of criticism and stimulation of public welfare relinquished by state boards when they assumed the administrative function was taken over by no agency in the country with the success ultimately achieved by the State Charities Aid Association of New York (organized in 1872), first under the brilliant leadership of John H. Finley, and then for a half a century under the no less able leadership of Homer Folks. Its purpose was to organize visiting committees in each county to do whatever was possible to improve the conditions of the inmates of the public charitable institutions of the state, including those under county or local authority. By 1897 three quarters of the counties had been organized, and Homer Folks reported that by virtue of the body of information gathered by these committees and the public opinion they had created, and by marshaling these resources into a single state channel, the Association had been instrumental in the passage of the law to remove the insane from almshouses; in the founding, at Sonyea, of Craig Colony, a specially equipped institution for the mentally deficient and epileptic; in the reorganization of the welfare structure of the city of New York by the establishment of a Department of Correction and a Department of Public Charities; and in transferring the care of the insane to state auspices. The central office of the Association in New York had also watched bills introduced into the New York Assembly touching on matters involving social issues, and through its wise and constructive relationship with the executive and legislative branches of the state government, it had become the most successful nonofficial adviser on matters of social legislation in this country. Its state-wide organization provided it with detailed and accurate data, and established, as well, a pattern for educating public opinion which, utilized through the years, became the broad basis for a sound and vigorous public opinion. The State Charities Aid Association demonstrated that

supervision and leadership, originally considered the functions
of state boards, can be quite effectively exercised over the years
by a nongovernmental agency. Pennsylvania has a Public Charities Aid Association which serves the same function for that
state, and New Jersey had a similar organization for a few years
at the beginning of this century. While speakers at the National
Conference often urged that such private, state-wide institutions should be established in every state to prevent the public
services from falling into a rut, and to provide lay leadership
and backing for their development, the movement did not
spread; the only organization in most states was the state conference, which in this period limited its activities to providing
a forum for discussion but was not a vehicle for social action.

The phrase "state board of charities" is used as if all states
entrusted the same tasks to its board. Nothing could be further
from the fact. Probably no two boards enjoyed identical
powers, and these powers were constantly being shifted about
in each state. As originally conceived, the boards were intended
to cover the four fields of health, penology, mental diseases,
and dependence; health, however, was usually separated early
from the other fields and cared for by its own board. In the
newer and Western states the grants of power were usually
more stable and more nearly inclusive of all the above functions
except that of caring for public health. In the Eastern states,
especially Massachusetts and New York, the allocations were
constantly shifting, and have continued to do so during the
present century. In Massachusetts, for example, the creation of
the Board of Health and Vital Statistics in 1869 separated public health from the Board of Charities. In 1875 care of the deaf
and blind was transferred to the Board of Education. In 1879
the supervision of institutions for delinquents was transferred
to the new Board of Commissioners of Prisons and its name was
changed to the State Board of Lunacy and Charity; in 1898,

with the creation of the State Board of Insanity, it became the State Board of Charity.

In 1895 Homer Folks, then secretary of the State Charities Aid Society (N.Y.), stated that all agencies caring for children should be under the supervision of the state board, or of a special children's bureau, in the larger states, with authority to visit foster homes and with the power of removal; to inspect town, city, and county institutions, including private agencies receiving state funds, as well as those who were not receiving any, and to be authorized to give publicity to their findings and, as a last resort, to revoke the charter of the offending agency. It was assumed by some of the state boards that the supervision of private agencies was included among their duties, but the question of their authority to do so did not become acute at this time. Later, it was called sharply into question, and a judicial decision given, based on a consideration that had not been thought of at this time. Folks's statement is significant as being the first to be made on this subject; moreover, it was presented by an executive of a private agency which would come under such official scrutiny.

In the twentieth century the interests of the Conference began to swing away from such close attention to the function of state boards, and while recent changes in state boards have been even more radical than those that had occurred in the first quarter of a century of the Conference's existence, less of its attention is paid to them; for the Conference widened its interests in the whole field of the public and private social services and paid less jealous regard to the pattern by which the states handled their problems of welfare.

The trend of the assumption of responsibility by the states for all their wards, begun by Massachusetts in 1863, has never been reversed. States have changed the functions of such boards and their forms with the accumulation of experience. They have expanded the one board which exercised supervision over all forms of public welfare into several boards; new boards have been established for oversight of the insane, the mentally diseased, the delinquent, and, in a few instances and for short times, over children, leaving the original board more specially concerned with the dependent wards of the state. State boards have taken on an increasing number of administrative functions, and, in general, the solely supervisory board is consequently a thing of the past. While the multiple-headed executive board, of which the board of control was one type, has nearly disappeared, its disappearance was largely due to its ineffectiveness in the face of the demands put upon it for leadership in the development of state social services. States have experimented with all forms of board, from a board of unpaid members, with only advisory capacity, without the governor, to boards which include him. In some states the boards have been abolished at the suggestion of political scientists, who generally regard them as useless encumbrances to efficiency, and a single Commissioner of Public Welfare has been appointed.

The increasing importance of the tasks undertaken by state boards is a measure of the public's acceptance of the state's responsibility to furnish protection or opportunity to those who cannot provide these services for themselves. At the present time approximately half the annual expenditures of most states are devoted to the varied services performed under the boards of welfare, health, insanity, and correction, and fully half of the personnel in the state's employment is on their pay roll.

5 · CONCERN OF THE CONFERENCE WITH THE INSANE AND THE FEEBLE-MINDED

THE INSANE

*D*URING its first ten years the National Conference of Charities and Correction was composed, for the most part, of members of state boards who were not primarily responsible for the administration of institutions for the care of mental patients; but the members were true to their function and exercised the right to comment, to criticize, and to suggest. There was a now-forgotten National Association of Superintendents and Members of Boards of Asylums for the Insane, whose members did have the duty of caring for the insane; and with this group the Conference had differences which at times deteriorated into severe conflicts. Specifically, the Conference was interested in the abolition of physical and narcotic restraint; in plans for separation of the chronically insane from the acutely insane; in building costs and arrangements; in personnel; in accuracy of statistics on insanity and its causes; and in an accurate statement of the percentage of cures.

Hospitals for the insane existed in the Middle Ages. In this country, however, except for one hospital erected by the state of Virginia in Williamsburg in 1773, and the one in Philadelphia started under the stimulus of Benjamin Franklin in 1775, care of the insane was usually entrusted to the almshouses until the second quarter of the nineteenth century. The first institution for the mentally ill in New York State was built in 1843, but so great was the increase in number of patients that by 1875 there were seven such institutions in New York; and a development of relatively similar dimensions took place in other states. This was the situation when the Conference was launched; and during its first twenty-five years a considerable portion of its time was spent in commenting upon the operation of insane asylums, as they were then called.

In the second year of the Conference, a paper was read on the success in treating mental patients without physical restraint. From that time to the end of the century, the development of the new method, from its inception at Bicêtre, France, under Philippe Pinel in 1793, and at the Middlesex County Asylum at Hanwell, England, in 1839, under Dr. John Conolly, was cited as demonstrating the therapeutic value—and safety—of removing all forms of physical coercion in mental hospitals. To this was added the suggestion that such freedom from restraint would call for a higher class of attendant; and the Conference asked for the development of outdoor work as a means of engaging the time and energies of the patients, and demanded, as well, a more accurate classification of the types of mental illness.

The cost of buildings for the insane engaged the attention of the Conference from the very first. In his address of welcome at the Saratoga meeting in 1876, Governor Samuel J. Tilden, of New York, said, "I . . . object to the magnificence of the public buildings being erected . . . for these purposes . . . unite in your action prudence, caution, frugality and economy of the thorough man of business . . . that the burdens for these objects shall not become intolerable." This sentiment was repeatedly expressed by Conference speakers who gave as a reason for their plea the fact that the costs of new buildings, such as that at Morristown, New Jersey, amounted to as much as $4,000 a bed. This high cost, so it was said, was the result of the ambitions of architects and of superintendents for monuments and imposing edifices without regard to the money of taxpayers, of which members and secretaries of state boards would be very conscious.

One point of difference between the association of superintendents and the Conference was on the matter of institutional housing. The former took the position that the chronically insane and patients whose insanity was of an acute nature should be housed together, whereas representatives at the Conference insisted that the two types of patient could be separated, reserving for the acutely ill the best equipment necessary for personalized service, and housing the chronically insane in cheaper and smaller units. Wines gave an illustration of the feasibility of such a plan for the chronically insane by recounting that when a building of a certain insane asylum was injured by fire, it was necessary to house its patients in small temporary units, which he expected would be resented by the patients. Instead, he found that they loved the arrangement. The smaller groups, easy access to the out-of-doors, the less institutional character of the buildings—all this gave the inmates a sense of greater freedom.

Similarly, the cottage system at Cranston, Rhode Island, was reported as being successful and commended as having many advantages. This system was later used in a modified form by Wines at the institution at Kankakee, Illinois. The practice of housing the insane in private homes at Gheel, Belgium, was known, and Gheel had been visited by at least four members of the Conference. Sanborn introduced a modification of the system by boarding selected harmless patients in private homes in rural areas of the state; but most of the Conference members did not believe that such a plan as that used at Gheel, or any modification of it, could be successfully put into operation in this country.

The Conference itself was divided on the matter of the use of the almshouse to care for chronically insane patients. Elmore, and his successors from Wisconsin, explained that it was pos-

sible to decentralize the care of this the largest group of the insane by state regulation and to grant aid to counties whereby
almshouses might be erected and maintained with valid standards for the care of patients. No one in the Conference agreed
with them except Sanborn, who stated that by such means Wisconsin had partly met the baffling problem presented by the
rapid increase in the number of patients and, as well, had been
able to offer the long-time patient more acceptable care, concentrating a smaller number of patients in one place and making possible greater individualization of treatment and nearness
to the patient's home. To most of the members of the Conference, whose long years of effort had been spent in removing
patients from the sordid surroundings of almshouses as they
knew them, the suggestion implied a return to the barbaric
conditions of the past.

In the discussion of causes of insanity, the members of the
Conference were in the midst of one of its central problems,
research; but the state of knowledge of the dynamics of behavior reached in the nineteenth century was not such as to
throw much light upon this puzzle. Physicians were early put
in charge of institutions for the insane; but there was a healthy
criticism both of the competency of the average physician in
this field and of the fact that, too often, physicians of inferior
qualifications and even charlatans were appointed to such posts.
The medical profession naturally explained insanity in medical
terms, and some speakers went so far as to say that all insanity
was caused by some impairment of the brain, although such
impairment could not at the time be identified. At the third
Conference, in 1877, Dr. John B. Chapin, of New York, asserted that the "care of the insane was better since physicians
had taken hold," but not because of any known therapeutic
method of treatment; and he even raised the question whether
the true nature of insanity could ever be known. Similarly, at
the Conference the year before, Dr. Louis A. Tourtelott, of the

Utica Asylum, came out flatly with the statement that insanity is not a medical entity, connected with certain bodily (cerebral) changes: it exists where there are changes, and also where none are observable. No drug or medicine "can minister to a mind diseased" had now been empirically demonstrated. As a result of this belief, he said, the declaration of insanity should rather rest on the moral judgment of a lay jury than be based on the judgment of a panel of specialists. Others, like Wines in 1888, favored court action based on specialists' findings. However, more realistic—if equally superficial—explanations for mental illness were usually given, such as inebriety, heredity, lack of ventilation, meager diet, neglect of moral culture, increased aging of the population, immigration, fast living, overwork, the competition of modern business, all of which recognize the emotional factors involved without identifying emotion itself as the area of research for causation.

Among the errors regarding mental hospitals called into question by the Conference were the exaggerated claims of cures made by their management, running from 75 percent to 90 percent of patients admitted. As early as 1881 Dr. Pliny Earl, of Massachusetts, showed that by taking into account the number of "cured" who later returned several times, and each time were discharged as cured, and the number of whom all trace had been lost or who had died, 10 percent was about the average of those whose "cure" lasted long enough for the institution to be credited with such an outcome. Similar criticisms were made from time to time by speakers, usually themselves superintendents of state institutions, thus indicating an improvement in the competency of personnel, much of which improvement can probably be traced to the leadership of the state boards.

At the Conference of 1899, two significant suggestions were made, one prophetic of later improvement and the other unfulfilled to the present. Dr. H. C. Rutter, of Ohio, recommended that the determination of sanity or insanity of persons accused of crime be the responsibility, not of specialists employed by the defense and by the prosecution, but of a commission of three appointed by the supreme court of the state to sit in such cases. Massachusetts adopted this very procedure in the third decade of this century, thus doing away with the unseemly procedure of one group of specialists trying to prove a defendant to be insane, and another group proving him to be sane.

The other suggestion was embodied in a paper by Dr. Jules Morel, of Mons, Belgium, who advocated the creation of guardian societies for the insane, such as Belgium had developed. Such a society would serve as an auxiliary to each hospital and its functioning would span the entire cycle of the patient's involvement: before commitment, as a sort of probation service for him; during confinement, to serve as a liaison between the specialists at the institution and the patient's family; and after release from the hospital, to act as counselors to the family, the patient, and the prospective employer. The plan was a modification of that practiced at Gheel, in that it used large numbers of volunteers as well as instructed aids to the medical authorities.[1] The only part of this scheme that has been adopted in this country is a psychiatric social service, on a professional basis, that is given after release and ignores the great value involved in creating a sound public opinion by inducing the patient's relatives and neighbors to share the process of restoring the patient to such place in society as he is capable of filling.

THE FEEBLE-MINDED

The story of the Conference's concern with the feeble-minded is simpler than that of its concern with the insane, involving no conflict between administration and supervision.

[1] Giraud and Ladame, *Guardian Societies for the Insane* (La Rochelle: E. Martin, 1893).

The principal speakers were the executives of institutions, who recited their hopes, disappointments, and accomplishments. Only one voice was raised in protest in this first quarter of a century, when the Rev. S. J. Barrows, editor of the *Christian Register*, in 1888 protested as a humanitarian against the theory of the uneducability of the feeble-minded.

The most noted paper in this period, perhaps in any field of the Conference's interest, is that of Richard L. Dugdale on the Jukes family, in which he summarized the findings of his study of kindred groups of criminals made in 1876 for the New York Prison Association, of which E. C. Wines was then the executive secretary. Dugdale's study shares with Adam Smith's *Wealth of Nations* the fate of being all but completely misapplied in its popular and, too often, in its scientific discussions. He demonstrated the familial continuity of delinquency and mental deficiency, as accurately as that could be determined at that time, and called the relationship "hereditary." He included in that term all the influences which shape the personality of the individual: family status in the community (he was very emphatic on this point), disease, standard of living, and education, as well as the unknown factor of physical relationship between the generations, which he did not isolate or even describe. He even went so far as to follow members of the Jukes family into more favorable environments and revealed that they had reached a satisfactory social status when given an opportunity to do so away from the frustrating environment in which they were handicapped by economic want and the social stigma of being associated with a criminal clan.

The distortion of Dugdale's thesis that placed all responsibility on genetic relationship caused Franklin H. Giddings in 1901 to bring out a new edition of the study,[2] showing this almost complete reversal of the fundamental contention.

[2] Richard L. Dugdale, *The Jukes* (4th ed., New York: Putnam, 1910).

Speakers at the Conference, in the period under discussion, shared Dugdale's basic concept of heredity, although there were traces of a more discriminating separation of the genetic from the social factors in later papers, such as the paper presented by Dr. James C. Carson, of Syracuse, New York, in 1898. Carson felt that no single cause, such as heredity, was adequate to explain feeble-mindedness.

Specialized care of the feeble-minded had not been attempted much before the time of the Conference. Beginning with Jean Itard's unsuccessful attempt to tame the wild boy of Aveyron in 1800, interest in means of educating the feeble-minded spread over France and Germany. Dr. Conolly, of Hanwell, England, who pioneered in removing the shackles from the insane, started a school for the feeble-minded at Bath in 1846. In 1848 the Massachusetts legislature made an appropriation to cover the cost of care of the feeble-minded at Perkins Institute for the Blind at Boston. This was done at the suggestion of Samuel Gridley Howe, whose name occurs often in the annals of early provisions for different classes of the state's wards. In the same year, Dr. Charles T. Wilbur opened a private school for them at Barre, Massachusetts, a school which was still in operation in 1888 when he reported his findings on the feeble-minded to the Conference. The spread of institutions for the feeble-minded was slower than for the insane.[3]

The first enthusiasm of the founders of these institutions was built upon faith in the educability of their wards. Some of this hope had vanished by the time the Conference was organized, Sanborn reporting many years later (1892) said that Howe had entered into his project at Perkins Institute with the conviction that many of the feeble-minded could be restored to normalcy, but was disappointed with the results. At the same Conference,

[3] Stanley R. Davies, *Social Control of the Mentally Deficient* (New York: Crowell, 1930).

Hastings H. Hart, of Minnesota, made a similar statement. Dr. Wilbur, however, said (1888) that at least as large a proportion of the feeble-minded could be restored as of the insane. Dr. Isaac N. Kerlin, of New York, one of the earliest to work with the feeble-minded, while saying that "mighty few" were restored (1888), did place some on parole, as did Alexander Johnson, who was equally pessimistic regarding the majority. Dr. Francis M. Powell, of Iowa, related case stories showing that remarkable improvement in intellectual and mechanical dexterity had been brought about. In the absence of mental tests, precise classification and probable prediction were impossible. Then too, as the institutions increased in age, they tended to fill up with the lower grades of feeble-minded, thus displacing those of greater educational possibilities. Whatever the reason, the tone of hope so noticeable in the early accounts was largely missing at the close of the century.

Although mental tests were not in use, and the precision of the science of heredity introduced by August Weismann and his rediscovery of the Mendelian formula was not available, the fatalism of a supposed inborn taint led specialists in its treatment to pronounce against the marriage of the feeble-minded; to urge the custodial segregation of all feeble-minded women of child-bearing age; and to recommend the permanent custodial care of all whom the institutions for the feeble-minded had not trained to meet the conditions of free society.

Even with this growing pessimism regarding the results of educational efforts, these institutions continued to be called "training schools." A relatively free experimentation was followed in their construction, even as early as 1884 when Dr. Kerlin recommended their establishment on a wide area, with many and scattered buildings, each group largely a self-contained community. This idea easily evolved into that of the colony: separate units, spaced far apart, on land that had, for the most part, been abandoned, affording opportunity for separation of the sexes and careful classification of patients on the basis of their mechanical potentialities (Dr. William B. Fish, *Proceedings*, 1891). This idea had its most brilliant application in the first and second decade of the next century at the hands of Dr. Samuel Bernstein, of New York.

It is not without significance that attempts were made to identify feeble-mindedness with behavior. Kerlin estimated in 1884 that 10 percent of the criminal element belonged to this class; tramps, "obviously"; all prostitutes and alcoholics; and in 1898 Dr. James C. Carson repeated the same list without indicating any percentage for criminals.

In a like manner, classification of the feeble-minded, as it became crystallized in words, sounds strange to our ears, although in the practical management of the training school it might have worked well. Various classifications and terminology gained acceptance and then lost ground to successors: "idiot," "imbecile (*a*) high, (*b*) medium, and (*c*) low"; "juvenile insanity." Other terms were "idiocy," and "idioimbecility, high, low, and medium." Arthur C. Rogers used classifications (1888) that remained in general practice until Henry H. Goddard invented the term "moron" at the beginning of the next century: "idiot," "imbecile," "feeble-minded," the third term being used generically to include all grades, and specifically to indicate the highest grade, the one now called "moron." A term invented by Kerlin in his first paper (1884), "moral imbecile," illustrates the confusion between intellectual capacity and behavior. Later (1890), he says that moral imbeciles are incurable; that they should be disciplined in mechanical dexterity, but that intellectual education leads to their "deterioration." These classifications are indications that determination of feeble-mindedness was largely based upon behavior rather than upon degree of intelligence. There was not then available any means by which the latter could be evaluated apart from behavior.

Confusion and a fumbling, groping search for the clue to good care of the feeble-minded are apparent in the records; but it is equally clear that the frontiers of knowledge and method in the care were pushed forward by the forum evaluation of various theories. The advance was slight, but it was progress in the light of present standards.

6 · THE PROTECTION OF CHILDREN

As THE Conference tried to discover means of preventing the ills with which it was dealing, "to train up the child in the way it should go" took a place of importance very close to segregation of the unfit as a way of stopping trouble at its source. Even though the philosophy of the Conference had swung away from theoretical speculation about society and its members to the practical question of what to do about existing ills, as practical men its members could not avoid giving at least lip service to measures designed to prevent the ills with which they were struggling. It was, therefore, inevitable that leaders of the Conference should be concerned with the child to keep him from the ranks of the broken and vicious as he reached manhood. So it proved. The section on children devoted attention to all phases of child welfare, from infancy through school and early work period: the child's health and behavior; early delinquencies and their correction; the orphan, or the deserted child; the deaf or blind child; the child of an immigrant with the peculiar dangers that surround him—these matters run through the entire set of *Proceedings* without a break from the first appearance of child welfare as a special topic at the Second Conference to the present. Many influences besides interest in preventing the ills of the future insured this close attention to the youngest members of our population. A child in trouble makes a strong appeal to anyone; and therefore children's institutions and children's agencies sprang up in large numbers all over the land. Their representatives found a forum in the Conference—a university, as Cardinal Newman aptly called it—in which they could learn and be taught how this unpredictable thing called a child could be corrected and directed. But before it paid much attention to methods of guiding the child, the Conference found itself a debating society discussing the advantages and disadvantages of the institutional method for his care as contrasted with foster home placement. The debate became very bitter at times and was complicated with arguments based on sectarian religious interests rather than on the welfare of the child himself.

The Conference, at this period, never stopped to examine the validity of this intense interest in children; to question whether the damage was not already done when a child became the subject of society's concern. It was not until nearly the end of the first fifty years of the Conference (1922), that J. Prentice Murphy, a children's agency worker, suggested that it might have been wiser for society to have directed its efforts toward conserving the home from which the child had been taken (and thus undertake a truly preventive job by preserving the immemorial function of the family as the institution which equips the young to participate in a world of adults), than to have all but exhausted its energies to save the child after he had been damaged. In the period under review, however, such a doubt was never expressed; nor has it come into serious consideration since Murphy issued his challenge. The National Conference of Social Work and its widely spread members are still emphasizing the importance of child welfare, rather than spending their energies in discovering why so many families fail in their primary social function and in experimenting with means by which familial breakdown may be prevented.

The major difference of opinion regarding the care of children during this period was concerned with the relative advantage of institutional and foster home care. In 1852 Charles Loring Brace, who devoted his life to rescuing abandoned children from the streets of New York,[1] began sending them to homes in the Western states in groups of about a hundred each, and distributing them to families of farmers who had gathered at designated places to receive them. By 1875, 35,000 children had been taken off the streets of New York in this way.

In 1863 the New York Catholic Protectory was established to receive (1) children under fourteen entrusted to it by their parents or guardians for instruction or reformation; (2) children between seven and fourteen years of age, committed by the proper officials as truants or as idle, vicious, or homeless; and (3) dependent children sent to it by the New York City Commissioner of Charities and Correction; with power to place at suitable employment, instruct them in suitable branches of knowledge, and to bind them out. The Protectory grew rapidly, and soon became the largest single institution for children in the United States. Its policy was not definitely against foster home care for children, but it claimed that there were no homes available for the children committed to it, for the Roman Catholics in New York were largely recent immigrants who had not established themselves in a sufficiently stable economic situation, or long enough, to provide places for the thousands of children of that faith received by the Protectory.

Whether rightly or wrongly, the leaders of the Roman Catholic Church believed that Brace's agency, the New York Children's Aid Society, was picking up children in New York City without regard to their religious faith, and they went so far, in some instances, as to accuse the Society of intentionally taking Catholic children and placing them in families of Protestant farmers in the West. Not all the bitterness reached by the debate appeared in the *Proceedings* of the Conference. The activ-

[1] Charles Loring Brace, *The Dangerous Classes of New York* (New York: Wynkoop and Hallenbeck, 1872).

ities of the New York Children's Aid Society were aired at great length before the Conference; whereas the resentment of the supporters of the Protectory found scarcely any echo in the deliberations. What may be called the final chapter of the sectarian phase of the dispute was registered emphatically at the 1899 Conference when Thomas Mulry, director of the New York Catholic Charities, stated without qualification that the best care for a child, if it is possible to get it, is in a home of his own religious faith. It piques one's curiosity a bit to know why Mulry, who at the Conference a year earlier had presented some vigorous but far-fetched arguments against foster home care based on instances that no one defended, should make this about-face; but it is at least safe to assume that no religious organization as realistic as any of the major Christian denominations could defend any other general thesis than that the home is the best place for a child.

The difference of opinion between those defending Brace's method of child placement and those criticizing it does occupy a large place in the Conference's records. For the most part, its defenders were from New York, including Seth Low (1879), later that city's mayor. Decreases in the number of juveniles arrested in the city of New York were cited as evidence of its effectiveness: from 5,880 in 1860 to 1,666 in 1876; while representatives from Illinois and Michigan in 1888 believed that the plan should not be judged by the few boys who turned out badly. The chorus of protest was loud and widespread. A. G. Byers, of Ohio, claimed (1879) that Brace dumped carloads of children in the West without solicitude for their real welfare. A public official from Illinois, in the same year, maintained that instead of supplying homes for hundreds of New York's children, Illinois should reserve its homes for the 1,200 children in Chicago who needed them. In the same year, John P. Early, of Indiana, declared that a large percentage of those

sent out from New York turned up ultimately in the penitentiary, and Elmore said that every child he knew about who had
been sent out from New York, with the exception of one
Negro boy, had gone "to the bad." "It might be very good for
New York, but it is bad for the South"; said a delegate from
South Carolina in 1880; while one from North Carolina made
the discriminating remark in 1882 that farmers used the children as slaves, and if any farmer wished to be honest and to
treat them decently, he found that they presented behavior
problems too difficult to handle. Wisconsin threatened to pass
statutes prohibiting the transference of dependent children into
the state, and by 1889 Michigan had forbidden any to be sent
into the state without first securing official consent. Sanborn,
with his usual judicial attitude, expressed the opinion in 1888
that the work of the New York Children's Aid Society was developing without the intimate supervision necessary in foster
home placement.

In 1875 or 1876, in response to criticisms by the New York
Prison Association that many of the children placed by the
Children's Aid Society had become criminals, Brace said he had
sent out an investigator who visited prisons, reformatories, and
children's institutions in Illinois, Indiana, and Michigan, and
found only four inmates who had been placed by the Children's
Aid Society. At a later date (1894), the state of Minnesota,
through the secretary of its State Board of Charities, Hastings
H. Hart, made a careful study of what had happened to the 340
children sent from New York in the three years previous, and
presented the results of his study in a carefully worded paper
at the Conference that year. Hart found that 58 percent of the
children had either turned out badly, could not be found, or
there was no report available. Specifically, he found that a few
vicious children had been sent out, probably without knowledge on the part of the Society; that the children had been

hastily placed; and that there had not been sufficient super-vision to afford the children reasonable protection. He closed his report with recommendations that supervision of the children should be improved and that no child over twelve should be sent out. Brace took the criticism kindly, and thanked Hart for the care with which the study had been made and for the courteous manner of presentation. He also promised to put its recommendations into effect. It is not clear just what changes were made in the plans of the Children's Aid Society as a result of this study, but they were too late to prevent some of the states into which the Society had been sending children, from passing laws prohibiting such a practice except as a bond were deposited with the state to reimburse it should the child become a public charge. It was long after Brace's death and well into this century that the Children's Aid Society took the only practical step to insure adequate supervision of its far-flung charges by appointing a competent children's agency in each state to accept that responsibility.

No other agency attempted to place children on such a wide front as did Brace, but in 1883 a Dr. F. M. Gregg, of Chicago, inaugurated a plan of children's home societies which he planned to extend throughout the country. His idea was to have a society in each state, with its board made up largely of members of Evangelical churches and with local advisory boards in local communities, covering each locality with local representatives, for the most part volunteers, "with so complete an organization that a child cannot be hurt or abused without being known." The agency was to be primarily a means of placement for dependent and neglected children; but it included an institution for reception and examination of the children who came into its care before the placement. Such an ambitious plan, superimposed upon extensive provisions already in existence for such services, could scarcely be realized;

but by 1892 ten states had organized children's home societies, ten receiving homes were in existence, and 1,500 local advisory boards were functioning. The idea had sufficient vitality to live to the present time by serving communities untouched by the efficient child caring agencies of the large cities, and by functioning where there is no state-wide public service for the care of dependent and neglected children. (The Social Security Act of 1935 encouraged the development of public service to children in states lacking that facility.) The growth of the children's home societies seemed to be generally favored west of the Pennsylvania line and north of the Mason and Dixon, and in some states, such as Michigan, Illinois, and Washington, the societies have been pioneers in good placement of dependent children.

Three states, Massachusetts, Ohio, and Michigan, had characteristic and widely varying systems for the care of dependent children. The first, although it had institutions for children, depended largely on placements in the care of dependent as well as of delinquent children. The particular plan used in Ohio and Michigan was for dependent children only; Ohio encouraged counties to build local institutions to serve as receiving homes for children who would later be placed in private families; and Michigan had a single state school at Coldwater with a similar function.

In Massachusetts a reform school for boys was established in 1846, for girls in 1854, and the State Primary School for dependents in 1866. In 1869 the state board appointed an agent to be present at all court hearings of juveniles, held separately from the regular service of the court, with the function of advising the judge on the disposition of the child. The agent had authority to have the child committed to himself for placement, or to make such other disposition of the child as seemed fit. In 1880 it was reported that about one third of all children before the court were committed to the agent of the board. The plan was most widely used in the handling of girl delinquents, for whom was developed a volunteer auxiliary group of about fifty women scattered throughout Massachusetts, mostly in the western part of the state. They made local investigations, supervised the probationers, kept case histories, and were permitted to pay board to the family taking the child. Institutes were organized for their instruction. Since, for the most part, they were neighbors of the child, their knowledge of their charges was likely to be intimate and accurate.

The Ohio system grew, as so many movements do, from the inspiration of one woman. In 1858 a Mrs. Catherine Fay, of Marietta, Ohio, distressed because of the inability to find a way to care for some homeless children, took them into her own home, and ultimately succeeded in getting the county to erect a home for dependent children. Ohio then passed a law authorizing counties or a group of counties to build such homes on the favorable vote of the taxpayers, superintendents and matrons to be appointed by the county commissions; and the whole project to be under the supervision of the state board, but without any state grant of financial aid. The legislation also required a county not having such a home to board its dependent children in a county that did have one. It was the intent of the law that children should be placed as opportunity offered. In 1880 eight of the eighty counties had such homes. Later (1888), it was said that the plan, if not always satisfactory, was at least commendable, for these relatively small homes gave opportunity for individualizing each child. The principal limitation of the county home as a child placing agency was that its meager and unequipped personnel at best could attend only to the tasks involved in the custodial care of their wards.

The Michigan Home at Coldwater is noted merely because it was the first of the state homes for children built about this time. It was primarily a receiving home, with its major function that of placement for indenture or adoption. It was built on the cottage plan, with a housemother in each unit of thirty children. This plan was copied by the neighboring states of Wisconsin and Minnesota, and was chiefly used by the rural and northern counties; Detroit and Wayne County especially are said to have sent few if any children because the state home was at such a great distance from the homes of the children.

At no time during this period was the right of the state to remove children from unsuitable homes questioned. In Mary Carpenter's paper (1875) she says that all children without proper guardianship should be removed from their residences by the state; an argument later enlarged by a discussion of the formative influence of early environment—they were thinking of the children over two years of age—and the benefits that society would gain by insuring a suitable environment to its imperiled children. One speaker (Albert S. White, *Proceedings*, 1888) was able to work off his hatred of the Federal Supreme Court in saying that an unfavorable environment is one of lawlessness, which pervades most of society from the "vacillating Supreme Court" down, and from which children could be saved by good placement. Ernest P. Bicknell, at that time secretary of the Indiana state board, did not believe that the state had gone far enough in this direction; but he was probably thinking of the reluctance of the courts to take from their parents mentally deficient children who showed no behavior problem. By 1898, however, the principle was clearly held that no child should be removed from his family because of poverty.

Throughout this period there are frequent references to the necessity of removing children from the almshouse, for much the same reasons as were advanced for taking them from dissolute parents. One of the first acts of the Massachusetts board was to issue such an order. New York followed in 1878, but the great weakness in these orders, and even in the statutes, was that they were almost necessarily without penalty, they depended for their obedience, to some extent, on the coöperation of the superintendent of the almshouse, or the guardians of the children, but to a greater extent upon the availability of places to which children could be transferred. So we find all through the records, statements that children are in the almshouse, the situation which called forth a strong plea by Letchworth in 1898 that more effort be made if "the great number of children still in the almshouses" are to receive a decent chance in life.

The institution had very few defenders, even in the early days of the Conference. A speaker at the 1879 Conference describes the private institution as "a pioneer institution in the solution of hereditary pauperism," but for the most part, discussion is limited to its comparative value with placement: it is better than poor family placement; it should be used before a child is definitely sent to a family; it is valuable for the child that cannot be placed, such as the physically handicapped. There were clear statements as early as 1887 that the institution is essential to study of the child before successful placement. There was preference for the cottage system of institution, or the family system (as Mary Carpenter and others called it), and there were descriptions of how it works. In the treatment of juvenile offenders, there was a much wider acceptance of the institution, not as an alternative when a home could not be found, but as the best place to effect the necessary reformation. Massachusetts, however, did use the foster home for certain delinquents.

In regard to availability of foster care, there was a wide divergence on details. Brace thought that no board should be paid to foster parents, for to do so would commercialize a relationship which should be kept on a spiritual and moral plane. He was almost alone in that sentiment, although Letchworth was afraid that paying board would dry up the supply of free homes, which he considered better. Sanborn cited a striking illustration of the radical drop in infant mortality when the policy of placing foundlings out to wet nurses was substituted for the foundling asylum, a drop in which fatalities decreased from about 90 percent to about 20 percent—a demonstration of a condition for infant survival which is now universally accepted. All speakers who were closely connected with the practical operation of foster care were emphatic in their insistence upon adequate supervision, although nowhere in this period was adequacy defined. Various opinions were expressed as to the supply of homes, Josephine Shaw Lowell stating that there were not enough to meet the demand. The speakers for the Catholic Protectory took the same position. It is not without significance that these two witnesses on the subject had received their experience in the highly congested city of New York and that Brace, although he believed that there were enough homes, did not draw upon New York City or its environs to supply them.

In general, the societies and institutions placing children did not seem so much concerned with the limited supply of homes willing to take children as with the tendency to narrow the geographical area within which the search for homes was conducted, combined with the failure to secure the advantage for the child of being placed in a home far from his own home in order to insure him an unprejudiced opportunity for a new start. By 1890 John H. Finley, secretary of the New York State Charities Aid Association, and Homer Folks, secretary of the Pennsylvania Society, pointed out the need for careful investigation, both of the potential foster home and of the child to be placed, in order to save the family and the child from the bad experience of a faulty placement. And by 1890 placement of some delinquent, as well as dependent and neglected, children was advocated by both the Philadelphia and the Boston Children's Aid Society, as well as by the state of Massachusetts.

Letchworth, at the meetings of 1883, reporting for the Conference Committee on Children, divided delinquent children into three categories: truants for whom schools for truants should be provided; petty offenders, who should be cared for at industrial schools; and the hardened, "hereditary" offenders who should be sent to a reform institution. At the next meeting of the Conference Dr. John D. Scudder, of the Boys' School at Pontiac, Michigan, suggested that all boys fall into three groups: the goody-good (and most of them die young!); the creative, from whom come the leaders of business, as well as some of the vigorous delinquents; and the born criminals, who cannot be aided.

In spite of these pessimistic outlooks, no one at the Conference ever suggested punishment as a means of treating the juvenile offender. There was no realistic explanation of the reason for the differential treatment of the young on the ground of their social and emotional immaturity; but there was a firm faith in the value of re-education of the youth who had fallen into the hands of the law as a means of restoring him to a useful place in free society. This was obviously a statement of a faith that should be practiced, rather than a description of the ordinary operation of a reform school. Abundant evidence was presented of cruelty, and especially of lack of imagination in the handling of children entrusted to the custody of reform schools. Such recitals were uniformly presented as horrible examples, attributed at times to the baneful result of political control of the personnel of the institution; and at times attributed to the incompetence of its warden. As late as 1891 Folks quotes Dugdale to the effect that "reformatories are the nurseries not the reformatories of crime"; and in 1897 one speaker asks, "Do reformatories reform?" and replies that for the most part they do not. This places in striking relief the uniformity of sentiment that their inmates should be treated as children in need of re-education, and that the efforts of its director should be solely so aimed. Dr. Walter Lindley, of the Whittier School, at Whittier, California, in 1896 placed responsibility for the effect of the institution upon the child squarely upon the behavior of the superintendent and of his aids. Others favored doing away with all barriers; maintaining a balance between industrial training and scholastic work; and breaking the group up into small units, as was also advocated in caring for dependent children in an institution; moreover, they stressed the importance of recreation, but not to such an extent and for such specific reasons as was done later. There were discussions of various forms of industrial activity, with emphasis on outdoor work, and the caution expressed that political influence should not interfere with the appointment of personnel, nor allow the test of the success of the institution to be determined by the amount of its earnings instead of by what would benefit the boys. Religious education was given conventional approval, but at least one speaker (1884) questioned the value of formal religious instruction as given by a minister, on the ground that it was inclined to favor an unrealistic standard of morality.

The idea of a special court to try children's cases, which came to legal fruition in 1899, was suggested several times in this period (as in a Massachusetts provision of 1869 that an agent of the Board of Charities attend all trials of minors); but the Committee on Children of 1896 definitely recommended that there be created a special court to try children's cases in which there would be no semblance of formal criminal procedure. The recommendation of the committee went beyond the mere establishment of a special tribunal, and proposed a commission whose responsibility would begin with the complaint against the child and not end until the child had been discharged from supervision by the state.

On the matter of subsidies by states to agencies caring for

children, the Conference was almost uniformly opposed. One speaker, Judge Richard Prendergast, of Chicago, argued in its favor (1886) that with subsidies the state could use the resources of private agencies at a lower cost than if it were itself to supply such care to children; but also that children in such institutions, especially under religious auspices, could be furnished religious instruction in a natural way, which a public institution finds it difficult to do. The backers of the New York Catholic Protectory were very active over a period of several legislative sessions, and in 1875 finally succeeded in getting New York State to give it per capita subsidies, on the ground that it was taking care of children who otherwise would be public charges. California adopted the policy of subsidizing institutions at a rate varying from $75 to $100 a year for each child instead of itself building a children's institution. In the debates on this matter its representatives several times expressed impatience with the strictures of Eastern speakers, defending themselves by the blanket assertion that the conditions in California differed from those in the East, and could not be appreciated by critics of the method of subsidies. C. D. Randall, of Michigan, pointed out (1888) that the effect of giving subsidies to institutions in accordance with the number of children under care, over which number the state exercised no control, was to swell the number of children taken with little regard to whether an institution was the place for them or not. He quoted startling figures: Michigan and Ohio, which granted no subsidies, had one child in 10,000 and one child in 1,000 of population respectively in institutions, whereas in California and New York, which had subsidies, the ratio was 268 and 250 per 1,000 population respectively. On the same occasion, Mrs. Lowell pointed out that the policy once established would be impossible to discontinue because the existence of institutions so subsidized depended upon subsidy. In this way, the public would always be under the necessity of paying heavily for services it could not control and in amounts it would be unable to limit.

In 1882 Hastings H. Hart presented an over-all view of the number of children under public and private care in institutions in the United States and the cost: the total number in institutions at any one time averaged 100,000; 12,600 persons were employed in their care; while the institutions occupied property with the value of $55,000,000 and with an annual maintenance cost of $12,600,000. Seventy-four thousand of these children were in children's institutions, 15,000 were in reformatories; 5,000, in institutions for the feeble-minded; 4,500, in institutions for the deaf; and 1,500, in institutions for the blind. This is the only known comprehensive estimate of the dimensions to which the provision for children had grown in the period under discussion. When taken in connection with the variety of needs as analyzed by Hastings H. Hart, it is not surprising that there was a great deal of attention paid to considerations of treatment by members of the Conference, or that differences of opinion on methods, and even on evaluations of method, should have found expression in this national forum. In 1893, in connection with the Columbian Exposition at Chicago, a special conference on child saving was held under the auspices of the Conference in which representatives of most of the different types of children's agency and institution gave descriptions and histories of their projects. The only information additional to that contained in the *Proceedings* of the Conference itself was a rather long description, presented anonymously, of the origin, operations, backing, and philosophy of the New York Catholic Protectory with a vigorous statement of the advantages it offered in caring for the dependent and predelinquent child.

Of child labor and its ills, but few comments were made at this early date. In a plea for tenement house reform, which reform was delayed by at least a decade, John H. Finley described vividly (1891) the sweatshops existing in the city of New York where thousands of families were crowded together in old and dark tenements, their miserable situation aggravated by "home work," in which even the youngest children were forced to engage in order to eke out the scanty family income. In 1896 that most valiant of all the fighters in the small company which eventually brought some mitigation of the ills of child labor, Mrs. Florence Kelley, made a characteristic attack upon all labor by children under sixteen, adding slyly that labor unions can be trusted to take care of much of the evils of child labor, but there is no cure for the philanthropic lady who wants a job for a child so as to help support his mother.

7 · THE ENGLISH POOR LAW IN AMERICA

*B*Y THE PASSAGE of the Poor Law Reform bill of 1834, said Disraeli, England announced to the world that it was a crime in England to be poor. The economic theory set forth by the Commission that framed the reform acts on poor relief— "that it is not the intent of the poor law to take care of the poor; that is, of those who can earn their living by labour"— had an even more rigid acceptance in this country than in England. Work was more plentiful here; everyone worked, or his immediate ancestors had. There was less tolerance of the able-bodied man out of work than in England where there had never ceased to be vigorous opposition to the philosophy of 1834, an opposition which finally triumphed in the 1909 acts that swept off the statute books forever the whole accumulation of punitive legislation toward the poor. We were the children of England, and like so many countries that started as colonial offshoots of an older and more stable nation, we held to the older traditions longer than they survived in the parent state.

Aside from these reasons, there probably was another factor that prevented us from taking a more generous view of the plight of our less successful citizens. The 1830 immigration brought to the United States people who were largely alien to the major culture; to most of us the needs of these newcomers seemed remote, and probably for a time they were hidden from view by the protective devices of mutual aid which aliens use to hide their weaknesses—much as the Plymouth settlers secretly buried those who died that first winter so that the Indians would not know how weak they really were. America was becoming a melting pot of peoples, which in the long run was to make America great, but in its immediate incidence it erected barriers of ignorance so high that a Danish immigrant of the latter part of this period felt called upon to write a book on *How the Other Half Lives*.[1] These considerations help to explain, if they do not justify, that hard, contemptuous attitude of the moderately successful person toward those who fail. The French and, to a certain extent, the other Latin peoples do not have this viewpoint. We have no word corresponding to the French word *misére* which means at one and the same time both the condition of wretchedness of the poor and the sentiment of mercy which moves to pity, identifying thereby the needy and the reliever of want as a single social unit. Nor have we what is largely common among the Jewish people of today, handed down from Biblical times, the identification of charity with justice, for which there was originally but one word. We probably do not have caste, unless Myrdal is correct in asserting that we have established it so far as Negroes are concerned;[2] but we do divide ourselves into two groups: the successful and the failures, with little commerce between them.

Seth Low, in 1879, said, "the poor must learn to help themselves," and at the same meeting another speaker asserted that relief should be given only in the almshouse, where the poor could be segregated and thus the propagation of paupers would be stopped at that point. Theodore Roosevelt declared (1877) that, "able-bodied tramps and paupers must work," and Professor Francis Wayland, of Yale, in the same year warned that receiving public assistance would come to be looked upon as a right, and that the recipient would come to believe that he was

[1] Jacob A. Riis, *How the Other Half Lives* (New York: Scribner, 1897).
[2] Gunnar Myrdal, *The American Dilemma* (New York: Harper, 1944).

living by "decent" means. Charles R. Henderson, then in Detroit, claimed (1891) that public outdoor relief tends to lower wages and excites hostility to the state, since the poor cannot be satisfied no matter how much the state gives them in relief, and such dissatisfaction leads them to crime. Another earlier speaker (1880) would permit the state to give temporary relief, and several shared his view, but then he would say to the man so aided: "We have helped you over this difficulty; now if you do not work, neither will you eat."

Most of these speakers would permit some assistance to be given by private individuals, private agencies, and religious bodies, on the assumption that with such sources of aid there would be a more accurate and continuing knowledge of the condition of the applicant, and that assistance from such sources could not be regarded as a right. However, some claimed that assistance was the monopoly of the church as was stated (1891) by a delegate from Pennsylvania: "I do not wish to concede to the state the wholesome duty to visit the sick, to comfort the widows and fatherless and to raise up those who fall."

These statements carry, as tacit assumptions, either that any able-bodied person can get a job at which he can make a living, or, if he is in want, that there are private sources of assistance open to him and adequate to meet his needs. Such assumptions probably represented the public opinion of the time, and they are far from extinct, even at the present. There were some who saw more realistically, and they were the forerunners of a new day of promise for those described in our time as "one third of our people ill fed, ill housed, and ill clothed." The position advanced by Sanborn as early as 1877, that proper criticism against public relief rests only on its maladministration, and that as relief comes to individualize its applicants it will increase in volume, not decrease, was echoed by several. Thirteen years later he quoted as his own sentiments the memorable position taken by William Pitt in 1796 relative to the English Poor Law:

> The law which prohibits giving relief where any visible property remains should be abolished. That degrading condition should be withdrawn. No temporary occasion should force a British subject to part with the last shilling of his little capital and to descend to a condition of wretchedness from which he could never return, merely that he might be entitled to a casual supply.[3]

Wines, in 1883, took even more specific exception to the theory that the state should leave the field of assistance to private and religious organizations, asserting that such an idea was "romantic nonsense." He went on to say that almost all states have some system of public relief; some problems are so great that only the state can cope with them, and under certain circumstances relief is a right. He added that the services of the state were the common concern of all its citizens, which was enlarged by another speaker, who pointed out that taxation spread the cost of assistance more equitably, since "the rich" could not avoid paying their share. This seems to be an answer to the more rigid assumption that all charity is bad, and that the poor should help each other, a conception that was not absent from nineteenth-century thinking. All defenders of public outdoor relief acknowledged that it was often very badly handled, but as one of the Massachusetts officials said (1878), "the mischief of pauperization alleged to be inseparable from a system of outdoor relief . . . is a myth." Even the much-quoted Dugdale had no fixed idea and thought that public outdoor relief could be handled well.

Relative to private relief, some of the speakers (1891) were positive in their belief that its resources were inadequate for such a task, while another speaker, Dr. Samuel G. Smith, head

[3] Sidney and Beatrice Webb, *English Local Government* (London: Longmans, Green, 1929), Part 8, I, 37.

of the department of sociology at the University of Minnesota and later president of the Conference (1905), asserted in 1891 that probably more harm is done by indiscriminate private charity than by any other way of giving.

A few voices were raised in favor of some discrimination based on consideration of the causes of the need of certain applicants. The secretary of the Pennsylvania board declared (1880) that the state should care for those who were poor through no fault of their own; eight years later a speaker felt that widows should be permitted to stay at home with their children and that sending children to a day nursery was un-desirable; and in 1891 the administrator of outdoor relief in Columbus, Ohio, laid down the rule now universally accepted —in theory at least—that poverty alone should not result in the breaking up of any family. Some of the speakers who had neat little formulas to solve the problem of poverty, such as work for tramps, institutions for dependent children, and hospitals for the sick, admitted themselves baffled in their attempts to square the theory of no outdoor relief with the facts of widowhood and deserted wives.

While most of the thinking on the matter of poverty was moralistic in tone, there were some exceptions. For instance, one Conference speaker looked upon the Louisiana lottery as absorbing too large a share of the workers' wages (1892), while others blamed the presence of poverty on a faulty currency— irredeemable paper money and speculation (1874). Seasonal unemployment and illness of breadwinners, too great prosper-ity, and conflict between labor and capital (1889) were some of the "causes" as they were then identified by observers who were more carefully checking what they saw and not blindly following a settled theory in explaining the condition of men and women who appealed for aid. Of course, at this time the once popular classification of the poor into "worthy" and "un-

worthy" was widely used, and it is probable that these im-
personal factors identified as causing the plight in which the
poor were found were used to broaden the category of the
"worthy," and were not in any real sense a breaking away from
the moralistic method of evaluating the need of an applicant.
Wines in 1886, as a social statistician, exposed a fallacy in
ascribing a factor discovered as present in an applicant to be
the cause of his trouble by pointing out the danger of falling
into an *ex post facto* error that because a man was a drunkard,
or shiftless or unemployed, the cause of his need was immediately known. It is the only instance in these first thirty-five
years of the Conference's activity that a rigid, scientific theorem
of social research was mentioned; and Wines apparently never
repeated it. Its careful observance, which would have led either
to a more rational analysis of causes, or to abandoning the idea
that a cause or any galaxy of causes could be found, might have
saved the "scientific" efforts of an entire generation of fruitless
searching for a definite clue to the perennial dilemma of why
some men succeed and others, whose lot is not so very much
different, fail. This is not to assume that we are any wiser today
than our forebears; unless accepting defeat along these lines
and concentrating effort on method of alleviation and piecemeal
prevention are better, or at least wiser, uses of intelligence.

The Conference noted several experiments as well as current
practices in outdoor relief. The sudden but complete abolition
of outdoor relief in Brooklyn in the midst of the winter of 1879,
without the faintest effect upon the amount of aid requested
from the private agencies, or from the public or private institutions, made a profound impression upon the Conference, perhaps not so much in proving that there were no needy persons
in Brooklyn, as that public relief was not going to them. Nine
years earlier, Baltimore had also abandoned public relief because it was so badly administered.

Other reports dealt with actual methods of administration. Two cities reported radical reforms: St. Paul had established a special Board of Control of unpaid members appointed for life which had responsibility for the hospitals, almshouse, foundling asylum, and for public outdoor relief, thus taking the administration of all the city's charities "out of politics." The Grand Rapids system, reported ten years later (1897), was apparently less ambitious and confined itself to public indoor and outdoor relief. It was described as an unpaid commission that was making careful investigations and keeping records of its beneficiaries and "saving a good deal of money." Josiah Quincy, as mayor of Boston, stated in 1898 that a city gets as good an administration of its public charities as it deserves, to which Joseph Choate, of New York, replied that his city could not get a Josiah Quincy as mayor but had to be satisfied with what Tammany gave it. During this entire period, public outdoor relief administration in Boston remained free from political patronage, according to the report of a St. Vincent de Paul representative (1895), and was quite satisfactory.

About this time Byers reported that Ohio had adopted the plan which has come to be identified with that state and Iowa, and severely criticized by some, of turning over investigations to local charity organization societies, and acting on their recommendations. This was a difficult relation for both the public official and the private agency because it left the private agency without authority to follow up its findings while placing responsibilities upon the public which it had no voice in defining. Incidentally, the plan was an admission that public officials could not be secured to do the work honestly and efficiently. It is not without significance that in 1897 Ernest P. Bicknell, secretary of the Indiana State Board, expressed himself as being helpless in the face of the political interests of a thousand overseers of the poor, and that within less than ten years, his successor, Amos W. Butler, did bring order out of the chaos of "a thousand overseers of the poor," establishing outdoor relief in Indiana on a plane of efficient and humane operation that was a model for the entire country, and did it without enlarging the authority of the Board from its advisory and supervisory function.

Very few words of praise were spoken of the existing almshouses. In 1884 Sanborn sympathetically reviewed the situation regarding the almshouses of New England. The towns were responsible for their own poor, establishing and maintaining their almshouses, of which there were about six hundred in the region. Keepers sometimes had charge of the town roads, or served the towns in other capacities, such as keeping the town records and transacting the town's business. Most of the almshouses were on farms, but the officials were not notably successful in getting the inmates to work, although some produce was raised. The average almshouse population in Massachusetts was seventeen, and of all those living in almshouses about 620 were insane, probably one fourth of the total number. In New Hampshire the number was as high as 60 percent; in Vermont it was the same. In Connecticut the number of insane in almshouses was small, and in Rhode Island it was even less. Buildings were from fifty to 100 years old, but they were being gradually replaced; some extravagant ones were being erected, such as the one at Lancaster which was costing $3,000 per bed. In Massachusetts the tenure of the keeper of the almshouse was long; one stayed more than twenty years. The average salary was $387 per year plus maintenance. There were fewer children in almshouses than there were insane, and half of them were feeble-minded. Sanborn did not think that there was any possibility of reducing the number of almshouses by supplanting the town system with a county almshouse, as was the custom in the newer Western states. On account of the complex settlement laws of Massachusetts, so confusing that only "a few specialists understood them," the state provided a state alms-house for the so-called "state's poor," as well as outdoor relief for them out of the almshouse, by means of reimbursing local overseers for expenses incurred in their behalf. This is prob-ably a description of the almshouse at its best. Other places had fine buildings and expensive equipment, as for instance, Balti-more, which, John Glenn slyly remarked (1889) was "very well supplied with extravagances."

There was general agreement that an almshouse should have sound but inexpensive buildings, located on good rural land, with a place for crops and for livestock; that admission should be granted only after careful investigation; that adequate records should be kept (without any statement of what such records ought to contain, apart from the reasons for admis-sion); that there should be careful classification of the inmates; and that varied employment should be available for the charges. Various comments on employment similar to those made by Sanborn were that "it would be possible to hire the work that needed doing more cheaply than to get the inmates to do it," but that for the orderly running of the place and for its benefi-cial effect on its men and women, employment ought to be provided of such a variety that all but the bedfast might par-ticipate. The facts, however, were quite different. The man-agement of almshouses generally was a disgrace to the country, owing to the thousands of small units over which the state supervisory authority had ineffective control; the habit of mak-ing appointments of personnel on a partisan basis so that loyalty to the party in power rather than the quality of service rendered was the test of acceptability was quite usual, and produced wretched administration.

We are given a picture drawn by a sensitive physician of the almshouse as he saw it (1890) in Maryland, where there was no state board of charity, and where the duty of supervision was placed on the secretary of the State Board of Health. He indicts the general public for the shame of the almshouse, whose condition is worse than any brought on by war or pestilence; in it are crowded many whose only defect is poverty, who are and always have been willing to work. Children born there have no chance to develop normal lives. He then goes on to contrast the almshouse with the way hospitals are able to develop interest among the wealthy, whereas both the well-to-do and the general public forget that there is any such institution as the place where the poor spend their last days. From this all but universal criticism of the almshouse, Wisconsin, as well as Massachusetts, and perhaps some other New England states, should be excluded. In Wisconsin, by means of its plan to make grants-in-aid to almshouses that came up to the state's standards for the care of the chronically insane, there was ample testimony that the institutional care of the aged indigent was humane.

8 · CONCERN OF THE CONFERENCE WITH THE DELINQUENT

*T*HE WORK of two men, Zebulon Reed Brockway and John Augustus, dominated much of the discussion that took place on delinquency, not only in the National Conference, but in other circles interested in penology, such as the National Prison Association and university classes on charities and correction. The history of the Elmira (New York) Reformatory was almost precisely parallel with the life of the Conference, so that reports of its progress, and especially references to it as the exemplification of ideal prison administration, constantly occurred in contemporary literature. John Augustus died fifteen years before the Conference came into existence, but the dramatic beginnings in probation which he developed in Boston were lively memories to men of that period.

John Augustus (1785–1859) was a bootmaker who visited the police and municipal courts of Boston and was led by an unusual interest in people, coupled with a natural gift of discrimination, to ask a judge to be given the privilege of going bail for certain convicted defendants, who would then be released in his custody. Augustus then arranged to have the men (later he included women, even prostitutes), report regularly to him. He secured medical attention for them and found work, keeping meticulously accurate records of each person for whom he became surety. Most of the cases were of drunkenness, and Augustus persuaded them at once to sign a pledge of abstinence; it is reported that this reform, together with his persuasive and diligent supervision, restored three quarters of his charges to respected citizenship. In the period between 1841, when he went bail for his first charge, and 1858, Augustus took 1,152 men and 794 women on probation. He is said to have made as many as fifteen hundred visits in one year, and his surrey rattling over the cobblestones of Boston was one of the familiar sights of his day. In 1846 he gave up his work as a shoemaker to devote his entire time to his work in the courts and financed it out of his own savings and the unsolicited gifts of fellow Bostonians. When he bailed out a defendant who had no place to live, Augustus took him into his own home. He was discriminating in choosing his charges, but what the basis of his selection was, he never could tell; to him, the choice was between one for whom his services would be useless and another whom he believed he might help. He met obstacles, mostly in the police court where, for every prisoner released on probation, the court officer lost the few cents a day he would have been allowed if the man had been committed to jail. Opposition to his work became so pronounced in the police court that Augustus finally left it and devoted all his time to helping offenders who had been haled before the municipal court.

These two men alone were not responsible, of course, for the attitude toward the treatment of the delinquent as expressed by the public opinion represented in the Conference, an attitude which differed so decidedly from that toward poverty held by the same section of the population. There was no economic theory, such as laissez faire, obsessing men's minds in the field of penology as there was in the field of dependency. European criminologists were coming to the theory that punishment of the criminal does not act as a deterrent of crime, nor does it return the convict to freedom in any way improved after his incarceration; on the contrary, he is more bitter and revengeful at best, and a graduate from a school for crime at worst.

These pragmatic reactions against the older, classical school had captured the minds of thinking men and women concerned with the treatment of the criminal in this country and made them willing to accept the practical wisdom of a policy of reformation as the only practical way in which to treat the criminal. It was natural for them to look upon the Elmira Reformatory administration as proving the theory that punishment did not protect society from its criminal members nor was it an economically wise policy for the state, since it only produced recidivists.

In spite of Augustus's demonstration, probation was not seriously discussed by the Conference, not even by raising the question, so pertinent today, of whether some of the convicted might not better be treated outside institutional confinement. Massachusetts alone seems to have carried on the tradition. In 1878 the mayor of Boston was authorized to appoint a probation officer; he chose a man who had been chief of police for many years, with responsibility to seven lower courts and one superior court. In 1880 the legislature authorized each city or town to make a similar appointment. One speaker at the 1880 Conference declared that aiding discharged prisoners was the equivalent of "giving them a new heart and a little money," and that it should be done by paid, well-equipped officers of the state, not by volunteers. He also stressed the importance of keeping records of all former prisoners under parole. Attention was fixed on the indeterminate sentence, with all its recognized imperfections, as giving to the institution the responsibility of determining when a man who had been adjudged a criminal should be returned to society, under parole (1878).

There was no delusion that prisons were being managed, in general, according to such principles. In fact, it was fully known how bad many of them were, and that one of the reasons for their maladministration was the habit of appointing prison per-

sonnel for political reasons. Actually, outside the suggestion
that a civil service selection of wardens and keepers would do
away with the spoils system and that through longer tenure
prison officers would be trained by experience, there was not
much recognition of the need for special educational and professional preparation for the difficult task of remaking men and
women who had become society's enemies. Yet, General Roeliff Brinkerhoff, in a general statement on what a prison should
be (1880), stated as his last criterion that it should be staffed
by men specially trained for that service. He did not specify
just what the training should consist of, but the context implied that it should be in-service instructions under intelligent
supervision. He quoted with approval a resolution passed by the
International Prison Congress of 1878, "that we favor the professional education, in some form, of prison officials and employees and the payment of such salaries as will attract and retain competent persons in prison service."

The Conference did debate—and comment—on prison labor.
The same year that General Brinkerhoff read his very careful
paper, the delegate from Tennessee summed up the situation
in that state by concluding: "The poor are sold out and the
prisoners leased out"—to which Tennessee's governor, Albert
S. Marks made violent objection. He was given opportunity to
offer a factual denial but did not take advantage of it.

Perhaps the most stinging indictment of the system of leasing
out convicts to private contractors, backed up by a broad investigation, was presented in 1883 by the novelist George W.
Cable, of New Orleans, in reporting his survey of the leasing
system as practiced in eight Southern states and Texas. He
concluded that the system of leasing to private contractors,
who use the labor for private profit, precludes all possibility of
establishing an efficient penitentiary system; it contents itself
with disgracefully equipped prisons; in practice, it is brutally

cruel and teaches people to be callous also; it hardens, debases, and corrupts the criminal; it is based on the "suicidal and inhuman error" that society must not be put to any expense for the treatment of the criminal; it inflicts on the criminal a different sentence from that imposed on him by the court; it sets up false standards of conduct, and seduces the state into the commitment of murder for money. These were facts well known to penologists of the country, although probably they had not been dramatized elsewhere in a single statement. The system of leasing prisoners never had any defenders in the sessions of the Conference. Governor Charles Anderson, of Kentucky, where the lease system had been abolished, supported Cable's statement and called it "a policy of murder."

It would be flying in the face of known facts to assert that this vigorous exposure of the inhumanity of the lease system resulted in its correction. Use of the lease system has gradually lessened through this more than half a century, but a traveler in the South or a reader of the current press has evidence that it still persists, especially, but not wholly, in the treatment of Negro prisoners.

There was a spirited debate on the so-called "contract" and "state use" system of employment for prisoners. There was a universal feeling that prisoners should work while incarcerated; and there was the parallel conviction, probably more strongly shared by the man on the street than by the Conference, that they should earn their own way. The prisoners were perfectly able-bodied men, capable of producing material for which there was a market; and the conclusion was inescapable that they should be put to work at producing goods whose sale would defray the cost of their custodial care. As a matter of fact, while this ideal was rarely realized, it was more nearly reached in the states that used the much-condemned lease system than it was elsewhere. When prisons began to engage in the "contract" system (in which the state contracted with manufacturers to hire out its prisoners on a per diem fee, the manufacturers installing machinery and foremen in the prison with prisoners as the labor force), it was found that the labor unions vigorously protested against the competition of prison-made goods with goods made in a free market. There was some accusation that the opposition really came from the employers of free labor, who found their merchandise undersold by products of prison labor. The truth of the charge was never cleared up; but there was a gradual abandonment of the contract system in favor of "state use," which meant that prisoners were set to work on making goods for use in their own and other state institutions, even including the erection of buildings and landscaping the grounds of institutions. There was some grumbling by labor unions, but not violent opposition to this work. However, it closed the institutions as markets for such goods made by free labor. No one, not even the strongest defenders of organized labor, denied that prisoners should work, and it was admitted that the more nearly the tasks approximated the skills that would be in demand after the men left the institution, the better it would be for their morale while incarcerated, and the more useful to them after their discharge. The debate evoked bitter criticisms from labor leaders. They called into question both the wisdom and the motives of Conference speakers. One wonders whether a solution more satisfactory to everyone concerned could not have been reached by mutual consultation and compromise. It is hard to see how prison labor can have a really constructive effect upon prisoners unless they are engaged in producing something of value—any more than the Work Projects Administration could have been limited to tasks which "private enterprise could not undertake."

In the treatment of women and girls, some new ground was broken. When the first state board was created in Wisconsin in 1871, Mrs. William P. Lynde (1819–97) was appointed a member, the first woman in the United States charged with a post of such responsibility in social welfare. Her major interest in the field of the social services was the treatment of the delinquent girl. She secured the establishment of the Industrial School for Girls of Wisconsin, one of the first of its kind in the Middle West. She read two papers before the Conference (1879 and 1880) that set the tone for the discussion of treatment for women offenders. Quoting Josephine Shaw Lowell as saying, "the most dangerous . . . cause of crime, pauperism and insanity is the unrestrained liberty allowed to vagrant and degraded women," Mrs. Lynde then went on to condemn the practice of sending young girls to jails, thereby jeopardizing the chance of their reformation, while paying no attention to their male partners. She recommended the establishment of prisons exclusively for women and administered by women. In 1879, Secretary Warren F. Spaulding, of the newly created Board of Prison Commissioners of Massachusetts, reported that the commission consisted of three men and two women, and that a new prison for women at Sherborn was staffed entirely by women. He also reported that an effort was being made to have the sentences imposed for longer periods since the short terms were usually worthless as a means of reformation. (It is probable that he had in mind the indeterminate sentence.) It is to be noted that Mrs. Lynde's plea for a woman's board was that women exclusively should be in control. There were no specific arguments for separation. Brockway (1882) believed that men and women were much alike, and should be treated alike, although he did approve of separation. The burden of the debate rested, however, on women Conference members, who, in season and out, insisted wherever their voices were heard that prisons for women should be distinctly separated from the men's institutions, and have a complete personnel of women.

Byers in 1889 said that women in a mixed prison are "at the mercy of a bad lot of men," and quoted Mrs. E. Cody Stanton as saying, "May the Good Lord protect us from our protectors." While the exploitation of women in the mixed prison was a reason for their separation, it is probable that a much sounder explanation was that women only could deal with women in a matter-of-fact and sound manner, being at the same time more just and more merciful. There was recognition (1883) of the therapeutic value of music, art, and warmly sympathetic overseers—only those words were not used! The work was graduated to fit the ability and vocational outlook of the inmates; some Conference speakers regretted that there seemed to be less choice of activities for women than for men; but from reports of the limited range of possibilities, production was more fully exploited in institutions for women than in those for men. There is another difference to be pointed out, but its reason remains obscure: Why did women's prisons suffer less from the corroding influence of politics? Even in the period under review, the women's prisons began to offer prison management as a career and not as a temporary political gift. To a large extent, these conditions still exist in institutions for men, where the entire personnel sometimes changes when the political party in power is turned out and another comes in.

Local jails were universally condemned as the prey of petty politics. A speaker in 1878 quoted de Tocqueville on the "vile nature of American jails . . . as schools of crime." Brinkerhoff believed that they should not be used to house convicted criminals, but should be used only as a place of detention. Because the jails housed both petty criminals and citizens held as witnesses, it was said that it was more hazardous to be a witness to a crime than to commit one (1880). In the latter case, the man had a chance of being treated in a reformatory, whereas the witness had no recourse so long as the law wished to keep him in a place of which it was said (1883), "that every abuse named by Hóward as found in jails in England a hundred years ago may be found to exist in some jails in every state of the union." The only solution offered was to take jails out of the control of local government and put them all under the state as a part of a comprehensive penal system.

In 1882 Sanborn suggested that a Federal Bureau of Identification be established to conduct a central registration of all persons convicted anywhere in the United States. Its information was to be available to any public police authority (similar to the system used in France). Sanborn's idea finally bore fruit in the second decade of this century.

In 1886 George Hoadley, after he had served as governor of Ohio, made a refreshing confession that the matter of pardons had been a nuisance. He pointed out that on the reasonable theory that all governors are ambitious politicians, petitions for pardon were decided by the vigor of the importunity and by the influential backing that it had; that a governor's consideration of a pardon had not the remotest semblance to a judicial process; and therefore his decisions were based on grounds other than the merits of the petition. He suggested that the attorney general of the state be required to advise the governor on all such requests; but better than any plan to improve the pardoning power of the governor, he felt, would be a system whereby the matter of the convict's release should be left to the processes of a well-administered law resting on the basis of an indeterminate sentence and competent supervision of the prisoner during his period of parole.

Toward the end of the period under review, the Conference Committee on Penal and Reformatory Systems made an inclusive report (1891), embodying the recommendations previously made by Brockway, General Brinkerhoff, and Spaulding at previous sessions. It summarized the best thinking of the day concerning the treatment of offenders. On the ground that juries would not convict on such a blanket grant of power to the warden of a penitentiary or even to a parole board the report did not recommend a strictly indeterminate sentence. The current version of maximum and minimum sentence was recommended. The report recorded the opinion of the committee that a prison should be organized strictly as a reformatory institution. Each man would be individualized. The teachable inmates would be encouraged to learn a trade at which they could later be self-supporting, a trade chosen with reference to their antecedent experience. Convicts of doubtful ability would be engaged, for the most part, in producing goods for sale; those of low-grade intelligence and the incorrigibles would be engaged in occupations connected with service to the institution. As a reward for good behavior, a prisoner would be paid a certain percentage of the profit from the goods he produced, to be spent as he chose. A record of each convict would be kept from the time of his arrest to his ultimate discharge from parole, and individual treatment would be conditioned by the content of that record. The prisoners would have daily hours for the usual classroom instruction, and would be allowed to attend religious services on Sunday.

Reporting on recent advances, the report stated that by that time (1891) the indeterminate sentence had been authorized in eight states, but only for first offenders, except in New York. In New York, however, the indeterminate sentence did not extend to women. The Bertillon system of identification had been introduced in Pennsylvania, Illinois, and Massachusetts, with provisions for exchange of information between states using it. The report concluded by saying that there had been no progress in penal legislation or administration in the South; and that no state had taken in hand the serious problem of local jails.

9 · PERSONNEL IN PUBLIC SERVICE

*The spoils system . . . a system of terrorism under which
the best and bravest men quail.*[1]

*U*NTIL the end of this period (1899), the interest of the
Conference in personnel was largely absorbed in criticism of
partisan administration of public relief. The speakers cited instances of its baneful effect upon the competency of particular
institutions, such as the almshouse, the jail, the state prison, and
even the hospital for mental diseases. Even so, the most scathing
exposé of the latter did not take place until 1926, when the
former chairman of the state board of Illinois recited chapter
and verse in the appointment of incompetent physicians, in their
retention by political influence, and the disastrous effect that
they had, in this riot of such mismanagement, on the services to
mental patients.

During the nineteenth century the task of uplifting the ban-
ner for civil service reform was carried largely by the American
Social Science Association, and since many of the Conference
members were also members of that association, one must turn
to papers of the American Social Science Association for the development of the idea of appointment on merit to public positions. By 1896 the scandal of the "spoils system," as it came to
be called, had drawn together this informal separation of interests, and the Conference appointed a Committee on the
Merit System which, at that Conference and at the 1898 meet-

[1] Report of National Conference Committee on Politics in State Institutions, 1898.

ing, brought in formal reports on the evils of the spoils system and arguments for the adoption of a merit system. Lucy L. Flower described (1896) a situation in Chicago, details of which she had secured as a member of a committee appointed by the chairman of the county board to investigate conditions in the county institutions. On the election of a new board of county commissioners, the following method was hit upon as satisfactory to all its fifteen members: A list of the many hundred officers in the county who were subject to appointment by the board was compiled, with a notation of the salaries of each. The list was then divided into fifteen equal parts, each part containing positions of as nearly equal salary values as possible. These fifteen lists were then placed in a hat, and each commissioner drew one from the hat; each commissioner was then entitled to fill the positions on his list as he chose. On the witness stand, it was stated that superintendents of institutions could not remove incompetent employees, and that a resolution passed by this same board whereby the heads of institutions were given such a right was said to have been passed "only for outside effect." One commissioner defended himself with the statement, "my friends worked for me to get this position, and it is only right I should pay them, the only way I can, by appointing them to any place I can control."

The effect of such partisan appointments at their worst was described by Philip C. Garrett, of Pennsylvania, chairman of the state board, who had been president of the Conference in 1883. In his report for the first committee on the merit system in 1896, he described some of the results of the spoils system under the corrupt Ellis Phipps regime of Philadelphia:

tickets for outdoor relief were given as compensation to houses of ill-fame; and the lying-in hospital was made the resort for the prurient curiosity of pot-house politicians . . . the organized and systematic attack by certain politicians and public thieves, with the aid of a shrewd but depraved superintendent, upon the public poor fund, resulted in a shocking loss of life, and in untold suffering to those who were compelled to seek shelter under the almshouse roof and survived its terrors.

The spoils system is a distinctly American institution. It is a heritage from President Andrew Jackson's administration, which was, however, on the whole successful in bringing a new concept of democracy into American life. Its slogan, "to the victors belong the spoils," rests on the assumption that any average American is competent to fill any political position, either elective or appointive. The spoils system brought into clear relief the dilemma posed by the place of the specialist in a democratic society. Through the easy acquiring of wealth, America had been able to afford the luxury of wasteful public administration in all governmental functions long after European countries, under the necessity of preserving their solvency in a less bountiful economy and at the same time securing efficient administration, had found they could not afford to assume that any average man could perform any governmental duty. Europe had therefore devised various forms of a merit system by which competent service could be secured. George William Curtis, the leading protagonist for civil service reform, could cite the notable advances made by England through the use of its system of appointment by merit. Carl Schurz could speak (1898) realistically of the many dangers to which the merit system was exposed by politicians who desired to circumvent its provisions. (Probably Schurz spoke out of his German experience, though he did not refer to it.) In his second report summarizing arguments for the merit system, Garrett said that it insured competency, skill and experience, and special adaptation to the duties to be performed; rendered permanency of tenure probable; and involved economy. It had a good influence on beneficiaries, diminishing the probability of robbery and corruption, and would redeem the country from the demoralization of party spoils.

The members of the Conference were engaged in combating a monstrous miscarriage of justice perpetrated under the guise of party loyalty. They had neither time nor perspective for a long view of the problem of personnel. Their fight was a stubborn one, in which only a partial victory was won at any single time. It is therefore not surprising that they did not recognize that the great opponent of the merit system is not really the politician but public opinion, which, on the whole, supports the spoils system; for appointees under the spoils system are very sensitive to what the general public thinks and, especially, to what it wants. Public opinion is not particularly concerned by what happens to prisoners, or to the insane or to the poor; it does resent the bureaucrat, immune because of his civil service protection.

The choice, as the public sees it, is between the spoils system and a bureaucracy; between a system which is quite aware of what the average man wants and a system in which public officials pursue their tasks quite independently of public opinion, merely because it is their duty to do so. Grover Cleveland, among all our presidents the most ardent supporter of civil service, once coined a clumsy phrase—"innocuous desuetude" —to describe the solution which the honest official finally reaches under the ever present pressure of public opinion. It was a state of the greatest possible inactivity, for whatever he does will be wrong and so considered either in the estimation of the public or in the judgment of his own conscience. An English public servant once said that it was possible to conceive of the civil service of England as operating independently of parliamentary criticism or of the hampering effect of a democratically elected local government. It would give England the smoothest and most efficient administration the country had ever known; but at the close of the first year the populace would hang every civil servant on the nearest lamppost! This is not an argument against the merit system; it is merely the recognition that in a democratic society there is no specific for good government. There is this practical difference between the merit and the spoils systems: under the merit system, a public servant may courageously administer the law as he understands it, disregarding threats or incidental expressions of criticism, secure in the knowledge that his policy has the long-time approval of his community; under the spoils system, he does not have a chance to render honest and efficient service.

*T*HE CHARITY organization movement is still the most successful answer to the frustration suffered by men and women of good will in urban communities when they attempt to exercise the immemorial heritage of sharing with their less fortunate fellow men, and find that it is not practical. They can share their goods and their time, but their efforts seem valueless, if not worse; not only is the total amount of need not lightened, but it even seems to increase. When first experienced, this frustration was not fully analyzed; the actual explanation resorted to was that giving to the poor made them paupers, unwilling to accept employment if by begging they could exist without toil. This is an instance of the *post hoc* fallacy against which Wines had cautioned. The poor did sink into pauperism, but it has scarcely been demonstrated that the receipt of alms caused them to do so!

The universal sentiment of mutual aid among thoughtful individuals was exercised successfully in early and simple societies, and it was probably one of the strong cohesive factors that made societies out of groups. That tradition grew up among those who knew each other well, and its exercise was controlled by such knowledge. When people were thrown together in the anonymous relationship of the urban community, those safeguards of mutual aid were absent; the giver did not know the receiver, and the receiver did not know the giver. The grantor became suspicious of the statements of the suppliant, who, in turn, was forced to "learn the arts of beggary" in order to impress the possible donor. This created a vicious circle within which the giver became more and more suspicious regarding each story told by the applicant in his attempts to establish the gravity of his need. Too often the thoughtful citizen was led to the conclusion that most need was fictitious and used as a means of avoiding work. If the early social workers in the field of urban charities had not acquired this "fixed idea" of the depravity of the poor and had been free to examine the phenomenon of dependency more closely, needy persons would have been more sympathetically regarded. Even more important, the hardness and callousness of the average citizen toward dependency might never have developed, and the heartless disregard of the plight of his fellow citizens which characterizes the "man on the street" could have been avoided.

The first hint of an independent approach to the solution of the problem of urban dependency was embodied in Vives's ordinance for the care of the poor, prepared at the request of the mayor of Bruges in 1532. There is no hint that Vives had any "fixed idea" of the character of the poor. He capitalized the common interest in poverty and the virtue of helping them. He never mentioned that they would be demoralized by alms but valued the human virtue of charity for both giver and receiver. He did not denounce dependents as beggars or parasites; rather he reserved his denunciations for the dishonest trustees of funds, both religious and lay, given for the care of the poor and diverted to the luxuries of the trustees. He laid down the only principle yet discovered by which helpfulness may be directed to need and be kept alive in an urban community: investigation, registration, and supervision of all applicants, combined with a free differentiation of treatment. His philosophy was forgotten, and only the negative aspects of investigation lived on in the administration of the English Poor

Laws. Thomas Chalmers, in the third decade of the nineteenth century, put on in Glasgow a demonstration of how vigorous investigation and supervision could keep down relief. Antoine Frédéric Ozanam, in the fourth decade of that century, demonstrated in Paris that it was possible to conserve the intuitive interest in one's fellow men in an urban commuity. The Conference of St. Vincent de Paul, which he organized, has since spread all over the world wherever the Roman Catholic Church is found.

Then, after a number of attempts to control or "prevent pauperism and mendicancy" in the city of London, the Charity Organization Society of London was constituted, in 1869. It had the double objective of bringing order out of the chaos of the city's charities by offering district conferences at which the agencies could discuss their common problems and coördinate their efforts; and of insisting on careful investigations of appeals for help and a city-wide registration of applicants. Although this program was violently attacked, it did appeal to the citizens of London as the way out of the complexities of endless appeals, and it was hailed by many as an application of scientific method to that particular problem in human relations.

The charity organization movement came to America in 1877, introduced into Buffalo by an Episcopal rector who had served on one of the district committees of the London society. It was taken up even more eagerly in this country than in England. Although earlier societies, such as the associations for improving the conditions of the poor, provident associations, united charities and relief societies, had used the methods of investigation and case records (but not conferences), the new movement displaced some of the older organizations, combined with others, and spread over unorganized urban communities with great rapidity. At the National Conference held three years following the formation of the Buffalo society, the movement was given a section on the program. It has remained an important subject in Conference discussions.

Five names stand out in this early period as creators of the charity organization method and molders of public opinion regarding the movement: Robert Treat Paine and Zilpha D. Smith, of Boston; Josephine Shaw Lowell, of New York; Amos G. Warner, of Baltimore; and the Rev. Oscar C. McCulloch, of Indianapolis.

Robert Treat Paine (1835–1910) was a prominent Boston lawyer; a charter member of the American Social Science Association and an intimate friend of Phillips Brooks; he was widely identified with civic and philanthropic projects. His strongly independent philosophy made him more liberal in economic matters than were most of his contemporaries. Although a man of considerable means, for instance, he believed that the benefits to the world of our country's adopting bimetallism, especially to China, would outweigh any depreciation of value based upon gold which such a broadened basis of currency would cause. Paine was the first person to propose and put into successful operation a scheme for making loans on chattels at one percent a month, and to organize what amounted to an adult education program by bringing workingmen and members of the leisure class together to discuss their common problems and to attend courses. He was the first president of the Associated Charities of Boston, retaining that office from 1879 to 1907, or for nearly thirty years, becoming president of the National Conference of Charities and Correction in 1895.

Zilpha D. Smith, the daughter of one of the early leaders in the movement for women's rights, was secretary of the Boston Associated Charities during most of Paine's long presidency. She had strong faith in the possibility of training the paid worker, and an extraordinary capacity for social inquiry which she combined with a clear and logical use of language. Long before there was any school of philanthropy, Zilpha Smith held classes on the background of American charities for members of the employed staff of the Charities, "drilling them thoroughly" in the English Poor Law. Paine said (1888) that the charter of the Boston Associated Charities excluded the giving of relief from its purposes because of the insistence of the older relief societies that it be given up. This policy, however, threw back on Miss Smith, and probably on Paine himself, the responsibility for justifying the function of the Associated Charities apart from relief giving. Theoretically, this was orthodox policy in England and America, but it was violated more often than it was honored in this country. The early case records of the Boston society are no longer available, but it is probable that Miss Smith used the records of its activities—case records, minutes of meetings of district committees, of which there were seventeen during most of this period—as source material in a pioneer project in research in method of working with dependents in an urban community. At any rate, by 1908, near the close of her long administration of the Boston society, she read a paper at the summer session of the New York School of Philanthropy on "Methods Common to Social Investigations." [1] The early texts on social casework, including Mary Richmond's *Social Diagnosis* (published nine years later and dedicated to Miss Smith), were based on this article. In further support of the theory that Miss Smith was working on the definition of the processes of casework, a term, incidentally, which she did not use in her 1908 paper, is the tradition which was strong in the first decade of the twentieth century that in Boston there was being worked out by Zilpha Smith a method which was proving its worth and spreading to other cities.

Amos G. Warner (1861–1900), while a graduate student

[1] *Charities and the Commons*, Charity Organization Society of the City of New York, Vol. II, No. 5, February, 1909.

at Johns Hopkins University, was persuaded by John Glenn to assume the secretaryship of the Baltimore Charity Organization Society in 1887. He held a professorship at the University of Nebraska in 1889. Two years later he was appointed by President Benjamin Harrison to the new position of Superintendent of Charities of the District of Columbia, to bring some order and efficiency into the welter of projects in that city. In 1893 he went to Leland Stanford University in California as professor of economics and sociology and while there he brought out his book, *American Charities* (1894). Said to have been written within two months, it is one of the few classics in the field of social service. Warner was primarily a scholar in this field of human relations, quickly seizing upon the essential strength of the new movement and using the special technique of the social sciences, statistics, as his means of interpreting the data with which their workers had to deal. He expressed some caution, though, as to whether the data to which he was limited really could be interpreted as he and others were explaining them. If he had lived, and had pursued that question, Warner might have saved the movement some painful mistakes. His great activity was more than his physical equipment could carry and he died of tuberculosis at the early age of thirty-nine, after more than three years of invalidism. His book, the only text in this field for a quarter-century, gave to those who were trying to find out what the movement in charity organization really was essaying an almost fatally statistical pattern that proved to be its undoing.

Josephine Shaw Lowell (1843-1905), left a widow by the death of her husband in the Civil War, only a few months after their marriage, devoted her life and great talents to civic causes, including an effort to bring together the competing forces of capital and labor. Governor Samuel J. Tilden appointed her a member of the New York State Board of Charities in 1876, the first woman to serve in that capacity in New York State, and probably the only one besides Mrs. Lynde, of Wisconsin, in the country. She was a member of the board of the New York State Charities Aid Association. As a member of the State Board of Charities she was influential in having introduced into the state legislature a resolution granting the charter which created the New York Charity Organization Society. The National Consumers' League and the Civil Service Reform League were among the projects to whose beginnings she devoted her energies. She is the only one of these early workers of whom a first-class biography [2] has been written, but enough is said here to justify the phrase that she was "one of the wisest" of the early leaders, in spite of her prejudiced idea of why men work at all—a bias all the more surprising because she felt that her main contribution would be in the adjustment of the difficulties between capital and labor.

The Rev. Oscar C. McCulloch (1843–91) unlike the other four, was a Western product. The son of a tradesman, he started as a traveling salesman and showed his remarkable gift in human relations by making an unusual success of that enterprise. He then switched to the ministry, becoming pastor of the Congregational Church at Sheboygan, Wisconsin, in 1870, and of Plymouth Church at Indianapolis in 1877, as successor to Henry Ward Beecher. A lover of good literature, he was also interested in the current philosophical discussions of the evolutionary theory; he had a natural gift for friendship, as well as for organization, and during his pastorate at Indianapolis he was responsible for starting, not only the Charity Organization Society (1879), but also the Children's Aid Society (1881) and the Visiting Nurses Association (1885), as well as other less well-known agencies. He proposed the organization of the first

[2] William Rhinelander Stewart, *The Philanthropic Work of Josephine Shaw Lowell* (New York: Macmillan, 1911).

State Board of Charities of Indiana, of which he became president (1889); and he was elected president of the National Conference of Charities and Correction in 1891. He died in 1891. The memorial tribute in the next year (1892) spoke of him as "the typical American, the outcome and fruition of many civilizations, nationalities and conflicting influences." Several years later (1916) Alexander Johnson, who knew him well, said: "Much of what he was the chief originator did not come to full fruition until he had passed away."

Not being in touch with the Eastern movement, the Charity Organization Society of Indianapolis differed from its contemporaries in its emphasis upon organization. It became the nerve center of all the city's philanthropic activities, public and private, a center of ideas and of planning; indeed, it more closely resembled the contemporary councils of social agencies than anything else. McCulloch added nothing to understanding those who applied for assistance; he accepted all the principles as well as all the philosophy of the movement. His genius was not shown by any special creative contribution, such as Zilpha D. Smith's project in social inquiry, but by the fact that all alone, a thousand miles from his nearest exemplars, he was able, nevertheless, to capture and to fix the essential nature of the movement so early into an organization. He delivered the first report on charity organization offered to the National Conference, when it met at Cleveland in 1880.

In some of the older Eastern societies, the investigational and supervisory functions of the organizations were performed by volunteers. The members of the employed staff were used in a clerical and, to some extent, in an administrative manner. It was the aim of such societies to afford opportunity to citizens who had no contact with the less fortunate in their community to get to know them, partly for the sake of the services that could be offered, but quite as much to break down the stratification of urban society and promote thereby a more realistic mutual understanding. Paine is quoted as saying that during twenty-five years of his presidency of the Boston society, it never had less than a thousand volunteer visitors, of whom he was one. No other organization in the country approached that number of volunteers. Some of the cities looked with envy on Boston. Miss Smith read a paper at the Conference in 1884, and another in 1887, on how to secure volunteers; probably in answer to worried requests from cities that had tried and failed to hold any considerable number.

Boston's success could hardly be described by a Bostonian; for there was in Boston a unique combination of circumstances that other cities did not possess. There had been a long period during which the custom of doing volunteer work with the Associated Charities had its effect. The devoted service of both the secretary, Zilpha Smith, and the president, Robert Treat Paine, over the years was heartening indeed. Moreover, there was the habit of the Massachusetts State Board of Charities, reaching back to the years before the organization of the Associated Charities, of using volunteers as supervisory agents in placement of children. All these factors could not be duplicated easily or in a short time. However, the paper which envisioned the ultimate social effect of volunteer workers was written in 1897, not by Miss Smith, but by Charles F. Weller, a district superintendent of the Chicago Bureau of Charities, who described voluntary work as pervading the whole social fabric of a city, obliterating the differences in point of view between rich and poor, with a new brotherhood arising from the spirit of the volunteer.

It is futile to imagine what development the use of volunteers would have reached, in the primary functions of the charity organization societies, had it not been blocked in the early twentieth century by the rise of a professional personnel. Baltimore

more nearly competed with Boston than did any other city, probably due to an able volunteer, Mary Goodwillie, who never lost confidence in the capacity of the "friendly visitors" or in the possibility of using them. In other cities, volunteers made substantial contributions as members of boards and committees, where policies were formed and the choice of employed personnel determined. Many of these board members were also volunteer visitors, and perhaps their soundest gift to the rapidly growing movement was the knowledge they gained by actual contact with the handicaps under which the lower economic groups were forced to live.

The most popular and most easily understood of all the methods of the charity organization movement was registration. The new societies endeavored to establish it on a city-wide basis, although the means for accomplishing this end were varied, and the obstacles to its accomplishment underestimated. One way was to have such agencies as would, register their applicants with the charity organization society, which would thus build up a master list. In the process of registration, duplication would be detected. Before 1879 Boston had organized a registration bureau which had no other function but that of listing names. When the Associated Charities was formed, it took over the bureau as one of its functions, and under its able leadership the bureau became, before the end of the century, a city-wide, joint registration center for all the principal agencies of the city, including the medical clinics. It was called the Confidential Exchange; its information was available only to member agencies, who received also what was called "information" service; that is, they were notified when a new agency asked about a family previously registered by them. No other city had advanced so far in the period under review, but in the new century the plan spread throughout the country. In the city of New York there was joint registration between the Charity Organization Society and the Association for Improving the Condition of the Poor which functioned also as a guide for the allocation of new applications. Detroit had a city-wide registration by 1884. Somewhat later (1887), a very interesting suggestion was made that there be set up in Buffalo a national registration of transients, with the adoption of a telegraphic code to be used by societies making inquiries; this idea came to fruition in modified form in the Transportation Agreement at the beginning of the next century whereby relief officials observed certain rules regarding sending transients on to another town.

Logically, the step following joint registration was coördination of the efforts of the charitable agencies of the community. At this point the records are filled with reports of half-successes and half-failures. A new society was placed in an almost untenable position by advocating the coöperation of all the communities' social forces, because it claimed to be able to set standards in the field in which, in common with relief agencies, it was functioning. The field of social work has found out by hard experience that coöperation between agencies rarely follows when one agency assumes that it knows how other agencies should operate. In the older communities, and specifically in Boston, the Associated Charities apparently found a place of leadership, won over the quarter-century, by patiently holding conferences, in every part of the city, on an endless number of cases. The charity organization movement spoke less of coöperation and more of the function of the district conferences. In the review of activities reported from time to time at the National Conference, the cities were inclined to report that they found these city-wide conferences difficult to keep up, that they met irregularly, or that they could not be maintained. Actually, for all the high importance it assumed in the project of charity organization, the matter of coöperation between social agencies had to wait for the new century and the genius of

Francis H. McLean to point out a new approach by means of the council of social agencies.

Although created for the purpose of promoting an easy working together of local agencies, in reality the district conference performed another and more suitable function by educating its own members through case discussion and reports on what ensued when decisions were acted upon. In so far as such district conferences were composed of representatives of agencies in the district, taking counsel did draw them more closely together. That function alone could hardly suffice to induce the conference members to meet regularly over the years. The knowledge, however, that the district conference was a place where difficulties could be freely discussed and the best practice defined kept their members loyal to it as an institution. Boston had what was probably the most elaborate of the district conference organizations, consisting of the representatives of the agencies and the volunteers in that district, and an Executive Committee and a Case Committee (1884). The Case Committee's position as a body secondary to the district itself would seem to indicate that the larger body was concerned more with general questions, such as community relationships, than with the problems of individuals; but no discussion of the actual activities of the committee—or, for that matter, of the district conference—got into the *Proceedings*.

While investigation, in the minds of many, had a negative function—to separate the worthy from the unworthy, prevent duplication, and to detect mendicants and impostors, there were voices that expressed the constructive side of the process. In 1899 Paine, objecting to the definition of the purpose of an investigation as a method to find out whether a man were "helpable," insisted that it was for the purpose of "finding out how a man might be helped." Mrs. Glendower Evans, of Boston, had stated earlier (1889) a variation of the same idea, "human na-

ture is far too subtle a thing to be investigated in one or two in-
terviews"; while Zilpha D. Smith had said the year before, "the
possibility of imposture is not so much to be guarded against
as the constant danger arising from misunderstanding the real
needs of a family." In such statements as these, there is to be
found a foreshadowing of the spirit of the social casework of
the twentieth century.

In the search for a means to put a family on its feet without
giving relief, societies early hit upon various devices, such as
operating an employment bureau; setting up a workroom or
laundry for women or a woodyard for men; establishing a day
nursery where working mothers could leave their children
while away from home; creating a free kindergarten; organizing penny savings and other projects in thrift; instituting a training school for domestic help; opening a low-price lunchroom;
establishing a department for making small loans; setting up a
legal aid service—the list might be extended indefinitely. Some
of these projects, such as legal aid, small loans, and visiting nursing, eventually split off into an independent status; but questions were raised very early whether all these activities were
germane to the work of a charity organization society, and
whether, by taking them up, the society were not so occupying
itself with tangential activities as to lose sight of its major task.

For the able-bodied man in need of financial aid, especially
during financial depressions, made work has been considered the
only justifiable solution. Its suitability was not even discussed in
the depression of 1893, so general was the belief that a man in
full vigor should earn what he gets. Philip W. Ayres, then secretary of the Cincinnati society, discussed in 1895 the question
"Is Emergency Relief Work Wise?" But at that early date the
demoralizing effect that results when men work on a job merely
because they are in want, not because the job needs them, was
not foreseen. The Ayres paper discussed who should and who
should not be given work, and, in particular, that a man on re-

lief work should receive enough money to support his family. And then he added a modern touch, saying "that public improvements should be so timed as to take advantage of the supply of labor at periods of depression." There is only a passing reference (1894) in the Conference *Proceedings* to the way in which the city of Pittsburgh, Pennsylvania, employed its workless men, in the depression of 1893, to lay out Schenley Park, one of the most successful and beautiful projects in the country.

There were occasional instances of a wider searching for the causes of poverty than those on the moralistic level all but universal at that time. Carroll D. Wright, of the Federal Bureau of Labor, speaking in 1886 of the 1,000,000 men currently unemployed, declared that there was need of a moral reformation in our industrial organization (since we permit such inhumanity as throwing 1,000,000 men out to starve) that would educate employers in better ways of conducting business. In 1888 Mrs. Lowell, commenting on the fact that wives of laboring men had to go to work to earn money needed for the support of the family, said that being a wife and a mother demands a woman's full time, and that when she is forced by economic conditions to compete with her husband for a job, she actually succeeds in lowering his wages.

The organization of relief work in times of disasters, such as fires, floods, and tornadoes, was a challenge which the charity organization early met and which demonstrated the validity of its methods in a manner that surprised the general public, if not its own friends. Relief measures for the victims of several tragedies were described at conference sessions: the fire at Lynn, Massachusetts (1890); a tornado that hit Louisville, Kentucky, and a flood which destroyed property and made thousands homeless in the same city in 1895; and the forest fire at Hinckley, Minnesota, in 1896. There was almost an air of surprise among social caseworkers that a procedure worked out for the normal pace of civic life should be so well fitted to establish order in a time of panic. An observer at the Johnstown flood reported (1890) that the hastily gathered committee in charge of distributing relief supplies would have none of the advice of the charity organization representative, until near the end of emergency activities when, "by some means," the distribution of stoves was placed in his hands, and he was able to demonstrate how an efficient and just distribution of the huge volume of supplies that accumulates at such a time can be accomplished.

The greatest amount of money gathered for relief of the victims of a disaster, up to the San Francisco fire and earthquake of 1906, was contributed to Chicago "from all quarters of the world," after the fire which destroyed a large portion of that city in 1871. Its distribution was entrusted to the Chicago Relief and Aid Society. At the 1880 meeting of the Conference it was stated that "after relieving temporary and immediate needs, a considerable sum remained." The interest of a charitable organization in community-wide projects other than its own was shown by the Society's distribution of some $176,000 of this surplus to seven hospitals, on condition that each hospital establish a free bed for each thousand dollars received.

Closely allied to disaster were periods of acute industrial depression, throwing hundreds of thousands out of work and causing much distress and want. Here, too, the new societies could arrange for the orderly management of such relief supplies as were available. Not all cities took advantage of the resources and, especially, of the experience of the charity organization societies. Usually, special citizens' committees, set up to take care for the needs of "the new poor," eventually made some arrangements with the established agencies and finally turned over the entire load to them.[3] Agencies found themselves involved in projects of work relief, often initiated by these self-

[3] See Leah H. Feder, *Unemployment Relief in Periods of Depression* (New York: Russell Sage Foundation, 1936).

same citizens' committees, with all the insoluble problems implicit in such projects. The charity organization section of the Conference of 1894 was given over to reports of how the flood of relief applications of the previous year had been handled by various cities. Nine cities reported, and, with the exception of Charleston, South Carolina, all had resorted to creating jobs for the able-bodied unemployed. In most cities the relief work was carried on by special citizens' committees, or mayor's committees, but all used some form of registration. In at least one city, Cleveland, the actual contact with applicants was made by the largely expanded membership of district committees, much after the Boston pattern.

By the end of the period, apart from Boston and perhaps one or two other places, charity organization was caught on a dead center. It had failed to develop new leadership to give the wider possibilities of social casework its broader and, especially, its more humane content. The movement had spread too rapidly to secure a valid demonstration in many communities in which it had been organized, and where its organizers were repeating formulas which were losing their meaning. On the other hand, confidence in the value of reform as a means of doing away with some of the evils with which relief societies were struggling had the effect of throwing the method of treating individual families into contempt, as a "retailing" process when a wholesale attack was possible. It was the period in which much was made of the contrast between prevention of injury and relief of the injured. It was the middle of the second decade of the next century before charity organization freed itself from its dead center and demonstrated the fallacy of the contrast between prevention and relief.

II · THE CONSCIENCE OF AMERICA

*J*ANE ADDAMS (1860–1935), compelled to abandon her
plans to study medicine, because of a breakdown in health
after her graduation from Rockford College, Illinois, was sent
by her family to Europe for a two-year period of rest. By
chance, she heard of Toynbee Hall, which had just been opened
in London, and decided to visit it. This sincere effort on the part
of fortunate people to share their lives with their less fortunate
contemporaries made so deep an impression on her, as on so
many other visitors in those early days at Toynbee Hall, that it
caused her to devote her life to the establishment of a settlement
in Chicago.

As a result of this decision, Hull House was opened through
the efforts of her friend Ellen Gates Starr and of herself on the
West Side of Chicago in January, 1889. Jane Addams freely devoted her unusual energies and gifts to its interests for the re-
mainder of her life, a period of forty-five crowded years. She
had the divine gift of style and a strong dramatic sense, giving
her writing and speaking an appeal that easily reached international proportions. More perfectly than anyone else in this
country, Jane Addams realized the ideal of the settlement
worker set down by Canon Samuel A. Barnett, the founder of
Toynbee Hall: "the helper and helped [should be] in friendly
relations." She lived with the constantly shifting cultures of
that changing West Side of Chicago, and loved them; she saw
the beauty of their folklore behind the façade of misery and dirt

in which they were forced to live; and she became the inter-
preter of their heritage to America. She was, in turn, adored by
the people she served. She wrote much; some of it scholarly,
such as *Hull House Maps and Papers;* but most of it interpretive,
like *The Spirit of Youth and the City Streets,* descriptive of the
piteous efforts of boys and girls to snatch some crumbs of happiness from the impoverished resources of an overcrowded
tenement district, and *A New Conscience and an Ancient Evil,*
an appeal for a single standard of morality in sexual relations.
Her books made a deep impression on her generation because
they grew out of her own sympathetic knowledge of the way
her neighbors struggled against unnecessarily bad conditions.
No one in the field of the social services among English-speaking peoples approached the widespread reputation which Jane
Addams achieved among all classes of people. She received high
tokens of recognition, such as sharing the Nobel Peace Award
in 1931 and being elected to the presidency of the Woman's International League for Peace. She presided at the conventions
of the League at The Hague (1915), Zurich (1919), Vienna
(1921), The Hague (1922), Washington (1924), Dublin
(1926), and Prague (1929). Miss Addams was the first woman
elected president of the National Conference of Charities and
Correction (1909), thus breaking the custom which had persisted for thirty-five years.

The settlement movement grew out of the same ground that
gave rise to charity organization: the tragic contrast in the conditions of life of the rich and of the poor. There were luxury,
ease, enjoyment, and absence of economic anxiety on one side
and squalid living conditions, inadequate diet, cheap recreation,
and economic anxiety on the other; it was a contrast difficult to
justify in view of the rapid increase in the total wealth of industrial nations which did not in any way improve the lot of the
laborer and his family. The leaders of the charity organization

movement had a plan for the resolution of the dilemma: teach the laboring man to make the most of such opportunities as he does have. The settlement movement was not sure of any method, but it was confident that if the more fortunate were to live among the less fortunate, they would learn to know realistically the problems of the poor and how to meet them. At the Conference of 1897, Jane Addams said, "You know the poor, if you take pains to know them; and you do not know the poor, if you do not take pains to know them." Then she drew a vivid picture of the deterioration of an honest workingman into a tramp, through repeated frustrations in his attempts to secure work in a trade which had left him without a job because of the invention of a machine. She went on to say,

I have not the great fear of pauperizing people which many of you seem to have. We have all accepted bread from someone, at least until we were fourteen. . . . If we can only make the medium of giving friendly enough . . . it does not make any difference whether you give an old Latin Grammar or a pair of shoes.

There was in the settlement movement, especially in England, a touch of the mysticism of St. Francis of Assisi—poverty is a virtue in itself; if voluntarily assumed, it would spread an ennobling influence on the actually impoverished. At any rate, several efforts to realize this identification of the wealthy and able with the disinherited were made during the middle of the nineteenth century. Out of Canon Barnett's living among his parishioners at St. Jude in London's East End, grew Toynbee Hall in 1884. The name chosen for the new venture in neighborliness is evidence of another line of thought contributing to the settlement movement, the liberal school of economics. Arnold Toynbee was a lecturer and tutor at Oxford University and lived "in half-furnished lodgings as far as he could after the manner of workingmen, joining their clubs, discussing with them (sometimes in an atmosphere of bad whiskey, bad tobacco, bad drainage) things material and spiritual—the laws of nature and of God." [1] He coined the phrase "Industrial Revolution," in his economic lectures, to describe the change that had come over manufacturing in the transition from handmade to factory-made processes. His fascinating personality exerted a strong influence upon Oxford men, including Barnett, who chose the name Toynbee Hall as a memorial to his friend, whose early death, at the age of thirty-one, was widely mourned.

Toynbee Hall was an exemplar to the settlements that spread all over the world. At least four settlements in the United States were started by persons who had their direct inspiration from a visit to it. Hull House; the Neighborhood Guild in New York, established by Stanton Coit in 1886; Northwestern University Settlement in Chicago, founded in 1891 by Charles Zueblin, professor at the University of Chicago; and South End House in Boston, founded by Robert A. Woods in 1892—all stemmed from Toynbee Hall. The settlement movement spread even more rapidly than the charity organization movement. In the short time before the end of the century, it was introduced into all of Western Europe, China, and India, as well as into all the dominions of the British Empire.

As pointed out by Julia Lathrop, who first presented the subject of the settlement to the Conference (1894), it had an opportunistic program and no set method. A group of persons took up residence in a neglected neighborhood, fitting their activities to its needs, and stimulating local interest. According to Miss Lathrop, who was a member of the Illinois State Board of Charities, and a volunteer resident at that time, Hull House started a free kindergarten, then a day nursery; established a playground; organized clubs for children and for young men and women; established Sunday lectures; strengthened the mu-

[1] Memoir by B. Jowett, *Lectures on the Industrial Revolution of the 18th Century in England by the Late Arnold Toynbee* (New York: Humboldt Publishing Co.), p. xv.

nicipal life of the neighborhood; operated a branch of the public library at Hull House; opened a boarding home for girls, without chaperon or "lady board of managers"; secured the passage of a law governing sweatshops; and offered rooms for the meeting of labor unions and other groups who could provide for themselves no suitable meeting place. This is a typical description of the lack of set pattern in settlements. As some of these activities, like kindergartens, playgrounds, and civic and religious community centers, were taken over by other agencies, a question was raised as to whether the settlement was not working itself out of a place in the community. This question is merely evidence that the settlement movement, like charity organization, grew so fast that some of its supporters and well-wishers substituted formulas for philosophy. A settlement is not only pageantry, classes, and clubhouses for those who cannot afford them. It grows out of an attitude toward the gross and unjust differences in opportunity enjoyed by different portions of the people making up our communities, and an irrepressible ethical drive on the part of the privileged to understand the under-privileged better and to attempt to do something about it. It is conceivable that the first leaders of the settlement movement might never have organized a class, but instead might have found other means of sharing the advantages of culture and wealth with their neighbors. So long as there remains this contrast, almost a chasm, between two widely separated groups in a community, there will be need for the thing the settlement seeks to do, no matter how many of the specific methods adopted by the settlement are, in turn, adopted by other agencies. There always will be, as Lillian D. Wald phrased it, "the need for a House on Henry Street," to which neighbors can go as to a bureau of complaints, with the assurance that the House is a friend able to interpret to the greater community and to put into motion forces for the

correction of the evils from which the neighborhood is suffering.

The promise of the settlement as a center of research has not developed as its earlier friends expected. *Life and Labor of the Poor in London,* by Charles Booth, a study that found much of its stimulus in Toynbee Hall, and *Hull House Maps and Papers,* by Jane Addams, are the two early instances of such work. The reason for the failure to continue in this line of activity may have been the same as led to the separation of the Conference from the American Social Science Association—the interest of its personnel in action rather than theory. There is the probability of another and more compelling reason, however, in the technical nature which social research was acquiring. It called for specialists and a great deal of time, as well as a growing appreciation that social research should be free, and not directed to demonstrate the existence of a problem, or the means for its remedy.

In another field, the advocacy and promotion of social reform, the settlement had an enviable record, even in the nineteenth century. In 1896 Dr. Katherine Bement Davis, then a graduate student at the University of Chicago, gathered a significant list of efforts put forth by English and American settlements in promoting civic and political measures. At once, a strong contrast appeared between English and American settlements. The schedule showed that half of the English settlements did not believe that such efforts were within their proper function, whereas only 15 percent of the American settlements expressed such a limitation. The English workers felt their greatest effectiveness to result from the presence of settlement residents on official boards, acting as individuals, and not representing their houses. The organization of settlements encouraged the use of such influence, since residents were for the most part persons whose main vocations were other than the social work of the settlement; they gave only their evenings and other spare time to their houses. For instance, Dr. Davis found residing at Hull House a state factory inspector, a member of the Illinois State Board of Charities and Correction, and a city garbage inspector; in Boston, the City Commissioner on Public Baths was a resident of a settlement as was also the Inspector of Streets and Alleys; and the list might be lengthened considerably.

Settlements in America, in general, took seriously their responsibility for informing their immediate neighbors on civic duties and privileges of citizens. This led to such political efforts as the attempt to defeat the "boodle" alderman in Chicago and the Tammany candidates in New York, and to place women on school boards in Philadelphia. Dr. Davis reported that most of these efforts were failures but that they did reduce the majorities of the winning candidates. It should be added that they were prophetic of the area in which the settlements would make their best known contributions in the next quarter of a century.

Lillian D. Wald established at Henry Street Settlement a unique variant of settlement functions—district nursing. When she and her classmate Mary Brewster graduated from the New York Hospital Training School, they decided to live in a district of tenement houses. They established the Henry Street Settlement in 1893 and there they instituted a service of visiting nursing, the first of its kind in the world. Henry Street Settlement came to be called the "Nurses' Settlement," although it also conducted the usual activities of a settlement. Miss Wald proved a vigorous and imaginative leader, with a flair for writing as well as for the initiation of new movements, such as the Children's Bureau. Like Jane Addams, she was a promoter of the movement for international peace, but her chief monument is her demonstration of the possibility of providing the best professional nursing to the sick who cannot afford to pay the salary of a private nurse.

The strength of settlement influence lay in the testimony or effort of its residents as members of the community, not as professionals. Florence Kelley was primarily a factory inspector for Illinois, and Julia Lathrop was a member of the Illinois state board. When they spoke, it was as specialists in their respective fields. Hull House was their alma mater in social ethics, but neither they nor Hull House felt their relationship to the settlement to be professional in any sense of the word. They were not studying a method or perfecting a technique, and they were not paid; rather they probably paid something for the privilege of living there.

The settlement, therefore, made no direct contribution to the professional development of social work. The movement formed no national association until 1911, although representatives of its houses met informally on a national scale three times before that date. It was represented on the program of the National Conference as a special section only eight times in the thirty years between 1894 and 1923, when the Conference ceased to be organized by functional fields. It was not, in fact, clear to workers in settlements whether their activities belonged to the area of interest covered by the Conference. When finally the technique of social group work was defined, neither the term nor its definition came from the settlement field, although the settlement has from the start operated with groups more realistically and experimentally than any existing institution. The settlement movement chose to remain the conscience of America, the laymen of this country reporting to its citizens on the lot of their forgotten fellows.

12 · MIGRATION, IMMIGRATION AND TRANSIENCY

*U*NDER the general heading of "migration, immigration, and transiency," discussions at the National Conference of Charities and Correction covered such related subjects as: why men migrate; immigration and settlement laws; and tramps and vagrancy.

At the meetings in 1877, Edward Everett Hale, of Boston, quoted from Richard Hakluyt's "Discourse on Western Planting":

. . . for want of sufficient occasion of honest employment . . . through . . . long peace and seldom sickness . . . we are grown more populous . . . so that [we] can hardly live one by another, . . . yea many thousands of idle persons are within this realm . . . having no way to be set on work [become] burdensome to the commonwealth . . . whereby all the prisons of the land are . . . stuffed full of them, where either they . . . pine away or else at length are miserably hanged, even twenty at a clap out of some one jail.

Hale added the invention of machinery and the aftermath of the soldiers' experiences in the Civil War, quickened by the reckless generosity of the people, as the modern conditions contributing to mobility of population and unemployment. Back of these statements is apparent the astonishment of the average man at the spectacle of idle fellows in the midst of what appears to be plenty of work and general prosperity. Frederick J. Turner had not yet come forward to point out how the frontier had absorbed the more venturesome of those who did not succeed in the settled areas, thus reducing the number of discarded men that America had to consider. Hastings H. Hart, however, in 1885, revealed one side of the picture in his statement that "the best folks go West," while dependent and delinquent persons remain in the East. The West should not object, therefore, to caring for those who go West—and fail! As Hart himself was secretary of the Minnesota state board, it was surprising that he should take that position.

There was but little discussion on migration in general. In 1886 Sanborn, the philosopher of the Conference, outlined the cultural and biological significance of migration throughout the evolutionary process, showing the benefits of cross-fertilization of cultures. He also pointed out that our country was settled by the "lower social classes," along with a criminal element—a movement of population then to be seen in California and Colorado, he believed. He then laid down certain generalizations regarding the control of migration. Sanborn assumed that every nation has a right to determine whom it will and will not receive; but such regulations should conceive of migration in the large sense, looking to the good of the human race. He recognized that all political levels are interested in who come within their borders; and while both state and local communities are immediately concerned, he thought the matter one largely for Federal regulation. He was speaking, essentially, not of the right to relief established by residence, but of the desirability of a person's being admitted into a community; and so, in general, he believed it to be a matter of Federal concern to stop the unwanted person before he reached the United States. He was either not interested in, or not thinking of, the undesirable citizen who attempts to enter a new community, against whom at that time there was no law, nor was any contemplated.

The attitude of the Conference, in general, was inclined to

be liberal in the matter of immigration, on the ground that the country needed more rather than less workers (1898), and that the only defenders of restriction were "labor agitators" (Philip C. Garrett, *Proceedings*, 1887). Garrett added (1888) that prohibition against bringing in immigrants by contract labor was unwise, as thereby some of the best workingmen were excluded. The principal danger of immigration, he believed (1890), was the creation of blocks of foreign voters, dominated by a *padrone*, which might become a menace to our democracy.

The most pessimistic view of the effect of immigration on American culture was expressed by a public school official from Massachusetts (1888). In speaking of the influence of the children of immigrants upon the native-born in the public schools he ventured the prediction that "universal suffrage, as practiced now, will end in ruin to our republic and in a revolution that will throw us back for centuries." Such a statement was more general in its condemnation of immigration than was, for instance, the agitation in California against Asiatic immigration, but it represented the feelings of a large section of the old-stock Americans, however, as they saw the French Canadian and Central and Southern European group displacing them from factories and farms. The agitation of the American Protective Association for the exclusion of all "non-Nordic" immigrants in the last two decades of the century found no other echo in the Conference. There was general approval, however, of the exclusion of certain classes, such as criminals, insane, feeble-minded, venereally diseased; and, by some, of anarchists and others holding antidemocratic philosophies. On this point, there was little discussion.

Shortly after the Conference came into being, the Federal Supreme Court ruled that the states' practice of collecting a capitation tax from each immigrant was unconstitutional. Congress therefore passed, "at the instance" of the Conference, a Federal law to levy a fifty-cent fee upon each immigrant, the money to be available to the states for reimbursement for the cost of caring for sick or dependent immigrants, or for their return to the countries of their origin; the administration of the tax remained in the hands of state officials. Sanborn felt (1887) that it should be left with state officials, except in New York, where the scandals connected with the Port of New York could probably be handled only by the Federal Government. From 1887 to 1890 efforts were made to transfer the whole business of immigration to the Federal Government. When Congress passed the Owen Law in 1890, transferring control of immigration to the Federal Government, some states, Pennsylvania especially, protested strongly. The states were doing a splendid job, so it was not in an attempt to increase efficiency that the law was passed, but merely to enlarge the power of the Federal Government (Cadwallader Biddle, *Proceedings*, 1890, 1891). The same law placed upon the United States consul at port of departure responsibility for certifying that the prospective immigrant was eligible for entry into the United States—a provision universally approved. This measure also required the immigrant to be able to read the Constitution of the United States. There was some protest on the ground that literacy does not measure one's usefulness to a country so greatly in need of labor as was the United States (1896). States bordering on Canada and Mexico were beginning to protest against the illegal entry of aliens across international boundaries, and they were urging the deportation of those so entering, in line with the policy regarding all illegal entrants pursued by the Federal Government since the early part of the century.

There were several Conference papers indicating that a disproportionate number of immigrants became public charges;

one paper was presented as early as 1876. Twenty years later, Hastings H. Hart, by a more careful statistical method, demonstrated that the foreign-born furnish a smaller number of criminals than their proportion in the population, but that the children of immigrants produce more delinquents. His was the first attempt to apply a valid statistical method to the question of the dependency of immigrants, and also to point out what has since become general knowledge, that the second generation presents the real problem of assimilation. He did not attempt to explain it.

The widely differing state laws on establishing eligibility for assistance, known as settlement laws, were noted by the Conference from the very first. In 1874 Edward W. Rice, of Boston, gave a careful history of such legislation, beginning with that of Massachusetts towns in which settlement could be acquired only by vote of the town meeting. Six states made the possession of property a condition of settlement. Some states established it by vocation, such as serving as clerk of town, officiating as a minister, or carrying on a trade for five years. In the matter of time, Maine required five years of residence; South Carolina, three years; Minnesota and Kansas, six months; Nebraska, one month; but most of the states required one year. With the general recognition of the dissimilarity of state laws regarding settlement, there grew up a sentiment that interstate migration should be handled by the Federal Government. In 1892 the Conference Committee on Nonresidents, acknowledging the inability of the states separately to deal justly with the transient dependent and at the same time to be just to the taxpayers of the state, tentatively suggested that Congress set up an Interstate Migration Commission. This would require the Federal Government to assume responsibility for the "nonsettled" poor, much as Massachusetts did for its "state's" poor; and also to establish a Federal poorhouse, much as Massachusetts had established an almshouse at Tewkesbury for those who had not acquired local settlement but were acknowledged as settled in the state. The committee went on to say that New York and Massachusetts had not succeeded in working out a plan of mutual comity in regard to the nonresidents in their respective states, and consequently the committee did not feel that progress was possible by means of interstate agreements. It was assumed that, since such a law would interfere with the rights of none of the states, there would be no difficulty in securing its passage. Hastings H. Hart agreed (1895) that only Federal action would be able to handle the matter, since there were complex problems of determination of residence involved. Because it is impractical for one state to sue another to enforce a claim for poor relief, he felt that such commission should be authorized to make decisions between states and enforce them by imposing penalties. The next year, the same writer said that an effort should be made to have the states adopt uniform statutes, instead of working for a Federal commission. The contents of such statutes, he thought, should contain the following provisions: independent residence of one year to constitute settlement; nonresidents of a state could be admitted to a state institution only by the state board; nonresidents, after investigation by state boards, to be returned to their place of residence by state boards; disputes between counties in the same state to be adjudicated, in the first instance, by the county commissioners concerned, with appeal then possible to the state board, and final appeal from state board to district court. Hart also believed that an effort could be made by each state to enter into mutual agreements with their neighboring states. In 1899 the committee accepted the position laid down by Hart that it was impractical for a state to sue another state on the issue of poor relief, but it went one step farther and gave as its opinion that a federal law on the subject would be unconstitutional. Then the committee added the constructive suggestion that state boards, by agreement, could create an arbitration device to pass on disputed cases.

The basic weakness of a poor law, harking back to the Elizabethan statutes, is that its provisions are not enforceable. The statutes on which relief is granted by the locality are usually permissive; if mandatory, there is no penalty attached. They do not confer upon the dependent person the right to assistance; rather they place on certain officials the responsibility of caring for those in need. From that point, decisions are made on an administrative level, from which the applicant had no way of appealing until the passage of the Social Security Act of 1935, and then only in three categories of assistance—the aged, dependent children, and the blind. This left an administrative official in the position of making judicial decisions, based on his interpretation of the law, and quite free from any check upon carelessness or dishonesty to which courts of original jurisdiction are subject. It is conceivable that the applicant might appeal to a court, if he could find one which would accept jurisdiction—and if he had the financial resources to pay the costs of such an appeal. Practically, of course, no such appeal could be made. In turn, the absence of such appellate decisions defining the intent of the law left the administrator without guidance or control in arriving at his own decisions as case after case appeared before him. Because the system was permissive, and without machinery for enforcement or even a dependable definition of what the law really intended, many persons lost settlement—involving the right to ask for assistance —in one state without acquiring it in another. This might be the result when a destitute person moved from a state which required a short term for establishing residence to one requiring a longer term; but usually it occurred when the state from which he came refused to acknowledge that he had a residence within its borders, or refused to honor any claim after he left the state, in spite of his not having established residence in another state. Conceivably, the state to which he had applied for assistance could sue the state where he was supposed to have had settlement; but the process is a clumsy and expensive one and has never been employed. Instead, the claim of the applicant is refused by both states, and he is helpless to remedy an obviously flagrant injustice.

In his effort to be just to an applicant, an administrator of the poor law is under a double disadvantage because his community is not primarily interested in caring for those in need. It is interested in low taxes and would generally oppose a policy that would raise them merely to take care of nonresident dependents. The administrator also knows that if he wants to do the just or even the generous thing, he is surrounded by communities which would take advantage of his generosity and send him, on one pretext or another, their dependent families; consequently, he has constantly to be on the alert against being imposed upon by his neighboring administrators. It is a vicious and insoluble dilemma for the workingman who has to move from place to place in search of work, and who finds himself and family dependent in a strange community. It is one of the efficient means of teaching him the "arts of beggary," which he has to learn in order to survive.

If the transient is a tuberculous patient trying to find a sanctuary in which he may ward off the fatal menace of his disease in the more favorable climate of the mountain states, his search ends only in death, unless someone, or some official, ignores the law of settlement and gives him a chance to gain the complete rest on which his cure depends. Begging a living and, at the same time, "chasing the cure" create an almost invariably fatal combination. Many mountain states complained of the burden thrust upon them by patients from the East, who placed on the authorities of those states the necessity of deciding whether to insist upon limiting assistance to residents, and therefore dooming the transient sufferers to death; or to spend their resources on nonresident tuberculous patients, with the knowledge that such a decision would attract a still larger number to swell the ranks. In the face of this dilemma, representatives of the Western states pled for some sort of recognition of their problem, and a method for its solution. The question at issue was whether the state from which the patient came should retain responsibility for his care, or whether the burden should be transferred to the Federal Government.

In the paper by Edward Everett Hale mentioned in this chapter it was suggested that overseers of the poor be empowered to offer the work test in all cases of vagrancy; that the same method be used by the police; and that workingmen seeking jobs ought to carry certificates of character. He thought further that societies of workmen (labor unions?) might protect the bona fide worker by some sort of identification. Brace, in the same year, noted that tramps flock to cities in the winter, and that a public employment bureau could separate the parasites from those looking for work. The policy of separating the honest seeker for work from those who make a living "by looking for work" was advocated by Washington Gladden throughout this entire period (1899), and Gladden generally recommended the work test. The inference that there is moral failure in the group avoiding work, received much emphasis. Rhode Island, in a law much praised during this period, authorized arrest for begging, and had the offender sent to work for ten days on the state highways; and for a second offense, the tramp was sent to the workhouse for thirty days. A representative from Boston asserted (1877) that tramps should be forced to work, should not be allowed to marry, and should be disenfranchised. Others later became more specific regarding the tramp himself, citing drink and vice, a roving disposition, laziness, desertion of wife, depravity and worthlessness, as among his characteristics or as reasons for taking up the life of a tramp. On one measure there was universal disapproval: the custom of passing—or driving—the tramp on to the next town. Even the severest critic of the workless man recognized that the custom offered no solution to the problem, but actually aggravated it by furnishing some slight answer to the tramp's need, without tackling the problem itself. In no area of the field of dependency was the "tacit assumption" more prevalent that any honest man could find a job if he really wanted it and that should he fail for a short time to do so, there were adequate resources in neighborhood and church on which he could rely.

There was general recognition that severe laws against tramps would keep them out of the jurisdiction within which such laws were enforced, but would also drive them to neighboring communities which had no such restrictions. Strict laws would be beneficial, therefore, only if they were generally enacted and fully enforced. The next step in thinking was not taken at this time: when this separation of sheep from the goats has been made, what are we to do with the goats?

Second Period. *1898-1924*

13 · THE UNIVERSITIES AND THE SOCIAL SERVICES

THE SOCIAL SCIENCES

*P*HILOSOPHY 11, taught by Dr. Francis G. Peabody at Harvard University, was the inspiration that turned many young men into social work. Seven men who later became leaders in their chosen calling came out of Harvard, and its Philosophy 11, in the short period between 1885 and 1893. Four of them became presidents of the Conference: Dr. Richard C. Cabot; Homer Folks, who also had the honor of being the only person twice elected to that office; Sherman Kingsley; and Robert A. Woods. One, Charles Birtwell, of Boston, was a pioneer in child welfare work in New England; one, William H. Pear, of Boston, was a long-time leader in the Boston Provident Association; and one, Harvey Baker, became judge of the juvenile court in Boston during its formative years (1906–15).

The description of Philosophy 11 ran as follows, "The Ethics of Social Reform. The questions of Charity, Divorce, the Indians, Labor, Prisons, Temperance, etc., as problems of practical ethics—Lectures, essays, and practical observations," and the content differed but slightly from that of courses elsewhere given in departments of economics or sociology. Dr. Peabody said that when he first gave the course, the suitability of its material for inclusion in a university curriculum was seriously questioned by the leaders of the university; and it was only the great reputation he bore—as well as his father before him —in the department of philosophy at Harvard that made it possible to offer the course in the oldest educational institution in America. None of the leading schools of the East, however, followed Harvard's example, nor have the others contributed anything to the project of education for social work. It may have been the great personal influence of Dr. Peabody, or it may have been the tradition of volunteer service in Boston that led this stream of brilliant men to catch the inspiration of this new field; but it is without parallel in this country.

In 1894, a year after Robert A. Woods graduated from Harvard, a professor from the University of Chicago reported at the Conference that data assembled at the Conference and by its member agencies were excellent source material for college courses in charity and corrections. He further reported that, as early as 1889, Yale and Williams Colleges were offering courses in sociology. From time to time reports were given of the universities giving courses in sociology, and prominent sociologists, such as Franklin H. Giddings, of Columbia University; Charles H. Cooley, of the University of Michigan; William H. Brewer, of Yale University; and Harry H. Powers, of Smith College, discussed the relationship of sociology to charitable work. Some, like Giddings, took a critical attitude, but most scholars pointed out that each subject was in a field of its own, although dealing largely with the same material (human beings in their relationships), and that each had its contribution to make to the other: sociology, to discover the general laws and principles governing human intercourse; charity, to furnish the data, to test the principles, and to attend to the practical, day-by-day work of amelioration and prevention.

This period might be called the honeymoon stage of the interrelationship between theory and practice; between the teaching of sociology and the practice of social work. It was often assumed that a thorough discipline in sociology was the proper educational preparation for social work, and ways by which more universities could be encouraged to offer such courses were suggested. A more concrete consideration was that if the courses were taught by the right instructors, they would prepare students to take up social work as their vocation, and in that way open up a means of securing recruits for the rapidly expanding vocation from among the very best possible sources of supply.

Some of this identification of the science of sociology with the art of helping continues to the present, but it is being resisted by both groups—by the sociologists, because of the need to dissociate research and theory from extraneously determined values; and by the field, because of this very theoretical trend in sociology. It was a trend which caused Mary Richmond in her first paper (and a long line after her), to warn against too close affiliation with a university. It also became clear that the art of helping, in common with all professional arts, is dependent not on one science, but on many, including such diverse subjects as biology and economics. The recent rise in the importance of psychology and, especially, of psychiatry has tended to crowd sociology as a useful science into the background, as a result of the immediate availability of psychology and psychiatry to the needs of the social worker. The neglect of sociology has not been without some loss, a recession that showed itself especially in perspective.

One of the results of this early association between certain instructors at universities and practitioners in the field was the opening of an outlet for college graduates, and their immediate reception by agencies. Charles Birtwell, the first of the series of brilliant men who found their inspiration in Philosophy 11, was probably the first practitioner to encourage college men to enter the field, and many of those seven men had their initiation into social work in the Children's Aid Society of Boston, of which Birtwell was secretary. Dr. Vida Scudder, of the department of economics at Wellesley College, who, according to Robert A. Woods, shared the Franciscan philosophy of the virtue of poverty, showed rare counseling skill in selecting girls from among the graduating groups and sending them each year to the agencies and settlement houses of the large Eastern cities. Many other professors, such as Charles R. Henderson at the University of Chicago, Cooley at Michigan, and Franklin L. McVey at the University of Minnesota, were doing the same thing, on a smaller scale. Doubtless there were many others whose names have been forgotten, but whose interest in the enlarging field of the social services (and in the West, especially, the public social services) was brought to the attention of their promising students. Before the professional schools were equipped to provide recruits to fill the vacancies calling for competent candidates, this association between colleges and agencies was the device used by progressive leaders in the field to secure their much-needed personnel.

Of less direct influence on the preparation of the practitioner, but of far-reaching impact on the practice of social work in the twentieth century, was the teaching of Simon N. Patten at the University of Pennsylvania. Working independently on the thesis, first suggested by Arnold Toynbee, that the economic problem of production had been solved by the introduction of machinery, he pointed out that the major economic question to be mastered was how to maintain the consuming power of the nation at the levels at which it was possible to purchase the goods made by the machines. He advanced what was considered quite an unorthodox theory, that the only sound economic program was to raise the purchasing power of the great body of workers so that they, the bulk of consumers, would be able to buy the goods the machinery was capable of turning out. Such a program would, of course, involve a pronounced rise in the standard of living for the ma-

jority of the population. The only prominent social worker
of this century to come under the direct influence of Patten
was Edward T. Devine, who was a teacher in the same department at the University of Pennsylvania before he accepted the
secretaryship of the New York Charity Organization Society
in 1896. The theory so nicely fitted the anxious hopes of many
who spent their days struggling to help the disinherited to a
better standard of living that it was eagerly welcomed even
though they were quite ignorant of its source.

While it would be an exaggeration to credit Patten alone
with the result, because there were other influences inherent
in the development of social work itself in America (illustrated
by Sanborn's philosophy), Patten's findings performed a still
greater service to the entire field of the social services by saving
it from identification with the conservative classes of society as
private social work in Great Britain and France had already
done. It preserved the unity of the front between the social
services and social reform which was to prove of such great
value in the years that followed the first decade of the twentieth century. This is not to say that there were no practitioners
in the public and private welfare field who were not conserva-
tives, or even that there were no reactionaries, nor that there
was none in the area of social reform who did not look with
contempt upon the efforts of the social worker. But there were
never absent from the field of practice those who embraced
the more general movements to increase the economic well-
being of the wage earner as being quite as much within their
function as service to those who had suffered from the effect
of the widely unequal distribution of wealth with the assurance that such maldistribution is economically wise as well
as ethically necessary. This acceptance of the dual task of social work reached such a point of general acceptance that John
Fitch, of the New York School of Social Work, could say

(1919): "The interest of the social worker in social action is a test of his integrity."

PROFESSIONAL EDUCATION FOR SOCIAL WORK

The two outstanding papers of the Conference on Education for Social Work were Mary Richmond's proposal, made at the meeting in 1897, that preparation of the personnel for social work should be undertaken as an educational function, and Abraham Flexner's paper, given in 1915, examining the question of whether the practice of social work can be correctly classed as a profession. However, before either of these studies, Anna L. Dawes, of Pittsfield, Massachusetts, prepared the way for an education for the social services, in a paper given at the International Congress of Charities and Correction in 1893. Miss Dawes raised the question why the men and women who were then departing from the field of active social work should not have an opportunity to transmit to their successors what they had learned during their years of service, so as to enable the new workers to take up the work where the older ones left off, without going through a long, hard period of learning by doing. This she urged also for the sake of the applicant, to save him from the needless repetition of the mistakes through which the earlier practitioners had learned their art. Her paper was a sound definition of the content and method of education for a profession, and while at times emphases have been placed on other aspects, the development of education for the practice of social work since then has confirmed her contention that there is something to be learned in the practice of human relations, and that something can be passed on to those who wish to master it.

Miss Richmond's paper took up Miss Dawes's thesis and defined the conditions under which such a school could be established, the sort of personnel needed to staff it, its cost, and something of its curriculum. The proposed project would be called a training school of applied philanthropy. Its activities were described more in the light of what it was to accomplish than how. She felt that there were no norms or standards of work arrived at by the practitioners in the diverse fields then being covered by agencies and institutions. If the common elements of what was then called "charity work" were to be established, it could only be accomplished by a school at liberty to undertake the task of defining the underlying processes common to social work. At that early date, she expressed her fear that exclusive attention to one's own task would be bound to defeat the real objectives of social work. Her school would have as a director "a university trained man . . . who has had wide practical experience in [charitable work]." Such a school would need a good deal of money, which she believed would not be too difficult to secure. It should be located in a large city and possibly affiliated with "some institution of learning." She was careful to point out that the curriculum should emphasize "practical work rather than academic" material. The school should be in close relation with the public and private charities of the city, where students could observe social work practice under the supervision of their instructors. Classroom instruction should parallel experience in the field. Mary Richmond felt that only by some such educational opportunity could college graduates, drawn into the field, feel a professional assurance of standards and vocational security. The suggested school would not provide merely an apprenticeship on a different level. But it did not specifically include the teaching of method by classroom instruction; method was to be taught in field experience which paralleled the classroom instruction. The latter was to concern itself with the general principles which governed all social work.

Miss Richmond's paper was apparently submitted to several

persons, and one of them, Frances Morse, of the Children's Aid Society of Boston, thought the plan too ambitious: salaries paid charity workers would not justify spending one or two years after college in a professional school. Miss Morse suggested as an alternative that the agencies of a city enter into a coöperative agreement whereby a student would pass from one agency to another on an apprenticeship basis, a certain amount to be paid as a scholarship. In this manner, the student would be saved from the worst hazards of the apprenticeship system.

Abraham Flexner's study, written eighteen years after Miss Richmond's paper and seventeen years after the first project in education for social work was started, and at a time when some fifteen or eighteen schools of social work were in existence, undertook to define the criteria of a profession. He set them down as: an intellectual operation with large individual responsibility; a basis of science and learning; progress toward practical ends; possession of an educationally communicable technique; a tendency to self-organization; and increasing altruism. As he observed the operations of a social worker Flexner could identify no method unique to the practice. It was rather a function of discovering the resources in the community and placing them at the disposal of the applicant. Therefore, he did not think that social work was a profession, since it did not have its own "technique communicable by an educational process," though it served as a mediator between the professions. In this essential criterion of a profession, Flexner was in agreement with Miss Dawes's major thesis: a professional must "know how" to perform the intellectual activities, and there must be a large degree of personal responsibility required in his area of work. It is perhaps not without significance that Flexner could not identify this activity, or "technique," as he called it; whereas Miss Dawes, who had spent a long life in its application, was so conscious of it that she felt the need to pass on her accumulation of "know how" to her successors, to save them from the mistakes she had made. Again, it is difficult to see how Flexner, applying this criterion as essential, could have admitted that two of the oldest professions—law and the ministry—are professions at all. They have no unique techniques communicable by an educational process or otherwise. Law uses the method of research more extensively than any other vocation, but it is not exceptional; the ministry is quite innocent of any special method.

The effect of Flexner's paper was profound and far-reaching. The challenge was accepted at its face value, and has set social workers to defining and perfecting their methods with a singleness of purpose that has all but blinded them to the fact that method is only one test. Philosophy—what it is all about; why it is undertaken; what are its ultimate goals and its relationships to other activities—is as essential to a profession as method. Method, however, is essential; anyone attempting to practice in a profession without acquiring the best possible skill in method is a charlatan; he is a danger to the profession and to the people whom it serves. Nevertheless, the practitioner whose sole objective is facility in a method becomes a technician, and fails to realize to the full his professional responsibilities. The danger is that a professional worker will look upon the perfection of method as its only end, neglecting the philosophical considerations of why there should be a method at all and what is the ethical responsibility of a professional to his age. Some practitioners in social work would have shared that narrowing of its conception, sooner or later, as workers in all other professions have done. It is tragic that an impetus in that direction was given social work at the very inception of its professional consciousness.

The establishment of schools of social work followed closely upon Miss Richmond's paper. The next summer, in 1898, the New York Charity Organization Society opened a summer session to invited practitioners, and it was followed the next year by one conceived on a broader basis. By the fall of 1903 the summer session had been expanded to an academic year; and by the fall of 1910 the curriculum had been further expanded to two years, at which point most schools of social work now arrange their professional instruction. In the meantime, other schools had come into existence: Boston, Philadelphia, Baltimore, Chicago, and St. Louis, each one organized by the practicing social workers of their respective communities. The schools might be affiliated with a local university, but the connections were tenuous, for each school wished to be free to develop its own curriculum unfettered by academic rules. This fact also made them, at the same time, not particularly welcomed by the universities.

In the Middle West, at Ohio State University, Indiana University, and the University of Minnesota, by 1915, schools were established on the undergraduate level, designed particularly for college students working for their bachelor's degree; in contrast were the older schools, whose interest was principally, although not wholly, to furnish the means of professional education to the worker in the field. Each of these schools developed quite independently of the others. The Russell Sage Foundation granted funds for research to the older schools during the years 1907–12, but it made no move to bring their curricula into any alignment.

Representatives of the schools met informally on the occasion of the Conference sessions, and at least once (1917?) appointed a committee to draft a plan for a national association. In the spring of 1919 Porter R. Lee, the director of the New York School of Social Work, invited the heads of the known schools, seventeen in number, to meet with him to discuss the advisability of creating a national association. The proposal appealed to those who were present, and they reached an agreement that such an organization be formed at the time of the June meeting of the Conference. Thus was established the American Association of Professional Schools of Social Work, which has continued to be the medium for the setting of standards of professional social work education in the United States and Canada and, to some extent, in the rest of the world.

The concern of the Conference for this development was only incidental during this second period. In 1911 Jeffrey R. Brackett, head of the Simmons College School of Social Work, in Boston, made a valid distinction between education and training. Training, he said, was the acquisition of experience under leadership; and education was the acquisition of knowledge. This distinction has not been observed by the schools of social work, which prefer to call themselves "educational institutions." Those who considered educational preparation for social work as an academic project phrased it (as Devine did in 1915), as a discipline in the data of contemporary society, with field work to offer opportunities to observe such conditions as had been discussed in class; though the people who thought of it as learning a method believed that class work should consist of discussion of method, with field work to give the student facility in its use. In the National Conference the discussion does not appear to have reached the degree of bitterness of the early days of the New York School of Social Work. It became merely a matter of historical interest after Abraham Flexner's paper of 1915, and especially after the appearance of Miss Richmond's book on *Social Diagnosis* in 1917. Her book was acclaimed by social workers, and by some people in other professions, as laying a sound basis for method, at least in social casework.

The older Eastern schools started out with what Felix Frank-

furter called (1915) a "platonic connection" with a university, which he criticized, as did also Abraham Flexner. They
both asserted that the only valid basis for professional training was an integral relation with a university, accepting its
standards for admission of students, for appointment of instructors, and for content of curriculum and conditions of
graduation. They were thinking not of a literal control of subject matter, but of the maintenance of the same standards for
selection as were applied in other university disciplines. Soon
after the Association of Schools was formed, this principle
was adopted, and no new schools were admitted that did not
conform to the rule. By the time that the fiftieth session of the
Conference was held (1923) each of the independent schools,
save New York and Pennsylvania, the National Catholic
School at Washington, and the National Jewish School of Social Service in New York, had become a part of an accredited
university.

Just to give evidence that the Conference was an open
forum, a dissenting opinion is quoted from an anonymous dis-
cussant of Sophonisba P. Breckinridge's paper of 1911 on "Securing and Training Social Workers": . . . "all useful work
is social work . . . there is danger of wrecking the useful lives
of young men . . . who ought to go into business or professional life . . . but whom someone persuades to drop work of
unquestioned utility in favor of a kind of work which is at
best of questionable utility."

14 . *TOWARD A PROFESSIONAL ASSOCIATION*

*T*HE NATIONAL CONFERENCE itself offered the first opportunity for practitioners in the social services to meet together for the professional exchange of experiences. It was not, however, composed exclusively of paid workers, nor did it have vocational criteria for selection of membership. Through the years, due to the expense in time and money involved in attendance upon its sessions, the tendency has been for the Conference membership to consist almost exclusively of paid employees, and only by the most persistent effort has the volunteer or the board member been induced to become affiliated with it. As a result, for nearly a half a century there was no other organization to bring together the employed personnel on a national scale, to consider the vocational questions faced by the employed staff, in contrast with the functional and social questions with which the Conference was concerned.

The first effort to provide an organization for the personnel was furnished on the local level by social workers' clubs. Even here, the distinction was not easy to make between special needs of the personnel and general needs of the community for a forum on social matters. Many cities, as well as states, had local conferences of charities (called "charities and corrections," and, later, "social work") modeled on the National Conference. In such cities a social workers' club might find itself regarded as superfluous. Probably the pioneer in such ventures was the Monday Club of Boston. Within the second decade of the twentieth century social workers' clubs had been established in New York, Detroit, Pittsburgh, Minneapolis, and San Francisco. The club names are somewhat indicative of their incidental character: Monday Club, in Boston; Hungry Club, in Pittsburgh; S.O.S., in Minneapolis. There doubtless were similar organizations in many other cities, but there was no formal communication between them, and practically no permanent record was kept of their activities. They did meet a local need, however, and they forced the organization of local chapters of the American Association of Social Workers, which contemplated no such structure at the grass roots in its pattern of organization adopted in 1921.

Zilpha D. Smith discussed the value of such a club at the Conference in 1911, when she urged that all communities having as many as a dozen paid social workers employed by several different agencies should organize a club, for the clearance of ideas, for a better understanding of each other's work, and for consideration of mutual problems. She urged, on the basis of Boston's experience, that its membership be limited to professionally paid workers, including representatives of all fields operating in the community, and that the fee be low in order to permit as many as possible to join; the programs should entail participation by the membership. So far as is known, representatives of these clubs never met at the Conference, or anywhere else, to form a national body for the promotion of the movement in other cities, or for exchange of ideas. The social workers' clubs, therefore, were not the direct antecedent of the professional organization, although the experience gained by many members in such clubs definitely influenced its initiation, its function, and, to a less extent, its structure.

The Intercollegiate Bureau of Occupations of New York City was the unwitting parent of the professional association, when the latter did come into existence. The Bureau was organized in 1911 by the New York alumnae of the Eastern women's colleges for the purpose of offering vocational counseling to graduates in search of opportunities in the field for which they were educationally prepared. Soon after the beginning of the Bureau's operations it was found that the field of social work was so heterogenous and undefined that a special department was desirable to care for applicants, and one was therefore set up with a social worker in charge. The department soon ceased to function exclusively as a project in vocational counseling and established a registry of all social workers, men as well as women, who were willing to affiliate themselves without reference to placement. In this way was laid the foundation for a national professional association. The logical step of separation from the Intercollegiate Bureau was taken in 1917, with the formation of the National Social Workers' Exchange. The Exchange, national in scope and with branches in two or three cities, was not limited strictly to professional workers, for its membership "was open to persons engaged in social work professionally, or as volunteers and others interested in the purpose of the Exchange." The entire matter of defining the requirements for membership in an association of social workers proved difficult, since those from whom the association would draw its members did not have any single educational preparation which could be used for their identification; a prospective member might be employed, for example, as the visitor for an agency, or as the executive of that agency, as the matron in an institution, or as the head of a national social work association, such as the Child Welfare League of America or Community Service, Inc. In fact, during the fall and winter of 1918–19, an abortive effort to create a national association of social workers, which would seek to capitalize the postwar enthusiasm for democracy and the important place that social work might play in its world-wide realization, came to naught largely because of the inability of its sponsors to agree on whom the proposed association should include.

In the interval between 1917 and 1921 the National Social Workers' Exchange avoided the pitfall of definition of a social worker, taking into membership quite freely those who felt themselves included in its terms of eligibility. It was, therefore, building up a small but clearly identified group which, in the end, defined eligibility in terms of the functions in which they themselves were engaged. While lacking all the elements of precision, the method probably conformed to the pattern that any emerging profession is compelled to follow. It consisted of a group of practitioners who stated that they represented current practice; they invited others to join. The criteria became stricter with the passage of time as the professional association discovered errors or laxity in its early rules, or was able to establish new standards of practice or of educational preparation. While the Exchange was primarily established for the purpose of furnishing vocational counseling and placement, it early felt that there was a wider function for such an association in "the development of professional standards and organization." Several committees were appointed from time to time to map out this development and to make recommendations looking toward a broader and stronger national body. Finally, at a meeting of the members of the Exchange held at Milwaukee, June 27, 1921, in connection with the annual meeting of the National Conference of Social Work, it was voted to change the name of the Exchange to the American Association of Social Workers. The professional association was launched and got off to a flying start. It already had a journal, the *Compass*, authorized by the Exchange six months previously.

The Exchange had been financed from three sources: fees for placements, dues of members, and gifts from friends and foundations. Because the new Association was confined strictly to employed professional workers, its leaders felt that if the organization were to be free to direct its own development, financial support should come solely from its own members. At the next Conference, held in Providence in June, 1922, such a resolution was passed, and in order to make up a substantial deficit in the budget occasioned by the withdrawal of foundation support, an appeal was made to the better-paid members for subscriptions much larger than the five-dollar membership fee. Enthusiasm for the project caught the imaginations of social workers, and about thirty of them pledged a hundred dollars a year, while increased contributions of fifty dollars or less swelled the total income. The membership unanimously decided that by 1925 the organization be wholly self-supporting. This goal was reached in 1927.

There was a saving clause in the Providence resolution, by which the Association would be free to accept special gifts or grants from foundations for special projects. Since the placement work of the National Social Workers' Exchange had always operated at a deficit, it was therefore decided that the Association would not undertake the functions of counseling and placement, but instead would allocate them to a separate agency, which could receive grants from foundations. In that way, the Joint Vocational Service was created in 1922, with its own independent board and with responsibility for establishing a placement service on its own merits.

Membership in the American Association of Social Workers was determined by one or more of three methods: all current members of the Exchange were "written in" as charter members; employment for four years in an approved agency (with certain personal characteristics); and professional education. A new class of members, the juniors, was set up which had professional education as its aim.

These liberal definitions proved at once too sweeping and, at the same time, too strict. The test of "four years' employment" opened the door too widely, and the qualifying prerequisite of certain "personal characteristics" proved too clumsy to be applied. Any educational test, when coupled with the condition that professional education must be gained in a school that was a member of the Association of Professional Schools of Social Work, could be met, in general, only by those engaged in social casework; for casework was the only area in which the technique had been sufficiently defined and had a sufficient literature to be "communicated by an educational process." This left out most of those engaged in settlement or community activities; it also excluded many subexecutives, or even executives, who had reached their positions without the intervening phase of an educational preparation. For persons who had given exceptional services in the field of social work, but were not otherwise eligible, the new Association made special provision, that the National Executive Committee of the American Association of Social Workers might elect them to membership. This provision is jealously guarded and has been used but rarely.

The *Proceedings* of the Conference carry no mention of this development of the professional association. Apart from Miss Smith's paper on local social workers clubs, not a single paper or comment on the discussions refers to this vital development, which so intimately concerned most of the members of the Conference. This omission was not because of any antagonism between the older body and the new one. William T. Cross, the executive secretary of the Conference (1914–20) and one of the influential movers in the ill-fated National Association of Social Workers, pointed out the entirely different func-

tions of the two bodies. During these years the presidents of
the Conference, and many of its former presidents, were on
the organizing committees of one or the other of the two projects. A good many meetings of the Exchange took place at the
time of the meetings of the annual Conference, since that was
the most favorable occasion to get a full national representation. By the second decade of this century, the National Conference had expanded from a single program of meetings organized around subjects in which its members were interested,
to a galaxy of conferences meeting at the time of its sessions,
and giving to its members a chance to meet with their own special groups. Furthermore, these special groups, unlike the National Conference itself, were not limited in function to conducting a forum. They were usually national organizations,
such as the National Probation Association, the Child Welfare
League of America, the Family Welfare Association of America, the Young Men's Christian Association, the Salvation
Army, and so forth, which passed resolutions, established
standards, and performed such functions as a national representative body would undertake at its annual meeting. But
their deliberations did not get into the *Proceedings* of the Conference, and only rarely was reference made to them in the
papers presented. The Conference, a forum for free discussion,
where any competent person might state his opinion or tell his
experience, was a nucleus about which clustered a large number of other national bodies, meeting at the same time to conserve the time and effort of several thousand men and women
who came from all over the country, representing all sorts
and forms of social work. Such were the meetings, beginning
with a few people that came together and ending with a large
session at Milwaukee, of the group that made up the American
Association of Social Workers.

15 · THE UNITED STATES
CHILDREN'S BUREAU

*I*T WAS RELATED, at the twentieth anniversary of the establishment of the United States Children's Bureau (1932), that when Lillian Wald happened to read in the morning paper one day in 1906 about a special session of the President's Cabinet being called to consider the menace of the boll weevil, she turned to her breakfast companion, Mrs. Florence Kelley, and said, "This is interesting. Nothing in the interest of children could or would bring about a special Cabinet meeting, or fix the attention of our legislators. We count the boll weevil, or the lobster, or a fish, or a pig as more important than a child." During the discussion that followed, the hope was expressed that someday there would be a Federal bureau that would be as much concerned about the welfare of children as we are about the menace to the crop of cotton. Mrs. Kelley then talked with Dr. Edward T. Devine, and he sent a telegram to President Theodore Roosevelt, who immediately wired back: "It's a bully idea. Come to Washington and let's see."

Miss Wald and Dr. Devine at once went down to Washington and talked over their suggestion with the President. After consulting with Congressional leaders, Senator Murray Crane, of Massachusetts, introduced a bill authorizing such a bureau. This was followed by hearings held all over the land. President Roosevelt then called the White House Conference on Child Welfare in 1909, which passed a resolution in favor of such a bureau.

In the interval between the first suggestion and passage of the bill in 1912, the National Child Labor Committee entered the lists as champion of the idea. Much of the opposition came from the forces opposed to the regulation of child labor. The bill as it was finally passed was introduced by Senator William Borah, of Idaho, and signed by President William Howard Taft on April 9, 1912, six years after its first suggestion.

When the proposed bureau was still in the stage of discussion, Homer Folks gave (1910) what could be considered a classical outline of the arguments of the opposition. He stated that some opponents claimed the proposal did not go far enough; and others, that it attempted to accomplish too much at one step; that the proposed purposes were already cared for by existing statutes; that the objective was good, but that it should be achieved under other than the proposed auspices. Then, the three final arguments (always brought out when other arguments fail) were that the bureau would cost more than the country could afford; that it would destroy our form of government; and that in any event it was unconstitutional!

This most discerning analysis of the delaying tactics employed to defeat legislation of a welfare nature could easily be used in dissecting the opposition to any proposal in this field. It is to be noted that none of the objections is based on the actual merits or faults of the proposal. Tactically, it is apparently not good judgment to oppose welfare legislation in that manner. It should be added that too often these delaying tactics work well.

In support of the proposed bureau, Folks employed a similar light touch. He stated that children were more important than animals, that a live baby is worth much more than a dead one. However, he insisted that the public took no recognition of that fact, in spite of Rochester's (New York) amazing feat in cutting the infant death rate by 50 percent: no attention was paid to the achievement, he claimed, and no delegations were sent from other cities to find out how such results had been brought about. He emphasized that facts are important, and that there is a serious lag in our knowledge about child welfare. Mr. Folks declared too that the proposed bill was not intended as a joke; and that clarity of information is better than confusion.

The creation of the United States Children's Bureau was the first occasion on which the Federal Government entered the field of the social services as distinguished from public health or education. The bureau was authorized to "investigate and report . . . upon all matters pertaining to the welfare of children and child life among all classes of people," but it was not set up to perform any child welfare service. It has adhered strictly to fact finding and interpretation. Under able leadership the Children's Bureau enlarged itself and set standards for the various areas of child welfare work. This has been accomplished, not by the grant of special legal power, but because the bureau's competence has become recognized and its advice sought by agencies whose function it is to perform the services on which the bureau was reporting.

During the bureau's first year under the capable hand of Julia C. Lathrop, it started to assemble materials pertinent to its field gathered by other departments, and to give them wider circulation; it also initiated studies in infant mortality. Discovering at the outset of such studies the imperfect condition of birth statistics in the various states, the bureau entered upon a campaign for complete registration of births in every state.

In this first period its staff numbered only fifteen, and its over-all budget was the sum of $25,640. In view of the limited budget and small staff, the head of the bureau was forced to select rigorously the few projects that could be undertaken, leaving to later years the inclusion of other fields of inquiry.

In 1919 the bureau presented at the Conference its first report on infant mortality. Based on a study of sample cases, it showed a definite relation between infant deaths of children under two years of age and the economic status of the family. The mortality rate was found to be 59 per 1,000 live births in families whose income was $1,250 a year and over, but it rose to 125 in families where the income was only $450–$549 a year. The disparity is exaggerated when the comparison is made between breast-fed and artificially fed children: in the upper income group, the infant mortality rate was found to be twice as high among the artificially fed as among the breast fed; but in the lower income group it was seven times as high.

The sample on which these startling findings were based was small, and later studies somewhat modified the results, although without substantially changing the demonstration that it is far more dangerous to be born in a family whose income is low than in one which is able to provide some of the medical and nutritional services essential to the safeguarding of infant life. There are parallel values, such as better parental care, in addition to the food and medical attention enjoyed by the child in the higher income family. On the basis of the bureau's first study, it was stated that it was twice as dangerous to life to be born in a family of poverty than in a family of moderate circumstances; and that in some circumstances it was three and a half times as dangerous.

At the meeting held in honor of the bureau's twentieth anniversary, J. Prentice Murphy, of Philadelphia, one of the great leaders in the field of child welfare and indeed in the entire area of social work, gave special praise to the bureau's long-range and patient investigations with unmarried mothers and their heavily handicapped children: "The Bureau has made us see that what has happened and is happening to these [3,000,000 illegitimately born] children is of immediate and far-reaching concern to all of us." In this much stigmatized branch of social work in which there has been, on the one hand, brutal and heartless exploitation of children and, on the other hand, a certain sentimentality to fight, the bureau, through its careful investigations, has established norms for the care of the unmarried mother and her children, for the responsibilities of the father, and for the later life of both the mother and her child, and thereby helped to rescue unmarried motherhood from the greed of the exploiter, the prejudice of the moralist, and the sentimentality of the weak. The Children's Bureau in performing this essential service enabled one phase of social work to make advances in method and improvements equaled by few other efforts in the social services.

In 1922, when Grace Abbott had been in charge of the bureau for a year, she laid down three fundamental tasks for the immediate future of the bureau: the passage of the proposed child labor amendment; the enforcement and spread of the services offered by the Sheppard-Towner Act (maternal and infant welfare services in rural areas); and the protection of children from the devastating influence of the economic depression which the country was experiencing at the time.

The effort to limit the labor of children to such work and within such hours as would not be harmful to their physical and intellectual development was not a new project to Grace Abbott. In 1916, while Miss Lathrop was chief of the Children's Bureau, Miss Abbott was induced to join its staff to administer the new responsibilities imposed by the Child Labor Law passed that year. That law forbade the transference in interstate commerce of goods in whose manufacture child labor had been employed. Two years later the law was declared unconstitutional by the Federal Supreme Court, in a five to four decision.

It was the Bureau of Internal Revenue that administered the

law passed in 1919, which set a tax on all mines and manufacturing plants employing child labor. This law was declared unconstitutional in 1922, by an eight to one decision. It is little wonder that as Grace Abbott succeeded Julia Lathrop as the chief of the Children's Bureau she should have placed foremost among the planks of her platform the passage by Congress of a joint resolution proposing that self-same child labor provision as an amendment to the Constitution and promotion of its ratification by the several state legislatures.

The Sheppard-Towner Act (passed in November, 1921), to the effective administration of which Grace Abbott next proposed to devote the resources of the Children's Bureau, interrupted the functioning of that bureau; for the bureau entered into a supervisory and promotional relation with the states on the execution of the legal provisions of the law. The act was devised to spread to nonurban centers the benefits which most cities had given mothers and their infants, by offering nursing, informational, and advisory services to mothers on the care and feeding of their newborn children.

By means of this service, as well as through advances in sanitation and in the protection of urban food and water supplies, the relative death rate of infants in cities and in rural areas had been reversed; and the cities, which historically had a higher death rate than that of the rural areas, had now remarkably reduced that rate. In fact, the rural areas now found themselves with a death rate of newly born children decidedly higher than that of the crowded cities, for all the fresh air and the access to cheap and good food supplies in the country. The objective of the Sheppard-Towner Act was to aid the states to establish maternal and child health services in the rural districts by offering grants-in-aid to states whose provisions for such services met specifications set up by the Children's Bureau.

By June, 1922, forty-two states had accepted the provisions of the act by passing legislation in conformity to its demands. Homer Folks, in his previously quoted list of methods by which legislation for social welfare may be thwarted, omitted the decidedly familiar device by which provisions already in force may be killed by legislative failure to grant the appropriation to carry out the intent of the law. That fate awaited the Sheppard-Towner Act. In 1927 the Appropriations Committee of the House expressed itself as unwilling to continue the money necessary for the administration of the act; but in response to pressure from many sources the committee consented to include it in the appropriations for the next biennium, with the statement that by 1929 the work would have to be completed.

And so this second plank in Grace Abbott's platform was brought to defeat, not by the process of debate in the Congress on its merits, but by the decision of the Congressional committee in charge of finances on the ground that it could not be afforded. This action took place in the most prosperous years the country had known to that time. It remained for the agony of the great depression of the 1930s, with its unmistakable evidence of the unjust manner in which the cost of the "recession" was borne, to bring back the same measure in the Social Security Act of 1935, and so again to enable a country-born child to secure a protection from the perils of infancy equivalent to that enjoyed by his city-born cousin.

Miss Abbott's third plank to protect children from the effects of unemployment did not prove so important in the first years of her administration because the short business depression of 1921–22 quickly gave way to one of the dizziest periods of prosperity this or any other country had ever known. That it was a sound objective, however, no one gainsaid; and its pertinency was abundantly demonstrated when, in the next decade, again a substantial percentage of the working population was unemployed, and their children exposed to the hazards of an uncertain maintenance.

The main task of the Children's Bureau remained through all these years the investigation of the conditions of child life, and the publication of these findings. Over the years it has produced hundreds of sound and carefully documented monographs on all phases of child welfare, including foster and institutional care; juvenile court administration and probation; mothers' allowances for dependent children; maternity homes and their regulation in the interest of the children born within them; recreation as a socializing factor, and also as a preventive of delinquency; day nurseries and their problems, and the possibilities inherent in nursery schools. All go to form an impressive library of source materials quite without equal, and a glowing tribute to the sound workmanship and vision of the bureau's first great leader, Julia C. Lathrop, and of her successors.

16 · CHILD LABOR

*T*HE *INDUSTRIAL REVOLUTION* changed the nature of the work of children from vocational preparation for adult responsibilities to mechanical and meaningless tasks. The compensation provided by schools in order to make good this vocational loss could not be enjoyed by the child who spent his daylight hours in a textile mill.

England, 150 years ago, noticed this deprivation of preparation for his life work suffered by the child, and her public-spirited men sensed the physical and moral hazards to be expected when many children work long hours under the harsh supervision of foremen rather than carrying out small tasks for their respective parents. The first law referring to child labor passed by England, in 1802, was called the Health and Morals Act.

Massachusetts took the lead in the United States, enacting restrictive legislation in 1836, at a time when it was estimated that two fifths of all employees in New England factories were between the ages of seven and sixteen. Up to the end of the nineteenth century it was said that less than a dozen states had passed laws to limit the legal age for working children and the hours within which they might work.

At this point the National Consumers' League was organized in 1899, and the National Child Labor Committee in 1904. The latter grew out of the interest in child labor which followed an address delivered at the Atlanta Conference (1903) by Edward Gardner Murphy, of Alabama, on "Child Labor as a National Problem." From this time, a determined effort built on national lines was made to bring the states up to some uniform and valid standard of regulation of the labor of children. The United States Children's Bureau furnished a great deal of information on the human costs of child labor, gained by its studies.

The memory of three persons should be honored for their courageous leadership in the crusade to rescue children from the stultifying bondage of child labor: Mrs. Florence Kelley (1859–1932); Alexander J. McKelway (1866–1918); and Owen R. Lovejoy (1866–   ).

Mrs. Kelley, a graduate of Northwestern Law School, served as chief factory inspector for Illinois from 1893 to 1897 and became the first executive secretary of the National Consumers' League in 1899. While in Chicago, she stayed at Hull House, and when she removed to New York she lived at Henry Street Settlement.

The "White List" of manufacturers, prepared by the National Consumers' League, is now largely forgotten, but it was compiled in an attempt to encourage buyers to limit their purchases of goods to those produced under approved working conditions. For a time the movement appeared to possess vitality, but the necessity of buying in the lowest market, inherent in a competitive economy, proved an almost insurmountable barrier to the League program. Mrs. Kelley, however, was a valiant and resourceful fighter who never knew when she was defeated.

Her vision was not limited to superficial aspects; insistently she searched for underlying causes. One could never forget how, in a debate on widows' pensions, she startled her hearers by the statement, "I don't believe we should have widows!" With this declaration she dramatically summarized all she had seen of the needless deaths of wage earners and, incidentally, expressed the belief that stress should also be placed on preventing those deaths in the first place. Florence Kelley occupied a unique place in her large circle of friends as a lovable, if fiery, personality.

Alexander J. McKelway, secretary of the National Child Labor Committee for the Southern states from its organization in 1904 to his death fourteen years later, was a Presbyterian minister who was born and educated in the South. He was a strong believer in the ability of the South to accept the standards of school attendance and child labor adopted by the more progressive Northern states. His territory covered the areas of most stubborn and successful resistance to improving the conditions of child labor in the country. The resistance was reinforced by the assumptive necessity of the South to build up its industry by paying low wages; and the citation of Northern experience did not help the argument. No one can measure the extent of effectiveness of McKelway's efforts in furthering such improvements as were made, but he maintained a courageous and loyal front through the extremely difficult years after 1915, when the National Child Labor Committee had decided it was hopeless to bring the South up to any decent standard and turned its effort to the passage of Federal legislation.

Owen R. Lovejoy, like McKelway, had come into social work from the ministry, both finding in social work a field for the exercise of their passion for humanity which the church did not offer. Each entered his unexpected career early enough in life to give it the vigor of his best years. Lovejoy is one of the unsung heroes of social work; a man who combined a singular purity of religious devotion with a loyalty to liberal philosophy, he achieved the distinction of being the only man against whose election to the presidency of the Conference a formal protest was made to the Executive Committee, a protest that failed. This opposition was on the ground of his expressed sympathy for Eugene V. Debs's candidacy for the presidency of the United States on the Socialist ticket (1919).

As chairman of the Conference Committee on Standards of Living and Labor in 1912, Lovejoy drafted a set of reforms in industrial relations that previsioned almost precisely the Bull Moose platform of the Progressive party on which Theodore Roosevelt ran that same fall. That platform reached the high-water mark of idealistic democracy scored by this country in times of peace and prosperity. Lovejoy's interests were not at all confined to his own quite lonely objective. He was a prolific writer of Conference papers on a wide range of subjects. He was greatly interested in the formation of the American Association of Social Workers in 1921 and became its second president.

Child labor has been said to be caused by "tradition and poverty." Children have always worked in one way or another. An economic system in which the wage scale tends to descend to what is barely necessary to support the wage earner forces families of the unskilled and the low-paid workers to send their children to work to supplement an inadequate income. Other factors have entered the scene, such as the belief that parents have a right to send their children to work, and, for many children, the relatively greater attractiveness of wage earning over school attendance (Jane Addams, *Proceedings*, 1908). Fundamentally, however, the maintenance of an adequate standard of living for the unskilled worker demands that his children and his wife contribute to the support of the household when they are physically able to do so (O. R. Lovejoy, *Proceedings*, 1923).

Edward Gardner Murphy in his Atlanta address (1903) pointed out that it was poor economy to hire children at low wages. He put the blame for this shortsighted policy, however, on Northern capitalists who had established mills in the South. Whether he was correct in his judgment is not particularly important, from the point of view of the regulation of child labor. The issue became one of the South against the North—and one which finally induced a reaction in the New England states. The latter could not—or claimed that they could not—adopt better child labor legislation because of competition with the Southern child workers employed at low wages in the textile mills. There was probably little basis of fact in the contention of either section of the country, but it proved in the end a successful method of blocking improvement in both the North and the South.

The first ten years of the work of the National Child Labor Committee saw the greatest advance ever achieved in this country (1914) in the adoption of state laws on child labor. From barely a dozen states with inadequate and badly administered laws, the roll had grown to forty states, each of them having adopted laws approximating the uniform child labor law proposed by the American Bar Association. The eight exceptions were five Southern states and Nevada, New Mexico, and Vermont. The last three were unimportant; for in New Mexico and Nevada there were but few children employed and in Vermont a well-enforced school attendance law insured the same result. A few states ignored the minimum age limit of fourteen years, and established it at sixteen.

The energies of the national and local child labor committees had been largely expended in securing the passage of these laws, and the committees had not successfully followed up on their enforcement. In many places factory inspection was weak and corrupt, the positions being filled by political hacks, some of whom had secured the jobs because of their activity in opposing the passage of child labor laws in their state legislatures.

In 1907 Senator Albert J. Beveridge, of Indiana, presented to the Conference the arguments for a Federal law to be based on the power of Congress to regulate commerce as the one way to handle the child labor problem on a national scale. The Supreme Court having upheld the power of Congress to prohibit the interstate distribution of lottery tickets in the interest of national welfare, Beveridge argued that the court would therefore hold that Congress has the power to pass a child labor law on the same principle. He showed that twenty-seven times, the Supreme Court had approved the exercise of such power by the Congress in situations analogous to child labor, that is, to prohibit the transfer across states boundaries of goods deemed in some way injurious to the welfare of the nation. (If he had spoken several years later, he could have cited the Mann Act, wherein it was not goods, but persons that could not be transported across state lines under certain circumstances, and that law was declared constitutional.) Beveridge believed that child labor could be stopped only by a Federal law because of the "handicap" suffered by a state whose legislation was much in advance of its neighbors.

After the two acts passed by Congress had been declared unconstitutional, as related in Chapter 15, advisers of the National Child Labor Committeee abandoned the effort to pass a law which might be approved by the Supreme Court, and turned their attention to securing a constitutional amendment that would definitely grant such power to the Congress. Herbert C. Hoover, then Secretary of the Department of Commerce, urged (1922), "that a final effort be made to bring all states into line to abolish child labor. If that cannot be accomplished quickly, I regretfully join with those in favor of Federal action." The context indicates that he meant an amendment to the Constitution. At the same Conference, Msgr. John A. Ryan, speaking in the shadow of the second adverse decision of the Supreme Court on child labor, said that "if the friends of better child labor legislation were compelled to choose between state action and federal action they ought to decide in favor of the latter."

These two opinions from widely diverse sources expressed the conviction of people intimately interested in suppressing the evils of child labor, and so attention was directed to the passage of a joint resolution by Congress looking toward an amendment to the Constitution. Such a resolution was passed in the spring of 1924, giving to Congress "the power to limit, regulate and prohibit the labor of persons under eighteen years of age."

The friends of such legislation looked forward with confidence to the ultimate approval by the necessary three fourths of the state legislatures, in view of the expected public support of regulation of child labor. However, the opposition marshaled an impressive array of adverse forces—conservative, industrial, religious, and even sentimental—and the required three fourths has never been reached. At the Conference of 1925, Owen Lovejoy and former Senator Charles S. Thomas, of Colorado, debated at a general session the pros and cons of the child labor amendment. The extravagant interpretation of the proposed amendment made by its bitterest opponents is well summarized in Thomas's plea: the structure of the nation will fall if the amendment is adopted. There must have been some powerful interests menaced by it, to call forth such wild—and at the time widespread—opposition.

In 1921, commenting on three proposed amendments submitted in 1789, 1810, and 1861 which had not received approval by the requisite three quarters of the states, the Supreme Court said that "approval must be within some reasonable time after the proposal." It has not passed specifically upon whether the child labor amendment is still before the states. Agitation for a Federal law against child labor ceased with the failure to secure the adoption of the amendment, and efforts to control child labor reverted back to the states, with the exception of certain

New Deal legislation of the 1930s and of the years of the second World War.

Two sore spots in child labor remain to claim attention: street trades and agricultural labor. Hawkers and "little" businessmen are accustomed to hiring child labor on the streets, but it is reserved to the power of the press really to protect its own interests! Newspapers have steadily opposed regulation of street trades, as well as the adoption of the child labor amendment. They have used all their resources to publicize the "energetic young merchant" as the valuable citizen of the future and on the whole they have been quite successful in blocking efforts to limit hours and territories within which the newsboy may operate.

The newsboy is not an employee but an independent merchant, so it requires special regulations to protect him against the perils of his work. License of the children by school authorities; prohibiting the employment of boys under a certain age (with a higher age for girls); districting a community—all have been tried, with some measure of success. But the evil still remains, and constitutes a very real problem in the general improvement of child labor conditions and regulations.

Agricultural child labor presents an anomalous problem. Often it consists of work by children for their parents at tasks which from time immemorial children have to some extent been accustomed to perform. In 1924 Wiley H. Swift, of the National Child Labor Committee, estimated that three quarters of a million children were employed in agricultural tasks instead of being at school. Swift, in the same article, pointed to the correlation of high illiteracy with the high percentage of agricultural child workers.

In rural areas, the point of attack is school attendance. As its enforcement is a matter for local school boards, whose members may be using their own children on the farm instead of sending them to school, the remedy for the situation can only be found (again in violation of the principle of local control) in some state programs of grants-in-aid. The subvention to local schools is based on the number of days of school attendance, not on school enrollment or on the length of the school year.

Felix Adler, president of the National Child Labor Committee, spoke (1920) of the regulation of rural child labor as a more promising field than regulation in factories or mills. If there are good school attendance laws, well enforced, the occupation of the farm worker, being full of variety, unlike the monotonous labor of the factory operative, makes the highest demands on the intelligence and education of those who fill it. The great development of the 4H Clubs among rural boys and girls seems to be some fulfillment of Adler's prophecy.

17 · THE JUVENILE COURT

CREDIT for the creation of the first juvenile court in this country is usually given to the state of Illinois, which established this special procedure in chancery for the consideration of children's behavior in the Circuit Court in June, 1899. On the other hand, according to Judge Benjamin B. Lindsey (1925), Colorado had granted the same authority to county judges a few months before. The roots of the legal procedure go back many centuries in English practice to the chancery function of the court over the property and welfare of minors.

The theory of chancery is that a girl or a boy who commits a delinquent act should be considered a child whose social development has been so faulty that the state is warranted to intervene as an authority superior to that of the parent, in order to insure to the child such corrective influences as will compensate for his previous upbringing. There are in the main, therefore, two functions belonging to a juvenile court. One is based on a determination of fact: does this child come under the legal definition of a boy or a girl in need of protection by the state? The other function is to provide such protection. The first is a judicial function; the second is an administrative one. Homer Folks, at the 1906 Conference, made clear the distinction, which Judge Julian W. Mack, of the Cook County Juvenile Court, at the same Conference entirely approved, and which Abraham Flexner in 1910 repeated in his lucid and logical manner.

Homer Folks and Judge Mack, at the Conference of 1906,

suggested as a corollary to their thesis that there should be an independent department of probation, consisting of a board with authority to set qualifications for probation officers and to select them by a merit system; such a department would be either local or statewide.

Flexner, laying more stress on the judicial function, questioned the wisdom of bringing to the juvenile court any cases except those of delinquency of a child or of an adult who has contributed to a child's delinquency. In view of such a position, he would entirely remove the function of relief—mothers' pensions—from the juvenile court and place it in an independent administrative agency. (This was the position that Massachusetts had taken.)

Judge James Hoge Ricks, of Richmond, Virginia, expressed the same opinion in 1920, merely adding that in cases involving guardianship, the question is one for judicial decision, with which Flexner's statement is not in disagreement. Some of the early juvenile judges, notably Judge Lindsey, of Denver, acted as their own probation officers, but ordinarily that expedient has not been recommended.

This negative attitude is based on the totally dissimilar function of the judge, whose responsibility is to pass on the law and the facts of the case, and that of the probation officer, whose duty it is to study the child in his entire setting, and to put into operation those measures he deems best fitted to provide the child with such assistance as will enable him to avoid the pitfalls of his past experience. It is a job in social casework (Grace Abbott, *Proceedings*, 1929)—the subtle task of understanding a unique individual, and of reinforcing his inner resources and environmental influences to his best advantage.

One of the primary difficulties in this dual situation is the selection of a competent judge. Judge Mack remarked (1906) that unless "the justice is interested in philanthropy, you might as well give up the Juvenile Court." He deplored the method of changing the juvenile judge every three months, not to speak of more often, and believed that the right person should be urged to sacrifice "his intellectual pursuits" and serve for one or two years. Nowhere in the *Proceedings* of the Conference is any mention made of a basic difficulty inherent in the effort to engraft upon an elaborate and well-seasoned practice in judicial procedure chiefly concerned with civil law a function almost totally alien to its interest, such as determining whether a socially handicapped child is in need of the protection of the state. The custom of rotating the selection of the judge to act in the juvenile court results either in the office being fixed upon the one least able to defend himself against such assignment, or in its acceptance as a necessary chore that must be done with as soon as possible; not as a new professional challenge. As Judge Edward F. Waite, who for twenty of his thirty years on the district bench of Hennepin County (Minnesota) served as juvenile judge, expressed it:

Time spent on the juvenile bench has little professional significance. From the legal point of view the cases heard are simple; whatever technical learning and acumen the judge may have is likely to suffer from disuse; contacts made in court do not add to his professional prestige; he is not in line for professional promotion, and after service as juvenile judge he is at least no better off as a lawyer than if the time had been spent in some wholly nonjudicial task. Reward for efficient service according to the standards commonly applied to trial judge is not to be expected.

William H. Hodson, after serving four years as director of the Children's Bureau of Minnesota (during which time he became one of the leading authorities on child welfare, including the operation of the juvenile court), was told by the foremost legal firms of Minneapolis and St. Paul that his experience not only did not fit him for employment by them, but, rather the reverse, all his experience and facility would have to be un-learned and he would have to start all over again.

This exclusive professional concern of law with civil law re-acts badly on its relation with criminal procedure, as well as on the juvenile court. No one has suggested a solution which, at one and the same time, is accepted by the legal profession and the broad field of the social services. Some courts, as in Ohio, have appointed referees, and chosen to fill the positions people well qualified to deal with the social in contrast with the legal questions involved in the cases.

New ground was broken in 1909 by the formation of the Psychopathic Institute as an arm of the Cook County Juvenile Court, with Dr. William Healy in charge. Credit for its estab-lishment is given by Dr. Healy to the initiative of Julia Lathrop, and to the generosity of Mrs. William Dummer. European criminologists had urged expert psychological examinations of criminals as a basis on which treatment should be given; but in the United States this was the first instance in which a court routinely used a competent psychiatrist. Credit should also be given to Judge Merritt W. Pinckney, of the Cook County Juvenile Court, for his courage in making such a radical change in procedure.

Dr. Healy's first interest was in determining the degree of in-telligence shown by the children examined by him (1911), but by the time his classic work, *The Individual Delinquent*, ap-peared (1929) his interests had widened to include the emo-tional and mental life of the child. His most significant sugges-tion, that "the boy's own story" had an important diagnostic value and was perhaps the most important of all sources of knowledge of the boy, has grown to be the capital stone in the structure of contemporary psychiatric examinations, as well as of social case inquiries. From the purely legal point of view, and because of the inability of the judge to evaluate its significance, "the boy's own story" would be looked upon by the judge as a fanciful fairy tale.

The services of Dr. Healy and his many successors furnish a bridge to span the gap between the legalistic determination of "fact" and its social interpretation, available to the judge who, like Pinckney, is wise enough to ask for it. Indeed, a new judicial procedure in juvenile cases as well as in criminal cases might develop in time. For the present, at least, the major service of the psychiatrist is to guide the probation officer in offering a clue to the personality of the child, together with suggestions as to his treatment. The psychiatrist then has a double function. He should present to the judge an explanation of the personality of the delinquent child, on which the judge can decide whether the child is to be sent to an institution or placed on probation. He then has also the task of expertly advising the institution or the probation officer as to the sort of treatment the child should receive.

This is a complex situation in which there is great variableness of the parts. If the judge is not overly defensive of his prerogatives, he welcomes the services of the psychiatrist, and leaves a good deal of authority in the hands of his probation officers. If the psychiatrist is proficient, he recognizes the limits of the areas of his competency, and leaves to judge and probation officers responsibility for their tasks. If the probation officer is a well-qualified social caseworker, skillful in the use of the services of the judge and of the psychiatrist and all the other factors on which treatment depends, he can ably fit himself into this difficult pattern.

Again, if all three parties in this joint operation were constant, they would probably weld themselves into a team of considerable efficiency; but in general, the one member of the team with ultimate authority, the judge, in most places, is frequently changed, and the other members of the team again and again have to learn the personality, the prejudices, even the defensiveness of a new judge (Frederick Moran, *Proceedings*, 1930). In such a difficult structural situation it is not any wonder that real efficiency in dealing with the subtle problems of a delinquent child is seldom reached; and that only too often the various services tend to crystallize into rigid formulas.

A serious limitation upon the juvenile court has been the absence of a tradition of supplying an adequate staff to the bench, and when it took on the task of probation there was no precedent to support its needs for a staff large enough to do the work assigned. Then, too, probation had been largely a volunteer effort; working at times under public bodies, such as the group of women in Massachusetts in the last century, or in the early days of the juvenile courts, representatives of religious sects were sent by their denominations to serve any member of their faith who was under court supervision. In Chicago, Judge Mack could call upon a private agency to furnish paid probation officers, but he felt that there were too few available for the volume of work; and so he recommended the use of volunteers (1906); the same action had been taken by Henry W. Thurston, chief probation officer of the Cook County Juvenile Court, in the previous year. Thurston stated that the case loads of each probation officer varied from 150 to 225 cases, and that it was humanly impossible to do justice to so many children. He therefore recommended the enlistment of volunteers as a remedy. Judge William H. deLacy, of the juvenile court in Washington, D.C., was not impressed (1909) by what he saw of the work of the volunteer probation officer, however. The experience of charity organization societies in the use of volunteers was roughly paralleled in probation. Some of the more enthusiastic early leaders were able to use them; but the inevitable trend to substitute the paid worker was already winning out.

The individual loads of probation officers, however, remain impossibly high even today.

An important change in procedure was advocated by Dr. Lilburn Merrill, of Seattle, in 1913: the hearing out of court of certain nonserious cases in order to leave the court free to consider the more important complaints and also to save many children from a court record. Dr. Merrill did not suggest how it might be done, but the procedure has become general practice in many juvenile courts. The chief probation officer, or someone deputized to act for him, hears the complaint and decides whether it is to go further or not. This cannot be done, obviously, without the full approval of the court.

Most lawyers resent the invasion of their domain by probation officers; as a matter of practice, lawyers are now actually excluded from the juvenile courts. The influence of the juvenile court on criminal and even on civil procedure was noticeable, however, throughout this period, although only incidentally. Parenthetically, it should be added that the opposition of the legal profession is not sound, for in general, appeals taken from decisions of juvenile courts on grounds of procedure have been decided by the higher courts in favor of their legality.

The first suggestion for extension of the jurisdiction of the juvenile court was that it cover all cases of domestic relations, and such a court has been established in Buffalo, in Cincinnati, and in certain other cities. The proviso that it should be inclusive of all juvenile cases, however, has not generally been carried out. The only change in the court handling domestic relations has been in the matter of procedure, and in the recognition that such cases call for the method of probation rather than imprisonment for their treatment. In 1925 Judge Lindsey made the interesting suggestion that a Court of Human Relations be established. Whether this should include all matters now covered in courts of criminal jurisdiction, as well as domestic relations and juvenile delinquency, is not clear, but the logical development of the juvenile court idea, as Juvenile Judge T. Munford Boyd, of Charlottesville, Virginia, pointed out in 1928, is to produce a revision of the general body of criminal law and criminal procedure of the future.

18 · MOTHERS' PENSIONS

*T*HE PRIOR CLAIM of the widow on relief, whether public or private, noted in earlier chapters, softened the almost rigid theory that relief is injurious and should be granted only in the almshouse. The plight of a mother left dependent by the death of her husband opened the heart, if only slightly the purse strings, of a nation beginning to be self-conscious of social causes and results. Logically, the next step would have been to consider the mother and her children as a preferential class of relief recipients, but some influence never identified ignored the mother and singled out the children for aid. The inference is almost inescapable that in some way the French movement of bonuses for children influenced the first legislation. Nowhere in the history of American welfare before 1910 had there been any indication of a philosophy that children living in their own homes were to be assisted apart from their parents.

The report of the first White House Conference on Child Welfare in 1909, from which the movement for mothers' pensions received inspiration, stated that "homelife is the highest and finest product of civilization," and on that basis it made the plea that no home should ever be broken up for reasons of poverty alone. Yet in 1911 when the first legal provisions were passed in Missouri, and the same year in Illinois, they were for grants to children alone; the mother and the home she sought to maintain were ignored in these early provisions, so far as recognition of their claim for assistance was concerned. In six states and the District of Columbia, this shortsighted policy has not been followed; instead, the need of the family is the basis of the grant. However, the general rule was to base grants on the number of children, and a policy so fundamentally unjust to the concept of the primary importance of the home is perpetuated in the section on Aid to Dependent Children of the Federal Social Security Act of 1935. The principle of allowing somewhat more for the first child than for subsequent children does not meet the charge that the plan ignores the mother and her home. The cost of caring for an only child is recognized to be greater than the cost of maintaining each subsequent child.

The Kansas City law of 1911 was entitled "Mothers' Pensions," whereas the Illinois law was termed the "Funds to Parents Act." The more conservative proponents of mothers' pensions would have limited the provisions to widows (James F. Jackson, *Proceedings*, 1914), but gradually the distinction between the needs of a family in which the father is dead and one in which he is permanently incapacitated or incarcerated for a considerable period of time became indefensible, and most laws were early expanded to include all but families deserted by the husband. However, as the casework services within this field improved, it was seen that deserted wives could be included without the danger of encouraging desertion by lazy husbands (Pinckney, *Proceedings*, 1912).

Most of the early laws were permissive; but if the cost of their operation fell exclusively upon the local government unit, mothers' pensions might have very scant application. Thus in Missouri, where the law applied only to Kansas City and St. Louis, there were in those two cities less than two hundred recipients of such aid at the time of the passage of the Federal Social Security Act in 1935, although in many states there was wider participation than in Missouri. Where the state shared the expense of the law with local units, there was much wider and more general participation, Pennsylvania being the outstanding example. In the few states under state-financed programs, there was more nearly statewide coverage than elsewhere.

The way in which the juvenile court entered the picture can best be described as an accident. The first Missouri law, applicable only to Kansas City, indicated the juvenile court as its administrator; the law for St. Louis placed it in a special body, the Board of Children's Guardians. The Illinois Funds to Parents Act designated the juvenile court as in command. Very early, a few states, such as Massachusetts, placed administration as a special mandate upon the overseers of the poor and so rescued the law from the handicap of being a provision that ignored the family and considered only the child. The same policy was originally adopted by Indiana.

But the trend toward placing the aid under the juvenile court prevailed in most of the Northwestern states of the Union, and its benefits were geared to the number of children, not to the mother's requirements. The juvenile court of Cook County, under the administrations of Judge Mack, and of his successor, Judge Pinckney, had made an enviable reputation for integrity and courage. Moreover, there was a belief that pensions for mothers should be regarded as earned, so as to avoid the stigma of pauperism that clung to the recipient of public charity. How much influence the Fabian Socialists of England, with their determination to break up the Poor Law and distribute its functions to other political institutions, played in the decision to separate mothers' pensions from general relief has never been shown. In accordance with their theory that maintenance of the home was a function of the chancery court, the juvenile court would have been the Fabian Society's logical choice. In the debate on mothers' pensions at the 1912 Conference, Julia Lathrop spoke of the Minority Report of the English Poor Law Commission of 1909 as setting the new philosophy for public assistance, indicating that she was well acquainted with the policy of the Fabian Socialists.

This new function, however, has never rested easily upon the juvenile court, and important authorities, including Judge Pinckney himself (1912), had opposed it as a function of the juvenile court on the grounds that determination of need is not a judicial, but an administrative function. Certainly, determining the amount of assistance and furnishing the casework services to meet it have little of the judicial nature. While not supported by strict logic, the choice of the juvenile court as the auspices under which mothers' pensions were granted probably did much to rescue that form of assistance from the stigma of public relief, and indirectly influenced a revaluation of the entire philosophy of assistance, the end of which has not yet been reached.

The National Conference's concern with mothers' allowances was chiefly limited to a debate in 1912 between its defenders in Chicago and its Eastern critics and an interesting summary of the situation in several states published in the 1914 *Proceedings*. The arguments opposed to mothers' pensions centered largely in the familiar criticisms of public outdoor relief: that it could not be done well by the state; that it was degrading to the recipient; that it became unmanageable in size because of its inefficient administration; and that the sense of "right" to assistance which it encouraged became a threat, although at least one speaker (Frederick Almy, of the Buffalo Charity Organization Society, 1912) raised the question of whether after all a widow did not have such a right. It was further claimed that private organization of charity could handle the problem more economically and efficiently, and with less injury to the families involved.

In their arguments for mothers' pensions the proponents denied that private agencies could, or ever did, handle adequately the relief needs of widowed families; that the new child labor laws reduced the potential income from children; and finally, that the state has a duty to such families which can only be met by providing an adequate and reliable income to insure the maintenance of the home.

The impression one receives after reading these old debates is that the leaders in the charity organization movement in the East were shortsighted in their opposition. In the face of such a sincere effort as Judge Pinckney's to break new ground for a sound method of social casework, it would have been the part of wisdom for the charity organizations to throw all possible experience and guidance into the endeavor rather than to stand on the side lines and predict failure.

There is a question, at present insoluble: What gave the tremendous vigor to the movement for mothers' pensions? It created a body of public opinion which swept the legislators from their feet. Bills of this sort, even in the Illinois legislature, passed without consultation with any social workers, public or private. There was an organization in the city of New York known as the Widowed Mothers' Fund Association, of which Sophie Irene Loeb was the dominant personality. The influence of this association spread beyond the borders of the city and even passed the boundaries of the state of New York. It may have been an aspect of the progressive spirit of the early years of the second decade, but it was specific: the Widowed Mothers' Fund wanted to secure for every dependent mother in America an assured income, which income should not be furnished through existing public or private agencies. The movement made a clean sweep of the country so that by 1913, seventeen state legislatures had passed substantially identical measures. Such well-defined movements do not just happen.

It is possible that the movement for mothers' pensions was the outlet for the nascent sense of social responsibility that sought expression in an object emotionally somewhat removed from the operation of prejudices that confused and encumbered other phases of relief giving. It was a thoughtful program of differentiated aid and—in no flippant sense—the child was father to the thought.

19 · THE RECOGNITION OF SOCIAL CASEWORK

*T*HE DEVELOPMENT of a social technique, such as social casework, has what might fittingly be called a "preliterate" phase during which its elements are tested out and made ready for the task for which it is designed. Yet of this period of probably intensive activity there is no record—much as our great human cultures seem to spring fully developed from an unrecorded past. Certainly, that is true of our most familiar technical term: social casework. Probably the first appearance of "casework" in the *Proceedings* was in a paper by Edward T. Devine—the first that he gave after becoming secretary of the Charity Organization Society of New York in 1897—in which he said that "good case work involves much thankless labor."

The term did not occur again in the title of a Conference paper until 1909 when Mary K. Simkhovitch, of Greenwich House, New York, suggested that there was a place for the use of the method of casework with families "above the poverty line," known to settlements. In 1901 Zilpha Smith and Mary Richmond read important papers describing the methods used and the scope of resources available in casework, but in neither paper did the term "casework" occur. Then in 1911 casework burst into full view as an accepted and well-known technique. Frederick Almy, of Buffalo, spoke of adequate relief as a factor "in case work"; Dr. Adolf Meyer, of Johns Hopkins University, spoke of "Case Work in Social Service and Medical and Social Coöperation in Nervous and Mental Diseases"; and Porter R. Lee read a paper on "The Social Function of Case Work." From that date, social casework entered the field of literate history, becoming the best known and, ultimately, the most widely employed skill in social work. Of the steps that led to this completed result, nothing is known, further than the inferential explanation given in Chapter 10.

What is social casework? It is perhaps significant that there has been no paper in the Conference on that exact subject. Mary Richmond wrote a book, published in 1922, with that title, and its definition gained general acceptance at first. Karl de Schweinitz, with his genius for words, calls it "the art of helping." Mary Richmond used to say, informally, that it was the use of common sense in uncommon situations. Already noted is Zilpha Smith's insistence that casework means leaving no stone unturned to find the trouble which drags a person down. In her 1901 paper she implied that it is a process by which a person becomes known, quoting Jane Addams as maintaining, "It is nonsense to say that one cannot know the poor who does not live with them. You know the poor if you take pains to know them." Miss Smith identified social casework by that statement as the method of taking "pains to know" the applicant. The word "individualize" was often used to describe the process of casework.

It is to be noted that, in these early explanations, the process of casework was limited to the investigation by which the visitor might come to know the family. Charles Birtwell spoke (1902) of the necessity of "knowing" the potential foster home, by the same means and for the same reason. It may therefore be said that social casework, in its early stages, was the process by which the visitor overcame the applicant's protective reserve and the obstacles to knowing the otherwise anonymous essential person, a result necessary in order to base whatever was advised or done on a foundation of fact rather than of fancy.

At this stage of its formulation, social casework was not developing the subject of treatment with as much care as that of investigation. In that rule-of-thumb age it could be assumed that, given adequate knowledge, the form which action should take would follow; and in some situations, just such a result did take place. If a man were unemployed, work would be indicated as the remedy. If sickness were present, the use of medical resources could be advised. In the cases of low-skilled workmen whose inadequate wages kept their family in a chronic stage of dependency, Mary Richmond used to say that it was better to spend a thousand dollars to teach the man a skilled occupation at which he could earn an adequate wage, than to spend a hundred dollars in relief to the family. Dr. Richard C. Cabot told the story of the child who repeatedly visited the clinic on account of pediculosis, which was permanently cleared up, not by the medical services at the clinic, but by the casework of the medical social worker who found the whole family afflicted with the same parasite. All these are examples of how suitable treatment followed almost automatically on discovery of the real difficulty.

Nevertheless, investigation at the hands of the unskillful worker was a dangerous tool. It tended to deteriorate into "snooping" about to see what unfavorable factors could be unearthed in a family. So long as the concept of worthy and unworthy, or any other moralistic jargon, dominated the philosophy of the caseworker, investigation was almost certain to become a means to discover the unfavorable features of people's lives—and whose life does not possess hosts of them? It might become a device to refuse appeals and cause the social caseworker, in turn, to become hardened and suspicious. With the rapid spread of charity organizations in which the principle of investigation was fully accepted, it is not surprising that social casework was looked upon by some people as a barren and dehumanized process from which all the warmth and love of fellow man that was supposed to characterize human relations had been plucked out by the roots. It is probably not going beyond the facts to state that such a result is a constant threat to the whole field of social casework, and it accounts for much of the opposition with which casework was greeted on its emergence into literate expression.

Between 1911 and 1917 the value of the method of social casework was becoming more widely appreciated by the actual practitioners themselves. Dr. Cabot and his chief medical social worker, Ida Cannon, were demonstrating its utility in the social treatment of the sick; Ada Sheffield, in Boston, was employing it in her work with unmarried mothers; C. C. Carstens, recently come to the Massachusetts Society for the Prevention of Cruelty to Children, was finding it essential in protective work with children; Porter R. Lee, who had succeeded Mary Richmond in Philadelphia, was developing that philosophical grasp of the function of social casework in contemporary society which was to contribute much to the establishment of the method on a world-wide basis.

In the spring of 1914, Mary Richmond gave the Kennedy Lectures in Social Case Work before the New York School of Philanthropy. The clamor for admission was so great that they were delivered to two different groups without satisfying the demand. The lectures, in turn, were followed in 1917 by the classic in this field, *Social Diagnosis,* acclaimed at once as meeting the most exacting requirements of professional and scholarly standards. The effect of Mary Richmond's book on the whole field of the social services was dramatic. Instead of being somewhat apologetically acknowledged by social workers, social diagnosis became overnight *the* process of social work, threatening to overshadow all other techniques in the field of human relations. Mary Richmond declared, recognizing this sudden tendency to limit social work to social casework, "I have spent twenty-five years of my life in an attempt to get social casework accepted as a valid process in social work. Now I shall spend the rest of my life trying to demonstrate to social caseworkers that there is more to social work than social case-work."

The coming of the first World War was destined to strengthen even more strongly the dominance of social casework in the field of social work. The psychiatrists and psychologists who laid the basis of the first application of psychiatry to men in the armed services who were severely affected by the emotional shocks incidental to war found in the well-trained social caseworker just the assisting personnel necessary for the examination and treatment of those suffering from battle neuroses and psychoses; and because psychiatry was then beginning to adopt the dynamic methods of the psychoanalysts, social caseworkers for the first time had guidance in the treatment of their applicants, as well as more subtle diagnostic processes available for understanding them.

Social casework had not been uninfluenced by psychiatry even before the war. Mary Richmond drew on Dr. Adolf Meyer, of Johns Hopkins University, for guidance in developing her theory of social diagnosis. In some cities, psychiatrists were members of case conferences, and contributed not only to the method of understanding clients, but also to the education of the professional staff. The influence had been only rarely felt before the war; but after 1918 it became essential for anyone practicing in the field of social casework to understand the dynamic functions of the emotions. It became apparent that it is not only men in the armed services who are made or broken by their emotional tolerance to stresses and frustrations, but that the behavior of the ordinary person can be better understood if we know how he meets environmental factors than if we limit our study to the nature of the environmental factors themselves.

It was fortunate for the existence of social casework that,

when psychiatry suddenly focused on the importance of the emotions in shaping personality, casework was already practicing in the field of human behavior, and had developed a valid method of understanding its problems. At once there was apparent the close interrelation between the method of evaluating social data as developed by the caseworker and the psychiatrist's method of defining the dynamics of the mentally ill person. Each was dealing with persons in trouble, and each had developed a method designed to understand more clearly the nature of the trouble and how the person might be enabled to overcome it. Even their methods of treatment followed a roughly similar philosophy. It is not what is done for or to the applicant which is significant, but what the applicant alone is enabled to do for himself that really matters. But back of the psychiatrist's technique were long years of experimentation and research in its mastery. Social casework as a distinct art was new; its practitioners had not been subject to so vigorous an educational discipline as had the psychiatrists; they did not even have an accepted vocabulary with which to express their concepts. The social caseworker did have, however, according to Mary Richmond (1917), "skill in discovering the social relationships by which a given personality had been shaped; . . . ability to get at the central core of difficulty in these relationships; and . . . power to use the direct action of mind upon mind in their adjustment."

Skill in mastering the method of social casework is acquired by practice under competent supervision and by classroom discussion of case records. Porter R. Lee pointed very clearly (1920) to the kind of record it would be necessary to have to develop facility in handling the problems of human adjustment with which the caseworker deals. Mary Richmond, in the first (unpublished) bulletins of the charity organization department of the Russell Sage Foundation in the first decade of the century, printed case records, and then circulated discussions by different persons and groups based on the records.

Case records of actual situations, edited for teaching purposes, have furnished an all but exclusive method of teaching social casework, both to the employee receiving in-service training and to the student at a school. Yet the conditions laid down by Lee as to what constitutes a teaching record have not been met. Records have given a statement of the situation, the steps have been carefully outlined, and the results honestly reported. For teaching purposes, the reason why each step was taken should be recorded, with some discussion of alternative possibilities and why they were rejected. The psychiatric social record, following the professional tradition of medicine and psychiatry, does that. As a contribution by the Judge Baker Foundation in Boston, Dr. William Healy, in 1920, arranged for the publication of annotated records of twenty children who appeared before the juvenile court in Boston. The Commonwealth Fund publication, *Three Problem Children* (New York, 1926), similarly described the actions that were taken, the reasons for taking them, and why alternative possibilities were rejected.

The current practice of teaching from bare case records limits the teaching possibilities to the competence of the instructor, not to the potential teaching value of the situation described in the record. When the same supervisor or same teacher uses a number of records, the apprentice or the student learns merely what one person conceives to be the reasons for the various processes used. Until casework is taught by a discussion of the reasons for adopting certain methods given by the very caseworkers who made the decisions in their repeated handling of their problems, use of the skill is likely to become a cult, not a profession; the reflection of the point of view of a leader, not the synthesis of all the best thinking in the field.

The other basic method of teaching in the area of human relations, the case conference, is not discussed in the *Proceedings.* The case conference as a device to secure mutual understanding and coöperation between agencies is mentioned, but although it was probably a method used by all the careful caseworking agencies before the advent of the school, it fell into disuse with the coming of the professional staff. Nevertheless, for professional purposes the case conference is even more vital than carefully annotated case records. It deals with current situations and is shared by the actual practitioners themselves.

The first case committees were composed of lay and professional members, with laymen taking the leadership. Now that the layman has stepped into the wings, there is a feeling among social caseworkers that it would be a denial of professional competency to rely on lay opinion, even in the give-and-take discussion of a conference. Whatever may be the merits of such a judgment—and it has a dubious side—the professional caseworker has not himself created any substitute on a professional level which would bring together, routinely, those engaged in the difficult and subtle task of understanding human beings; discussing cases as they arise; and subjecting their decisions to the criticism of their peers. (Exception must be made in behalf of the psychiatric social worker, who uses the medical terminology for "staffing a case.")

To be of influence wider than that of the group participating in the symposium, such discussion should be recorded and available to all social workers. The probabilities are all against the assumption that such a natural method of improving one's practice in the art of helping might be extinct. It is more likely that under one auspice or another, by staff meetings in agencies, or by case conferences called by councils of social agencies, or by case conferences called by national bodies such as the Child Welfare League of America, or the Family Service Association of America, social caseworkers would be constantly maturing their grasp of their problems and improving their practice by use of the method of the conference. Seldom, however, would their conclusions be published or the results of this work become known, except by word of mouth. If this hypothesis is at all in accord with fact, to that extent the development of the method of social casework is still in the preliterate stage.

20 · THE COUNCIL OF SOCIAL AGENCIES

ONE OF THE causes that brought about the charity organization movement was the need to create some sort of order in the many unrelated public and private agencies dealing with the poor. In pursuit of this aim, the general idea of organization was broken down into several parts, one of which was to coordinate the task of raising money by social agencies, which was tried early in Liverpool, England, in 1869, and taken over in Denver in 1889.[1] This phase of coöperation, however, did not make any progress in America until money raising was put on an independent footing in Cleveland in 1913. Another means adopted by the early societies was that of joint registration, whereby societies might avoid duplicating the efforts of other agencies. Use of this device had a steady growth in the more progressive societies, and it was retained as one of their primary functions until taken over by the council of social agencies. Another novel feature was that of endorsement of charities. It is not known how widely this function was incorporated into the activities of the early societies, but in the larger cities, such as New York, Boston, and Chicago, as well as London, it became an important service, and in many of the smaller cities, the contributors to the local charity organization society look to it to advise them on their charitable gifts. And so the situation remained, till the councils of social agencies or the community chests took over the function of endorsement.

[1] See Chapter 21.

These various supplementary functions of "organizing" the charities of a community might be flattering to the leaders of the charity organization society, but the duties not only added a heterogenity of tasks, they also imposed a serious handicap on the original objective of the society, planning for individual families. For, being a social agency, with a specific charitable function, the society could not without bad grace set itself up also as a commentator and critic of its peers. Other agencies did not relish being criticized by an authority in whose selection they had no choice, and in the framing of whose judgments they had no share. It was an arbitrary assumption of superiority —to some extent pushed upon it—on the part of the charity organization society that fatally handicapped its substantial success.

Credit for finding a solution should probably be given to Francis H. McLean, associate director of the charity organization department of the Russell Sage Foundation, for his suggestion that the two functions be separated: the charity organization should concentrate on its services to families; and to set standards, there should be a new organization, to be called a "central council of social agencies," composed of representatives of social agencies that wished to unite in a common project of establishing and improving standards, thereby taking the ungracious and impractical responsibility of setting standards away from a single agency, and placing it upon the entire group. This was, obviously, the only pragmatic method of doing the job, but its suggestion was evidence of the democratic faith of McLean in the integrity of the individual agencies.

The structure of the Charity Organization Society of New York, chartered by the New York Assembly in 1882, provided for an over-all governing body called a "council," composed of representatives of the leading charitable agencies of that city. Within such a pattern it was expected that the agencies would work together and mutually agree on procedures for improvement. However, the device produced but little effect upon the relationships among the city's agencies. McLean's project differed from that of the Charity Organization Society of New York in two important respects: it would create a new agency whose only function was that of improving standards of work; and its membership would be open to any agency that could qualify.

In 1908, in connection with the establishment of the Associated Charities of Pittsburgh, this new form of agency was adopted, thus separating the original functions of the charity organization society into two parts. Thus the agency was set free to perfect its services, but in its initial stages the new procedure placed upon all member agencies the so-called "organizing" function, through a mutually controlled council. Pittsburgh was probably not the place where the first council of social agencies was planned. Rochester, New York, seems to have had one somewhat earlier than Pittsburgh, and Elmira seems to have developed even earlier a plan whereby social agencies effected a coöperative device to promote coördination of effort. Pittsburgh's example, however, served to set the standard for council organization and function, but neither the beginnings in Pittsburgh nor in these other two cities finds any mention in the *Proceedings* of the Conference.

The program of a council of social agencies, like the services of a secretary of a state board of charities, is limited only by the imagination and leadership of its management. McLean cited (1921) thirteen different functions of councils actually in operation, such as passing on new projects, reorganization of old agencies, abandonment or combination of existing agencies, improvement in relationship between agencies, advice to agencies on publicity, and advancement of standards. Since progress, if it is to be made in these projects, depends upon arriving at a common agreement, it required much time spent in conferences and a willingness of board and of leading staff members to give time and effort in that way rather than in the direct promotion of the work of the individual agency, and so the movement made slow headway.

Council financing has always been bothersome. A council should be staffed by persons whose judgment is respected; and that means high salaries. Most communities were unable properly to finance their operating agencies, and money to finance an efficient council, which by definition performed no direct services, was all but impossible to obtain.

As matters stood, McLean suggested that the Associated Charities of Pittsburgh lend its general secretary to act as executive of the Council of Social Agencies. The Chamber of Commerce of St. Louis and the Civic and Commerce Association in Minneapolis furnished executive service for their councils. In the larger cities, such as New York, it was possible to secure ample funds for research from foundations, a very important aspect of any council's activity as it settled down to its work. Even in New York, however, the late William Hodson, when he was director of the Welfare Council, declared that getting more money for the operating budget was an all but impossible task.

In the first years after their organization, therefore, the growth of councils was slow and uncertain. It is a fair query whether the movement would have lived in any but the largest cities if it had not been for the advent of federated financing which created the necessity for such a coöperative method of determining standards on which to distribute the federated fund. The promoters of joint financing believed that their duty to contributors to insure a just allocation among the different agencies of the funds so raised was of equal importance to money raising itself. Therefore, the budget committee found itself in need of the best available advice, if distribution was not to deteriorate into mere logrolling; and while there was not unanimity at first on the use of this representative body from the social agencies for determining how to handle the problem of distribution, the council has proven itself the best source of information to the budget committee and, in many places, the best means of appointing the committee.

Under this close association between the community chest, the organization responsible for raising the community's funds for social work, and the council of social agencies representing such work, the question of financing the council has been as satisfactorily solved as possible, within the framework of the times. In its need for valid advice, the chest must depend upon a body representing the specialists in the field. More adequate financing by the chest has given the council a certain freedom to develop its own work, to improve the standards and efficiency of its own members. Thus the chest, in turn, makes its appeals for funds with greater assurance that the work of the agencies is well and truly done, an assurance not possible on any other basis of judgment. Councils have not been limited, however, to the interests of agencies participating in chest financing; they have come to include the planning of the social resource activities of the entire community (William Hodson, *Proceedings,* 1929; A. Wayne McMillen, *Proceedings,* 1932), including public and private, sectarian and nonsectarian agencies. Development of any one agency when undertaken by the council of social agencies is coming to be evaluated in the light of the needs of the entire community and its resources rather than primarily with respect to the agency's own fate (Lyman Ford, *Proceedings,* 1944).

So far, councils have been largely dominated by private social agencies, but there is some thought that public rather than the private agencies should take the lead in community plan-

ning (A. Wayne McMillen, *Proceedings*, 1932). This is
roughly parallel to the principle of the English Local Government Act of 1929, which provides for public assistance committees in each county, with broad supervisory powers over
local authorities in the field of health, assistance, and education. In this country it is quite clear that the very important
section of the social services performed under public auspices
is but weakly represented in the social planning of our councils
of social agencies. It may be that the brilliant but ill-fated Board
of Public Welfare of Kansas City (organized in 1910), which
attempted much the same sort of task as the English public
assistance for counties, will set the pattern for a later development when public agencies will take the lead (Leroy A. Halbert, *Proceedings*, 1913).

In the brief time that councils have been in existence, entirely new values have come into social work. Some of these—
especially in budgeting, accounting, and methods of raising
money—have come about through the influence of the chest.
But the ideal of charity organization is in process of accomplishment to bring the operations and development of the social services into close relationship with each other; and to
make it possible for the most efficient and humane methods to
permeate all operating agencies—an impossible objective for a
single society to reach.

Still, it would be flying in the face of facts to say that the
council has won everyone to its cause. Its method of arriving at
judgments through conferences shared by the forces concerned
is too slow and sometimes too timid to suit those impatient for
decisive results; nor have all agencies appreciated the strength
of coöperative effort. Some agencies, strong ones, are quite content with their own standards and skill in leadership. Some
weak societies fear the loss of their identity in the process of
sharing with others the determination of their plans. Neverthe-

less, none, the independently strong agency or the defensively weak one, can ignore the council. It represents, through its official structure, the agencies of a community; and the impact of its judgments is ceaselessly exerted over an area that is approximating the socially conscious life of the community. In its hands lies most of the future of social work under private auspices, and it will be a significant influence on social work in the public services.

PROBABLY the most characteristic development of social work in this country is the plan of joint financing of social agencies, known as the "community chest." Denver had the credit for having started such a movement in this country when, in 1888, fifteen or sixteen relief-giving societies united their appeals for funds and named the joint project the Charity Organization Society (Mrs. A. Jacobs, *Proceedings,* 1892; Izetta George, *Proceedings,* 1894). Before Denver had launched its plan, however, Liverpool had made an experiment in joint collection of contributions, but it bore only a faint resemblance to the later American community chest. In 1869 a clergyman in Liverpool, noting that a relatively small group of contributors was giving the larger part of the money necessary to finance the private agencies, persuaded each giver to combine all his gifts in one check and deposit it in one of the local banks, which would then distribute the total in accordance with the wishes of each donor. This plan was no more than a time-saving method of collection and distribution useful to the givers. It was never adopted at any time by the charity organization movement in England and was not a part of the program of that movement when it came to this country.

The Denver experiment never assumed responsibility for raising all the money needed by its constituent members, and, consequently, it could not promise its donors immunity from further solicitation in behalf of its member agencies. A halfway measure, it tended to suffer from the defects of joint solicitation without capitalizing its benefits. As the years passed by, the member agencies found it possible to obtain from sources other than the joint fund an ever increasing portion of the money they needed. Thus by 1905 the amount independently raised by member agencies in Denver exceeded the amount granted by the joint fund, and the fund president seriously questioned whether the plan had not lost its original usefulness.

By 1900 the Chamber of Commerce of Cleveland had organized a Committee on Benevolent Institutions which did for Cleveland what the "organizing" function of the charity organization movement set out to do, for it acted as an endorsing body on social organizations. In the process of endorsement, the committee attempted to evaluate the work of agencies in the light of their competency in their chosen field; their co-operation with other agencies; the activity of boards of administration; methods of collecting and accounting for money; and the availability of financial records to inspection by the committee. According to the report of its secretary, endorsement by the committee at the beginning of its activities was of little value to the agencies endorsed, but "after years of education . . . the community has come . . . to rely almost universally upon the Committee's [judgment]" (Howard Strong, *Proceedings*, 1910). From this supervision of the way in which agencies collected and accounted for their money, it was only a step before the agencies themselves questioned the adequacy of the current method of raising money. The committee responded to this overture by proposing a plan for joint financing of all agencies through an appeal sponsored by a board of thirty created for the purpose, ten to be chosen by the agencies themselves, ten by the givers, and ten by the Chamber of Commerce. Although proposed early in 1910, it was March, 1913, before the Cleveland Federation was launched. It was reported (Edward M. Williams, *Proceedings*, 1913) that old subscribers to agency funds had increased their gifts by 57 percent, and more than ten thousand new subscribers had been secured.

The Cleveland experiment was early followed by other cities, of which Cincinnati probably offered the most interesting variant. In Cleveland the movement was wholly lay; none of the professional social workers was on the board of the Federation. In Cincinnati the initiation for joint financing came from the professional workers and was promoted by the Council of Social Agencies. However, the plan was started tentatively and was joined only by agencies wishing to participate.[1] Cincinnati also established budgetary control, a precaution which Cleveland had failed to adopt. In many ways, these two early projects were similar: the preparation of a total budget covering the anticipated needs of member agencies; the pledge on the part of member agencies that they would not solicit money from anybody who contributed to the federated fund; and the use of an unprecedented number of volunteers to solicit money from citizens in behalf of the agencies in the federation.

The first World War profoundly influenced the chest movement. Newton D. Baker, President Woodrow Wilson's Secretary of War, had been mayor of Cleveland at the time of the launching of the Cleveland Federation. When the United States entered the war, a number of national agencies, such as the Young Men's Christian Association and the Young Women's Christian Association, the Knights of Columbus, the American Library Association, the Salvation Army, and some of the national organizations for foreign relief made independent appeals for war relief or service. At the local level it caused much confusion to receive so many national appeals regarding whose validity and relative merits most communities were ignorant. In 1918, the second year of our participation

[1] William J. Norton, *The Coöperative Movement in Social Work* (New York: Macmillan, 1927).

in the war, Secretary Baker induced seven national agencies to join a United War Activities Fund, to establish a joint national budget, and to assign local quotas to be raised locally by war chests. Although the period set for raising the money was the week of Thanksgiving, and the Armistice was signed on November 11, the war chests throughout the country were a tremendous success, both in amounts raised and in numbers of contributors. It is supposed that more than three hundred communities organized war chests, in contrast with the less than twenty cities which had adopted federated giving by 1916. Some of the new war chests absorbed the budgets of the peace-time agencies; most of them did not. But the experience of donors in combining all of one individual's contributions in one pledge exerted a powerful influence on the chest movement; and although most of the war chests went out of existence with the end of the war, the development of the chests kept on at an accelerated pace, until at the present the principle of the chest has been more widely adopted than almost any movement in social work.

Solicitation and distribution of welfare activity funds during the second World War repeated the experience of the first World War with an advantage: by 1941 federated solicitation had been adopted in most American cities, and the war chests consequently had a wider basis of experience and a more popular acceptance on which to capitalize. War, or any calamity, evokes a response for the relief of its victims out of all proportion to any other appeal, and the great outbursts of generous gifts, through the war chests and through the American National Red Cross, can be explained for the most part by the dramatic appeal of the incalculable suffering of war. It is, however, pertinent—and not depreciative—to point out another reason for this great outburst of giving to the war chests, especially by the wealthy. The Hollis Amendment to the Income

Tax Law was passed about this time, permitting the deduction for taxing purposes of 15 percent of one's otherwise taxable income; and with surtaxes rising to 60 percent of income in the highest brackets in the first World War, and to 90 percent in the second World War, gifts might represent very little actual money to the giver.

Some of the representatives of the older and stronger social services did not look with favor upon the chest movement, which caused both its advocates and critics to define their reasons. It was said (William J. Norton, *Proceedings*, 1917) by its supporters that the ways of agencies were chaotic and unbusinesslike; that the cost of collection of their money was wasteful; and that the agencies were losing out in the race between expanding needs and the income possible under the appeal of the individual agency (Edward M. Williams, *Proceedings*, 1913). It was also claimed that larger total sums could be secured by the method of joint solicitation; that more contributors could be secured and a valid basis could be established for distributing the total gifts with the interests of the whole community in mind.

The opposition, much of which did not get into the *Proceedings*, centered around three fears. Foremost was the fear of loss of the agency's autonomy. W. Frank Persons, of the New York Charity Organization Society, said (1910) that the chest plan was equivalent to putting the individual agencies in the hands of a receiver, i.e., the authority of the chest being responsible for the allocation of its funds. The second point made was that the plan would place the fate of social work in the hands of financial interests, whose major concerns would be to keep down costs and suppress troublesome movements. And the third objection was that it would promote mediocrity (Fred R. Johnson, *Proceedings*, 1917) by a process of leveling down to the average standard.

In the perspective of three decades of experience, it is clear that the chest movement came in because those on whom rested the responsibility for raising substantial sums for individual agencies became confused by the increasing number of agencies which laid claim to their efforts; and they finally declared that they would continue to spend their energies only on condition that all requests be united into one. Another factor leading to the same end was the rapid and bewildering increase in the number of agencies, which left the potential giver confused and frustrated. In other words, the task of raising money to finance private social work had outgrown its early methods, in all but the largest cities, and the chest offered the only available solution. Many social workers of those days (the second and third decades of this century) did not welcome the chest; but they accepted it as the way out of a difficult situation.

The chest has tapped new sources of contributions, especially in the phenomenally successful industrial field. In the picture it presents to the potential contributor its inclusion of the community's need makes a valid claim at once upon the national corporation and upon the individual workingman. This the individual social agency never could have done. The ratio of givers to the increase of the total amounts secured raises the question whether the chest has been as successful in obtaining —or even in retaining—the gifts of the larger contributors as it has in interesting the smaller ones.

In the comparison of time—and money—costs of fund raising before and after the chest was established as the money-raising organization for social work, proponents of the chest system have arrived at results that are not quite valid. Even assuming that some agencies spent a large share of their income in getting it, and that the chest reduced that expense materially, a high cost of securing gifts was not universal. Some agencies, the ones that had learned their task the best, spent less than one percent of their income in this manner, by building up a list of continuing contributors—a device that was not patented!

The fear that social work would be dominated by financial interests is, after all, not absent from the independent agency. A few chest agencies have suffered from such influences. No one knows how many independently supported agencies have also suffered; but it is a fair inference that the coercion that can be exercised through a complex agency such as the chest is less than can be exerted by the board of an independent agency.

The great contribution of the chest movement has been through its function of distribution. By establishing budgetary control, it required each agency to budget its expenses, a practice that almost none of them had adopted before the coming of the chest. This meant the keeping of a system of accounts on which the chest was able to base its assurance to givers that all money was honestly spent and accounted for. Distribution went ever farther than that: "Money raising involves budgeting. Budgeting involves decisions as to program, which soon reveal themselves as being without any sound basis unless some method is devised for looking at the individual agency . . . in relation to the whole community position" (Lyman S. Ford, *Proceedings,* 1944). This probably is placing the agency in receivership, as W. Frank Persons suggested, but does not all co-operative effort involve some surrender of sovereignty?

There is still dispute as to whether the council, on which the budget committee depends for guidance, should be a member of the chest, or independent of it. In the early days there was wide variation of structure. Cincinnati organized the joint financing scheme, at first as a function of the council, but later it created the chest, which absorbed the council. In Cleveland there was no council on the occasion of the formation of the Cleveland Federation; and the Committee on Benevolent Institutions of the Chamber of Commerce performed that function for the Cleveland agencies. The consensus among council people and, to a less extent, among chest personnel is that the council should be independent of the chest if it is really to consider matters of moment to all the social work of a city, and not to confine its interests principally to the welfare of the private agencies in the chest. Various devices whereby the chest may receive the advantage of the knowledge of social work have been developed, but any simple means providing for a comity of services between the two has been found to work satisfactorily, even to the point of the chest's accepting from the council the nominations of a certain percentage of the members of its budget committee.

*A*MOS W. BUTLER (1860–1937) was ornithologist
for the state of Indiana when in 1897 he became secretary of
the State Board of Charities. In this capacity he served the state
for twenty-six years. He was president of the National Conference in 1908, vice-president of the International Prison Congress during its meetings of 1925 and 1930, and founder of the
International Committee on Mental Hygiene in 1930. Butler
was the last outstanding personality to guide the destiny of a
state administrative body whose authority was limited to supervision. During his long administration, the authority of state
boards gradually changed from the primarily supervisory to
the primarily administrative, with the supervisory function receiving decreasing emphasis and, in so far as it affected private
agencies, meeting increasing resistance.

The achievement for which Butler will be primarily remembered was his success in changing the politically dominated
handling of outdoor relief by the thousands of township trustees to a well-organized and carefully supervised distribution
of assistance to the needy comparable with the method used
by the private urban charity organizations. He demonstrated
what men like Wines, Sanborn, and many others had claimed:
it is not inherently impossible to conduct public outdoor relief
in a satisfactory manner, given the necessary personnel and
the guiding philosophy that are required.

In 1903, in a brief discussion following papers on public and private assistance, Butler gave the first report of the method used in Indiana to reform local administration of poor relief. He credited the State Board of Commerce with initiating the steps that brought about the reformation which resulted in "Indiana . . . [applying] the principles of charity organization to the whole state." In 1915 he gave a more complete account of the situation preceding the reform, and of measures taken to bring it about. Previous to 1895 local township trustees granted relief upon their own authority and received reimbursement from the county commissioners. The latter had no authority to control these expenditures. In 1895 a law was passed by which township trustees or overseers of the poor were required to keep "full records of applicants' aid, of the relief spent for applicants and to send copies of such records to the office of the State Board." These reports showed that for 1895, the trustees had spent $630,000, distributed to about thirty thousand persons. The board published these figures, and the next legislature (1897) charged the cost of relief to the town supplying the money, and so eliminated the irresponsible manner of giving relief whereby one authority granted it, and received reimbursement on sight from another authority. In 1899 the legislature required full investigation of each case, and coöperation with existing agencies was made mandatory, as was also the requirement of developing any natural resources possessed by the client.

These laws were codified in 1901, and the plan put Indiana in the lead in the administration of public outdoor relief. The actual results in money were striking: from $630,000 spent in 1895, the expenses of public assistance dropped to $355,000 in 1896, and to $210,000 in 1900, with an average annual cost from 1896 to 1914 of about $284,000. The average number of persons who were receiving relief was 32,627.

By modern standards of public assistance, an examination of

these figures shows that neither the number receiving relief (a little over one percent of a population of 2,250,000), nor the amount received per capita per year ($30 in 1895 and $10 in 1914) was excessive; in fact, the number on relief was small, and the amount granted was niggardly. The significant features of the demonstration were that the philosophy of charity organization could be as well applied to public outdoor relief throughout a state as in an urban center and that this statewide reform could be effected without any basic change in the character of the board's authority. Administration of public outdoor relief remained a local responsibility.

When search is made for the source of knowledge that made possible this extraordinary reform, one is left with conjecture only. Oscar C. McCulloch had been dead six years when Butler was appointed secretary of the state board. It may be that his influence still lived in the theory of charity, since the reform was secured largely by a process of administrative vigor. On Butler's board were two men who were prominent in the Conference. One was Timothy Nicholson, a Quaker with strong philanthropic interests, who was president of the National Conference in 1901; a publisher of books by occupation, he was called the "Nestor of American publishers" when he died in 1924. The other was Demarcus C. Brown, a classical scholar, state librarian, and a translator of Lucian. And the reform was carried through, patiently but with striking ability, by a zoölogist who was a specialist in birds! The net gathering in the early leaders for the social services was widely cast.

The Board of Public Welfare of Kansas City was organized in 1910 with Leroy A. Halbert as its executive secretary and with a membership of liberal and forward-looking citizens who conceived the idea of such a board and secured passage of the enabling act by the City Council. William Volker (1859–1947), the ruling spirit on the board, was born in Germany, came to this country at the age of twelve, and began an unusually successful business career in Kansas City, eleven years later. He unquestionably contributed the liberal philosophy combined with an unyielding belief in the government's capacity to serve which characterized the political faith of so many Germans who had come to America because the Germany of Bismarck had become intolerable. The guiding theory back of the board's organization was that dependency and delinquency are caused by economic conditions and not by the moral weakness of the poor and criminal (Leroy A. Halbert, *Proceedings*, 1913); and that therefore government should concern itself with those factors which produce such evils: housing, hours and conditions of labor, and the environment in which youth receives its recreation. In its original charter, the board was "given broad powers to devise and execute plans to fulfill the duties of the city toward all the poor, the delinquent, the unemployed, the deserted and unfortunate classes, and to supervise the private agencies which solicited money from the public . . ." (Halbert, *Proceedings*, 1918). In putting these powers into operation, the board concerned itself with the usual methods of care or amelioration of the lot of those who could not help themselves, establishing a legal aid bureau, an employment bureau, and a loan agency. While it did not enter the field of outdoor relief or of child welfare, it did attempt to weave into the municipal pattern the activities of the private agencies concerned with such services.

Halbert, like most successful leaders, was a pragmatist, and although he believed that the function of outdoor relief was one which the community as a whole, through its elected officers, should handle, he was content, temporarily, to let it rest with the well-organized and strongly entrenched private agencies. Moreover, he believed that since "the causes of dependency are social . . . relief . . . should not . . . reflect on the character of its beneficiaries."

Halbert gathered about him a group of able young men to head the various activities of the board, some of whom, such as Charles C. Stillman, afterward head of the School of Social Service Administration at Ohio State University, became leading figures in the developing field of social work. The powers of the board were not restricted by later legislation; indeed, they were even increased (Halbert, *Proceedings*, 1918). However, opposition to the vigor of law enforcement in factory and tenement house inspection, and probably to other activities of the board, such as supervision of commercial recreation, created enemies which even the influence of the prominent members of the board could not neutralize with the City Council. The latter progressively cut the board's appropriation so that by 1919 Halbert had left Kansas City, and the brilliant promise that the board held under Halbert became only a memory. In spite of this apparent failure, coining the name "board of public welfare" and recognizing the philosophy of governmental social services behind such a body marked a new era in the theory and practice of government as an instrument designed "to promote the general welfare." The Elizabethan Poor Law was doomed, and a broader, more generous concept of the state's responsibility for its citizens was supplanting it.

Gertrude Vaile, who demonstrated that municipal government could maintain an efficient and humane administration of charity, was a member of a prominent family of lawyers, one of her brothers becoming a Representative of Colorado in Congress. Encouraged by her family's interest in public affairs, Gertrude Vaile attended the Chicago School of Civics and Philanthropy in 1909, joined the staff of the Chicago United Charities in 1910, and spent two years in the stimulating West

Side district of that agency. The strong influence of Wines's faith in public welfare was still evident, not only in the Chicago Graduate School of Social Service Administration, but also in the West Side district. Consequently, when Mayor Robert W. Speer, the reform mayor of Denver, asked her to serve on the Board of Charities and Correction, Gertrude Vaile gave up her professional work to assist in guiding the policies of the social services of her native city. Within a year, she was appointed the executive of the board, charged with responsibility for administering its functions. The policies of the board were under the constant fire of politicians, who succeeded in defeating Mayor Speer; but his successor found the board so firmly entrenched that he thought it wiser to permit it—and Miss Vaile —to handle the affairs of public assistance and correction as it saw fit, and not as dictated by the politicians who had elected him. Again, at the next election, her position was in jeopardy, and again she and her board weathered the storm. When in 1917 she left to assume the position of director of civilian relief of the Mountain Division of the American Red Cross, the nonpolitical, honest, and humane administration of the public social services had won the approval of public opinion in Denver, and Gertrude Vaile's successors have continued the policy she inaugurated.

Gertrude Vaile's philosophy was, like Halbert's, that poverty is largely a matter of the economic setting, for which society, not the individual, is responsible (1915). Consequently, the state, as the organized representative of society, should assume responsibility for its treatment. The Denver experiment never went the length of attacking many of the factors in society that so unfavorably affect the lives of persons with low incomes. What Gertrude Vaile did was to demonstrate in the state of Colorado that the methods found successful by charity organization in the private society could be applied to the public municipal agency, as Butler demonstrated in Indiana. She gathered about the project a board of influential men and women who first learned how honest administration could be organized, and then defended it against the attacks of the spoilsmen.

When the enemies of the board in Denver made an effort to compel Miss Vaile to make public the confidential material accumulated in the clients' records, which would have driven every self-respecting client away, Miss Vaile secured legal advice that the law required publicity only for certain routine data, which she meticulously supplied. As for the confidential records of the clients, not only did the law not compel her to disclose their contents, but she found that she would be rendering herself liable if she did so.

She was able to gather volunteers to serve the Denver public agency quite as successfully as she had seen it done in Chicago. She was also able to establish case conferences, at which the volunteers and representatives of other social agencies met to discuss the problems presented by clients of the public agency and the possible marshaling of available medical, educational, and vocational resources for their care.

The significance of the work in Denver lay in the fact that it was a successful demonstration at the beginning of a trend in a situation which had known only the run-of-the-mill sort of political administration. Moreover, it was dramatic and compelling enough to rivet attention on the change. So, with the new day ushered in by the heavy public commitments of the first World War, followed by the great depression and its insistent demands on wise public welfare administration, Denver established a bench mark that did not need to be fixed anew in the hurry and confusion of a crisis.

*T*HE WIDESPREAD and diverse interest in children had led to the establishment of many organizations equipped to provide for their care or protection. These took the form of institutions for delinquents, defectives, handicapped, and, too often, dependent children; and every important urban center had agencies for furnishing services to these same classes of children. When the juvenile court entered the scene, some of its legal personnel were astonished at the chaotic aggregation of child welfare agencies. "Some are now antiquated, some are meaningless, many, excellent in themselves, are to the general mass, unrelated and conflicting." In these words, Judge George S. Addams, of the Juvenile Court of Cleveland, described the situation that he found in 1910. Succinctly, he characterized the uncertainty facing the bench in its use of these "unrelated and conflicting" child welfare resources. To meet the challenge, he suggested that all child welfare workers in a state get together to codify the laws in their field. "If there is a code of evidence and of commercial paper and of Insurance Laws, why not a Children's Code?"—these were the words of a lawyer, accustomed to see order and dependability in the materials with which he dealt, who, as a juvenile judge, saw only disorder and nondependability in the material with which as a juvenile judge he was concerned. Judge Addams went on to say:

A Judge can commit [a child] to a State institution . . . but . . . cannot compel the institution to receive it. If suffering from two defects . . . the probabilities are no institution will receive it.

. . . Children can quit school at fourteen if they can read, but
. . . cannot work until sixteen. . . . All our public institutions are
footballs of politics, and a woman cannot superintend even an industrial school for girls.

Rarely had a suggestion received such a prompt and enthusiastic response. The next Ohio legislature authorized the
governor to appoint a commission to frame a children's code.
By the middle of the summer of 1912 it had completed its report, and the legislature of 1913, after making several amendments, adopted the first children's code in the United States.
Without in any manner detracting from the credit due Judge
Addams for the creative imagination which suggested the way
out of the morass of child welfare legislation, it should be mentioned that the hard, detailed work was probably performed
by the secretary of the State Board of Charities, H. H. Shirer.
His was undoubtedly the task, first, of persuading the legislature to authorize the governor of Ohio to appoint the commission, and then of safely guiding the report of the commission through the legislature. By 1930, twenty-nine states and
the District of Columbia had appointed similar bodies to codify
their laws relating to children.

Roger Baldwin, at that time secretary of the Civic League of
St. Louis, but previously secretary of the Board of Children's
Guardians of the same city, outlined in 1914 the scope of legis-
lation that should be embraced by a children's code, which he
said should be broader than the Ohio code, or the Children's
Charter of England. Specifically, it should include:

Eugenics: marriage laws; and the care of the defective
Infant welfare: birth registration and compulsory reporting of
  abnormal births
Provisions for neglected and delinquent children
Protection of the unmarried mother and her child
Supervision by court of adoption and placement of children

A juvenile court in each county, with jurisdiction over adults in children's cases; dependent children

Mothers' pensions and placement on a county basis, with provision for a state agency to assume responsibility for children whom the county fails to protect

State supervision over all public and private institutions for care of children

Probation work of the juvenile court and the placing of children by public or private agencies

Education: compulsory school attendance law and an attendance officer in each school district

Special schools for defective children

A statewide school system, with state aid and state supervision

This catalogue of legislation—compiled by only one social worker, to be sure—brings out vividly, nevertheless, the wide range of legislation for the protection of children, the many state and local agencies concerned with child welfare administration, and, by implication, unless all the laws were drawn and administered as part of an inclusive child welfare program, how chaotic and bewildering either the laws or their execution might become.

The Committee on Children at the 1915 Conference, under the chairmanship of C. C. Carstens, general agent of the Massachusetts Society for the Prevention of Cruelty to Children, analyzed in a series of three papers the need for comprehensive planning for children's services. The chairman laid the groundwork by outlining a possible pattern of public and private organization in the child welfare field. The salient feature was a board of children's guardians, under the state board of charities, with supervisory powers over all local public and private child welfare administrations. It was to be concerned specifically with mothers' aid; to assume custody of dependent children and properly place them; to assume guardianship, *ipso facto*, of all illegitimately born children; to license maternity

homes; and to maintain a reception home for children awaiting placement, or for children not suitable for adoption. He
suggested that the local administrative body should be the
county board of public welfare, patterned after the Kansas City
board, performing the functions relative to public health, public assistance, child protection, probation, and recreation. (He
included also in this list education, but it is possible that he
meant educational supervision of classes for retarded pupils,
and such social services of public education as attendance records and medical inspection.)

Mr. Carstens's second major suggestion was the organization
in each county of a court of domestic relations, which should
include in its functions the juvenile court and be properly
staffed with competent probation officers. Such a court would
have jurisdiction over cases of cruelty or neglect of children,
arraignment of adults contributing to the delinquency of children, cases of nonsupport, desertion, or separation, custody of
children in divorce, cases of heinous crimes against children,
and of complaints by either spouse against the other. To such a
court he would attach the juvenile court, so that there would be
but one legal authority to deal with any case in which a child
is involved. Having gained his experience in a private society,
Mr. Carstens expressed his conviction that the major portion
of the services to children should be assumed by public authorities, leaving to the private agencies areas of experimental work
to be turned over to the public authority as soon as methods are
established and public opinion is favorable.

In another paper, Dr. Edward N. Clopper, of the National
Child Labor Committee, suggested (following the wording of
the report of the White House Conference on Children) that
there should be a children's charter, nationally conceived, covering services in behalf of children under the headings of "preserving life and health," "protection from want, abuse and

crime," and "education and recreation." He did not recommend that the charter contain rules or proposed statutes, but only principles to be observed in drafting laws in the individual state. He was not clear as to what groups should undertake the actual administration, since there were already in existence school and health authorities exercising child welfare functions which varied widely in their scope between states. Nor did he say who should draw up the children's charter, or be responsible for its promotion.

At this point, Julia C. Lathrop, chief of the United States Children's Bureau, described the efforts of the Children's Bureau to secure uniform legislation in specific fields, such as, for instance, registration of births. Her practical suggestion was that a movement be inaugurated for the creation of children's code commissions "to review existing legislation in each state and to make recommendations." She then suggested that representatives from such commissions should meet with members of the National Child Labor Committee, of the American Bar Association, of "this Conference," and of other national bodies, to discover "the common needs, and . . . the various legislative expedients by which they can be met."

Finally, in closing this first phase of the growth of the movement for a children's code in 1920, Hastings H. Hart, now director of the child helping division of the Russell Sage Foundation, listed the national agencies prepared to offer advisory service to state code commissions: the Division on Children of the National Conference, the Russell Sage Foundation, and the Federal Children's Bureau. If he had made the list a year later, he would have added the Child Welfare League of America, which was organized late in 1920 with C. C. Carstens as executive. It proved to be a major factor in bringing order and standards into the child welfare field.

Outside of Mary Richmond's Conference paper in 1897 suggesting a school for training social workers, no other paper was followed so quickly and so wholeheartedly as Judge Addams's idea of a children's code, by the whole field of social work. His contribution was the more remarkable, since he was primarily a lawyer; through his suggestion, taken from his own field, was found the formula that is gradually bringing some order into the child welfare field with its many separate but related parts.

The subject of the children's code was left alone after 1920, but not because it ceased to be a matter of vital interest. In fact, the movement is one that will continue indefinitely because of the need for the constant revision and codification of laws relating to children. Several such state commissions are probably in existence and at work in the current year of 1947. But the need was demonstrated, and the method fairly well worked out; and the United States Children's Bureau (now a function of the Federal Security Agency), together with the Child Welfare League of America, is equipped by long experience to furnish to any state code commission the national guidance necessary for wholesome functioning.

24 · CONCERN OF THE CONFER-
ENCE WITH REFORM

IS IT TOO BOLD a paradox to say that, while the revolutions of 1688, 1775 and 1792 liberated man, the revolution of our day in the world's best progress has again enslaved him? [1]

The independence and unplanned, unregimented, freedom of action of its rich and powerful members is not the test of a free society. . . . [It] will be found in the scope of right and privilege preserved to, and possessed by, its weakest elements. . . .[2]

It was inevitable that a body such as the membership of the National Conference, whose paramount object was to search for the causes of human ills, should be concerned with the economic conditions of the age. Paine, the first one to be elected to the presidency from outside the membership of boards of charities, himself a successful businessman, placed responsibility for the economic suffering of society on the unrestrained pursuit of the profit motive, or, as he put it, because business is run on the principle of "charging all the traffic will bear." Eleven years later, Edward T. Devine, whose training was in theoretical economics, was more specific in his analysis. He followed the same theory, however, when he charged that back of each one of the evils is some group which profits by exploitation: "Housing reform would be easier than it is . . . if there were not strong pecuniary interests at stake . . ." Child labor would come to an end in a twelvemonth if there were no money to be

[1] Robert Treat Paine, in his presidential address at the National Conference of Charities and Correction, 1895.
[2] A. Delafield Smith, Assistant General Counsel of the Federal Security Agency, at the National Conference of Social Work, 1946.

made in the exploitation of child labor. He set it down (1906) as the duty of social work "to seek out and to strike effectively at those organized forces of evil, at those particular causes of dependence and intolerable living conditions which are beyond the control of individuals whom they injure and whom they too often destroy."

Paine described himself as a socialist in so far as he defined socialism to mean that "the forces of society shall unite, and delight to remove hard and unjust conditions, and give just opportunities of life to all men." No one else at the Conference identified himself definitely with any of the "proposed roads to freedom," [3] except the advocates of a single tax, who were represented in all their certainty at several sessions during this period. Paine himself scarcely assumed that his definition of socialism was orthodox. Pragmatism, not doctrinaire logic, was the philosophy of the Conference members interested in reform. Evils were to be understood and their sources uncovered and destroyed, if possible. While most of the first workers in the field were inclined to consider causes in terms of morals and personality, in less than a generation, a knowledge of environmental factors came to be generally recognized as essential to an understanding of social problems. Not only that, but there were a sufficient number of Conference members by 1896 to secure a special place for the subject on the program. Since 1910 programs on economic and social problems, together with discussions of means for understanding and treating them, have been a regular part of every Conference.

In 1912 Owen R. Lovejoy, as chairman of the Conference Committee on Standards of Living and Labor, submitted a report covering the position taken by progressive thinkers of the time which was practically identical with the economic and

[3] Bertrand Russell, *The Proposed Roads to Freedom* (New York: Holt, 1919).

labor planks of the Bull Moose platform of the Progressive party on which Theodore Roosevelt was defeated in the fall of that year. Just what influence the report had in the shaping of the Bull Moose platform is not clear. Lovejoy at no time made claims to that effect. William Allen White, who treats the Bull Moose campaign very sympathetically and fully in his autobiography, makes no mention of any of its planks having been proposed by the Conference. But it is inconceivable that coincidence alone could have produced two such similar documents.

Paul U. Kellogg said on August 24, 1912, "the men and women . . . who drew up at Cleveland . . . a series of labor planks which they could stand for collectively, little thought that in less than two months their platform would be adopted bodily as the practical economic gospel of a new political party," [4] but he did not explain how the transfer was made. Specifically, the report "demanded" that a living wage for the workingman be secured by the establishment of minimum wage commissions in every state. It demanded that the working day be limited to eight hours and the working week to six days; that the safety and health of workingmen be safeguarded, and, furthermore, that compensation be provided for industrial accidents and disease; that the right to a decent home be not denied to the workingman; that sweatshops, as well as industries employing the labor of children, be abolished; and that the cost of old age assistance and unemployment relief be borne by compulsory insurance. According to Kellogg, this platform was not a flash in the pan, but had been labored over for three years. Nor was the Conference committee a rump committee. There were, of course, followers of the single tax on it (Dr. Alice Hamilton and Benjamin C. Marsh) who sub-

[4] Paul U. Kellogg, "The Industrial Platform of the New Party," *Survey*, XXVIII (August 24, 1912), 668.

mitted an addendum advocating a tax levied on the value of land irrespective of improvements; but persons as diverse as Mrs. Raymond Robbins, John B. Andrews, Edward T. Devine, Lee K. Frankel, Pauline Goldmark, Mrs. Florence Kelley, V. Everit Macy, Walter Rauschenbush, and Msgr. John A. Ryan, among others, insured its representative character as speaking for the liberal social work of America.

During the next ten years, no such summary of economic objectives was discussed at the Conference. In 1914 Devine amplified his thesis that business is not competitive but exploitative. The next year, Professor Harry R. Seager, of Columbia University, summarized the advanced thinking on the treatment of employment. He explained regularization of industry, the dovetailing of industry, and smoothing the curves of consumer demand. He also discussed the use of public works and social insurance. The following year (1916), Isaac M. Rubinow appealed to social workers for a more intelligent and cordial backing of health insurance; and finally, in 1922, Lovejoy, as chairman of the Committee on Industrial and Economic Problems, sadly reviewed what had happened in the decade which had intervened since the comprehensive platform of 1912, and balanced gains and failures, with the weight falling on the negative side. He recognized that the first World War had badly upset the expectations based on the continuation of peace; and regretfully he saw an opportunity in the war and its aftermath for the resurgence of "our political leaders and lords of the market place."

There was, however, another side to the picture. Theodore Roosevelt was defeated; but Woodrow Wilson's election did not mean reaction. Though Democrat in name, Wilson's philosophy approximated that of Roosevelt, the Republican Bull Moose. The revision of the system of Federal taxation, by bringing about the graduated net income tax, furnished a basis for a wide and effective control of "the lords of the market place," or, to use Theodore Roosevelt's phrase, the holders of "predatory wealth," more flexible and effective than any of the proposals in Lovejoy's program. It assumes that America's great capacity to produce what consumers need may be directed to the common good.

Specifically, workmen's compensation for industrial accidents was in the full tide of adoption by the different states when the Conference address was given by Lovejoy in 1912. Nine states had adopted workmen's compensation laws the previous year, and by 1920, forty-one states had enacted such a law, although in general the laws afforded imperfect coverage.[5] Probably this sweeping reform was due less to such pronouncements as the Progressive party's platform of 1912 or the agitation of reformers than to the shocking revelations of neglect or injustice suffered by the injured in the mills of Pittsburgh disclosed by the Pittsburgh Survey of 1910.[6]

The recognition by workmen's compensation laws of industrial disease, which Lovejoy would have classed in the category of "accidents," has been long delayed, and stormy arguments have taken place in discussions of its coverage. In fact, it is today only partially recognized as compensable, and this in spite of the brilliant advocacy for its inclusion by Dr. Alice Hamilton, an international authority on the matter. The insurance provisions for old age and unemployment had to wait for the shock of the great depression of the 1930s and the Social Security Act of 1935 to become a reality.

The other items on Lovejoy's platform, such as the eight-hour day and the six-day week, have on the whole been taken up largely by labor unions. The United States Steel Corporation's final surrender in 1924 to an eight-hour day after a twelve-

[5] See Chapter 27.
[6] Crystal Eastman, *Work Accidents and the Law* (New York: Russell Sage Foundation, 1910).

year battle was not due to organized labor, however. Up to that time the corporation had successfully resisted all efforts to organize its workers, but it submitted to the forces of public opinion and, possibly, to a conviction that it was good business to adopt the day-and-hour limitation.

Again, minimum wages did not secure legislative sanction until considerably after the period under review. The advance in wages to the point of insuring a decent standard of living was won, if at all, by the efforts of organized labor in its own restricted field. Provision for the safety of workers was achieved principally because it was more economical to the employer to prevent accidents than to pay the higher rates of insurance charged in the absence of safety devices; while the regulation of home work, or elimination of the sweatshop, again was brought about by local health and safety ordinances.

In regard to the remaining demand, which was for the outlawing of child labor, social workers suffered the most serious point-blank legal defeat in the entire history of reform, when the amendment to give the Congress power to regulate child labor failed to receive approval from the requisite number of states. But although social workers were defeated on the national front, and faced many discouraging delays and some defeats on the state front, the protection of children from the hazards of unregulated employment has made substantial progress toward its ultimate goal of securing to every child under sixteen the opportunity of education and recreation (Raymond G. Fuller, *Proceedings*, 1922).

During this period the discussions on housing were based upon the assumption that, given proper conditions, the housing needs of the lowest paid worker could be met, and that public housing subsidies were an unnecessary evil (Harlean James, *Proceedings*, 1921). As early as 1885, Alfred T. White, president of the Brooklyn Bureau of Charities, pointed out the evils of overcrowded tenements, and described philanthropic projects in housing that rectified evils of bad housing and demonstrated "that Reform . . . [may] make possible a return of 5 percent on the investment." Harriet Fullmer, of the Visiting Nurses' Association of Chicago, in 1908, and Jacob Riis, of New York, in 1911 and 1919, argued that poor housing was expensive since it caused many of the ills with which the Conference was dealing. It was pointed out that unskilled workers were forced to live in unsanitary, cast-off dwellings (Bleeker Marquette, *Proceedings,* 1923). The Conference devoted a good deal of space to the discussion of the single tax as an economic measure to enable the workingman to rent or to purchase decent housing (1912, 1915, 1916, 1917).

The movement which stood in the foreground of social work, however, was the establishment of building codes that would avoid, in future construction, the evils disgracing the uncontrolled erection of the multiple dwelling—in other words, tenement house reform. New York State's code, applicable to cities of the first class, adopted in 1901, set the standard of desirable features in such legislation; and it has been widely followed. It limits the percentage of the lot that a building may occupy; provides for an open space in the rear of each building; requires windows in each room; and provides that there shall be a water supply, sewer connection, and separate toilet for each dwelling unit. However desirable—or even essential— may be these minimum standards for the construction of dwellings, they entail at least two consequences that have fatally injured their effectiveness in supplying housing for the lower income group. The demands of the code have increased the cost of new construction to the point where it is estimated that only those in the highest third of the income groups can afford to live in quarters that meet these standards.[7] Even more dis-

[7] Article on housing, *Encyclopedia of the Social Sciences* (New York: Macmillan, 1932), VII, 515.

heartening, the passage of a model tenement housing law at once places a premium upon the substandard houses that are in existence at the time of the passage of the tenement house code, and also postpones still further the disappearance of the ramshackle buildings. If the new dwelling could be rented as cheaply as the old and outlawed type, the unfortunate effect of the tenement house laws would not follow.

In spite of these facts, no speaker at the Conference before 1930 proposed a public subsidy for housing. Nor did the housing activities of the Federal Government during the first World War demonstrate much to the speakers at the Conference but that government-sponsored housing was uneconomic. Rarely was public housing advocated in the Conference papers. Rather it was something to be avoided (Harlean James, *Proceedings*, 1921). Even Lawrence Veiller, whose life was devoted to the reform of the evils of the overcrowded and unsanitary tenement, saw only an aggravation of housing evils in public housing.[8]

In 1912, that year which seemed to promise so much to progressive leaders, Warren D. Foster described a project of the Massachusetts Homestead Commission to purchase land, and to erect thereon houses to be sold or rented to workingmen. (The State Supreme Court, however, declared the plan to be unconstitutional, in an opinion given to the legislature at its request just as the law was about to be passed.) Foster was of the opinion that "this was the first admission by an American State . . . that [it] had the responsibility to provide for its citizens who could not properly house themselves." He further gave it as his opinion that, "perhaps negative regulation and passive encouragement" are all the state can do in the way of rectifying "housing conditions . . . [that] have long been a shame to the State."

[8] Lawrence Veiller, *Housing Reform* (New York: Russell Sage Foundation, 1910), Chapter 7.

The ills of excessive usury, whose charges ran to 360 percent and more a year, bore most heavily on the poorest, and Paine started the movement for making reasonably priced loans available by organizing the Remedial Loan Association of Boston. It made loans on pledges at one percent a month as early as 1886. This plan was followed in 1894 by the organization of the Provident Loan Association of New York. The importance of the field was recognized by the Russell Sage Foundation (established in 1909) in the establishment of its division on remedial loans, one of whose early directors was Leon Henderson. Under the stimulus of the Sage Foundation the growth of remedial loan societies was rapid. The societies formed an association, more or less under the guidance of the Russell Sage Foundation, with the primary object, so far as the Foundation was concerned, of protecting borrowers from the various forms of exploitation immemorially practiced by moneylenders (Arthur H. Ham, *Proceedings*, 1910).

The credit union, a more interesting, as well as possibly a sounder method of handling the business of small loans, was described by Pierre Jay (*Proceedings*, 1910); but of its future in the United States he was not so confident. In 1909 Massachusetts passed the first law in this country authorizing credit unions and placed them under the supervision of the state banking departments. By 1916, Arthur H. Ham, then director of the division of remedial loans of the Russell Sage Foundation, was able to give a necessarily sketchy account of successful advance of similar laws in several states of the Union.

In spite of state regulation of interest that can be charged for small loans, its various provisions for lending money have a very serious handicap. Sufficient to say, they protect the borrowers who can meet the legal conditions or who can borrow from a remedial loan association or a credit union. However, because of lack of collateral, or in the absence of any other satisfactory security, there are people who are forced to run into debt, and they borrow in the "black market" which knows no controls. To assert that such people should not borrow is no answer, and no help at all to the partial protection offered by these devices.

The list of proposals advocated by Conference speakers for improvement in the lives of the lower economic groups is a long one. The need for such betterment was often shown, as, for instance, by Msgr. John Ryan in his statement (1907) that 60 percent of our nation's workingmen have an income inadequate to furnish their families with even a minimum standard of living. Perhaps the most radical suggestion, however, was made by Frank Tucker in his presidential address in 1913. He declared that if it is not possible for "private enterprise to furnish [transportation, heat, and light] . . . to the humblest homes . . . at prices that represent a reasonable return on the actual investment of capital . . . social justice demands public ownership." Frank Tucker was president of the Provident Loan Association of New York, and before that executive of the Association for Improving the Conditions of the Poor of New York City.

*J*UDGE *JULIAN W. MACK* drew up the Soldiers' and Sailors' Insurance Law of 1917, and thus made history in this controversial field. It covered both the care of the family of the enlisted man and his protection from handicaps in civil life that might arise because of his military service. The reason leading to its formulation was the desire to avert the scandal of war pensions that had followed every American war. It was felt that could be accomplished by making provision for the foreseeable economic handicaps from which an enlisted man suffers, such as loss of earning power during his period in service; reduction of earning power through injury; deprivement of the family's income through the man's death and forfeiture of eligibility for the enlisted man's life insurance. In the first place, the basic wage of the enlisted man was raised from $15 a month to $33. The act provided that on condition of his making an allotment to his family of not less than $15, the government would make an additional allowance to dependents of the serviceman varying in amount according to the degree of their relationship to him.

The injured serviceman, moreover, was furnished with medical care, vocational re-education and guidance, and a monetary compensation dependent upon the degree of his disability. In addition, the enlisted man was eligible to purchase term insurance at a very low cost; later this could be turned into regular life insurance issued by the government.

The act was the most liberal and comprehensive provision for the protection of servicemen that was ever offered to that date by any government. It was drawn up after careful study of the way in which other nations had made provision for their fighting men and it placed on government the responsibility for meeting the foreseeable costs to servicemen and their families rather than leave their need to the uncertain care of private benevolence. Judge Mack had a strong advisory committee assisting him, containing such outstanding persons from the social services as Julia C. Lathrop, of the Federal Children's Bureau, and Lee K. Frankel, second vice president of the Metropolitan Life Insurance Company, who had been general manager of the United Hebrew Charities of New York City from 1899 to 1908.

The positive objectives of the act were accomplished: families of soldiers, sailors, and marines received some economic support while the war was in progress. Among low-income groups, notably rural families, the support was quite adequate and even placed some Southern Negro rural families upon a new and higher plane of living. Compensations under this act for disabilities and for death have been generous, and were liberalized in 1931 to include certain disabilities and deaths not resulting from military service. By 1942 the government was paying nearly three hundred million dollars annually in disability compensations to more than four hundred thousand ex-servicemen, and nearly sixty-five million dollars annually in death compensations to the dependents of nearly one hundred and twenty thousand deceased veterans.[1]

While these comprehensive provisions for the care of the injured serviceman did prevent a movement for a general pension to all servicemen, such as had been granted after all pre-

[1] *Statistical Abstract of the United States for 1943*, pp. 170–71, Washington, D.C., 1944.

vious wars, they did not preclude the passage of bills granting a bonus to all returned men, both by the Federal Government and by most of the states, in addition.

Among the major scandals of the Harding-Coolidge Administration, however, were the corrupt practices of the Veterans' Bureau which was set up in 1921 to consolidate all governmental services to veterans. These irregularities showed up especially in the medical care of the disabled. Then, too, there was bribery in letting of contracts and choice of sites. The exposure finally sent the chief of the Veterans' Bureau, Colonel Charles R. Forbes, to the Atlanta Penitentiary in the fall of 1924.

The United States entered the first World War in April, 1917, but the Soldiers' and Sailors' Insurance Act was not passed until six months later. In the meantime, the American National Red Cross had achieved the well-nigh impossible task of organizing every county in the nation and directing these local chapters to protect any dependents of servicemen suffering from want. This service, however, was on the basis of need, although the Red Cross interpreted "need" liberally. After the act was passed, and each family knew what it was entitled to receive, the Red Cross advanced the money to families that had not yet received their allotment and allowance (Eugene T. Lies, *Proceedings*, 1917). Since the Federal bureau handling the allotments and allowances had been set up six months after the war started, and since a signed authorization to deduct a portion of his pay had to be secured from a serviceman before any money could be sent to his family, most dependents had to wait months after the soldier was enlisted before they received the money due. Indeed, a few did not receive their checks from the government until after the Armistice; so that filling in the gap by the American Red Cross proved to be a heavy and relatively thankless task.

Incidental to this service, the Red Cross national headquarters relayed to each chapter the substance of any new legislation, administrative order, or judicial decision affecting the rights of the families of enlisted men, thus supplying promptly to the home folks much vital information on which their welfare depended.

In connection with its military service by which the Red Cross had a representative in each Army and Navy post branch of the armed services, the national office served as a medium of communication between the relatives in this country and the enlisted man, so that news of any emergency occurring at home could be communicated to the enlisted man, within bounds of military safety. Of all the services rendered by the Red Cross to the enlisted man and his family, perhaps none was more appreciated than this means of getting in touch with one's loved one, who was not only in the armed forces, but, in many instances, thousands of miles from home in a foreign country, his whereabouts hidden by the veil of military secrecy.

The Home Service Bureau of the Red Cross, as this service was called to distinguish it from the other activities of the division of civilian relief, was named by Mary Richmond, and it enlisted many social workers from the private agencies into the ranks of the American Red Cross. It created a special literature defining the duties of the Red Cross Home Service worker, and placed the rapidly accumulating factual information in convenient, loose-leaf handbooks.

The Home Service Bureau instituted training courses for chapter chairmen and their assistants (Joanna C. Colcord, *Proceedings*, 1917). These training courses ran usually from two to six weeks. They were held at some university or a school of social work, and were the means of developing a tolerably adequate staff for the more than three thousand chapters over the country.

Home Service, its rapidly instructed personnel, its handbook "hot off the griddle," and the supervision it received from divisional and national headquarters constituted the first introduction to modern social work for most localities, especially rural districts and small towns. Many saw in it the answer to the problem of how the rural region was to secure the benefits of the modern methods of dealing with social ills which are relatively as common in rural areas as in urban communities (Gertrude Vaile, *Proceedings,* 1918). On the other hand, Home Service units were stronger and more self-sufficient in urban centers than in other places, and Home Service had invented some new and valuable lines of service, such as communication between the home folks and the fighting front. Moreover, it had awakened many urban centers to an appreciation they had never enjoyed of the possibilities of vigorous, competently supervised social service as part of a national scheme.

In 1919 three papers were read by J. Byron Deacon, Margaret Byington, and Anna King on the future of Home Service in peacetime. It was officially stated that a Red Cross chapter wishing to continue Home Service on a civilian basis might do so, since the local chapters were largely autonomous. This was viewed by many persons as a statement of intent on the part of the Red Cross to enter the family welfare field on a national scale, and it drove off some of the early supporters and promoters of Home Service in the war years. Neither the fears of its critics nor the hopes of its promoters were realized; for the American Red Cross was preoccupied with wars and disasters, and looked askance at any development of professional social work.

No more interesting figure ever appeared in the orbit of social work than Douglas C. McMurtrie (1888–1944), who from 1912 to 1919 became an authority on treatment of the physically handicapped, and then, comet-like, disappeared from social work to devote his tremendous energies to typography and its history. In the quarter of a century remaining after his work for the disabled, he must have written at least a book a year in the technical field of typography. But during the eight years that he spent in the care of disabled, he compiled a *Bibliography of the Education and Care of Crippled Children* (1913), and wrote *The Rehabilitation of the Disabled Soldier* (1918), and *The Disabled Soldier* (1919). In addition, he edited the *American Journal for the Care of Cripples* from 1912 to 1919; was president of the Association for Cripples from 1915 to 1919; and director of the Red Cross Institute for Crippled and Disabled Men from 1917 to 1918.

The field of social work should learn something of why it draws to itself brilliant innovators in human relations, as well as why it sometimes fails to keep them. Was it, in the case of McMurtrie, the passive resistance of the medical profession which resented the intrusion of this lone layman, who probably said some unorthodox things about physical disabilities? Or was his abandonment of social work evidence of the unwillingness of the American Red Cross to pay the cost of courageous explorations in human nature?

From hearing McMurtrie at the National Conference in 1917 and from reading his writings, the impression is clear that he was a man of brilliant imagination and rare judgment as well as one possessed of profound faith in the human capacity to surmount handicaps, given wise guidance. His outstanding contribution was his insistence—possibly he was the first person in the field to point it out—that the emotional frustration suffered by a cripple is more serious than the physical one.

According to McMurtrie,[2] the first school for the training of the physically handicapped was established at Charleroi,

[2] American Academy of Political and Social Science, *Annals*, 1918, LXXX, 62.

Belgium, in 1908. Then none was established until the outbreak of the first World War, when both Germany and France set up elaborate equipment for salvaging the industrial skill of the injured. That was followed in this country very shortly after America entered the war, by a less extensive, but after all a steady development of facilities for the care of the serviceman who had been injured in line of duty, to save him from that dependence on the pity of his fellows which had been his lot after previous wars. The inclusion in the Soldiers' and Sailors' Insurance Act of the section on compensation, with its provisions for vocational re-education and guidance, is evidence of the acceptance of the message of McMurtrie and his fellow workers.

The difficulties attendant upon adjustment of the returned soldier to civilian life were detailed in 1917 by Helen R. Y. Reid, of the Canadian Patriotic Fund, and other representatives from Canada; and in a measure, the members of the Conference were prepared to recognize the problems, if not to treat them intelligently. The withdrawal of Federal appropriations for the combined Federal-state-local employment agencies, in early 1919, destroyed a promising resource for meeting the endless difficulties the returned serviceman faced in attempting to find a place for himself in the quiet tempo of civilian life.

From reading the plans made by the American Red Cross, or from observing the leadership it offered to localities, it is apparent how inadequate were the resources and even the imagination of leaders to help the returned man whether able-bodied or disabled (Arthur F. Sullivan, *Proceedings*, 1919). The same story is told about the care and treatment of those who returned as neuropsychiatric patients (Mary C. Jarrett, *Proceedings*, 1918). In their cases, knowledge of what should be done was more realistically possessed, but the resources were pitifully meager. The government was rapidly preparing buildings for their hospitalization; but the special psychiatric guidance that they needed after discharge—or that was needed by those not physically ill enough to require medical treatment—was almost totally lacking.

The effect of the war upon social work was of deep concern to many speakers at the National Conference. Robert A. Wards, its president in 1918, took for his presidential address "The Regimentation of the Free." He foresaw "the stupendous organization of the nation for relief and service" in the American Red Cross, the promise of a new day in governmental functions, in foreign relief, and most of all in the splendid responses of the civilian population to war services. People would "carry over into the future the associated power which the war . . . evolves . . . a duty so profound that it stands indistinguishable from the objects of the war itself."

Julia C. Lathrop, president of the Conference in 1919, spoke of the necessity of the nation's being willing to invest heavily in the welfare of the common people during the coming years if the promise of advance in the social services was to be realized. She did not venture a prediction as to the outcome.

Professor James H. Tufts, of the University of Chicago, listed (1919) some gains made by the family as an incident of the war, and he assumed for them a certain degree of permanence. These were the establishment of new standards of public health, particularly with regard to health of children and to venereal disease; the coming of prohibition; the improvement of standards of living; the greater entrance of women into industry and responsible public service; and the drive toward equality for women.

In discussing the social problems of the war, Edward T. Devine, however, warned (1917) that we may "win the war, but lose the social gains"—a prophecy that has all the unpalatable quality and realistic foresight of a pronouncement by Cassandra. His usual optimism prevailed in his final appraisal though: "We shall do our ordinary social work better after the war." It required the perspective of a few years, however, to realize the full effect of the reaction against Wilson's idealism.

Third Period · *1924-1946*

*A*LTHOUGH the American Public Health Association
and the American Medical Association antedated the Conference, the subject of health, both in its individual aspect and in
the broader trends toward public health and liberalized health
services, stood next to the welfare of children in the number
of papers presented at the Conference.

At an early session (1881) Dr. James Knight, of New York
City, in recounting the establishment of the New York Society
for the Ruptured and Crippled started a train of thought that
became prominent in the twentieth century. It was this: Disease and physical injury are symptoms, but they are, as well,
primary factors in the causation of dependency. Efforts to treat
and cure the cause are therefore worth while, not only in themselves, but also as a means of preventing destitution.

We did not hear that note again for twenty-five years in Conference discussions of provisions for the care of the needy sick.
Two themes supplanted it: the exploitation of clinics by those
who could pay for their own care; and the injustice of free
service to the private practitioner. At this early date, no word
was spoken concerning the quality or method of the care given
by the clinic. In the state of New York, Dr. Frederick H. Wiggin, vice president of the American Medical Association, reported (1898) on efforts to secure legislation making it a misdemeanor to receive treatment at a free clinic if one is able to
pay for it. At the same Conference, Dr. Stephen Smith, a mem-

ber of the New York State Board of Charities, speaking in favor of such a measure, stated that acceptance of free service at a "dispensary" was the "first step in pauperism."

The woes of the private practitioner faced with the competition of free clinics and public health services received scant notice in the program of the Conference, but at least one voice was raised against the whole system. Dr. James Stewart, of St. Louis, declared (1910) of medical inspection of schools that it was "neither right nor proper for a corps of doctors, living at public expense, to treat our patients and work into our families, after we have spent years working up a practice." If in 1910 medical inspection of schools extended to the treatment of children found to be in need of it, that injustice to the medical profession—if, indeed, it is inequitable—is carefully avoided in current practice of school inspection. The significant feature of Dr. Stewart's statement is the claim of the proprietary right of the physician in his patient; and his resentment at any interference, quite independently of the quality of the needed service which he might or might not be able to give.

This is almost an isolated example of the expression of this sentiment during the sessions of the Conference, not because the feeling had died out among the private practitioners, but because those in charge of the Conference program were more likely to be guardians of the interests of the common man than jealous of the protection of the rights of any group of specialists. Nevertheless, the opposition of the private physician—and to a certain extent the resistance of the private lawyer—to professional services in behalf of those in need has been constant. In certain areas, such as health insurance, it has been determined and bitter. Perhaps, as an open forum, the Conference should present both sides of the question. However, in a body actuated by the philosophy held by the National Conference, there is only one side to the argument that, so far as possible, the common man should have easily available those services necessary for his fullest self-development, such as education and health.

In 1906 Dr. Charles P. Emerson, of Johns Hopkins University, struck a new note. After describing the deplorable condition of medical services to the poverty stricken before the Flexner study of medical education, when all sorts of charlatan preyed on poor and ignorant people, he recommended that a clinic be located in each settlement house and in each district office of every charity organization society, staffed with well-paid physicians and nurses. Dr. William H. Welch, dean of the Johns Hopkins Medical School, commented in 1915 on the excellent service to indigent persons given by the clinics of first-class hospitals, which he declared, however, was of more interest to social workers than to physicians. In the same connection, he added that with the present organization of medicine, the wealthy get good service, the poor have an even better grade of benefit, but the large middle class has been somewhat neglected.

In 1929 Dr. William P. Shepard, of the Metropolitan Life Insurance office at San Francisco, renewed the early request of Dr. Emerson and asked that, in the interest of good organization, doctors be paid for their services in the clinic, and that there be one or two full-time physicians in charge of its administration. He asked also that the clinic limit its intake, in the interest of the patients as well as of the physicians on the service. By that time, all discussion of the supposed evil effect of free treatment on the patient had vanished. The entire interest was directed toward improving the services of medicine for the final good of lessening destitution.

Dr. Walter Lindley, public health officer of Los Angeles and vice president of the Conference in 1892, in describing (1905) the California Hospital at Los Angeles, a coöperative venture maintained by fifty physicians where patients could be treated for fees ranging "from $10 a week and up," pleaded for the erection of a coöperative hospital at which patients who could pay no more than a dollar a day might receive care. He did not discuss the financial arrangements that would make such economical services possible.

The possible growth of such coöperative medical services under a plan of prepayment has been greatly hampered, however, by the antagonistic attitude of the American Medical Association. Andrew J. Biemiller, a state legislator of Wisconsin, describing the Milwaukee Medical Center, reported (1938) that doctors had been expelled from membership in that association because of their connection with the Center. In a similar coöperative project at Enid, Oklahoma, the physicians, who were members of the county medical association, suffered a similar fate. It is a little difficult for a layman to understand the opposition of a professional body to a group of good medical men who have associated themselves together for the purpose of promoting the services that they and they only are competent to give.

In the same connection, suggestions were made for the establishment of pay clinics by Dr. Walter H. Brown, director of the Child Health Demonstration, Mansfield, Ohio, in 1922 and by Dr. Michael M. Davis, of the Boston Dispensary, in 1915. Dr. Davis said that the clinic was started as an experiment at the Boston Dispensary with eye patients, and then extended to venereally diseased persons. He believed that the service could be even more widely extended. Yet development of the pay clinic runs squarely into conflict with the interests of the private physician, and, possibly on that account, its enlargement as a special sort of medical service has not been noticeable. The regular clinics have begun to make slight charges which, initially considered as registration fees, have gradually increased to the point where a charge of one dollar a visit is not unknown.

So far as the Conference represents the attitude of the medical profession, there has been a great change in determining the knowledge that the social worker should possess of disease and its treatment, since the pioneer days of the social services. Early social workers were inclined to take the position of many medical men that it was dangerous for them to dabble in medical knowledge, that all matters of illness should be left to the physician. However, doctors themselves pointed out that the social worker's task was incompletely done unless it was guided by some knowledge of disease, its symptoms and prognosis (Dr. James Alexander Miller, *Proceedings*, 1912).

Dr. Richard C. Cabot, of the Massachusetts General Hospital, a member of the faculty of the Harvard Medical School and president of the Conference in 1931, was an outstanding advocate of the coördination of the medical and social services and the reciprocal education of the practitioner of each in the other's field; and of the philosophy that the human being is indivisible, and one aspect, such as the body, cannot be treated apart from the social grouping. He even went so far as to be specific (1917) with respect to the medical knowledge that all social workers should have. The year previously his book on the subject,[1] designed especially for the guidance of social workers, had been published. Although he recognized the difficulty that medical men labored under in accepting his point of view, Dr. Cabot insisted (1912) that the social worker and the doctor constituted a team of peers in the treatment of a patient; they did not hold the relation of a superior and subordinate, like the relative position of physician to nurse.

In 1916 Dr. Charles P. Emerson, now dean of the Medical School of the University of Indiana, while agreeing in part with the idea that social workers should possess some medical knowl-

[1] Richard C. Cabot, *A Layman's Handbook of Medicine* (New York: Houghton Mifflin, 1916).

edge, pointed out the dangers of their assuming a greater competency than they possessed. Real competency, he declared, was possessed only by a qualified physician. In 1920, from the point of view of mental hygiene, Dr. C. MacFie Campbell, then at Johns Hopkins Medical School, directed attention to the importance of the diagnostic significance of behavior to the social worker. Finally, in 1933, Helen Crosby, of New York City, from the vantage point of her position as social worker in a medical setting at the Metropolitan Life Insurance Company, indicated the difficulties encountered in the effort to create a real parity between the physician and the social worker.

In attempting to cast up the gains and losses of this combination, it is apparent that at times the social worker has assumed competency that he did not possess and has attempted to use the doctor as his aide in working out his own plan. The physician, however, does not find it easy to work with anyone else as his peer. Even though largely intellectual, the autocratic habit of treating his patient as an inferior too often carries over into the doctor's relations with social workers as well, leading him to identify their shortcomings rather than to welcome them as fellow workers in a common task.

The causative relation between disease and poverty, first pointed out at the Conference by Dr. Knight in 1881, had again come into prominence by 1919, when the results of state health surveys and studies by the United States Public Health Service had begun to be available. In that year, Dr. C. E. A. Winslow, of Yale, and Karl de Schweinitz, of the Philadelphia Family Society, reported on several such studies, showing, as the researchers of the United States Children's Bureau had pointed out in discussions on infant mortality, that the incidence of sickness varies inversely with the income of the family, even more startlingly than does the infant death rate. Illness occurred nearly four times as often in the lowest income group as in the highest. Bailey B. Burritt, of the New York Association for Improving the Condition of the Poor, lamented in 1923 the fact that social workers were deficient in health education in view of the large part disease had played in the poverty that drove clients to the offices of the Association.

As we come down toward the present, we see that finer and more intricate statistical methods are used to discover the relationship between income and poverty. Thus at the 1930 Conference, Dr. Herbert L. Lombard, of the Boston Department of Health, reporting on a study of a sample of 46,000 cases of chronic illness in aged people, declared that the poor, as they became old, were afflicted with disabling chronic disease twice as often as those who were economically better situated. In a report on a method of analyzing social and health data by census tracts, Howard W. Green, of the Cleveland Health Council, found (1934) that deaths from tuberculosis were six times as frequent in census tracts of the lowest rental as they were in those of the highest.

Dr. Knight's thesis of the intimate relationship between disease and poverty has been fully demonstrated in the years since 1881. Whatever else may be true of those who are forced to live on the lowest income level, they are sick more often than are the economically better situated people; when ill, they are incapacitated for a longer period; and the death rate, for nearly all diseases, usually is at the top of the scale. Tuberculosis has become almost a rare disease except in the lower income groups.

As early as 1925, the Conference asked the question: Is there adequate medical service to meet the needs of those who require it most? The answer has been "no," with increasing certainty as the years pass. Professor Irving Fisher, of Yale, asserted in 1917 that "millions of American workmen cannot at present avail themselves of necessary medical, surgical and nursing aid. When they most need it they cannot pay for it." The Rochester survey of the Metropolitan Life Insurance Company showed that 39 percent of the cases of illness did not have a physician in attendance. Dr. Haven Emerson estimated (1925) that the average American city spends between 40 percent and 80 percent of the minimum amount necessary to protect the health of its citizens. John A. Kingsbury, director of the Milbank Memorial Fund of New York, claimed in 1934 that "the proportion of serious illnesses which goes unattended is more than three times as great among the poor as among the well-to-do." In 1938 George S. Perrott, of the Office of the Surgeon General, reporting on a survey of 750,000 families, stated: "Low income families, in comparison with the higher-economic groups, receive less intensive medical care of illnesses, for the treatment of which they depend on the . . . voluntary service of private practitioners."

At the 1945 Conference, Dr. Thomas J. Parran, Surgeon General of the United States Public Health Service, declared that "counties with per capita income of more than $600 have eight times as great a proportion of physicians to population as do counties with income of less than $100 per capita." Finally, we come to a statement of philosophy, showing how far the social services have traveled since the early days of the Conference. Dr. Joseph W. Mountin, Assistant Surgeon General of the United States Public Health Service, said in 1946: "A position no longer tenable is that a person should be permitted the benefits of medical service in proportion to his financial position . . . ," and he insisted that "all people of this country should have as a right of citizenship, health services appropriate to their needs."

The Conference had heard no contradictory voice during this period of thirty years since Irving Fisher made his statement regarding the inability, not of the penniless, but of the "workman" to pay for the medical services he needed. No one knows better than the worker in a settlement or a caseworker who spends all his days with fellow creatures in straitened circumstances or in trouble, what neglected or uncared-for illness means; that what the long-drawn-out attack of tuberculosis does to a patient and to his family, in suffering and in reduced standard of living, is tragic and terrifying.

It is to be expected, therefore, that the social worker should espouse any movement that could make provision for the amelioration of these conditions or prevent such tragedies. As Homer Folks observed in 1917, a social worker, Edwin Chadwick, the secretary of the Poor Law Commission of England, was the initiator of the movement for public health, becoming the commissioner of the first English board of health. And it was but prophetic of the lay promotion of public health that Chadwick so infringed upon vested medical interests that he was driven out of office after six years. Although a physician, Dr. William C. White, of the Pittsburgh Tuberculosis League, pointed out (1917) that there was almost an inherent antagonism between the worker in the field of preventive medicine and the practicing doctors. The layman is the one who sees the need and presses for action in the field of public health. Harry Hopkins, when he was director of the New York Tuberculosis Association, developed this same thesis (1926) by reviewing the influence of the knowledge of social conditions gained by the social worker on the advancing standards in the field of preventive medicine. As an illustration he said:

Homer Folks . . . has become probably the most influential single individual in the promotion of adequate health facilities in New York State. . . . Lee [K.] Frankel, trained in the family case work field has, as Director of the Welfare Department of the Metropolitan Life Insurance Company, inaugurated a health educational campaign . . . . that leads the world in health education.

Social work, as represented by the *Proceedings* of the Conference, has been especially concerned in two sectors of the field of public health: tuberculosis and the venereal diseases.

The early advocates of better provisions for the care of the tuberculous and for the elimination of the ostracism of the patient afflicted with a venereal disease and for their more sensible treatment were Edward T. Devine, general secretary of the Charity Organization Society of New York, in tuberculosis; and Dr. Prince A. Morrow, clinical professor at Bellevue and University Medical College, New York, and Dr. William F. Snow, general director of the American Social Hygiene Association, in the venereal diseases. None of these men was the inventor of a method. Dr. Edward L. Trudeau, himself a tuberculous patient, demonstrated in the last decade of the nineteenth century that the disease could be best treated by rest. Dr. Robert Koch had discovered the germ of tuberculosis in 1882, and Wassermann perfected his method of identifying syphilis in 1907. The social significance of these discoveries was demonstrated by others. There is a certain amount of moral enthusiasm and idealism necessary in a promoter of such movements. Dr. Morrow had it in a high degree, although his Society for Moral and Social Prophylaxis is now remembered only as a historical curiosity; but Dr. Snow, for many years the moving spirit in the American Social Hygiene Association and an international authority on the venereal diseases, has amply realized the high hopes that actuated Dr. Morrow.

Many persons, lay as well as professional, joined in the campaign for the eradication of tuberculosis, but Edward T. Devine's share in its early development never will be fully known. He gives a modest account of it in Chapter 5 of his *When Social Work Was Young*.[2] Without his dynamic leadership, probably the movement would have taken on quite a different form. As Devine stated in his paper of 1905, the first occasion on which the subject was presented to the Conference was only six years

[2] Edward T. Devine, *When Social Work Was Young* (New York: Macmillan, 1939).

previously when Dr. George F. Keene, of Rhode Island, based his plea on the newly discovered germ origin of the disease, and urged early diagnosis, isolation, and state responsibility for the care of its victims.

In 1902 there was a series of papers on the subject. One was by Dr. S. Adolphus Knopf, senior visiting physician of the New York City Health Department's Riverside Tuberculosis Hospital, in which he described the special importance of caring for the indigent tuberculous patient and providing him with economic assistance; Dr. Knopf even suggested a plan of social insurance for the support of tuberculous patients. Others gave a good picture of the situation at the time: the high hopes based on the noninheritability of the disease; and the possibilities of rest as a cure, for although the number of sanatoria was still pitifully small, they were increasing in number rapidly.

Devine spoke in the main of sanatoria, special clinics, and local and state tuberculosis associations. He perceived especially that these associations, gradually covering the entire country with their influence, would be the most promising of all the agents in the fight against the disease. Devine could not tell of a contribution made by Jacob I. Riis to financing such organizations because it was not given until the following fall. Remembering the Christmas seal sale in his homeland of Denmark, Riis persuaded the American Red Cross to issue Christmas seals, the income of which should be devoted to an antituberculosis campaign. That project, which has become the annual Tuberculosis Christmas Seal sale, now finances both the national and the local associations so amply that critics have questioned whether the public is wise to place so much of its money in one national health project in view of the many other national health movements that are in straitened financial conditions.

The problem of the transient tuberculous patient and the cost of his care in the few places whose favorable climates are supposed to be beneficial to the invalid received considerable attention in 1925 and again in 1929. Papers were presented on the incidence of such transients; on the expense of this invalidism and their ultimate fate; on who is responsible for them; and whether any legal means was possible to secure support for them from the places of their original residence. The consensus of opinion in all the discussion was that nothing could be done, given our present settlement laws. The localities where they went in their illness would have to struggle as best they could with the problem; and the tuberculous patient might pay with his life for our indifference.

An interesting problem confronts these widely spread and amply financed tuberculosis societies since the death rate from the disease is dropping, and much of their educational work is fairly well done. Dr. J. Arthur Myers, of the Lymanhurst School for Tuberculosis Children in Minneapolis, made the interesting suggestion (1931) that they adopt the program of spreading the knowledge of the communicable nature of disease and promote the various means for controlling it. This, of course, would change a tuberculosis society into an agency for the promotion of public health in general, which would bring it at once within the field of the American Public Health Association. That would not be fatal, if a plan for joint operation were worked out, as the Tuberculosis Association did with its branches in every state. Many hundred local branches could widely extend and intensify the activities of the older organization.

On the subject of social hygiene, the Conference ran full tilt into the strongest taboo which social heritage has thrown about conduct in Western civilization. Social hygiene has many and important ramifications, such as the significance of extramarital sexual relations; prostitution and its control; the so-called "double standard"; the method of transmission and control of venereal diseases, salacious literature, and other means of perverting the ideals of youth; education in matter of sex; and even eugenics. As Freud has amply demonstrated, the topic also touches the deepest springs of emotion, affecting behavior in the most unexpected situations and in ways that are unpredictable. No adequate analysis of the social significance of the taboo or of the sexual origin of such a large section of human dynamics has ever been made. The taboo has been denounced and called a conspiracy of silence. Efforts are made to counteract it, but none at all to understand it. The same comment in different phraseology might be made of the basic emotional drive so brilliantly explored by psychoanalysis.

Charles W. Birtwell, at that time secretary of the Massachusetts Society for Sex Education, made a plea (1912) for a new and harmless (but not named) nomenclature to be used in teaching matters of sex to children. He declared that much research and experimentation would be necessary before it was known how such education should be given and by whom. He was quite aware of the wide implications of the subject; but he also had implicit faith that these problems would be solved by the substitution of knowledge for tradition, superstition, and ignorance.

At the same Conference, Dr. C. B. Davenport, of Cold Spring Harbor, speaking of the importance of eugenic selection of parents, advised the charitably inclined layman to "give your alms to organized charity as it will be able to distinguish between those who can be helped and the eugenically unfit." This was too much for good old Alexander Johnson, at that time secretary of the Conference, and himself a believer in eugenic selection. He protested in a footnote, "that it was the farthest from an accurate statement . . . that had ever appeared in the *Proceedings*."

Dr. Ira S. Wile, who has become a national authority on sexual education of young people, broke down the problem by pointing out (1912) that the method would vary with the age of the child, its sex, and its general sophistication. If she is properly equipped, the mother is best situated to give such information. The physician, and in some instances the pastor or priest or rabbi, may be used. Dr. Wile was convinced that sexual education had possibilities for good if it were wisely guided.

As experience accumulated in the results of sexual education, a note of caution was beginning to be heard. Dr. Max J. Exner, of the American Social Hygiene Association, declared (1924) that such information is essential to the education of a child, but in 1931 Karl de Schweinitz, who wrote one of the most successful books on the subject,[3] laid down the obvious principle that character is not formed by knowledge, but by the way knowledge is utilized. He asserted that urgency on the parent's part to give his child such information may only reveal the parent's anxiety. He then went on to say that while there are many avenues through which a child receives sexual information, some of them in connection with study of the biological sciences, he thought a parent wise who assumes that a child knows more than he talks about and that he will ask, when he wants more information. Karl de Schweinitz was assuming in this very important paper that the parents will be the guides to conduct, as well as to knowledge, in this new area of formal learning, just as they fix the standards of conduct for their children in the world outside the home.

Without exception, the segregated district was denounced by all speakers who touched on the subject. While there were many factors working toward its elimination, the Conference reported on but two of them. One was the Iowa injunction law (H. S. Hollingsworth, *Proceedings*, 1914), modified later by the so-called "padlock law" by which the premises were

[3] Karl de Schweinitz, *Growing Up* (New York: Macmillan, 1928).

precluded from use for purposes of prostitution. The second factor recorded in the *Proceedings* (Dr. C. C. Pierce, *Proceedings*, 1919), was the work of the Federal Interdepartmental Social Hygiene Board set up during the first World War to establish standards to which communities within certain distances of camps should conform. This was cited, not only in describing the standards themselves, but also in discussing their educational effect on public opinion.

But repression and prosecution are not in line with the spirit of the Conference, and we find in 1921 two descriptions of a procedure of individualization of the prostitute, used in Washington and in New York, whereby she was treated as a person, on a humane plane of understanding and of exploration of the possibilities of rehabilitation. Arthur Fink, of the Federal Security Agency, returned to the theme nearly a quarter of a century later (1944) with the observation that the adoption of humane methods is yet too meager for comfort. In 1946 Mazie F. Rappaport, of the Baltimore Department of Public Welfare, asserted out of her experience that it is possible to use the methods of social casework successfully in such situations, even though the client is under the control of the court.

Any complacency with which a community may tend to consider the elimination of the segregated district—the decreased use of hotels for commercialized vice and other evidences of success in the effort to destroy prostitution—should be tempered, according to Eliot Ness, of the Federal Security Agency, by the evidence of increasing promiscuity, especially among teen-age girls (1944). He did not point out that the coming of the automobile changed the whole character of illicit sexual behavior, by scattering it all over the countryside. If there is any concentration now, it is not in segregated districts in the metropolis, but in the automobile camps situated on the periphery of nearly every town and city.

By and large, the interest of spokesmen on the matter of

health is in the person afflicted: who he is; what his illness does to him; how the resources for his treatment may be provided. Even in the first moralistic days, there was concern with the demoralization which it was assumed that free clinical care produced. How is a poverty-stricken human being who is known to the social services to benefit by the great advances made in scientific medicine? That is the challenge which has emerged from all these years of discussion. Illiteracy is by way of being vanquished; now let us undertake in earnest to free from disease the person lacking means of livelihood, not as a gratuity, but as his right in a free democracy.

27 · SOCIAL INSURANCE

*T*HE *GERMAN* invention of social insurance in 1884, credited to Bismarck, to cover the losses to the worker caused by accident, sickness, and old age, had spread over much of Western Europe by the end of the nineteenth century. It was known and discussed in this country. A full report of "every phase of it" was given at the St. Louis Fair of 1904 (John Graham Brooks, *Proceedings,* 1905), and its outlines were probably known to some of the leading social workers. In the early days, however, the *Proceedings* were not concerned over the debatable features of social insurance. It was still a matter of indifference to Conference members where the cost should rest: on the employer alone; or on both the employer and the employee; or whether the state should share the expense. Nor was there an early discussion of the difference between insurance as a means of meeting the economic costs of these contingencies and a system whereby the cost would be met wholly by the state.

After graduating from the Harvard Divinity School, John Graham Brooks (1846–1938) spent three years in Germany and apparently was deeply impressed by what he saw there of the radical economic and political philosophy of the bulk of German workingmen and by the efforts of the government to counteract this unrest through the device of social insurance. He spent the rest of his life lecturing on industrial subjects at various universities, such as Harvard, Chicago, and California. He also acted as special adviser to the Federal Bureau of Labor, in connection with which, in 1893, he wrote the first description in this country of the German system of social insurance. His subsequent publications dealt largely with the plight of labor in an industrialized society: *The Social Unrest*, in 1903, which made a deep impression on the liberal thinking of that generation; *American Syndicalism*, ten years later; and *Labor's Challenge to the Social Order*, in 1920. Like the other Boston liberals, Frank B. Sanborn and Robert Treat Paine, he was considered by many of his contemporaries a dangerous radical, and one catches echoes in the papers of such men as Frederick L. Hoffman, of the Prudential Life Insurance Company, of a certain amount of discount to the claims for social insurance because of Brooks's advocacy (1905).

In 1902 Charles R. Henderson, of the University of Chicago, commented on the German method of social insurance and suggested that the National Conference appoint a commission to study "the best practicable method of insuring the working people against extreme need in case of accident, sickness, during the period of invalidism and helpless old age." Timothy Nicholson, president of the Conference, appointed to the commission Professor Charles R. Henderson, as chairman, Frederick L. Hoffman, Dr. Samuel G. Smith (head of the department of sociology at the University of Minnesota, and elected president of the Conference for 1905), John Graham Brooks, Amos W. Butler, Frank A. Fetter (professor of economics, Cornell University), and Edward T. Devine. As chairman of the commission, Henderson reported in 1903 that all appointees to the commission had accepted and had been assigned specific phases of the subject.

In his report on progress at the meeting in 1904, Henderson indicated that social insurance was a subject of wide interest; that many national associations of charity in Western Europe were discussing it; as would the International Congress on charity at Milan the next year; and that it had become a political issue in England. He stated that the commission would have some sort of a report at the Conference of 1905; instead, two of its members, Hoffman and Brooks, presented reports on their special assignments. Hoffman had been assigned "criticism of government insurance on financial, actuarial and economic grounds; with a recommendation of the best non-governmental substitutes"; and Brooks reported on "the recent forms and development of workingmen's insurance in Europe—their financial principles and economic justification apart from any charitable motive."

Hoffman centered his criticism on the great cost of the German social insurance system to the government, so great as to imperil the business prosperity of the country. In his opinion, it placed German products at a disadvantage with products of other nations which did not have to burden themselves with the expense of such insurance.

Brooks submitted other reasons why it might be unwise for the United States to embark on a system of social insurance. It was assumed to be unconstitutional, anyway, for the Federal Government to enter the field of welfare. Because of the inefficient and wasteful conduct of most public administration it would be difficult to bring the question to a successful issue. He gave as an example the corruption that had accompanied the granting of Civil War pensions. "The German success, such as it is, has been owing to a strictly competent and independent administration. . . . With an administration like that which has controlled our army pensions, what would become of social insurance?" Brooks also believed that the scale of German pensions would be utterly inadequate for the American workman. He took strong objection to Hoffman's statement that social insurance was crippling German industry and cited the "astounding progress [that] has been [made in Germany] during the years in which this insurance has been in force" in refutation of any such assertion.

Henderson made a report for the commission at the meeting of 1906; it was a weak and vacillating endorsement of the principle of social insurance, though he saw no chance of Federal action. Social insurance "should be fostered by state legislation, though that does not necessarily mean insurance at cost of government and by means of state administration. . . . The best methods must be found by experience and by experiment guided by expert actuarial advice." He ended with the words: "In the general statement of facts and tendencies the members of the Committee [Commission?] agree. In relation to the extension of governmental supervision and compulsion it is probable that two or three are in doubt or antagonistic."

It can readily be seen from this report that the lines of debate between proponent and opponent of social insurance were already drawn. Social insurance must include "compulsion" to be effective; that is, all within the defined class of eligibles must be covered; it must be under "governmental supervision" and not left to voluntary initiative, if it is to protect the economically weakest workers. The implacable opposition of private insurance, which has distorted the administration of workmen's compensation laws, and has fought so strongly against any extension of social insurance, was made clear in the most positive terms at this early date.

Several other papers by members of the commission were presented at this same meeting. Professor Fetter made a strong, and even indignant, argument for insurance against accident, on the ground of the utter inadequacy of the liability laws. The high wages which the common law assumes that a worker can demand on taking a job known to be dangerous, in matter of fact, "he doesn't get." We must have "industrial insurance to bring our social legislation abreast of that of the leading countries of the civilized world . . . but most of all it is needed to justify us to . . . our own conscience."

Frank A. Vanderlip, president of the National City Bank of New York and not a member of the commission, after reciting the advance made by private corporations in granting pensions to their employees in case of accident and old age, added, "that there is to be development in the industrial pension idea is as inevitable as the working of the law of economic progress . . . whether that development should be directed by the government, or . . . through the individual action of corporations, I am not prepared to say."

In this early phase of the discussion certain prophetic trends in attitudes toward social insurance are clear, in addition to the opposition of private insurance companies. Perhaps the most noteworthy is the testimony of business, through Vanderlip with his assertion that some form of insurance of workingmen against the economic insecurity of their situation is inevitable on economic grounds alone, and that it might take the form of governmental action. If there had been more businessmen, broad gauged enough to appreciate the economically helpless position of a wage earner in the uncertainties of a competitive system, the story might have been different. Fetter's caustic criticism of the utter farce of the protection offered by common law against accidents is one of the highlights of the whole debate. Crystal Eastman [1] cited in 1910 chapter and verse of the actual machinery of such defense endured by Pittsburgh workers and so brought about such imperfect laws on accident insurance as we now have.[2]

In contrast, Henderson shows up badly, either through lack of assurance in handling the subject, or because he was cowed by the imposing position of the private insurance companies.

[1] Crystal Eastman, *Work Accidents and the Law* (New York: Russell Sage Foundation, 1910).
[2] See Chapter 20.

His report was a first-class example of "double talk," an attitude of seeming approval, for some time in the future, and by means to be made clear by later research. These are precisely the tactics of skillful opposition. It is all the more reprehensible because Henderson was the one who first proposed the commission; he took four years to bring in his report, and then, in effect, said that he did not know the answer.

Brooks, on the other hand, represented the nineteenth-century liberal who lacked faith in governmental action and looked to labor itself to force from employers the concessions necessary to gain economic security. For many years this was the point of view of the American Federation of Labor; but by 1912, the president of the Ohio Federation of Labor, Harry D. Thomas, reported at the Conference that his organization had tried, but failed, to have inserted in the new constitution of the state authority for the state to enact legislation on unemployment insurance.

The first full unqualified argument sounded for social insurance was voiced (1911) by the late Louis D. Brandeis, who afterward became associate justice of the United States Supreme Court. He brought to the consideration of cases before that tribunal his deep interest in the problems of making democracy work in a highly regimented industrial system. Justice Brandeis, without specific knowledge of how a system of social insurance should be run, believed, nevertheless, that it should cover all those contingencies in a wage earner's life which endanger his economic independence, such as sickness, old age, accident, unemployment, and provision for his dependents in case of death. He based his argument on the supposition that workingmen "are not free while financially dependent on the will of other individuals." He later said that "the cost of attaining freedom is usually high, and the cost of providing . . . [an] adequate system of insurance, will prove to be no exception to this general rule." He estimated that complete coverage would cost 25 percent of the pay roll, of which 10 percent would be needed to protect against unemployment alone.

Using the analogy of some mutual fire insurance companies of New England which had decreased the fire losses of their policy holders by 90 percent, Justice Brandeis suggested, as one of the arguments for social insurance, that it would decrease the incidence of need for such insurance because of the great reduction in actual financial outlay that could thus be saved: "If society and industry and the individual were made to pay from day to day the actual cost of sickness, accident, invalidity, premature death or premature old age consequent upon excessive hours of labor, or unhygienic conditions of work, of unnecessary risk and of irregularity of employment, those evils would be rapidly reduced." Brandeis arrived at his real argument for social insurance on the basis of justice to the workman, so that he might be protected against the insecurity caused by his dependence on an uncertain wage.

An equally forthright argument for social insurance was advanced by Royal Meeker, United States Commissioner of Labor Statistics, at the Conference of 1917. After making a careful analysis of the essentials of genuine social insurance he asserted that there was not any at all in the United States, at that time. He excluded workmen's compensation because competition for profit in the private insurance companies precluded it from serving its full purpose. "The . . . cure for this serious condition which threatens to break down the effectiveness of workmen's compensation is to socialize our workmen's compensation laws. . . . The making of private profits out of the misfortunes of the worker is intolerable." He then proceeded to develop the argument for health and old age insurances, which he felt were imperatively needed since existing voluntary plans were entirely inadequate. In so far as he was competent to express an opinion, Meeker excluded Vanderlip's possibility of "the individual corporation" assuming responsibility for such provisions, and believed that the government alone could secure the coverage necessary to provide the needed protection.

By the middle of the second decade of the century, the American Association for Labor Legislation had taken up the cudgels in earnest for health insurance (John B. Andrews, *Proceedings*, 1917). After considerable discussion, a tentative draft of a bill was made by 1915, and introduced into three state legislatures in 1916 and "in a dozen states in 1917." Massachusetts and California appointed commissions on health insurance which brought in reports favoring action similar to that proposed by the association. Andrews reported that Governor Hiram W. Johnson, of California, declared in his message to the state legislature, "I believe in health insurance, and that ultimately it will be established in our nation, and this within a brief period."

At the same Conference (1917), Professor Ernst Freund, of the University of Chicago Law School, discussed the constitutionality of the proposed measure. He pointed out that there was no legal precedent for such a law, and that such features as compulsion and limitation of benefits to those earning $100 a month or less raised certain constitutional questions. However, he believed the law might be sustained on the basis of its essential equity. As a matter of fact, the question of the constitutionality of a compulsory insurance law was not passed in review by the Supreme Court until nearly twenty years later, in 1937, and then the favorable decision was based on "its essential equity."

How is it possible to account for this promising start in the field of health insurance when even now, thirty years after such a beginning was made, there is no social insurance provision for health on the Federal or state statute books? The reason is simple: all the enthusiasm and promise of the second decade collapsed in the reaction following the first World War. Taking advantage of the popular distaste for governmental activities, first the private insurance companies, then the agencies interested in opposing the adoption of health insurance, and soon thereafter the American Medical Association, found that powerful business forces were their natural allies. It would require exploration far aside from our field to do justice to this wave of cynicism and resentment against control that followed the first World War—and is developing anew after the second. It succeeded not only in holding off the threat of social insurance until the great depression in the 1930s, but it was also successful in excluding health from the insurance provisions of the Social Security Act.[3] The United States and Canada are the only industrialized countries in the world where there is no assured provision for citizens when sickness strikes.

When the Committee on Economic Security submitted its recommendations to President Franklin D. Roosevelt, which later were incorporated in the Social Security Act of 1935, the Committee, too, sidestepped the question of health insurance. Again the inference is inescapable that the opposition to health insurance in the large and widely representative Committee on Economic Security was so determined and forceful that the whole program would have been endangered if the proponents of health insurance had insisted upon its inclusion. Such an inference is buttressed by the Committee's including in its report unemployment compensation, a far less satisfactory form of social insurance.

The Congress has had before it almost continuously since 1937 various proposals for a comprehensive revision of the Social Security Act, whose major suggestion has been the inclusion of health insurance. Up to now [4] the proposals have

[3] See Chapter 32.
[4] December, 1947.

uniformly failed, and have been honored by the opposition of the combined reactionary forces of the country as well as by the American Medical Association and the private industry of insurance. Prophecy is dangerous, but if the tremendous popularity of President Franklin D. Roosevelt and his brilliant leadership of the country in its hour of despair were not sufficient to secure this well-tested means of providing medical services and handling the economic losses incident to sickness, the outlook for its adoption in the near future is not bright.

Economic provision for the aged assumed political importance in the third decade of the century. In 1923 Pennsylvania, Montana, and Nevada passed laws granting pensions to the needy aged (Abraham Epstein, *Proceedings*, 1925). Although these laws were either declared unconstitutional or repealed, the movement gained momentum with the years, so that by 1934 Professor Paul H. Douglas, of Chicago University, could say that "approximately half the states" had adopted them. The provisions for old age pensions varied widely. Eligibility was usually made severe: ordinarily, it was attainment of seventy years of age. The aged person had to have very long residence in the state: as long as twenty years in some states. All the more serious, some state laws merely gave permission to local political units to grant pensions, if they so wished.

The strong political drives for pensions to the aged, of which the Townsend Plan was the most vigorous, never extended to the promotion of social insurance for the aged. When the Committee on Economic Security made its report in early 1935, it included two provisions for the aged: a system of pensions based on need, and a contributing form of old age insurance. Both recommendations were incorporated in the Social Security Act, and the old age insurance feature was liberalized in 1939 to include the surviving widow and children of a deceased beneficiary, thus indicating the political strength of the proponents of provision for the aged.

Insurance against unemployment was the last project in social insurance to be tested in Western European countries. France established it on a voluntary basis in 1905; England, on a compulsory basis in 1911. The difficulty of establishing any actuarially sound and complete system of insurance against unemployment is practically insurmountable. Even England's limited plan had not covered the real crisis of unemployment and had to be financed by loans from the government during the period from 1922 to 1934—despite the fact that it had had eight years in which to accumulate its reserves. (The law was passed in 1911 and was not to go into effect until 1913; by 1914 the first World War had abolished unemployment, and the plan was not called upon to function until 1919.)

Wisconsin, in 1934, was the first state in this country to pass what was called an "unemployment compensation law," which placed the entire premium on the employer. In practice, it followed Justice Brandeis's theory of social insurance by regulating the premium in the light of each industry's experience or rate of unemployment. In this way, there was an incentive to the employer to reduce the amount of unemployment. This is called the "reserve system" of insurance.

There is another school of thought which claims that such a system distributes the cost of unemployment insurance unjustly; that many perfectly stable industries are stable in their very nature, and the unstable ones are inherently dependent upon factors largely out of their own control. The reserve system would, therefore, penalize such industries as are inherently unstable even more heavily than they are penalized by the fluctuations in demand for their goods or services. Therefore, a general agreement seemed to be reached by the time the Social Security Act was passed that it would be more just to all industries to treat them together as a whole, and tax them uniformly. This system is called the "pooled fund."

Because the administration of the unemployment compensation section of the Social Security Act is in the hands of the several states, each state may choose either method of handling its funds (Aubrey W. Williams, *Proceedings*, 1936; Joseph P. Harris, *Proceedings*, 1936), and thus there can scarcely be said to be a national system of unemployment insurance in this country. The systems are unified only by the fact that each state must meet certain standards of eligibility in order to draw on the Federal Government for the payment of benefits to the unemployed. These requirements include an integration between the state's employment service and its compensation administration; the merit system in appointing personnel; and certain accounting standards, such as an actuarial basis of benefits. In 1941 Edith Abbott, in her paper on "Work or Maintenance," quoted William Haber, of the University of Michigan, as saying, after a survey of the workings of unemployment compensation in the several states, "coverage under Unemployment Compensation is illusory for a substantial proportion of wage earners."

Thirty-five years after Justice Brandeis declared the need for social insurance, his vision of a complete coverage of the foreseeable contingencies that menace the wage earner seemed foredoomed. Only two categories had been covered in the Social Security Act: old age with fair adequacy, and unemployment only in its transitional or incidental occurrence. For the real protection of the unemployed worker caught in the maelstrom of a depression, there is still absolutely no Federal provision, and no apparent conviction that any protection is necessary against the most frightening menace that the wage earner faces.

Justice Brandeis anticipated that it would cost 25 percent

of the national wage roll to offer complete coverage. In 1944 New Zealand passed a comprehensive insurance and relief act to cover all contingencies, foreseeable or not, and established the total tax at 10 percent of the pay roll to cover the cost, dividing it equally between worker and employer. It would be well to watch this courageous effort to treat need as a unity, to prepare for it beforehand, and to establish a right to receive benefits on which any citizen may lay claim.

28 · SOCIAL GROUP WORK

*L*IKE SOCIAL casework, social group work was practiced long before it was defined. The end that social group
work seeks to accomplish, the realization of the social capacity
of the individual, is a goal attained by numberless devices
throughout all recorded history. Among the Greeks, games
were so important that the Greeks measured time by the Olympic festivals. It is not stretching the term unjustifiably to say
that the Olympic games came under the general heading of
group work, even though we know nothing of their organizers.
These games included music, dancing, oratory, pageantry, and
dramatics, as well as games of physical skill. Who would venture to enumerate the many contributions made by those national occasions to the sense of unity and comradeship among
the Greeks of the classical period? A similar claim may be made
for the miracle plays of the medieval age, that of Oberam-
mergau being the one which has persisted to the present.

After all, the ethics of social relationship are learned by the
activities of social groups, as an incident to the major purpose
of the group. An athletic team learns a skill, but incidentally,
its members learn, by practice, the ethics of working together.
Morals are better taught on the playground than in the Sunday
school.

It is assumed (probably correctly) that as part of their culture, the earlier, more stable societies developed certain activities which would now be called group work, such as national
games, dancing, plays, and music. It is a matter of record and

tradition that cultural groups have done so. As observers noted the absence of such customs in the modern city, and also the occurrence of juvenile and adult delinquency, men and women of good will initiated various group devices to make good the loss. Some of these customs that have come to this country are the *Turnverein* of Germany; the *Sokol* of Jugoslavia; the celebration of the saints' days of Italy; and the Feast of Walther celebrated by the Southern and Roman Catholic Germans, of which the many Schuetzen parks in American cities are, however, the only surviving evidence. Leroy E. Bowman, of Columbia University, asserted (1931) that the "recreation movement was a compensation for the deprivation of human expression . . . forced on us by urban and industrial civilization."

So we come to the reason for social group work at exactly the same point we reached in social casework; a social technique is made necessary by the loss of those devices and controls for the realization of personality that are automatically supplied by the customs of an earlier and more stable society. There is, of course, a certain romanticism about this. Early society too had its rogues and criminals, its unnecessary suffering and indifference, and most of the early cultures had only partially learned the strength of mutual aid or the art of developing personality through group activity. The gain achieved by our contemporary analyses of social dynamics is the isolation of those factors that can be understood and developed and on which depended such services as the earlier cultures had imperfectly achieved. It is the introduction of scientific planning into the cultural mores, with all the tantalizing reformulations to which the scientific method constantly subjects its material, in contrast with the intuitive stability of the mores.

Social group work, like social casework, was fairly well established as a method before mention of it appeared in the

Proceedings. In 1931, in the paper quoted above, Leroy E. Bowman spoke of the ways in which social group work was being influenced by progressive education. Also in 1931, Helen Hart, head worker of Kingsley House in Pittsburgh, in speaking on the "Changing Functions of the Settlement," declared that "the central objective for settlement programs, which satisfies a no less universal hunger of the human heart, than the love of beauty . . . is the objective of personality through group relations."

It is to be noted that Miss Hart, of the settlement field, did not use the term "group work," but rather defined the objectives of the activities of groups. So dimly had the term "group work" entered either into the field of the social sciences or of social work itself that the *Encyclopedia of the Social Sciences* has no article on social group work or group work; and Paul U. Kellogg, editor of the *Survey*, who wrote the article on the social settlements for that encyclopedia (1934), himself a resident of Henry Street Settlement in New York City and a member of its board, did not use the term either.

Perhaps the term was difficult to define; moreover, it ran into competition with other phrases of which the word "group" was a part. Sociology, also, had developed its own technical usage of the word, defining it as an association of individuals bound together by a common interest. Sociology's concern with groups included the phenomena created by the contact of two or more groups, such as conflict, accommodation, assimilation, and so on. In this meaning, "group" was early used by speakers at the Conference. In 1925 Thomas L. Cotton, of the International Community Center, Inc., of New York, spoke on the "group approach" as a means of dealing with immigrants, in which he used "group" in the sociological sense.

In 1927 Paul L. Benjamin, secretary of the Family Service Organization of Louisville, Kentucky, spoke of the necessity of knowing the interests of a family or of a community, as a condition of effective relationship, under the title of "Individualizing the Group Approach"; and in 1928 Alfred S. Sheffield, of the *Inquiry* of New York City, spoke on "The Organization of Group Thinking," in which he analyzed the processes that go into creating the "common interests" which bind groups together—and sometimes make them belligerently defensive.

It is only natural that a word such as "group," which had a large number of common usages and, in the social sciences, one technical usage, should suffer a heavy handicap in securing accurate and general acceptance, as compared with the term "social casework," whose only competitors were law and medicine. The usage of the term "case" in either of those professions clarified rather than clouded its meaning.

By 1935 the process of group work had come to be sufficiently agreed upon so that Wilber I. Newstetter, of the School of Applied Social Sciences at Western Reserve University, Cleveland, could present a paper on "What Is Social Group Work?" By that time the term had been so thoroughly accepted as defining one of the major activities of social work that the Conference itself, in reorganizing its program, placed social group work on a parity with the other three major functions of social work: social casework; community organization; and social action.

Newstetter defined the group work process as the development and adjustment of an individual through voluntary group associations, and the use of this association as a means of furthering other desirable social ends. He conceived the whole as an educational process.

Grace Coyle, also of the School of Applied Social Sciences at Western Reserve University, was quoted at the same Conference by Leonard W. Mayo, of the New York School of Social Work. She defined social group work as "an educational process aiming at the development and social adjustment of individuals through voluntary group association." This is substantially in agreement with the first part of Newstetter's definition and is, in general, the definition accepted by the field. There is a different philosophical implication in a process which aims at "other desirable social ends," as Newstetter sees the technique, than there is in one which considers the development and adjustment of individuals as ends in themselves. It is probable that the field of group work follows Miss Coyle's conception rather than Newstetter's more complicated definition.

There is implicit in the idea of a process called "group work" that there be someone skilled in directing it, so that the term "group worker" came to define a person versed in the dynamics of group life, just as a caseworker is assumed to be one who understands the dynamics of the individual. One of the sharply defined differences characterizing the professional group worker from his predecessor, who merely led groups, is the careful limitation of the functions of the social group worker. In the field of recreation, which preceded social group work in the matter of time, it was learned early that recreation carried on without a leader is likely to create a mob. Consequently, the movement stressed the qualification and functions of the leader to the relative neglect of the group. Social group work, reacting against the tendency to ignore the group in the recreation movement, placed its emphasis on the leader's sensitivity to the interests of the group itself; his ability to begin any program from those interests, and to leave to the members of the group as much freedom of initiative as possible in the development of the program (Arthur L. Swift, Jr., *Proceedings*, 1935; William Kalodney, *Proceedings*, 1936).

A special handicap facing the social group worker is that a

great deal of the actual direction of group activity is still in the hands of volunteers, usually leaving to the professional group worker supervision only and not activity on the operating level (Roy Sorenson, *Proceedings,* 1937). While there are some parallels between the leader of a group and a supervisor, essential differences between the two exist. With the increasing number of professionally equipped social group workers who become available, and with more adequate support for agencies engaged in social group work, the professional group worker himself is increasingly assuming responsibility for the operation of the social group work process.

As social group work and casework often deal with the same person, it becomes clear to both fields that there is need to study their common objectives as well as the different methods in reaching them, if confusion and even actual conflict are not to develop in the person served by both agencies. Several papers on this matter were presented at the Conference. Claudia Wanamaker, chief of recreation service at the Chicago Institute of Juvenile Research, in her paper on "Integration of Group Work and Case Work" (1935), discussed in a general way the difficulties which beset both group worker and caseworker in a common use of both services. In 1937 Gertrude Wilson, of the School of Applied Social Sciences, Western Reserve University, reported on several joint committees of group workers and caseworkers who had studied their common relationships over the previous four years. They learned each other's vocabulary, shared each other's concepts, and grasped the meaning of their respective philosophies.

In 1939 Mary Hester, a caseworker with the Cleveland Family Society, and Dorothy Good Thomas, a group worker at the Alta Social Settlement, reported on a project in coöperative work on a girl known to both the Settlement and the Family Society. By means of their own special avenues of knowl-

edge, both agencies were able to contribute to a fuller understanding of the girl than either alone could have gained. Moreover, by reason of this close relation of the two workers, plans
for either's services could be reached by mutual agreement, and
the results evaluated. Many such joint undertakings, with their
processes and results made available to professional workers,
would greatly strengthen and more sharply define the respective functions of each agency; but even more important than
any effect on the agencies, they would clarify and make more
effective their common service to the client.

Following out the second part of Newstetter's definition of
social group work "as a means of furthering other desirable social ends," certain group workers, strongly influenced by
psychoanalytic theory, have used social group work for its
therapeutic influence upon children who showed behavior
problems. In 1938 Samuel R. Slavson, of the Jewish Board of
Guardians of New York, read a paper on "Group Therapy"
in which he described the way in which achievement in a group
may compensate a child for failure to secure the love and appreciation he needs in his own home.

In 1941, following the same conception of a function of social group work, Grace Coyle described it as a means of socializing some of the predelinquent characteristics of late
adolescence through satisfactory group experience. And in
1946 Gisela Konopka, a social group worker with the Pittsburgh Child Guidance Center, explained in some detail the instances which called for use of play in the treatment of the
child showing problems of behavior. She illustrated, especially,
the manner in which a properly selected group may supply
that security to the child in his relation with other children or
adults, the absence of which caused him to build up antisocial
behavior to secure attention, or to protect his self-respect.

One of the most interesting practitioners of group therapy,

Fritz Redl, of the Wayne University School of Governmental Administration and Social Work, Detroit, is not represented in the *Proceedings*. Apart from the courage with which he accepts difficult problems in behavior, his work is significantly interesting in that he is a pupil of Alfred Adler, the Viennese psychoanalyst, whereas elsewhere the Freudian School has influenced practice in this country in both social casework and social group work.

It is needless to add that only the professionally equipped group worker is employed in the use of social group work for therapeutic purposes. It would be dangerous to use volunteers, however skilled and proficient they may be in ordinary group activities, in a project requiring specialized training as well as demonstrated skill.

Two summaries of the development of social group work, from its early efforts to the time these were written in 1940, are presented in the *Proceedings*. They are entitled "A Review of Group Work's Affirmations," by Charles E. Hendry, director of personnel and program, Boy's Club of America, New York City; and "An Examination of Group Work's Practices," by Ray Johns, of the program service staff, National Council, Young Men's Christian Association, Chicago. Together, these two tell the story of social group work, its hopes, its frustrations, its false starts, and its accomplishments. As seen from the inside, it is a thrilling story by two men who were themselves influential participators in the developing movement.

29 · THE EVOLUTION OF SOCIAL CASEWORK

The mystery of personality is not a new discovery.[1]

$\mathcal{S}$OCIAL CASEWORK, it is sometimes thought, had its origin in a general method of conducting the professional relationship with a client, and from that branched special forms of casework. The terms "generic" and "special casework" were in fairly common usage at one time.

There is no historical basis for the assumption. The systems of social casework were being developed simultaneously in the first decade of the century in several fields: childrens' services, medical and psychiatric social work, and family welfare. If the term "generic" clung to the field of family welfare, it was because some of its early exponents, such as Zilpha Smith and Mary Richmond, were in that field. Since the term describes a method used by a professional worker in his contact with a client, there can be only one basic process.

Porter R. Lee, in his presidential address at San Francisco in 1929, on "Social Work, Cause and Function," described the way in which professional method grows out of the initial lay attempts to meet social problems. He said that social work begins by someone seeing an unmet need, and setting about providing for it. If it is a neglected child that arouses his sympathy, he makes arrangement for its care. In this phase, the worker is a missionary, a propagandist, rousing his fellows to see a need,

[1] J. Prentice Murphy, "Certain Philosophical Contributions to Children's Case Work," *Proceedings of the National Conference of Social Work* (Chicago: Chicago University Press, 1933).

and then to join with him to meet it. When the project of caring for neglected children has been established, and there is a permanent personnel, the members of the staff begin to consider critically the methods used in caring for neglected children. It is at this point that social casework is born. The workers, then and there, change from propagandists to technicians.

This transitional period may be met and provided for at a certain stage in an agency's development, although it is dependent upon the degree of freedom the full-time personnel of the agency can exercise in a careful examination of the process upon which they are engaged. Some welfare societies never reach the transition: either the agency is not at liberty to examine the validity of its methods, or else it is intellectually incapable of doing so. It may be prevented by tradition or by vested interest from calling its procedure into question.

In the first decade of the century, a sufficient number of agencies, in different fields of work with individuals, in numerous cities, were actually studying their processes. They were exchanging experiences and, in some instances, interexchanging records of their work. Members of their staff were passing back and forth from one agency to another, so that the method of social casework began to have common elements, and a professional basis of practice was laid down.

In actual operation, however, the comprehensive nature of social casework was not always recognized. Agencies were training their own personnel by apprenticeship, without the corrective experience of other practices. It was this danger of provincialism in preparation that Mary Richmond believed could be avoided by a transfer of training from apprenticeship to schools, and so she proposed, in 1897, "a school of applied philanthropy." The provincialism was not avoided, and that it even crept into the organization of the curricula, especially of the early schools, is quite clear from the paper delivered by

Walter Pettit (then associate director of the New York School of Social Work), at the Conference of 1929, on "The Integration of Specialized Fields of Social Work in Professional Schools." And this, as an objective of schools of social work more than thirty years after Mary Richmond's paper!

More valid than the distinction between generic and specialized social casework is one based simply on the auspices under which it is performed; whether it be an agency whose only task is social casework, such as an organization established for public welfare, children's aid, or family service; or whether it be an institution in which the major responsibility is in a field other than social casework, such as a hospital, a school, the court, an industrial plant. Porter R. Lee was fond of labeling these differences as "extramural" and "mural."

In a school, for instance, it is obvious that the major task is to bring about the progress of its pupils in an orderly fashion from grade to grade. Any services rendered by social casework with laggards or problem children which facilitate their progress are welcome; but they must not interfere with the established routine of the school. In industry, if social casework can transform an indifferent employee into an industrious worker, it is acceptable; but if the social worker should raise questions of hours, working conditions, or wages, he would find himself out of a job in two shakes of a lamb's tail.

It was, indeed, a fortunate day for social caseworkers when other professions invited them to practice under "mural" auspices. Each of the learned professions had endeavored to understand the mystery of personality and each had an answer to that age-old problem, colored by its special approach. The physician knew the person in sickness, as well as the sickness from which the patient suffered. The church, throughout the ages, had struggled with much the same riddle of human behavior that faced social casework, and had arrived at an answer. It was not the same answer that the social worker had found, but contained, as did the answers of the older humanistic professions, wisdom distilled from centuries of experience, with facets of insight which might widen the concepts of the new profession.

Calling upon social caseworkers to assist the other professions was a recognition that the technique of "knowing a person" developed by social work was a specialty of its own, and could be used with profit by the other professions in dealing with human beings. The welcome to social workers extended by these older professions varied with each group and between members of the same group. In those such as psychiatry, whose professional pattern did not deviate greatly from that of social work, there grew up a cordial relationship amounting almost to partnership. In others, where the pattern was somewhat different, and quite self-contained, as in medicine, the relationship, while vital when it did exist, was entered into with more reluctance. In still other professions, where there is a deep philosophical basis, grown sacred with age, such as may be found in the ministry, the relationship has somewhat the nature of armed neutrality; each works on its specific tasks to attain a common end, but each labors with mental reservations.

However partial or complete may be these coöperative efforts between social work and the "mural" auspices under which it is practiced, the older professions have profoundly influenced social casework by broadening its perspective, acquainting it with the codes of professional ethics the older professions had developed, and by sharing so much of their specialized knowledge with social workers as was practical.

As it happens, the one social institution with which the objective of social work is in closest agreement is the church, and yet the give-and-take between the two has been less significant than between the other professions and social work. This is probably because of the absolute character of the philosophy of the church which finds in the pragmatism of social work an uneasy yokefellow. The church accepts social workers, but largely that it may promote its own objectives by the professional methods of the newer vocation. Social work, on the other hand, has not been influenced particularly, as to method, by the church. It would take more wisdom than is available at the present time to explain this fatal dichotomy between two such allied institutions as the church and social work. All that can safely be asserted is that there is much the church could contribute, in method, to social work, out of its age-long experience in human relations; but as yet the way to its utilization has not been found.

Another of the three ancient professions, law, presents somewhat the same picture of an apparently sincere but sterile relationship. The point of contact with law is the probation officer. He has been brought into the criminal and the juvenile court as a means of enabling the court "to know" the person concerning whom it must make some decision; but the procedure of the court in evaluating evidence is so far different from that of social work and, on the whole, is so well established that Dr. Henry C. Schumacher, of the Cleveland Child Guidance Clinic, who had an excellent opportunity to see it in action, declared "that probation had never been tried" (quoted by Dr. Milton E. Kirkpatrick, *Proceedings*, 1935). There are very few Judge Pinckneys or Judge Bakers.

So far as the development of social casework is concerned, it is only a matter of secondary concern whether another profession—the "mural" auspices—accepts what casework has to give, or bends it to its own usages. What is more important is

that these older disciplines share with social work the wisdom
of their craft. And on this point social work has no cause to
complain. (Again, an exception must be made of the church.
While the church claims that the ethical concepts of charity
are inspired by religion, it must be acknowledged that ethical
ideals are not the monopoly of any one religion, or of all of
them.)

Medicine has taken the lead in sharing its knowledge. It early
claimed that physical well-being is fundamental, and that the
development of any person must take into account his physical
condition. It was said to be the evidence of physicians regarding the effect upon the health of Thomas Chalmers's parishioners in Glasgow that led to the abandonment of his experiment in poor relief at the beginning of the nineteenth century.
Reference has been made to Dr. Richard C. Cabot's vigorous
and generous insistence that social workers be equipped with
medical information. The influence of Dr. Cabot, and of other
physicians who advocated a similar education (James Alexander Miller, *Proceedings*, 1912), has resulted in providing the
well-trained social worker with a body of medical information not shared by any other layman at the present time.

The legal profession, regardless of its reluctance to modify
its procedure by adopting methods used in social work, is quite
as emphatic in its insistence that social workers should be acquainted with pertinent knowledge of the law. Roscoe Pound,
Dean of the Harvard Law School, discussed in 1923 the relation
of preventive justice to social work, urging upon his hearers enough knowledge of law to enable them to use it effectively in their efforts to improve living conditions. John S.
Bradway, of the National Association of Legal Aid Organizations, was very critical of social workers, in 1927, for their
ignorance of legal remedies available to them through legal aid
societies, or even through practicing lawyers, if the social

workers knew how to make use of them. It is only fair to the efforts of the legal profession to admit that while the competency of the average social worker in matters of the law is far less than in matters of medicine, this inadequacy in the use of legal material is not due to any failure on the part of the lawyers themselves.

The greatest enrichment that social work has enjoyed has come from psychiatry. When the alienist ceased limiting his investigations to the legally insane and turned his attention to the emotions as the motive force in human behavior, and thus became a psychiatrist, he was working along lines almost precisely parallel with social casework. Very early, both disciplines recognized their common elements. Mary Richmond consulted frequently with Dr. Adolf Meyer, of Johns Hopkins, in the development of her principles of social casework. (It should again be noted that in 1911, the year in which social casework was first mentioned in the program of the Conference, Dr. Meyer read a paper on "Case Work in Social Service and Medical and Social Coöperation in Nervous and Mental Diseases.") In a few favored cities psychiatrists were being consulted by social caseworkers as early as 1915.

When the Training School for Social Workers was started at Smith College in 1919, to prepare workers for psychiatric social work in connection with the treatment of former servicemen, and the Bureau of Child Guidance of New York was established to study delinquency in children in 1922, psychiatry was recognized as a valid discipline for social work. In 1919 Mary C. Jarrett, of the Smith school, could present to the Conference a paper on the "Psychiatric Thread Running through All Social Case Work." The recognition of the validity of Mary C. Jarrett's thesis has resulted in an enrichment in the psychiatric content of the curricula of schools of social work quite out of proportion to their other subject matter. The knowledge that the emotions furnish a key to behavior has proven a discovery of the first order in social work, as well as in many other fields.

This sudden capture of the field of social casework by psychiatry, and especially by psychoanalysis, has not been without danger. At the 1935 meeting of the Conference, Grace Marcus, speaking on "The Status of Social Casework Today," was inclined to dismiss all previous methods as aimless and captured by random fads, and to believe that with the coming of psychoanalysis social casework was for the first time established on a scientific foundation. "In view of the possibility of development of social casework," according to Bertha Reynolds, of the Smith College school, who discussed the paper, these principles "have prophetic significance for centuries to come."

On the same program of the Conference of 1935, Dr. Frederick H. Allen, director of the Child Guidance Clinic of Philadelphia, recognized the invaluable contributions that psychiatry and psychoanalysis have made to the understanding of behavior. He believed, however, that the psychoanalytic explanation had become mechanistic and rigidly deterministic, leaving no play for individual creativeness in its present dependence upon primitive urges and the conflicts to which they give rise. He quoted Dr. Meyer with approval: "The philosopher who thinks that man will not act unless prompted by pain and conflict maligns nature." In this give-and-take between social work and the other humanistic disciplines lies the most hopeful promise that social casework will develop into a well-rounded and mature technique for understanding human behavior.

Aside from its usual setting in social agencies, social casework has come to be used in a number of unexpected projects. Of course, its acceptance by the Army and by the Veterans'

Bureau since the last war has become well known (General Omar N. Bradley, *Proceedings*, 1946; Saul Hofstein, *Proceedings*, 1946).

During periods of labor shortage, personnel work in industry (Louise C. Odencrantz, *Proceedings*, 1923) and counseling in industry (Carolyn M. McGoan, *Proceedings*, 1943) used social casework in an attempt to understand the personality of workers. At such times of crisis it is economically sound to spend money to discover and to develop latent possibilities in employees. However, any hope raised by the experience with such service during the first World War that careful selection and development of workers' potential capacity would be carried over into peacetime practice was rudely shattered. At no cost to itself industry quickly reverted to its traditional reliance on competition between workers to eliminate the laggard and to spur the efficient.

The National Maritime Union of America was probably the first group to incorporate social casework services as a democratically controlled function of its organization (Constance Kyle, *Proceedings*, 1944). While it has been the ideal of social work to develop the democratic way of life, social casework, at least, is ordinarily performed for someone other than the governing board or the personnel of an organization, and under specialized auspices, such as clinic, welfare department, and children's aid society. Yet if casework were logical in its operations, social case service would be made available to a member of any group, by the group itself. Perhaps the best way to demonstrate this universality of casework procedure in behalf of people in trouble is for the social work agency to have a counselor, competent in the method of casework, available to any member of the staff. Executives and supervisors in a social agency know that there is need for such service.

Among the nearly three hundred papers on social casework

appearing in the *Proceedings* from 1924 to 1946, four special topics should be noted: the new outlook on mental deficiency; the possibilities of social casework in public welfare; social casework in institutions; and social casework in an authoritative setting.

As early as 1922, Dr. Charles S. Little, Superintendent of Letchworth Village, Thiells, New York, quoted the principal of a school of ungraded pupils as saying that "the feebleminded were not all potential criminals, and that a great many of them were self-supporting, self-respecting citizens."

In 1928 Florence Sytz, of the Institute for Juvenile Research in Chicago, described the experience that the Walter Fernald State School for the Feebleminded had with parole. It showed, among other findings, that twenty-seven women had married and had borne fifty children, each one of whom seemed normal "in the light of the child's school history and a history of his behavior." Her conclusion, drawn from day-by-day contact with children of defective intelligence, was that the emotionally immature person is of more danger to the community than the intellectually retarded one. It is indicative of the neglect of the statistical method, characteristic of the practice of social casework, that Miss Sytz's paper was the only one in this period in which an effective inference having real social significance was made from statistical data.

In the midst of the depression of the 1930s there were some who voiced the judgment that it was not desirable and perhaps not possible to use social casework in the treatment of the unemployed. This judgment was not expressed in the *Proceedings*, but it was reflected in the answers given to the problem by several speakers. In 1935 Elizabeth Dexter, of the New York Temporary Emergency Relief, examined the assumption that giving relief to the unemployed does not involve social casework, and demonstrated the absurdity of such a position.

In 1938 Esther E. Twente, of the University of Kansas, who had been the administrator of public welfare in Wyandotte County, Kansas, told of the ways in which social casework is conditioned by the lack of resources in rural areas, and by the fact that rural communities are largely places of primary, direct contact. She summed up her experience by saying that "there is . . . enough rural social case practice to show that there can be" work of the finest quality, if there is a sufficient number of skilled caseworkers.

As the late J. Prentice Murphy, of the Children's Bureau of Philadelphia said, "Social casework is the foundation of all constructive work for children." [2] Progressive institutions for children have taken up the challenge, and many papers at the Conference have described the varied uses of casework which have been adopted for the care of exceptional, problem, and physically handicapped children. The use of the institution as a diagnostic center for the examination of children has also received attention.

In 1938, however, Ethel Verry, secretary of the Chicago Orphan Asylum, analyzed from the point of view of a well-equipped social caseworker what the orphanage does to a child, even when that orphanage is staffed with people competent to individualize each child. Her paper raised anew the persistent query whether any normal child should spend his formative years in an institution, even though it is equipped with the latest pedagogical aids and is staffed by highly skilled personnel.

Under the theory held during this quarter of a century (that all that one can do for a client in the professional relationship is to give him emotional support in the direction in which he wishes to go), it seemed to be a contradiction to assume that social casework could be used by a person who represented

[2] J. Prentice Murphy, "Foster Care of Children," *Social Work Year Book* (New York: Russell Sage Foundation, 1935), p. 162.

authority, such as a probation officer. Such a statement has never actually appeared in the *Proceedings,* and we gain that impression only as efforts are made to disprove it. In 1935 Dr. Milton E. Kirkpatrick, of the Worcester, Massachusetts, Child Guidance Clinic, asserted his belief that given the right approach, the probation officer can use social casework with his probationer. He emphasized, however, the therapeutic rather than the diagnostic function of the process. But, he added, "there are too few good juvenile courts and . . . they are seriously handicapped by the political and legal traditions which surround them."

In 1938 Harrison Allen Dobbs, of the Chicago School of Social Service Administration, discussed the subject of "Case Work in Difficult Behavior or Delinquency Situations." He assumed, without argument, or proof, that the method is applicable to the treatment of the delinquent child, basing his assumption on studies made by psychiatrists on the emotional background of delinquency and on methods of treatment.

Finally, David Dressler, Executive Director of the New York State Division of Parole in 1942, tackled the problem directly in his paper "Case Work with the Adult Offender." He placed the blame for the assumption that social casework was not suitable for use in an authoritative setting upon a faulty definition of casework, which has had the individual as its sole concern. He insisted that the welfare of society is just as essential to the social caseworker as the welfare of the individual; and that being so, the process is just as applicable to the offender as to anyone else in trouble.

This is an important statement, and distinguishes the ethical responsibility of the social caseworker from that of the other humanistic professions. In social work it is implicit in the word "social" that the practitioner must maintain a dual obligation: to society—the body of opinion roughly entitled "mores"—

and to the individual served. The members of other professions define their responsibility as pertaining solely to the client or patient, leaving with the latter the responsibility of adjusting himself to the "mores." This dual nature of the social workers' code has never been adequately explored, but it renders inapplicable the literal acceptance by social work of the codes of the other professions.

Perhaps the best description of the field of social casework in the area of the social services was given in 1937 by Gordon Hamilton, of the New York School of Social Work, in her paper "Basic Concepts in Social Case Work." Miss Hamilton said, "The issues just ahead lie not so much in the mastery of physical resources, although much still must be done, as in the management of human relations so that people may not only have true economic security, but may work and rest and play and be at peace with themselves and with one another."

No summary of contributions to the field of social casework in this period would be complete without noting J. Prentice Murphy's article, "Certain Philosophical Contributions to Children's Case Work," in 1933, from which the quotation at the head of this chapter is taken. With that mastery of the subject and beauty of diction that marked J. Prentice Murphy as a unique figure in the profession, he reviewed the various philosophies and schools of thought that have enriched the art of human relations. After he had paid his compliments to them all and to some of their great teachers, he concluded with the thought that the possibilities of casework are only reached as it is lit by the warm human insight of the social worker himself.

30 · THE JOINT COMMITTEE ON METHODS OF PREVENTING DELINQUENCY

*U*NDER THE auspices of the Commonwealth Fund of New York, and with financial support supplied by the Fund, a Joint Committee on Methods of Preventing Delinquency was organized in 1922 (Barry Smith, *Proceedings*, 1922). The committee consisted of the New York School of Social Work, the National Committee for Mental Hygiene, and the National Committee on Visiting Teachers of the Public Education Association of New York. The National Conference of Social Work did not have any part in originating it, but the members listened with attention to the graphic accounts of Barry Smith and Howard W. Nudd.

The objectives of the Joint Committee were the promotion of the psychiatric study of the child showing difficult behavior problems; advancement of the movement for visiting teachers in the public schools; and development of opportunities for the preparation of psychiatric social workers needed by the staffs of the enlarged services which were proposed. In pursuit of these objectives the Committee underwrote the establishment of the Bureau of Child Guidance, affiliated with the New York School of Social Work; opened demonstration child guidance clinics in certain selected cities; assigned visiting teachers to certain school systems; established training scholarships for psychiatric social workers; and, on request, offered consultation services to communities, both on guidance clinics and on visiting teaching.

In 1927 the Commonwealth Fund reported that following its demonstrations, in the six years during which this program was in operation (1922–27 inclusive), seven cities had established child guidance clinics and, in accordance with the recommendations of its consultant services, four other cities had established clinics. Also, twenty-one cities adopted the services of visiting teachers following the Committee demonstration; and thirty-seven more cities received advisory services in organizing or developing such service.[1]

In July, 1929, the London Child Guidance Clinic was opened with the financial support of the Commonwealth Fund. In 1926 the Fund had tentatively proposed a British child guidance council to be composed of representatives of medicine, education, and social work; and it encouraged psychiatrists, psychologists, educators, and social workers to visit the United States that they might see clinics in operation. Fellowships were also given British social workers for training in psychiatric social work in the United States. When, therefore, the London clinic was opened in July, 1929, it enjoyed the benefit of American experience in its operation.[2]

To these demonstrations the widespread interest and growth of the movement for child guidance clinics and visiting teachers can be directly traced. The Joint Committee on Methods of Preventing Delinquency had an unusual combination of favorable circumstances to aid it. The Committee's work was preceded by a year's study of the child welfare field, authorized by the Commonwealth Fund before deciding on any specific plan. The study was made by Henry W. Thurston, head of the children's department of the New York School of Social

[1] Commonwealth Fund *Annual Report* (New York: Commonwealth Fund, 1927), pp. 46–47.
[2] *Ibid.* (1929), p. 78.

Work and chief probation officer of the Chicago Juvenile Court from 1905 to 1909. The study gained the interest and advice of many groups that later joined the Committee.

In addition, the Committee had the advantage of the greatly increased interest in the psychiatric approach to the study of behavior which the coming of psychoanalysis had stimulated. The Committee also had unusual leadership, in such men as Dr. Victor V. Anderson, formerly of the Boston Psychopathic Hospital and an authority on the application of psychiatry to penological work; Porter R. Lee, the head of the New York School of Social Work; and Howard W. Nudd of the Public Education Association of New York City.

Decidedly, the Committee was fortunate in that it was amply financed by the Commonwealth Fund; it secured support for its projects to a degree never before enjoyed by any private experiment or demonstration in social work. The program met with the hearty backing of social agencies over the land, and the demonstration clinics awakened much enthusiasm in the localities in which they were placed. The personnel of these clinics conceived their function to be quite as much the education of the public—including social workers—to the possibilities inherent in psychiatry for the understanding of human behavior, as the examination of children at the clinic. They gave a series of lectures to social workers, and local agencies as well as schools were invited to send children to the clinic. Their co-workers—social workers, teachers, and school administrators—were advised of the nature of the diagnoses and were used to follow up the aftercare of the child. All in all, the six-year period of demonstration educated social workers throughout much of the country in the possibilities of psychiatric social work.

Barry Smith, in his paper before the Conference (1922), disclaimed any belief that the program "will revolutionize the world." In the Annual Report of the Commonwealth Fund, announcing the plan, a similar but more specific disclaimer is recorded: ". . . if marked progress in the direction of [preventing delinquency and crime] can be made, it will be but slowly and the results of many efforts in many different fields." [3]

Emphasis was placed on the preventive character of the plan. In contrasting the function of the child guidance clinics with the heavy cost of treating delinquency, the Annual Report commented, "Only recently has the idea gained strength that perhaps we shall some day have to spend less [in treating the delinquent] . . . if we make an intelligent effort to discover and remove some of the causes of these conditions."

Historically, of course, it was incorrect to say that "only somewhat recently" has attention been paid to preventing crime, poverty, and mental and physical ills. The purpose of the founders of the National Conference was to find out the causes producing the ills with which it was concerned and to put into operation preventive forces to check the supply of dependents at the source. Homer Folks pointed out at this same Conference (1922), in his paper on "Team Work in Mental Hygiene," that it was implicit in the English Poor Law of 1601 that the state, when it assumed responsibility for the support of the dependent, also would do all possible in the field of prevention.

That the point of attack on delinquency is when it appears in the child can be questioned on its intrinsic merits. Strategically, is the most promising time to attack delinquency when it occurs in its predelinquent stage in the school child, or when the delinquent appears in court? Does not the economic insecurity of the family have something to do with delinquency? The wretched housing which most workers must endure; the uncared-for illness of one or both parents; the foreshortened

[3] *Ibid.* (1922), p. 24.

educational and recreational opportunities—do not all these factors have to do with the delinquency of a child? Would it have any effect on the incidence of delinquency to determine that they do, if treatment is centered on the child?

The psychological explanation of behavior, of course, is that a child's conduct is framed by his experience with his family, especially during his early, formative years. If delinquency can be prevented, should not attention be directed to understand the members of the family, especially the parents, and the treatment, directed so far as possible to those unfavorable factors in the life of the family that create the conflicts, fears, and insecurities in the child, applied at the source of the child's behavior?

J. Prentice Murphy once said that if one tenth of the money spent in caring for the child after he comes to the attention of a social agency or public authorities had been spent in trying better to understand the family from which he came, we would be farther along in our effort to prevent the ills of children that we now ineffectually try to alleviate.

Both the child guidance clinic and the visiting teacher existed before the Commonwealth Fund launched its program, and the Fund has insisted many times that they are not its creations. Dr. William Healy's work at the Juvenile Court in Chicago, begun in 1909 under the auspices of the Chicago Juvenile Psychopathic Institute, is credited with initiating the method of examining children by means of the combined services of a psychiatrist, a psychologist, and a physician. Judge Harvey H. Baker, of the Juvenile Court in Boston, was so impressed by Dr. Healy's work that he recommended a similar clinic for the Boston court. Judge Baker died before it could be established; but by 1917, a foundation was created in his honor to achieve such service for the Boston court, and Dr. Healy was brought from Chicago to take charge of it.

At neither of these two courts was the term "child guidance

clinic" used, and it was not until after the launching of the program of the Commonwealth Fund that the term came into acceptance. The first clinic, in connection with the New York School of Social Work, was called the Bureau of Child Guidance; but otherwise, at least during the first few years after 1922, "child guidance clinic" was the ordinary title.[4]

The story of visiting teaching is less definite. Howard W. Nudd, of the National Committee on Visiting Teachers, New York City, presented a short history of the movement (1923). The first visiting teachers began their work in New York, Boston, and Hartford in 1906, and by the beginning of 1923 there were about 140 visiting teachers attached to school systems in fifty political units within twenty-six states.

The title "visiting teacher," apparently, rested uneasily, both upon the school and upon the visiting teacher herself as a term that did not explain her function. It has been superseded by a more accurate term, the "school social worker" (Ruth Smalley, *Proceedings,* 1945).

The child guidance clinic and visiting teacher movements are excellent, and almost contemporary, illustrations of the way in which new ventures in the social services are started under private auspices. A fairly long period of experimentation is undertaken during which the method is improved and public approval secured; when these aims have been reasonably fulfilled, the projects reach their further development under public auspices. Whether any other project in social work backed by similarly ample funds and adequately fostered during its maturing period would achieve the same success in popular acceptance and widespread adoption awaits demonstration!

[4] George S. Stevenson, *Child Guidance Clinics* (New York: Commonwealth Fund, 1934).

31 · UNEMPLOYMENT AND THE CARE OF THE UNEMPLOYED 1921-33

When the history of these times comes to be written, it will be said of social workers of America that they did their duty without flinching and that they deserved well of their country.[1]

*T*HE SHARP rise in unemployment in 1921 and the many emergency measures taken to meet the needs of its victims— the unemployed man and his family—found not even so much as a trace in the *Proceedings* of 1922 and 1923, even as the panic of 1893–95 failed to be reflected in the earlier sessions. There were, indeed, two articles in 1922 on employment and wages that reflected the anxiety the country had just experienced. One paper was by George Soule, of the *New Republic*, on "Is There Enough Work and Income to Go Around?"; the other, by N. I. Stone, of the Hickey-Freeman Co., Rochester, New York, on "Can the Worker Be Guaranteed Continuous Employment?" Later conferences continued the examination of the conditions of employment and the various suggested remedies, such as, for instance, the coöperative movement and methods and experiments in stabilizing employment, as well as social insurance.

During the period of surprising prosperity (1922–29) that followed the depression, when, however, the number of the unemployed was actually rising in every large city in the country, and when both public and private resources for assistance

---

[1] Walter Lippmann, "Poverty and Plenty," *Proceedings of the National Conference of Social Work* (Chicago: 1932), p. 234.

to the unemployed and their families were strained to the utmost, the current *Proceedings* was silent. (David Adie, Commissioner of the New York Department of Social Welfare, referred to the rise in unemployment in a paper given in 1933.) It was as if the public really believed that the rapidly increasing national income was filtering down to the lower income groups, and that those who had a desire to work, could find means of establishing or improving the standard of living.

Those years presented, not only the amazing spectacle of a dizzily prosperous America in an impoverished world, but also the rise of what Herbert C. Hoover aptly defined, when he was Secretary of Commerce, as "technological unemployment": the displacement of men by machines at a faster rate than they were being reabsorbed by the new industries and the new services called into existence by the increased rate of production. The automobile industry is often used as evidence that a new industrial process employs more men than it displaces (in this case, the horse-and-carriage industry). Economists insisted that there was no such thing as technological unemployment. The fact remains that the number of the unemployed, judged by such imperfect statistics as were available, rose steadily from 1922 to 1929; and that in 1929, relief agencies, both public and private, were struggling with a volume of unemployment that approximated the number of unemployed at the peak of the depression of 1921.

In the field of public welfare, important changes were taking place that proved valuable when the disaster of 1929 threw unprecedented responsibilities on public agencies, especially. North Carolina, in 1917, took the lead in creating a well-integrated and broadly conceived state department of public welfare (described by its commissioner, Mrs. Clarence A. Johnson, in the *Proceedings* of 1922). At the same Conference, Dr.

James E. Hagerty, of Ohio State University, described the so-called "cabinet" form of administration of the functions of a state government, whereby a commissioner of public welfare is appointed by the governor with responsibility for all the activities in the field of public welfare within the state. This system is generally recommended by political scientists and was adopted by Illinois in the year that North Carolina created its state board.

Social workers, on the whole, are not in favor of the "cabinet" form of administration of public welfare. Hagerty, in his article, developed the argument against it; as did also Gertrude Vaile, at the same meeting, in her paper, "Some Organization Problems of Public Welfare Departments." Although each type has certain serious political weaknesses, either form is capable of providing better state administration of the welfare functions of a state than is the supervisory board. When buttressed by a good civil service law governing appointments to all positions but that of the administrator, each method has proved its competence in handling the heavy duties that public welfare has had to assume since 1930.

In these years, attention was paid to personnel rather more in detail than formerly. Robert W. Kelso, who had been executive director of the State Board of Charity of Massachusetts for the decade of 1910–20, spoke (1925) of poor pay and political interference as the influences which result in securing services of a mediocre quality.

James H. Pershing, who had been a member of the Civil Service Commission of Colorado, and later became president of the Denver Board of Charities and Correction (1912–14), recounted how the best drawn provision for civil service may be prostituted to political ends by politically minded governors. In spite of the disastrous experience in Colorado under two

partisan governors—one from each major party!—who successfully demonstrated that civil service rules could be violated in
the interest of partisan politics if the state executive wished to
do so, Pershing was a firm believer in the merit system of personnel appointments, designating it as "a new declaration of
political independence for the people of these United States."

In 1924 Fred Telford, of the Bureau of Public Personnel
Administration, Washington, D.C., from his experience with
examinations and ratings of personnel for the public services,
discussed frankly with social workers what was to be gained
by adherence to the merit system for choosing personnel. He
deplored the preference rating given to veterans in Federal examinations since it was a serious compromise with the principle
of appointment by merit.

In 1928 Belle Greve, of the Ohio Department of Public Welfare, gave evidence that state departments of welfare were
really making progress in improving standards of service in the
child welfare field. She cited Connecticut, Pennsylvania, Massachusetts, Georgia, North Carolina, New Mexico, and several
other states, showing that the development was not an isolated
occurrence, but country-wide. Miss Greve did not discuss
factors that effected this change, but parallel with the increasing
interest in "efficiency and economy" in government, two na-
tionwide and wisely led bodies steadily encouraged better public work in the children's field: the United States Children's
Bureau and the Child Welfare League of America.

The great depression of the 1930s revolutionized social work.
Instead of being the Cinderella that must be satisfied with the
leavings, social work was placed by the depression among the
primary functions of government. Public welfare was greatly
expanded in scope, so that by the end of the 1930s social work
was an acknowledged obligation of every city, hamlet, and village in the land. Nevertheless, when the blow first fell, in

August of 1929, the depression was considered an "emergency." It would soon pass, and prosperity, then thought to be established for all time, was only "just around the corner." No one foresaw the long and terrible years ahead, although America had been an isolated area of prosperity in a world of economic distress since the first World War; and a thousand prominent economists had predicted the economic hazards of the Hawley-Smoot Tariff Act of 1930.

The first realistic statement of what the lack of work was doing to the country was made in 1931 by Jacob Billikopf, of the Philadelphia Federation of Jewish Charities and impartial chairman of the men's clothing industry in New York, in "What Have We Learned about Unemployment?" After recounting how the Federal and local governments had refused to face the disaster, he told of the experience of Philadelphia, whose federated fund campaign had failed, and whose mayor, in response to an appeal for $300,000, had said succinctly in refusing, "I'd rather be just than generous." Before the year was ended, however, the city was forced to appropriate $3,000,000 for relief. An additional $4,000,000 had been raised privately, and all moneys were exhausted by January 1 of the following year.

Then Billikopf pointed out how tragically inadequate was our provision for the unemployed, and that they had no security such as social insurance would offer against starvation. He then quoted Paul Douglas, referring to "the spectacle of a country which for a decade . . . did not want unemployment insurance because it was a dole . . . slowly realizing that under its boasted American methods all it can offer . . . is the real dole of public or private charity."

At the same Conference, Harry Lurie, of the Bureau of Jewish Social Research, maintained that the care of the workless was a public responsibility, to be financed by taxation. He enunciated the principle that "taxes must be levied where wealth resides; they should be distributed where there is social need."

Also at the Conference of 1931, Linton B. Swift, of the Family Welfare Association of America, took occasion to disagree sharply with President Hoover's statement that "the American method of assisting the unemployed is through private charity." "We all know," Swift asserted, "that between 70 and 80 percent of all the relief spent in this country comes from public tax funds."

The Conference meetings of 1931 and 1932 did not report on the great deal of aimless activity—and inactivity—of the Federal Government in this serious crisis, typified in 1930 by the President's Emergency Committee for Employment, of which General Arthur Woods was chairman; in 1932 by his Organization for Unemployment Relief, of which Walter Gifford, of New York, was chairman; and by the $300,000,000 fund made available through the Reconstruction Finance Corporation to states on a lending basis for relief. The Conference itself had no delusions on the seriousness of the situation, and it was convinced that public funds, and public funds alone, could meet the need.

The new development reported at the Conference of 1932 was the entry of state governments into the relief picture, by means of the device of grants-in-aid for relief needs to localities. Stanley P. Davies, of the State Charities Aid Association, reported on the creation of the New York State Emergency Administration in the fall of 1931, and on the success that had attended its efforts to bring public relief for the unemployed up to an acceptable standard throughout the state. Grants-in-aid had been used before by states to strengthen and improve local administration, especially in public education. New York, however, was the first state to use grants-in-aid in the area of public assistance. By 1933 the practice was followed by the majority of the states.[2]

During the administration of President Hoover, social work was finding itself increasingly in conflict with Federal policies, as well as with the philosophy of state responsibility represented by the dominant political party. It was accepting the philosophy of the social responsibility of wealth and of its corollary, learned through hard experience, that such responsibility can be enforced only by the state. In the title of his paper, "Poverty and Plenty," Lippmann expressed the paradox for which he could see no other solution but government interference in the distribution of wealth. Social workers saw the millions of the unemployed, and knew the desperate straits to which they were driven to keep body and soul together in a land so rich that its surplus food had to be destroyed to bolster prices! Accumulated wealth had reached an all-time high, but the contention of the classical economists, that these inequalities would rectify themselves in time, fell on deafened ears that had been forced to listen for four years to the tragedy of families starving because of lack of work. The cost of the classical, laissez-faire rectification was too high because the theory assumed that the worker existed for industry, and not industry that man might live.

By this time, also, the professional associations of social workers and the national associations of agencies had arrived at a certain maturity of development. They could speak as a voice from the entire country, expressing an opinion well thought out and generally agreed upon. When, therefore, President Franklin D. Roosevelt entered the presidency in March, 1933, and almost immediately embarked upon a national policy of grants-in-aid for relief of the unemployed, social workers for the first time since the dark days of 1929 began

[2] Josephine C. Brown, *Public Relief, 1929–1939* (New York: Holt), p. 96.

to see their way ahead. They perceived that their clients would no longer be dependent upon the inadequate and uncertain aid of separate authorities, that now the resources of the whole people could be tapped to meet the needs of the millions out of work.

The Conference of 1933 did not spend much time in listening to the new provisions for the unemployed made possible by the Federal Emergency Relief Administration, but set itself at once to the problem of state and local organization, created by the entrance of the Federal Government into the picture. An essential condition of receiving Federal aid was that there should be a state authority, to insure its distribution to all localities in the state needing it; that the state authority should base its requests for reimbursements on actual expenditures for unemployment relief; and that it should also certify that certain standards of personnel, administration, and records were maintained.

Since no state had any official body experienced in handling such a function, most of the states used their recently created emergency—or temporary—relief administrations as the state agency to receive and allocate Federal funds. As long as relief of the unemployed was looked upon as a phase that would soon pass, the injection of a new agency into the field of public welfare was not too disturbing. However, as early as 1933, Dr. Ellen C. Potter, of the New Jersey Department of Institutions and Agencies, pointed out the confusion which would be caused by the intrusion of such an important function as relief to the unemployed into the complicated organization of public welfare existing in most states. Dr. Potter saw as the only solution of these uncoördinated functions the creation of a strong, central, policy-making and administrative body, "democratically modified by an official advisory board." David C. Adie, Commissioner of the New York State Department of Social

Welfare, referred to the same confused situation in New York State and reached the same conclusion.

There were other problems associated with the sudden rise in importance of relief to the unemployed and with Federal participation in providing it. No satisfactory matching formula had been worked out to govern the portion of the whole that would be supplied by the Federal Government. Allocations to each state were determined on a bargaining basis between the governor and the Federal administrator, Harry Hopkins. Still more graphically, as Edith Abbott, Dean of the Chicago School of Social Service Administration, is reported to have described it, the situation constituted a poker game between Harry Hopkins and each governor, with each governor holding the aces. Theoretically, the allocation from the Federal Government was intended to make good that portion of the total need that the state could not supply. In a violent difference of opinion between a governor and the Federal administrator, however, the "ace" was that the governor could always claim that his state had done its best.

During the three years in which Federal emergency relief funds were granted, from 1933 to 1935, thirty-one states appropriated from their state treasuries less than 10 percent of the total amount spent for relief in their states; and only three states, Connecticut, Delaware, and Rhode Island, spent more from their own treasuries than they received from the Federal Government. With respect to the Federal Government's assuming an increasing portion of the total cost, the situation became worse in each succeeding year: in 1933 the government met 62.2 percent of the unemployment relief bill of the country, 71.6 percent in 1934, and 74 percent in 1935.[3]

In view of the very unsatisfactory conditions attendant upon Federal participation in the care of the unemployed, President

[3] *Ibid.,* pp. 204-5.

Roosevelt in the spring of 1934 asserted that the government was going to get out of "this business of relief." In August he appointed a large and representative Committee on Economic Security, with Edwin E. Witte, of the Department of Economics of the University of Wisconsin, as its executive director. Its commission was to prepare a program for the promotion of "greater economic security," and to have its report ready for submission to the President by January 1, 1935. This, completed according to schedule, was later published by the Social Security Board under the title of *Social Security in America.*[4] It contains an account of the insurance provisions for unemployment and old age, and of public assistance in various European countries, together with the Committee's recommendations for legislation. The Congress debated these recommendations for seven months and modified them to a considerable extent. The Social Security Act was finally passed in August, 1935. How the name of the total project was changed from "economic security" to "social security" is one of the mysteries surrounding the processes of legislation; but it is possible that "social" security seemed less menacing to conservative interests than "economic" security. Certainly, "social security" is an ambiguous title.

The passage of the Social Security Act marked the end of a period during which public welfare, which had carried the major burden of the assistance and care of the unfortunate, emerged from its semi-apologetic obscurity into full acceptance by social work. Yet public opinion lagged—and does still—in this matter. Nevertheless, professional associations and national bodies, both in the public and in the private field, acknowledged the change, and threw their fullest support behind the new concept of public social work. A new national body, the American Public Welfare Association, consisting of the

[4] Washington, D.C.: 1937.

professionally conscious workers in public welfare, had come into existence. This organization afforded, not only means of defending good standards in the public social services, but also the sort of dynamic, national leadership which the public social services needed.

A new sort of leadership was needed in the field of public welfare because the task to be performed assumed unprecedented proportions. At least fourteen million persons were unemployed in 1933. When the FERA was carrying its full load, 4,000,000 families, representing 18,000,000 persons, were on public relief, and in some states as much as 40 percent of the population was on relief. The parochial system that had stood firmly for three centuries and a half in the face of the national development of industry, which cared nothing for local boundaries, was shattered, and at last public opinion recognized that a new and just system of public assistance would have to take its place. The new system had no precedents to guide it, and it called for unusual courage and sound administrative ability to secure the advantages of a national system and to avoid the dangers, so often predicted, of taking the responsibility for assistance off the shoulders of local communities and placing it on national authority.

Wisdom was needed in the selection of personnel to staff the greatly extended work, and while the widespread unemployment included persons of ability who could be selected to fill many of the positions, yet this selection called for good judgment as well as a most economical use of all available competent personnel for supervisory tasks. The very extent of the job, measured in millions of persons and in billions of dollars, demanded that public assistance be conceived of in different terms than had previously been possible. Leadership and its policies were compelled to secure the acceptance of public opinion. They could no longer pursue their minor responsibilities in a neglected field of public administration, but had to work in the pitiless light of full, and not always favorable, publicity.

The degree of success attained by this new form of public welfare may be considered as evidence of the efficiency of the democratic way of life. Concerned with differences in method during President Herbert Hoover's administration, the leaders of public welfare discussed among themselves and with representatives of the public the wide range of possibilities the emerging organization should assume, so that when President Franklin D. Roosevelt's measures called for a new and greatly extended administrative structure, they were ready to submit valid proposals and to furnish surprisingly able personnel.

*I*F THE Social Security Act had been passed by the British Parliament instead of by the Congress of the United States, it would be pointed out as an excellent example of the British method of "muddling through." It is a series of miscellaneous provisions in the field of public welfare which altogether do not furnish a logical plan for social security. Frances Perkins, President Roosevelt's Secretary of Labor, said (1935), "it constitutes a very significant step in grounding a well-rounded, unified, long-range plan for social security"; but that is the best that can be said for this long-debated and hopefully expected means of mitigating the economic hazard of the wage earner.

This is by no means a criticism of the Committee on Economic Security, and even less of the Federal Administration's judgment. The Committee suggested something more logical and comprehensive, but, wise in the ways of politics, they knew the limits of the game, and accepted what could pass through the legislative mill. It is simply a statement of fact that an act which calls itself "Social Security" contains merely two proposals for social insurance, three proposals for general assistance, provisions for child welfare services and maternal and child welfare, a plan to strengthen public health work in the several states, and systems for the care and re-education of crippled children and for vocational rehabilitation of injured persons. The Social Security Act can only be called a measure to furnish such means of security as do not arouse serious opposition.

The act has two glaring omissions: provision for the unemployed able-bodied worker, and provision for the care of the acutely and the chronically ill. The Congress passed an emergency measure for the unemployed by authorizing the Works Progress Administration, based on the three months' experiment of the Civil Works Administration in the winter of 1933–34, which had put 4,000,000 men to work. The WPA, as it came to be called, was a temporary measure, and constantly the target of attack or of legislative restrictions. It was abolished as soon as the war industries reduced the number of the unemployed to less than a million.

If it was the hope that the act was but the beginning, and that later Congresses would correct its deficiencies, such an expectation has proved fallacious. In minor matters only has any article been improved. The section on Federal old age pensions has received the most substantial amendment; the original provision which practically made it meaningless for workers over fifty-five years of age at the time of its passage, has been changed to one establishing minimum benefits per month and including surviving widows and children among the beneficiaries. The act has been somewhat strengthened on its administrative side better to insure state selection of personnel on the basis of merit.

In one respect, there has been actual retrogression from the original intent of the law. The unemployment compensation pay-roll tax on employers, which, under the act, was to increase by one half of one percent a year, so that by 1947–48 it would amount to 2.5 percent, has been frozen each year by successive Congresses at one percent. This action has been taken on the basis that balances in state reserves are growing beyond any present need, and entirely ignores the fact that a serious depression such as the country experienced in the 1930s would bankrupt every one of these state funds. England's experience in

1921–22 fully demonstrated that a sudden drain on reserves which were ample to meet unemployment in ordinary times would cause them to disappear almost overnight in a period of cyclical unemployment. If this larger provision is not made, millions of workers who thought they were insuring themselves against unemployment will have been deluded when such a time of crisis comes. In very truth, it is living in a fool's paradise to assume that such a depression will not recur, and it would be shortsighted not to make provision for it in a period of high employment.

At the Conference in 1936, the shortcomings of the Social Security Act were pointed out for the first time. Edith Abbott indicated the weakness in omitting any civil service method of selection of personnel to implement the act; and that warning was heeded, to some extent, in the revision of the Social Security Act in 1939. She also pointed out the flagrant omission of any provision for general relief, or, as she called it, "the home assistance bureau."

Also in 1936, Solomon Lowenstein, of the Federation of Jewish Philanthropic Societies, voiced a more fundamental criticism of the act. In so far as the tax for old age security and for unemployment compensation rested on employers, it would be passed on to the consumer, and increase the cost of living; and in so far as it was laid on the worker, it would act as a sales tax, resulting, in either case, in making "the poor pay for the poor."

In her presidential address to the Conference, Edith Abbott suggested in 1937 that the "means test" be removed from relief and from categorical assistance, and insisted that contributory systems of social insurance are "not the American way." In 1940, in her paper, "Relief—No Man's Land and Its Reclamation," Miss Abbott came out squarely for nationalizing the care of the unemployed, the cost to be borne by taxation and to provide for maintenance, retraining, and placement of workers. Miss Abbott cited the experience of the English Unemployment Assistance Board in dealing with that country's heavy responsibility for the unemployed as an example of the success of such a method.

In this outline, Edith Abbott's philosophy was that of the English Fabian socialists, who would break up the administration of relief into separate categories. She would put responsibility for the unemployed under the Department of Labor in accordance with this theory. Her suggestion at that time did not receive general acceptance, in either the administrative or the professional associations.

Almost all the other speakers at the Conference, such as Jacob Fisher, of New York, and Walter West, secretary of the American Association of Social Workers, at the 1936 sessions of the Conference; C. M. Bookman, of the Cincinnati Community Chest, and Harry Greenstein, of the Associated Jewish Charities of Baltimore, at the 1940 sessions, urged a revision of the Social Security Act whereby there might be created a new category, known as "general assistance," or that all categories be abolished and replaced by one covering all forms of need. Whatever the suggested remedy, all speakers were emphatic on the point that to turn back to the states care of the groups which were not provided for in the Social Security Act would sacrifice the gains in standards of assistance established by the Federal Emergency Relief Administration.

For the most part, the states ignored their responsibility for general relief, as they had been wont to do before 1933, or gave only niggardly assistance. The monthly reports of the Social Security Board, showing assistance given through the act, and then by states alone, fully bear out the accuracy of such a statement, even to the present. In her paper of 1940, Edith Abbott said that if the relief of employable persons, who were ineligible for the WPA, were turned back to the states,

large numbers of local communities will do nothing for them. They are people in need; they are without money for rent, for shoes, for clothing, and they are eating surplus commodities or remnants of food picked up here and there, and hunting through garbage cans. These are the indignities to which we have subjected these honest, hard working people, who are unemployed through no fault of their own.

Senator Robert F. Wagner, of New York, who in 1943 introduced the now famous Wagner-Murray-Dingell bill to establish a system of social insurance covering health, included provision for general assistance to make good this glaring defect. Neither that bill nor the one introduced in 1945 by Senator Theodore F. Green, of Rhode Island, designed to avoid some of the criticized features of the Wagner bill, has passed; nor is there any indication of their passage in the near future.

One of the most stubborn delusions popularly held regarding recipients of relief is that they are inferior stock, and will work only when compelled. We have seen such a sentiment expressed by Josephine Shaw Lowell,[1] one of the leaders in social service of the last century. In his autobiography, William Allen White gives the point of view of a "liberal" twentieth-century newspaperman who was generally to be found on the side of the angels. He says this about beneficiaries of relief:

The exercise of the thrift and diligent persistence in the old century gave the children of the poor who lived below the tracks qualities which made them dominant in the town. But, on the other hand, those families who did not develop those virtues, who still are on the townsite, have filled the ranks of the W.P.A. the last ten years,

[1] P. 102 *supra.*

and their children will be the chronics on whatever poor list we have for centuries to come. A few breed out of it, but mostly the handicap of blood holds them in low estate.[2]

This fallacy regarding the recipients of relief was vigorously attacked by Dorothy Kahn, of the Pennsylvania School of Social Work, in the paper "Democratic Principles in Public Assistance" (1939) in which she said,

> . . . a belief that under ordinary conditions people are in need through some fault of their own, a belief rooted in our culture, fostered by religious injunctions, nourished by education, a belief that could be routed by the most elementary understanding of the economics of an industrial society, as modern psychology has replaced the belief in witchcraft . . . [is a] significant indication of the outmoded doctrines influencing our social structure.

Yet these men and women on the relief rolls of the 1930s are the ones who filled out our supply of labor when the time came to utilize every resource of manpower to staff the "arsenal of democracy." They did their full share in making possible that "miracle of production" which enabled the Allied armies to overwhelm the Axis powers with the sheer weight of matériel.

In city after city, where social agencies screened 1-A registrants for selective service, from 60 to 70 percent of this accurate cross section of the population were identified in the social service or control registration index. This means that in communities with adequate social agency records or free health facilities, some two thirds of the population have received help within the last generation. A look at America will say whether so large a majority of its citizens are inferior or whether "the handicap of blood" has held them in low estate.[3]

This blind and dangerous contempt for those who fail is probably a price we pay for our highly competitive and strati-

[2] William Allen White, *Autobiography* (New York: 1946), p. 357.
[3] Louis Towley, "Screening Out the Potential Psychiatry Case for Selective Service," *Public Welfare*, I (November, 1943), 348-49.

fied society. Prosperous people do not know "the poor," in the sense that Jane Addams used the phrase,[4] and the tendency is inevitable that thriving and successful folks should rationalize the failure of the poverty-stricken individual, as well as their own success, in a manner satisfactory to their own self-esteem. The cause of such an alarming misconception between the successful and the unsuccessful may be even deeper than that; but the successful who are vocal on the matter of taxes and their spokesmen in the legislative bodies have acted on this theory of the moral nature of poverty. The belief still holds that anyone can get a job. If they are hungry enough they will bestir themselves; but at any event, "they are a no-good lot!"

As C. M. Bookman observed at the Conference, "we find it even more difficult in 1940 than in any one of the depression years that preceded it to get intelligent consideration of a long-range work and relief program." The years that have followed 1940 have seen the unwillingness increase rather than decrease. All the resurgent sentiment that capitalizes the political and economic hostility to the policies of the Roosevelt Administration finds favorable support in its effort to prevent a further liberalization of the welfare activities of the Federal Government.

It would be unfair to the political statesmanship of Franklin D. Roosevelt and of those senators who stood so stanchly by their convictions—the late Edward P. Costigan, of Colorado, in the early days of the depression, and Robert F. Wagner, who has faithfully carried on in these less favorable years—to leave the discussion of the Social Security Act at this point. The act is a landmark in the history of the social services in the United States. It reversed the policy followed for a century and a half by the Federal Government, of leaving the fate of the indigent to the states. Justice Benjamin Nathan Cardozo,

[4] P. 114 *supra*.

of the Federal Supreme Court, in expressing the majority opinion of the Court, declared on June 24, 1937, that the section of the Social Security Act granting the Federal Government the right to establish old age insurance is constitutional.[5] This ended the long controversy over whether or not the Federal Government could legally enter the field of the social services. In a general situation of need, Justice Cardozo said, "only a power that is national can serve the interest of all."

From the time the Social Security Act was declared constitutional, the country can be said to have won the possibility of developing a national policy in public welfare. The act promoted the spread of public welfare units in every locality in the United States. It also established, in general, a national pattern for eligibility, competency of personnel, and protection of the self-respect of clients.

Perhaps the most dramatic change, however, has come about in the legal status of the applicant for relief. In establishing categories, the act also defined eligibility; and then by requiring that anyone in a state should be allowed to apply for specific assistance, if he believed himself eligible, and by granting to the client the right of appeal from the decision of the administrator, the applicant, for the first time in Anglo-Saxon history, was allowed to bring his case up for judicial decision.

Implicit in the applicant's right of appeal was the assumption of his right to public assistance. It was no longer a gratuity to be given or withheld on the unquestioned decision of the administrator, but a right that could be legally enforced. By this means the imperishable virtue of social insurance has been secured for public assistance. The late Justice Louis D. Brandeis could have said of it what he claimed for social insurance (1911): "Men are not free while financially dependent upon the wills of other individuals. Financial dependence is con-

[5] *U.S. Reports,* CCCI, 619–46.

sistent with freedom only where claim to support rests upon right and not upon favor."

State administration of the public assistance provision of the Social Security Act, as of the Federal Emergency Relief Administration, was not immediately and in all states incorporated into the functions of the state boards. As Robert A. Lansdale, of the Social Science Research Council, said (1936), the way in which the various provisions of the Social Security Act were allocated to different authorities in Washington offered no example for integration on the state level. He was of the opinion, however, that all functions of public assistance of a state should be administered by one board, or by a division of public assistance under a state board. He would consolidate the state's relationship with the Federal Government, and develop in an efficient and serviceable manner its responsibilities for state organization, for its service program and personnel, for its financial administration, and for its work in statistics and research.

In the years that have elapsed since 1935, no other paper on this subject has been presented at the Conference. It would have been of the utmost importance and concern to the members of the Conference during its earliest years. The logic of the situation has forced the Federal Government to consolidate its strictly welfare functions into a Federal Security Agency, absorbing within that body all the activities of the United States Children's Bureau, except those connected with child labor. In the interest of efficient organizational structure each state as well is integrating these new duties into a single administrative unit. In this state reorganization, the board is losing ground, both for advisory and for administrative purposes. A reason for that is the strong case made for the appointment of single commissioners of public welfare, coördinate with commissioners of other executive functions. Whatever the administrative form, the vastly increased importance of public welfare is forcing states to clean house and to prepare themselves for doing a really first-class job in the social services.

Two other results can be credited to the awakened interest in the public social services brought about by the great depression and the Social Security Act. The greatly increased demand for competent personnel initiated by the Federal Emergency Relief Administration and the merit provisions of the Social Security Act placed new responsibilities on schools of social work.

In 1936, at the first Conference held after the passage of the act, Florence Sytz, of the Tulane University School of Social Work, pointed out that public welfare, now greatly expanded by the Social Security Act, would make unprecedented demands on the professional schools, and especially upon their resources for field experience. Two papers presented at the same Conference (1936), one by the Commissioner of the New Jersey Department of Institutions and Agencies, William J. Ellis, and one by the Secretary of the New Jersey Civil Service Commission, Charles P. Messick, described realistically the new level of performance which the public official must reach, or "administration ends in failure."

In 1939–40 the American Association of Schools of Social Work, under a grant from the Rockefeller Foundation, conducted a study of the resources of the member schools in preparing personnel for the public social services. Marion Hathway, the executive secretary of the Association, reported on this project at the 1940 Conference, although the report was not published until two years later.[6] The report indicated the wide spread between the demand for qualified personnel in the greatly enlarged public social services and the capacity of the existing schools to meet it. The report spurred the schools,

[6] Study Committee, American Association of Schools of Social Work, *Education for the Public Social Services* (Chapel Hill: University of North Carolina Press, 1942).

not only in the direction of a more careful examination of their curricula with reference to the new source of demand for their graduates, but also into ways and means for augmenting their capacity to something more nearly adequate to the demand.

As the war drew to a close in 1944, Grace Browning, of the University of Pittsburgh School of Applied Social Sciences, again called attention to "The Responsibility of the Schools of Social Work for Training for the Public Welfare Services." She quoted studies that showed the slight impression which the professional schools had made upon the personnel for public assistance, and especially upon the workers who held beginning positions.

The ending of the war witnessed no easing up of the demand for social workers. Immediately, the Veterans Administration announced its comprehensive program for the employment of social workers, which absorbed all, if not more, of those who had been attached to the armed services (General Omar N. Bradley, *Proceedings*, 1946).

During the war, the general manpower shortage sharply reduced enrolment in the schools of social work, so that even with the best of intentions—and with sufficient equipment—they could not prepare the numbers necessary to staff the rapidly expanding public social services. Now that the shortage has been relieved, and our educational institutions, including schools of social work, are enrolling unprecedented numbers of students, the public welfare field looks more hopefully to the schools to furnish, if not enough personnel to fill all positions, still a supply liberal enough to staff their supervisory needs.

The other issue brought about by the great depression and the Social Security Act was the awakening of social workers to the importance of politics. In the presidential campaign of 1928, national committees of social workers were organized to promote the candidacy of each nominee. William Hodson, of the Welfare Council of New York City, was criticized for heading one of these committees. He defended his action before the Conference of 1929 in his paper, "The Social Worker and Politics." On the analogy of other professions, Hodson stated that since the social worker is accepted by the community as one skilled in adjusting human relationships, he will be "looked to for [a] leadership . . . [that] will depend upon his willingness to accept the responsibility incident to it and his capacity . . . gained in many fields of service to the wider problems of governmental policy and administration."

In 1936 Edith Abbott, in discussing "Public Welfare and Politics," pointed out that the original purpose of state boards of charities was to save public welfare administration from the corrupting influence of partisan politics. After recounting all the many ways in which politicians thwart the plain intent of the law by corrupt practices, she continued: "The stage is now set for a great political campaign. What is to be our policy? Surely it should not be a passive one." However, her advice was for social workers to work with both political parties to secure acceptance as part of their platforms of a civil service plank; to win a permanent Federal-aid policy for a home assistance bureau; and to obtain a pledge to broaden and extend the social security program.

Finally, in 1943, Joanna C. Colcord, of the Russell Sage Foundation, detailed by chapter and verse the vital part played by professional social workers in bringing about and in directing the framing of the first Federal relief programs. There was no debate on the merits of Federal participation. From the first suggestion by the National Social Work Council proposing a steering committee in the summer of 1931 to the passage of the first Federal Emergency Relief Act in May, 1933, social workers gave generously of their time and of their knowledge of the administration of public welfare. It was the realization of Hodson's prediction that the social worker would be "looked to for leadership . . . in the wider problems of governmental policy and administration."

The Social Security Act ushered in a new era for social work. Henceforth, the profession will use all the refinements of skill developed by the practices of the social services, but they will increasingly be available to all who need them as a democratic sharing of services that America may be strong.

33 · TRANSIENTS, IMMIGRANTS AND REFUGEES

$\mathcal{W}$E SHALL take care of transients. . . . Any state or group of states that wishes to present a plan for the care of transients can submit such a proposal . . . and if approved, we will finance it 100 percent." So said Harry Hopkins, at the Conference of 1933, within a month after the bill authorizing the Federal Emergency Relief Administration was passed. Apparently, no state or group of states took up the challenge, and in the fall of that year the Federal administrator established, according to C. M. Bookman at the next Conference (*Proceedings*, 1934), "the remarkable . . . federal program for transients . . . [although] from the beginning this program faced the opposition of local officials and encountered prejudice against nonresident dependents [it] . . . gave promise of a national transient program, adequate in scope and effectiveness."

With the liquidation of the Federal Emergency Relief Administration by the end of 1935, the only decent, adequately financed plan for the care of the transient dependent came to an end after less than three years. The care of the transient then reverted to the localities in which he happened to be. It would be more accurate to say, perhaps, that he again became a man without a country, with no right to assistance from any source.

During the years of the economic depression (1930–39) the incidence of transiency was greatly increased by the migration of unemployed men and women in search of jobs; and it was swelled by uncounted thousands of farmers from the South and

Middle West whose land had been scorched by the drought. In 1939 the utter distress of the farmer who had lost his holding was dramatized by John Steinbeck in one of the great American novels, *Grapes of Wrath*. Aroused public opinion demanded that something be done about the plight of the "Okie," the dispossessed farmer. In 1940 Congress appointed the Committee on the Interstate Migration of Destitute Citizens, popularly known as the "Tolan Committee."

The Committee assembled a mass of evidence, putting into official form the data on who transients were; where they were going and why; and what, if the worst should come, would be their fate on arrival. Edith Abbott quoted from the Committee's report in her paper on "Work or Maintenance" (1941), to the effect that "a body of stateless people is appearing, existing in a limbo of lost settlement rights and forced to migrate in search of elusive employment opportunities."

The Committee had no suggestion for solving the problems on the basis of separate action by the states faced with this great movement of dependent population. The conclusion reached by the Committee was that an amendment to the Social Security Act should be provided establishing a general category of public assistance, with grants-in-aid to states for transient relief as well as for the resident needy. The Green bill, referred to in Chapter 32, included a provision which went even farther than that: it made a state's eligibility to secure such Federal assistance dependent upon its abolishing the residence requirements.

Yet the problem of the dependent transient is now just where it has always been: it is still an affair of the local community, neglected, or dealt with in a niggardly manner. Year by year it becomes more serious; for the requirements of industry know no state lines, and the number of migrant workers increases. During the second World War and in the years immediately following, the demand for workers absorbed any employable surplus that might be seeking jobs. It is a shortsighted judgment that assumes this condition to be permanent.

During this period, though, the transient dependent made one definite gain. The California law making it a misdemeanor for a person to bring a dependent into the state was declared unconstitutional by the Federal Supreme Court (Leonard W. Mayo, *Proceedings*, 1942). The case on which the decision was based was representative of a problem faced by certain states in that period of economic distress. By reason of a favorable climate and industrial conditions better than in other parts of the country, California was struggling with a large flood of dependent or semidependent persons whose support taxed the financial capacity of the state. In the hearing before the Federal Supreme Court, Congressman John H. Tolan, who had been conducting the Congressional investigation of dependent transients, appeared as a friend of the court to give his reasons for holding the California law unconstitutional and to present evidence on the volume of migration then in progress.

If the Supreme Court had held the statute constitutional, it would thus have declared that each state has a right to exclude from its borders anyone whom it considers likely to become dependent. The state of California had given no relief in the particular case under review, and assistance was being provided by the Federal Farm Security Administration. A decision in favor of the state would have legalized in the United States the situation created by the English Settlement Act of 1666, now obsolete, whereby, eventually, a person might be confined to the state or region of his birth. It is significant that in the decision of the court given on November 24, 1941, the justices were, with one accord, for "unconstitutionality." [1]

From Leonard W. Mayo's report of the case, however, it

[1] *U.S. Reports*, CCCXIV, 160–86.

should be noted that the defendant, who had transported his indigent brother-in-law to California, had the assistance of the American Civil Liberties Union in preparing and presenting his case to the Federal Supreme Court. In situations of potential violations of civil rights, the injured party is usually precluded by poverty from taking legal action to secure redress and is ordinarily helpless against an unjust administrative decision or arbitrary laws. The statutes governing the care of the poor are rarely interpreted by appellate courts, and consequently their real intent and limits are not determined. Only when a case becomes as important as the one under discussion is it possible to command the considerable resources necessary to carry it to the court of last resort. Such a situation is a matter of serious concern to many thoughtful judges of appellate courts.

A landmark was established by Rhode Island with the passage of the General Public Assistance Act in 1942, abolishing residence requirements for general assistance and, in 1943, extending the provisions of the act to the categorical assistances (Glenn Leet, *Proceedings*, 1944). Rhode Island, therefore, becomes the first state to apply the philosophy of Supreme Court Justice Cardozo announced in the opinion of the Court previously mentioned: "The peoples of the several states must sink or swim together, . . . in the long run prosperity and salvation are in union and not in division." [2] Leet had some pertinent comments to make on settlement laws: "Some people think that the settlement problem can be solved by simplifying the laws. This is a snare and a delusion. I have tried [it]. . . . Settlement laws represent a Gordian knot. . . . The only practical solution is to . . . abolish settlement laws completely."

Thus the story of the transient ends: one rousing constitutional decision given, which removed all doubts that the indi-

[2] *Ibid.*, p. 174.

gent transient is, notwithstanding, a free American citizen; one little brave state daring to establish the policy that its assistance laws know only residents of one country.

IMMIGRATION

According to Roy L. Garis, of Vanderbilt University, Nashville, Tennessee (1928), the severe Quota Law passed by the Congress in 1924, which reduced immigration from 706,000 in 1924 to 294,000 in 1925 (J. A. Fluckey, *Proceedings*, 1926), was induced by the anticipation of 2,000,000 immigrants a year following the first World War. It was believed that the country could not assimilate that number of aliens. The only expert adviser of the House Committee on Immigration and Naturalization named by Mr. Garis was Henry H. Laughlin, a eugenist of national reputation. This fact raises the question, partially at least, whether the issue was not decided on a false basis. Garis said that the "opinions of various authorities, investigations of state and national commissions, the statistics on naturalization, the army tests, and the report of Dr. H. H. Laughlin, convinced the advocates of restriction . . ."

The new Quota Law of 1924 created some unexpected difficulties. While the wife and children of a naturalized immigrant could enter the country on a nonquota basis, this privilege was denied to the dependents of the nonnaturalized alien. A Congressional report indicated that 173,192 persons were so affected (Cecelia Razovsky, *Proceedings*, 1927). The husbands were caught in a vicious circle, for when a man applied for naturalization, the courts, under instructions from the Bureau of Immigration (Cecelia Razovsky, *Proceedings*, 1925), refused the application because he had a wife and children abroad!

The great depression, however, followed by the second World War, temporarily suspended immigration and its problems. According to Read Lewis (1933), of the 150,000 quota immigrants that might have entered the country in 1932, only 35,000 arrived. In the same year, nearly 105,000 left the United States. Although the flood of immigration to this country is now dammed back by other factors than our immigration laws, it is a fair question to ask how long the sharp difference in standards of living between wealthy America, on one side, and the impoverished Eastern Hemisphere, on the other, will continue without causing serious international complications.

During this period voices were not lacking to remind the Conference of the value of the foreign-born to this country, nor of the responsibility of a rich and well-fed America to a starving Europe. Edith Abbott, almost on the very day the new Quota Law went into effect (1924), presented a strong argument for keeping the doors of America open for those who wanted to enter. Miss Abbott reminded her audience that America is a unique nation. Other nations had been formed by the conquest of a number of peoples and cultures. In America alone the assimilation had been of people who had wanted to come here and become a part of the new nation. She pointed out that this was a precious tradition which should not be sacrificed lightly.

Jane Addams, in 1927, spoke on "Social Consequences of the Immigration Law," and pointed out how the wheat and corn which were being destroyed because of overproduction could have been sold to the two or three million immigrants who were excluded under the law of 1924; and that the United States would have been stronger and richer for their labor. She also implied a lack of moral sense in destroying food in America, when so much of the world was hungry.

In the tangled controversy on immigration, when racial prejudice plays such a strong part, where competition for jobs inevitably maintains a fringe of the unemployed as a reserve pool of labor, one thing is certain: the record of social work speaks for itself. The social worker puts immigration, like so many other things, to the test of its effect upon people; if they are harmed directly or indirectly, he enters a protest, even when he knows that the remonstrance will fall on the deaf ears of the mighty in high places! The social worker stands firmly opposed, however, to a policy dictated by prejudice, or one based on the false assumption of racial inferiority or superiority.

Another serious situation was created by the law of 1924, which excluded from quota regulations countries in North and South America. Consequently, Cuba, on the south of the United States, and Canada, on the north, became refugee camps of persons awaiting the time when they could come in as citizens of those countries.

REFUGEES

It was but natural, in view of the dominant interests of social work, that when Adolf Hitler and his gang began to make a shambles of all the human traditions of tolerance, the Conference should register its protests. In 1939 Solomon Lowenstein, president of the Conference in the previous year, in speaking on "The American Principle of Tolerance," contrasted the situation in this country with the spectacle of most nations driving certain cultural groups from their borders. He entered a plea for a more liberal administration of our immigration laws, so that some of the refugees from other lands might find a home in America.

In 1946 Max Lerner, of the editorial staff of *PM*, returned to the same theme, then complicated by the five years' infiltration into American life of some of the bigotry that had made Hitler and his Nazism a stench in the nostrils of the world. "When President Truman," he said, "had the wisdom and courage to issue an executive order assigning the unfilled immigrant quotas for Central Europe to the Jewish refugee groups, a bill was presented to Congress to cut these quotas in two."

In the days of the Nazi terror there was not much that the United States could do but protest and repudiate, and having uttered its denunciation once, it served no good purpose to repeat the protest. In 1940, when saving some of England's children from the slavery that seemed imminent was proposed, the Conference appointed for the following year a special program Committee on Refugees, with Eric Biddle, executive secretary of the United States Committee for Care of European Children, as chairman, to give a chance for discussion of the subject before the country. Three of the four papers prepared for that special program were included in the *Proceedings* of 1941. Katherine Lenroot, chief of the Federal Children's Bureau, described the regulations established by the United States Department of State for accepting English children in this country, and Charlotte Whitton, of the Canadian Welfare Council, reported for Canada: regulations to shield the children from exploitation, to provide competent supervision over them, and to protect the rights of their English parents or guardians.

Looking at the larger question of refugees in general, Arthur D. Greenleigh, of the National Refugee Service, outlined the extent of the problem of refugees, and the plight of the wanderer who has succeeded in reaching America. The way in which the refugees are distributed over the country and, through the medium of the National Refugee Service, the coordination of many special agencies, such as those for physicians, musicians, foreign scholars, and social workers, was presented in some detail. Finally, Greenleigh closed with an expression of the caution that has controlled the operation of the Service: by no means do anything that would stimulate antialien legislation!

Japan, Italy, and Germany declared war on the United States in December, 1941, and consequently America was itself involved in hostilities. The danger of England's being overwhelmed had been averted, and the special Committee on Refugees was therefore not continued.

The immediate and urgent question of the displaced person, that distressing problem to which there appears to be no answer, is concerned with the same subject as immigrants and refugees. The displaced person fights shy of resettlement in the land of his birth, now taken over by Soviet Russia. In any event, his plight does not find a place in this record, which ends with the spring of 1946. Still, there is not the slightest doubt what the response of social work will be.

*T*O *PHILIP C. GARRETT* (1834–1905) belongs the credit of having organized, in 1887 and in 1892, the only two Conference programs dealing with Indians and Negroes in the last century. A Philadelphia manufacturer who retired at forty-four, Garrett devoted the rest of his life to civic and social responsibilities. His first venture in Philadelphia as chairman of the committee to reform the Republican Administration did not, seemingly, appeal to him as an activity to be continued. Thereafter he was a member and served as president of the State Board of Public Charities, and as chairman of the State Lunacy Commission. Toward the end of his period of service he occupied himself primarily with the Indians, being a member of the Federal Board of Indian Commissioners. He was one of the organizers and president of the Mohawk National Indian Conference, which did so much to create a favorable public opinion in behalf of the Indian at the end of the last century.

At the Conference of 1887, his thesis was that while the Indian and the Negro may possibly be inferior, it is by no means certain that they are. He claimed that we have a special responsibility toward both of them: toward the Indian, because we have displaced him; and toward the Negro, because he is here through no wish of his own. He contrasted the white inhabitants of the country with these two races, pointing out that the white population represents a long tradition of Western European and Christian culture, while the Indian and the

Negro have very different backgrounds. This difference makes assimilation more difficult; but Garrett believed that assimilation ought to take place, for both benevolent and prudential reasons: "because they cannot protect themselves" from us, and to develop their strength as part of the resources of the nation. He went on to say, "There is a subtle sophism in denial of equality to the African and the Indian. . . . The interest of the country . . . lies most clearly in the direction of their perfect assimilation."

Appearing on the same program was General Samuel C. Armstrong, president of Hampton Institute, which he had founded in 1868 in the belief that a practical education of the Negro's "hand, heart and mind" was his only means of emancipation from slavery. "The outrages [of the Ku Klux Klan] did not touch his self-respect or lower him in the eyes of others," but "the purchase of his vote and the opening of whiskey barrels on election days . . . [are] a terrible snare, pulling down his manhood."

Franklin B. Sanborn also spoke on the same platform, and his judgment in the main was that "the past twenty years are the best evidence that the future of the American Negro will be decided in a far easier manner and in a far shorter time than was considered possible when the [Civil War] ended."

The Committee's program in 1892 was devoted entirely to the Indian. Garrett recounted the injustices to which the Indians had been subjected, as did also almost all the other speakers. He believed that education, citizenship, and land that they could call their own were the means that promised the greatest hope for eventual assimilation of the Indian.

A novel feature of the program was the presentation of the Indian point of view by an Indian, James M. Stuart. He recommended that the Federal Government "give them citizenship . . . no longer disregard their attainments by subjecting them to regulations which are only advantageous to savages; allow them to contend with the realities of independence and freedom; let them improve their lands in any way they can, and provide for themselves a way to meet taxation."

A significant historical statement was made at the same Conference by General Richard H. Pratt, founder of the Carlisle Indian School and superintendent from 1879 to 1904. He was convinced that the only solution of the Indian problem was close association between the two races, and gave several illustrations of its effectiveness. He placed upon President Jefferson the blame for creating the system of Indian reservations. The Indians were to be placed west of the Mississippi, which was to be the dividing line between the whites and the Indians. On the other hand, he said, "Washington believed that commerce freely entered into between us and the Indians would bring about their civilization, and Washington was right." He contended that any show of anxiety to civilize the Indians was "making a great pretense."

However, except as it was implied in the long story of the barbaric treatment of the Indians, there was no discussion of the hunger for land on the part of the whites that drove the Indians from one reservation to another, and a poorer one, nor how such a strong economic pressure, which becomes ultimately a political influence, ought to be met. What a "century of dishonor" we might have been spared, if Washington's and not Jefferson's plan had been followed. At least, the large sections of desirable land that were held by the Indians would not have been a constant temptation to the white men to violate their solemn treaties with the Indians.

After the Conference program of 1892, the fate of the Indians was touched upon only in one period, 1929–33, except for a paper on "Case Work with Indians," by Henrietta J. Lund (1923). From 1930 to 1933, inclusive, the Conference set up a special program committee on the American Indian, with Lewis Meriam as chairman. In 1928 Meriam had served as the technical adviser for a survery of Indian affairs, made by the Institute for Governmental Research of Brookings Institution at the request of the Secretary of the Interior, Hubert Work. The papers in 1929 were presented in the program of the Committee on the Immigrant, Meriam giving a report on "The Indian Problem: the Old Order Passes; What of the New?"

In this three quarters of a century of the Conference it remains true that only two men presented programs regarding the state of the American Indian and suggestions for dealing with their difficulties: Philip C. Garrett, a retired textile manufacturer, and Lewis Meriam, who describes himself as a statistician; the latter owed his interest in that neglected segment of the population to the accident of his acting as a technical adviser in a task which the Brookings Institution took on routinely. There could be no better confirmation from the Conference of the unwisdom of Jefferson's policy (if, indeed, it was his policy) of placing Indians on reservations away from sight than this almost total neglect of their fate by the Conference.

In his paper of 1929, Meriam laid down the good social work principle that the Indians' wishes should be consulted and, in line with them, different programs should be adopted. The Indians in the Southwest treasure Indian culture and industry as a precious heritage, and they should be respected as Indians who do not wish to become assimilated. In their case the government should offer those aids that it makes available to agriculturists which will enable them to pursue their farming and stock raising efficiently on a long-time program.

California Indians, Meriam continued, who have been deprived of their land by a treaty which the Senate has never ratified, "because the discovery of gold led to the fear that the treaties might give the Indians valuable gold deposits," are without property and "pressed back to remote and barren hillsides." For them, much more radical measures are necessary to stem the tide of deterioration. They have no tribal traditions to which they can return after these years of neglect. They can only be assimilated by the long, patient, and very expensive method of education.

In his paper of 1931, Meriam outlined the difficulties the Indians face in the process of assimilation where the free and the protected Indian intermingle in the same community. The latter is still a ward of the Federal Government, and the former is not; but both may be equally caught by disaster, such as the extreme depression in agriculture which existed in 1931. Meriam proposed coöperation between the Federal and state governments through grants-in-aid for such Indians.

Ben Dwight, chief of the Choctaw tribe in Oklahoma, presented a similar picture of a considerable section of his tribe, caught in the dust bowl of Oklahoma, and in the deflation of agricultural prices.

At the Conference of 1932, John Collier, at that time secretary of the American Indian Defense Association, but appointed the next year as Commissioner of Indian Affairs, discussed the misuse of Indian property by the Federal Government. He estimated that the government held in trust for the Indians at that time $750,000,000 worth of property; and that the original value had shrunk between 50 and 65 percent under government mismanagement. He went on to say, "It is worth while mentioning that in Canada, where tribes control their income from tribal resources, and where tribal capital is expended only with tribal consent, the capital and its income increase with each year, in contrast to the . . . United States, where tribal resources . . . vanish with each . . . year."

NEGROES

Discussion of the Negro was of a more realistic character than that of the Indian. The Negro was not far away on a reservation, nor so easily forgotten. He was in our midst, and, by the beginning of this century, his welfare had become an important topic at the Conference.

The discussion on the Negro's health started out on a note of pessimism. In 1908 the Rev. Beverly Warner, of New Orleans, quoted an analysis from the United States census of 1890 and 1900, and showed that the decrease in the death rate between the two periods was less among colored people than among white people, and that the death rate was practically twice as high as among non-Negroes. Dr. Charles S. Grandy, of Norfolk, Virginia, gave as his opinion that the Negro was inherently susceptible to tuberculosis, and that bad habits aggravated the tendency.

The health of Negroes was not taken up again until 1923, when Eugene Kinkle Jones, of the National Urban League, credited the inauguration of National Negro Health Week in 1914, by Booker T. Washington, as the greatest single factor toward improving the health of Negroes, a judgment confirmed at the next Conference by Dr. Algernon B. Jackson, of Howard University. In 1924 Dr. Louis I. Dublin, of the Metropolitan Life Insurance Company of New York, cited some supporting statistics from the experience of Negro policyholders of that company. Between 1911 and 1923, the death rate among Negroes decreased 27.9 percent; deaths from tuberculosis, 41 percent; and the infant death rate, 45 percent. An interesting comparison was made by Jones in 1928, in commenting on Frederick L. Hoffman's prediction in *Race Traits and Tendencies of the American Negro* (1896), that the mounting death rate among Negroes would eliminate the race in America. Jones pointed out that the death rate among Negroes was then about where it had stood fifteen years before among white people. In the same year, Charles S. Johnson, then with the National Interracial Conference, after offering a bewildering mass of statistics that showed the gains and losses of

Negroes in the struggle for health, had this to say: "The differences among Negroes are frequently greater than between Negroes and whites. This suggests that the same influences are operating upon whites and Negroes, but upon Negroes with greater intensity. It also suggests that these influences are largely environmental and thus controllable."

In the matter of educating Negro physicians and nurses, the statements are discouraging. Dr. M. O. Bousfield, president of the National Medical Association, reported (1933) on the great scarcity of first-class medical schools for Negroes. He urged that medical schools and hospitals admit Negro students and physicians, in the interest of the improvement of medical service among Negroes. Dr. John A. Kenney, editor of the *Journal of the National Medical Association,* was similarly urgent in 1928.

At the Conference in 1928, Abbie Roberts, of the George Peabody College for Teachers, Nashville, reported that of all accredited nursing schools in the South, only 3 percent admitted colored students; and not a single graduate course in nursing in the South was open to Negro students.

The migration of Negroes to the North was discussed first in 1917 by Robert R. Moton, of Tuskegee Institute, who said that it was caused by the exploitation of the Negro wage earner in the South, as previously Booker T. Washington had claimed in 1914. Moton saw many dangers in the movement. George E. Haynes, of the National Urban League, Nashville, went one step further and stated (in 1917) that "the Negro [migrates because he has] greater protection for his life and his hard earned although limited property" in the North than in the South, and that such motives, together with better schools, more freedom, and protection from injustice in the North, are motives that had been operating in such a migration for the previous twenty years. The great demand for workers in war industries had stimulated, but not created, the migration from the South to the North.

James Weldon Johnson, of the National Association for the Advancement of Colored People, had some striking comments (1918) to make on this migration, its causes, and its effect on the race. The Negro is asking himself, said Johnson, "Can full and unlimited democracy be realized for all the people, or is the hope of it a mere dream?" As he goes North, the Negro is faced with the fact that the unions are closed to him. He has to work as a "scab," or in unskilled and unorganized jobs. Johnson went on to say, "the Negro has . . . two choices: that of living in the South where most of his manhood and civil rights were denied him, but where economically his condition was secure, or of living in the North, where his rights were guaranteed him, but where his economic condition was always precarious."

In 1924 George E. Haynes (now with the Commission on the Church and Race Relations, Federal Council of Churches), noted the impact on Northern communities of the migration of Southern Negroes, from the race riots in East St. Louis, Omaha, Chicago, and Washington, to the strictest segregation of Negroes everywhere in the matter of housing. At the same Conference, Isaac Fisher, of Fisk University, Nashville, stated that "practically all careful studies of . . . Negro migration . . . agree that . . . the South does not propose, at any early date, to change the general attitude of the whites toward the Negro . . ." In the nearly quarter of a century since Fisher wrote these words nothing has happened that could change the argument or the conclusion that the migration of Negroes will continue.

Throughout the meetings of the Conference there has been much discussion of the difficulties faced by the Negro in adjusting himself to his place in Northern communities, but the subject of his migration and of its causes was not taken up after 1924, in spite of the new disturbances and riots that the Negroes' pilgrimage northward caused during the second World War.

In several addresses at the Conference, Negro speakers expressed their various views of what the Negro wants of America. These were well summed up by Dr. R. R. Wright, of the Colored Protective Association, Philadelphia, at the meeting in 1919. Essentially, he would substitute a true democracy for the "whiteocracy" that so widely prevails, by erasing "For Whites Only" from those avenues of opportunity now closed to Negroes. Specifically, he wants for the Negro:

1. A chance to vote
2. Justice in the courts
3. Representation on juries
4. Representation in government
5. Better living conditions
6. Fairer wages
7. Better educational advantages
8. Protection of colored women
9. Abolition of lynching
10. Repeal of the remaining special laws
11. The use of public privileges for which the Negroes pay through taxation
12. Democracy within the church
13. Recognition of Negro leadership
14. Mutual self-respect among the races of this country

There is not a word here about social equality; but insistence upon that is unrealistic to a degree, in any race. It is significant that the publication of the National Urban League is *Opportunity*. It expresses the deep and justifiable wish of every independent human being.

Long before anthropology had exploded the myth of racial

differences, Philip C. Garrett had questioned whether any inherent differences existed between white persons and those of other races; and the Conference speakers have steadily followed the assumption that there were none. There does not occur in the *Proceedings* any assertion of such a philosophy: it was so generally accepted that it did not have to be asserted. The potential equality of the races was not a debatable question.

JAPANESE RELOCATION, 1942–45

After the Executive Order of February 19, 1942, ordering the evacuation of about one hundred and twenty-five thousand Japanese to relocation, aliens and citizens alike, the Conference asked two people who were familiar with the situation to tell about it: Robert K. Lamb, of the Committee to Investigate National Defense Migration (successor of the Tolan Committee); and Jane Hoey, of the Bureau of Public Assistance of the Social Security Board. Robert Lamb voiced guarded criticism of the whole procedure; Jane Hoey limited herself to a description of the difficulties faced by the Japanese in their new setting, which consisted of one room to a family, a common eating hall, work arranged by officials, and medical care and other services supplied by the government.

In 1943, however, when the experiment had been in operation for one year, Edward J. Ennis, of the Alien Emergency Control Unit of the Department of Justice, admitted to the Conference that the decision to remove Japanese was the result of hysteria roused because "we could not know to what extent various types of fifth column activity . . . might be embarked against us." However, John W. Powell, director of community activities at one of the Relocation Centers, after describing the industriousness and law-abiding character of the Japanese, said that there had been no trouble at all in Hawaii, even during the attack on Pearl Harbor. He went on to state in no uncertain terms that the Japanese "major crime [in California] was to have created hundreds of millions of dollars of agricultural wealth, which some of their neighbors sought to control by forcing the racial issue." He further declared that such action was "dangerous to ourselves as a democratic people." To this, Clarence Pickett, of the American Friends' Service Committee, added at the same Conference: "Many wonder if the Four Freedoms are intended to apply only to remote places."

America's ruthless treatment of the helpless minority groups in her midst calls to mind the famous saying of the historian Lord Acton, "All power tends to corrupt, and absolute power to corrupt absolutely."

35 · SOCIAL REFORM, 1924-46

*D*URING THE third quarter of a century of the transactions of the Conference, social reform was incorporated into the body of social work, and named "social action." This change of status was not accompanied by any defense of the effort to control behavior by law in the interest of the common welfare. Almost habitually, social workers had used the power of government to rectify evils since the first statutes regulating child labor were passed in England in the early part of the last century. Although there were occasional voices raised against dependence on law to control behavior, they were heard, for the most part, outside the ranks of social work. Theoretically, social workers recognized that there were other ways of controlling mass behavior: propaganda and the influence of personal service, such as that furnished by settlement workers and by the so-called "friendly visitors" of the past generation. But in the main, social workers relied upon the enactment of law to rectify the evils of exploitation and neglect—much as Edward T. Devine had counseled in 1905.

A philosophical evaluation on the place of law as a means of social progress was given in 1926 by Judge Marvin B. Rosenberry, of the Wisconsin Supreme Court. He quoted Lord Moulton as dividing human action into three domains: first, actions defined by law; second, free actions; and third, actions controlled by custom. It is Lord Moulton's third "domain" that includes the scope of what social work calls "social action."

European observers have often noted how much of behavior

that is regulated by custom in the more stable countries of Europe comes under the control of law in this country. Judge Rosenberry explained that the need for law as a control was due to the rapidly changing form of industrialized society. "The movement being too rapid for change in the traditional attitude of the people, resort to legislation was the only method by which a speedy adjustment could be made." However, he pointed to the imperfection of obedience to a new law that changes the habits of a whole people; and declared that it must be enforced against a recalcitrant minority, who will violate it if they can.

Despite this reliance upon the imperfect control exercised by such laws, he said, "English and American law, from the time of Cromwell down to the middle of the nineteenth century, was a struggle to enlarge the rights of the individual, and to reduce to a minimum the privileges and immunities of the privileged class." There the argument for social legislation may rest. It had no other defender at the Conference, and indeed, it did not believe that it needed any.

Economic situations and data were presented by various speakers—situations and data that inherently called for social action, but usually without indicating what that action should be. The significant studies of the Brookings Institution, on this country's capacity to produce goods and its ability to buy them,[1] were presented by Dr. Harold G. Moulton, president of Brookings Institution, in 1933, and by Karl Pribram of the same Institution in 1936. By statistical research they showed what the second World War was amply to demonstrate, that our capacity to produce far outstripped our normal capacity to purchase. While Pribram's paper was a sort of red flag cau-

[1] Edwin G. Nourse, et al., *America's Capacity to Produce* (Washington: Brookings Institution, 1934).
Maurice Leven, et al., *America's Capacity to Consume* (Washington: Brookings Institution, 1934).

tioning social work not to go full speed in planning to bring these two capacities together, the lessons so painstakingly taught by the Brookings Institution in those dark years of the depression have been deeply engraved on the minds of the American people, as well as of the members of the Conference.

In 1930 though, Wesley C. Mitchell, president of the National Bureau of Economic Research, anticipated the findings of the Brookings Institution: "What keeps our income down is not inability or unwillingness to produce more goods, but inability to market what we can make. . . . We can raise the standard of living just as rapidly as we can remedy the defects of our economic organization . . . [which will depend] upon keener scientific [economic] insight . . ." This is certainly a call to social action, as well as to economic research!

William Haber, professor of economics, University of Michigan, who was closely in touch with the economic problems of the depression and of the second World War, both on the state and on the national level, confirmed our tremendous capacity to produce in his paper at the Conference in 1945: with "twelve million of the most productive members of our normal labor force . . . in the armed services . . . we are now producing goods and services nearly double that of 1940. . . . Our objective is really something more than 'reconversion.' If we 'reconvert' . . . we will again have millions of unemployed workers, side by side with idle plants and unused resources."

Haber rounded out the picture of what is ahead of us. No one as yet knows the answer, even for the immediate future. The wide prediction of a recession, which would again find able-bodied workers on the streets selling apples, has probably done its share to stimulate private industry to prevent such a deflation. The heavy backlog of unmet consumer's goods and unprecedented savings has furnished a market for goods as rapidly as plants could be changed from production of material for war to manufacture of goods for peace. Whether any fundamental change has taken place in industrial organization, whereby the primary function of industry is now to serve the needs of people, rather than, as heretofore, to use people in the interest of business, may seriously be questioned.

William Stead, of the United States Employment Services, presented the case for government economic planning in 1939. He showed that about six hundred thousand men had been added annually to the total of the unemployed, "in recent years," that the labor demand in agriculture was decreasing and output per man-hour increasing; that machines were displacing workers faster than they were being reabsorbed; and that unemployment hits unevenly, bearing especially hard on the young people seeking an entrance into industry and on the older worker. Yet, in the face of such conclusions as these of Dr. Stead's, the full and temperate report of the National Resources Planning Board (described by Eveline Burns in the 1943 *Proceedings*) was studiously ignored by Congress, and the appropriation necessary to continue its work was cut off.

The opposition to economic planning was bitter. In the debate in the House on the report of the National Resources Planning Board, Congressman John E. Rankin, of Mississippi, is reported to have said, "If this program proposed by our so-called National Resources Planning Board were put into effect, it would wreck this republic, wipe out the constitution, destroy our form of government, set up a totalitarian regime, eliminate private enterprise, regiment our people indefinitely, and pile upon their backs a burden no nation on earth could bear." [2] While such sentiments were uttered only by the more reckless opponents of economic planning in the Congress, all

[2] Rilla Schroeder, "Here in Washington," *Survey*, LXXIX (June, 1943), 178.

evidence points to an increasing body of articulate criticism and even of downright denunciation of the idea that free enterprise would benefit by national governmental planning. Such protests are the primary evidence of the form which social and economic reaction has taken following the second World War.

Coming to matters more closely related to social work, Owen R. Lovejoy, that brave champion of good causes, said in the dark hour of the depression (1932), "If poverty cannot be met and conquered under the system of private enterprises and so-called political democracy, then at any cost—*poverty delenda est.*"

In the winter of 1932–33, the American Association of Social Workers issued a statement of "Economic Objectives for Social Work," prepared by a committee of which Harry L. Lurie, of the Bureau of Jewish Social Research, was chairman. It was summarized at the 1933 Conference by Helen Crosby, of the Metropolitan Life Insurance Company. It contained the mature thought of the members of the professional association, and grew out of social workers' contact with the despair and suffering of the victims of the great depression. There was nothing philosophical or even scientific about "Economic Objectives of Social Work." It was a direct and to-the-point platform for certain reforms.

The report demanded that the "social order . . . provide a minimum standard of living for all . . . a comprehensive plan of social and economic organization"; and that these objectives can only be obtained by "more than a number of scattered legislative victories."

Specifically, it proposed:

1. Labor standards should be maintained through creation of labor boards and the abolition of child labor.

2. Relief should be adequate, with provision for relief, when necessary, for transients; methods of self-help should be encouraged.

3. There should be a program of public works, so planned as to meet the shock of periods of unemployment.

4. So far as possible, social insurance on a national scale should be substituted for assistance as a means of meeting sickness, old age, and unemployment.

5. Taxation should fall on unearned increments on land, on income and inheritance, and be lifted from consumers.

This is the most comprehensive program yet produced by social workers, though it could probably be agreed upon by such a widely diverse group only at a time when severe unemployment and attendant suffering swept aside more cautious counsels.

Under the bright hope of the early days of Franklin D. Roosevelt's Administration, Katherine F. Lenroot, chief of the Children's Bureau, chose as the title of her presidential address "Social Work and the Social Order" (1935). "The great task of the twentieth century is the reconciliation of individual freedom and social security," she declared. After discussing the evolution of the objectives of social work, Katherine Lenroot stated that "government may prove to be the only [agent] having the range and power necessary for dealing with the most complicated and difficult situations. A basic problem, therefore, is that of making government an effective agency of social control." So again we come, in the words of one of the most experienced workers in the public social services, to that phrase which promises to be the battle cry of future workers in the interest of the common man—"economic planning."

The disparity between wages and the minimum family budget was pointed out by many speakers. In his carefully prepared paper of 1930, Wesley C. Mitchell reached the conclusion that the average wage falls between $500 and $700 short of supporting a family of four; and that such a family can only receive an income adequate to support a minimum standard if it includes more than one wage earner. Dr. Paul H.

Douglas, professor of economics at the University of Chicago, suggested the "family wage" (1926), and gave a logical analysis of its advantages. He also suggested, as an alternative, a state allowance to families based on number of children. He did not seem to favor such a plan, but it has been adopted by England, Canada, New Zealand, and most of Australia, whereas the "family wage" has dropped out of existence to all intents and purposes. In Canada, allowances for children vary from five dollars a month for a child under one year of age to eight dollars a month for a thirteen-year-old child, for families whose income is $1,200 a year or less, with benefits on a sliding scale for families whose income is between $1,200 and $3,000 a year. This is, of course, a form of the bonus for children, adopted in France at the close of the last century to check the falling birth rate. Probably the first advocates of mothers' pensions in this country copied the French plan. The amount granted to each family in England and the British Commonwealth, in the current allowances, is not great, but for the low-income earners it does compensate to some extent for the economic handicap assumed by marriage and the birth of children.

At one time, a good deal of attention was paid to minimum wage boards, no less than five papers on the subject being presented between 1933 and 1939. However, with the great increase in strength, and the more sound legal basis that organized labor has enjoyed since the series of labor acts were passed during the Roosevelt Administration, greater dependence for securing adequate wages is placed on the process of collective bargaining than on decisions of *ad hoc* minimum wage bodies.

Roger N. Baldwin, of the American Civil Liberties Union, made a prophetic statement in 1924, to the effect that labor is a new force in industry, and is coming into a larger share of control of the economic forces of the country with every year. Therefore, it would be well for social workers to strengthen their relationship with "the producing classes." He even went so far as to suggest "building up a political class party of the producers, committed to such economic reforms as . . . public control of natural resources and public utilities, public control of money and credit, preservation of civil rights, and reform of the judiciary."

This is not a matter on which one can be dogmatic, but the unwillingness or inability of "the producers," as well as social workers and liberals, to form a political party leaves any gains achieved at one time subject to the mercy of the control of the political party in power.

The Conference discussions on housing illustrate how far removed from the phase of propaganda social work had moved since its preoccupation with "technique." While every country in Western Europe was eliminating its slums and erecting subsidized or publicly owned housing for their citizens of low income, there was only one Conference paper from 1928 to 1946 which even touched the subject in a realistic manner. Yet the members attending the Conference saw at first hand the vilest housing in the industrialized world; and they knew what it did to the health and morale of its dwellers.

An architect, Henry Wright, of New York City, said in 1928 that low-cost housing was a myth, due in part to the high cost of the real estate business, and in part to the demands of tenants.

In 1933 William W. Biddle, of the School of Applied Social Sciences at Western Reserve University, cited a statement issued by the President's Commission on Low Cost Housing, to the effect that housing for the lower income groups "could only be erected by use of public subsidies." Biddle's report went on to say that private contractors will actually do the work for the housing for one third of the population, but "the profit motive . . . cannot begin to solve the problem of providing adequate shelter for the low income families of our nation."

At the Conference in 1937, B. Charney Vladeck, of the *Jewish Forward* and of the New York City Housing Authority, made a careful analysis of the situation in New York City as shown by the investigation of its Housing Authority. He reviewed some of the efforts at tenement house reform, which he felt were misdirected; discussed, all too briefly, the experience of Germany and England with housing; and asserted that the only remedy is public housing, with the government guaranteeing the investment. Vladeck stated that the highest rate of interest paid by any city in England for its investment in housing was 3.1 percent and that over a billion dollars of private capital was so invested.

"One of the troubles of the housing problem is not that some of our people are so poor, but that some of our rich people are so ignorant," in not appreciating that under public guarantee, a long stride can be taken in solving the housing situation for the low-income group, by promoting such sound projects. "The greatest menace to any housing program today is the owner of slum property." Vladeck did not say how this "menace" is to be met. He did state, however, that 30,000 owners of tenement houses in New York City had flatly refused to comply with the requirements of the Multiple Dwelling Law, which went into effect in January, 1936.

All the other papers on housing delivered at the Conference meetings dealt with the benefits of new housing, or with some of the problems associated with it. In 1936 Mary Lumsden, of the New York Housing Authority, spoke of its beneficial effect on health. In 1939 John Ihlder, of the Alley Dwelling Authority of Washington, D.C., discussed the many problems of public housing and said that public assistance authorities must be willing to pay the current rent charges for their clients in public housing. Stanley M. Isaacs, president of the Borough of

Manhattan, in the same year described the stormy experience of getting through the New York Legislature a bill authorizing the state to borrow up to three million dollars and also to empower municipalities to borrow for the purpose of erecting low-cost housing.

Jean Coman, of the United States Housing Authority, commented in 1941 upon social problems created by the sudden coming together of people in a new housing project, and the ways in which such difficulties were met.

In addition, the Conference created a special program committee on social aspects of housing, in 1940, which discussed such problems as racial policy; neighborhood coöperation; and the relation between welfare and housing officials.

Somewhat aside from the matter of housing itself, Sidney Maslen, head of the Housing Committee of the Community Service Society of New York City, in 1944 analyzed the functioning of a private agency in such a project as public housing.

The coming of public housing, creating new communities of people who have never before associated with each other, puts forward issues with which social work is admirably equipped to deal. It is, therefore, quite fitting that when such housing appears, social workers be used to meet the challenges presented by these new and artificial communities; and that they consult each other on their successes and failures. Still, it is surprising that a Conference which represents the grand strategy of social welfare should give such scant place on its programs to the way in which to secure suitable housing for families known so well to its members.

In 1940 John Fitch, of the New York School of Social Work, who has so stanchly insisted that social action is an integral part of social work, dealt with "The Nature of Social Action." In reviewing the programs of the Conference section on housing since its inception in 1934, he pointed out that of the sixty-odd papers presented on these programs ". . . [only] six of them have, to some degree, dealt with method and technique in social action." They have been, for the most part, "excellent . . . discussions of social problems," but have "done little to define or outline the field."

He defined social action as "limited to legally permissible methods in the direction of legal objectives." He saw three types of activity in the field of social action: the activity of a group to improve its own conditions—such as labor unions; propaganda to influence public opinion; and governmental action to secure new laws or to improve public administration.

Fitch would not rule out the discussions of situations calling for remedy. He quoted approvingly from a personal letter, "social work . . . is the expression of an intangible force, evolutionary in character, engendered by the entire social body in its struggle to improve the individual and total lot of its members." As a part of this evolutionary force, shared by far many more than social workers, Fitch's position is that the role of the social worker in social action is that of a professional specialist in how to bring about a desirable change. This lines up social action with the three other acknowledged methods of social work: community organization, social group work, and social casework, to which welfare administration would be added by others, especially in the field of public welfare.

36 · THE NATIONAL CONFERENCE
OF SOCIAL WORK

*P*ORTER R. LEE used to say that social workers learn through their ears rather than through their eyes, thereby classifying social workers with persons of action rather than of reflection. The United States is peculiarly a nation of conferences. They compensate for the great distances that separate workers in the same field. They also neutralize the division into states which might have Balkanized this country if the local provincialism inherent in such a political structure had developed unchecked. Coming into existence almost at the very time that charity was emerging from an undifferentiated practice of good will to a specialized function of the state and of society, the Conference furnished a means whereby the developing practice took on a national character.

As an activity of the American Social Science Association, the Conference was simply a Conference of Charities; on attaining its independence it named itself "Conference on Charities and Correction." In 1882 it took the name "National Conference of Charities and Corrections," but dropped the plural in the last word of its title in 1884. So it remained until 1917, when, in line with the newer vocabulary then being adopted, the name was changed to "National Conference of Social Work." So it has remained to the present and will remain until a new fashion in words declares the title outmoded.

The control of the Conference in its early years was in the hands of members and executives of state boards of charities.

For twenty-one years all presidents of the Conference were elected from that group. When the break was made in 1895, it was almost total. From 1896 to 1916, six presidents were elected from state boards, and then none until 1945, when an executive of a state board again filled the office. The political significance of the state board is shown by the election of three governors of states as early presidents of the Conference: John J. Bagley, of Michigan, in 1875; Samuel J. Tilden, of New York, in 1876; and Richard M. Bishop, of Ohio, in 1878.

Passing to the general subject of presidents of the Conference, it had an Episcopal bishop in 1889, the Right Rev. George D. Gillespie, of Michigan, who was also president of the state board; two Protestant ministers, the Rev. Oscar C. McCulloch, of Indianapolis, in 1891, and the Rev. Myron W. Reed, of Denver, in 1892, both members of their state boards; two Monsignors of the Catholic Church, the Right Rev. Francis H. Gavisk, of the Indiana State Board in 1916, and in 1936 the Right Rev. Robert F. Keegan, of the Catholic Charities of New York City; one Federal district judge, Julian W. Mack, of Washington, D.C., in 1912; and three physicians, Dr. Miriam Van Waters, of Los Angeles, in 1930, Dr. Richard C. Cabot, of Boston, in 1931, and Dr. Ellen C. Potter, of Trenton, New Jersey, in 1945.

No woman was elected to the office of president of the Conference until 1910, when that honor was awarded to Jane Addams. At intervals of about five years thereafter, to 1930, five other women were chosen to that position: Mrs. Mary Wilcox Glenn, of New York, in 1915; Julia C. Lathrop, in 1919; Grace Abbott, in 1924; Gertrude Vaile, in 1926; and Dr. Miriam Van Waters, in 1930. Seven of the thirteen presidents between 1935 and 1947 have been women, affording a striking recognition of the importance of the part women are playing in the leadership of social work.

Two persons have twice filled the office of president: John
V. L. Pruyn, as president of the New York State Board, acted
as host to the first meeting in New York in 1874, and was
elected to preside. He was elected president in 1877, the only
person not a governor of a state who was elected to that office
during the Conference's first five years. Homer Folks was
elected first in 1911, and then again elected to preside at the
fiftieth meeting of the Conference in 1923, an honor conferred
in recognition of his long and outstanding contribution to the
field of the social services.

Geographically, presidents have been elected predominantly
from states in the North Atlantic and the upper Mississippi
Valley regions, with New York State accounting for twenty-
seven, or more than a third of the whole number. The South
has had one representative; and from west of the Mississippi
have come five. The concentration of national associations in
New York City accounts in part for the outstanding record of
New York, with the District of Columbia in recent years
threatening to become a serious competitor because of the new
value placed on public welfare and upon national concern for
its promotion and standards since the Administration of Franklin D. Roosevelt.

Presidents of the Conference have been a healthy lot. Only
two died within a year after the end of their service: Albert G.
Byers, of Ohio, and Oscar C. McCulloch, of Indiana. J. Prentice Murphy was elected to serve the Conference of 1937, but
he died before its sessions were held. The second World War,
indirectly, claimed one past president, William Hodson, who
was killed in an airplane disaster as he was flying to Africa in
1941, the first American representative of the United Nations
Relief and Rehabilitation Administration.

Perhaps a more reasonable measure of the representative
character of the Conference is the geographical distribution of

chairmen of committees in charge of programs. From the first session in 1874, the Conference has been organized by committees. From 1874 to 1946 there have been 609 chairmen appointed (not eliminating duplicates). Five hundred and sixty chairmen came from thirteen states, and 49 chairmen from sixteen states, leaving twenty-one states unrepresented.[1]

Breaking down the totals, it is shown that while New York still leads in number of chairmanships (164), the percentage is 26, rather than the 37 percent in the case of Conference presidents. The other states in order are: Illinois (72); Ohio (60); Massachusetts (56); District of Columbia (38); Pennsylvania (33); Minnesota (32); Indiana (23); Michigan (22); New Jersey (17); Missouri (15); and Maryland and Wisconsin (14 each). This analysis indicates that the concentration occurred largely in the older centers of professional social work, that is, in the Atlantic states north of the Potomac and in the North Central States.

During the three periods into which this history of the Conference is divided, the relative position of these thirteen states remained relatively constant, except that the District of Columbia moved up to its present fifth place from the eighth place, at the close of the second period (1898–1924), thereby exhibiting further evidence of the increasing interest in social work shown by the National Administration in the last two decades.

The distribution of committee chairmen shows that they were assigned from nine North Atlantic states, three South Atlantic states, six North Mississippi plains states, two South Mississippi plains states, and eight states west of the Mississippi, and one from Canada.

Women were given earlier recognition as chairmen of committees in charge of programs than as president. In 1886 Mrs.

[1] The District of Columbia, for this purpose, is counted as a state.

Virginia T. Smith, of the State Board of Connecticut, was appointed chairman of the Committee on Preventive Work with
Children, of which William P. Letchworth had been chairman
the previous year; and, in the same year, Anna Hollowell, of
the board of the Philadelphia Society for Organizing Charity,
was appointed chairman of the Committee on Kindergartens.
During the first period (1874–98), women were assigned ten
chairmanships, or about 8 percent of the total; in the second
period (1899–1923), thirty-two chairmanships, or about 15
percent of the total; and in the third period (1924–46), seventy-
eight chairmanships, or 41 percent of the total. In this way
evidence was further given of the increased significance of
women's participation in an advancing profession. It is almost
impossible to capture the social customs of an earlier age, and it
doubtless seems strange to the present generation that many
early leaders, both professional and lay, were opposed to granting suffrage to women; and that full political rights were
granted to women only as recently as 1919. Such customs with
regard to "the place of women" should be taken into account in
evaluating the status women have acquired in the Conference,
and in the social services generally. So far, the profession of
social work is one of the very few in which there is a minimum
of handicap imposed on its women members by reason of a
vocational tradition which would separate tasks into "women's
work" and "men's work."

In choice of meeting place for the Conference, thirty-nine
cities have been selected since 1874, with a better geographical
distribution than shown in the election of presidents or the appointment of committee chairmen. Twelve cities in North
Atlantic states have been chosen, two in South Atlantic states,
ten in the North Mississippi area, four in the South Mississippi,
nine west of the Mississippi, and two in Canada. Two cities,
Buffalo and Cleveland, have been its host four times; and San

Francisco, Atlantic City, Detroit, and Indianapolis have acted as hosts three times. Otherwise, no city has been visited more than twice.

From its beginnings, the policy of the Conference has been to visit as widely scattered cities as possible, but during the third period, the Conference grew to a size beyond the capacity of many cities to handle. By 1936 a special committee was appointed to consider the problem of selecting the Conference city with reference to its capacity to accommodate the meetings, and also to work out some formula whereby each part of the country would have the meeting in its area once in five years. The committee reported in 1938, and, in so far as the disturbed condition of the country made it possible, the choice of meeting place has been governed since then by available meeting places in the area which the Conference is due to visit.

As long as the Conference was primarily an organization of state boards, its programs were arranged by special committees on organization appointed each year by the president. In 1895, when Robert Treat Paine was president, the first reference was made to a plan whereby the president regularly appointed a standing committee to make the needed preparations for the program of the following conference. Such a plan, with minor modifications, continued until 1934, when the By Laws made special provision for a Program Committee, having some continuity, not only to have general charge of the very complicated task of planning the program of the Conference itself, but also to make the general pattern for the many other conferences meeting with the National Conference of Social Work.

During its first fifty sessions, the programs of the Conference were apparently selected in response to the interests of the Committee on Organization or the Program Committee and followed no general outline. Certain subjects, under different names, were carried year after year, such as "Children," "Prisons and Prisoners," "Charity Organization" (after its first appearance in 1880); "Insanity and Feeblemindedness" became "Mental Hygiene" after 1914 or 1915. Of the fifty-odd subjects that can be classified, less than a half a dozen were represented in as many as twenty-five Conference programs during that half century.

In 1924 the Conference adopted nine topics to be followed each year, and added two more in 1925 and one in 1926. These twelve sections, as they were then called, continued unchanged and with no additions through 1934, when the Conference made the radical resolution to limit itself to four permanent topics, or sections: "Social Case Work," "Social Group Work," "Social Action," and "Community Organization." At the same time, the Program Committee was authorized to add special committees for any one Conference as seemed desirable. In the eleven Conferences during which this regulation applied, twenty-two special committees were created for temporary periods. One of them, however, Public Welfare Administration, was admitted to the big four in 1939.

The limitation to four—or five—regular program committees proved too much of a Procrustean bed for the widely sprawling interests of the Conference, so, beginning with 1946, the Conference reverted to twelve committees. The new organization includes, substantially, the previous five, four taken from the twelve used in the decade 1924–34, and three that represent either new interests in current social practice or the revival of old ones.

In this review of the Conference and its times no mention is made of one of the most striking developments of twentieth-century philanthropy, the philanthropic foundation. It is omitted, partly because it finds only faint reflection in the *Pro-*

ceedings, but also because the Russell Sage Foundation has published an excellent account of its origins and development.[2] As for the Russell Sage Foundation itself, which has been at once the godfather and the father confessor to almost every interest in social work during the nearly forty years of its existence, John M. Glenn, its first general director, is preparing a history, making further reference unnecessary.

No discussion on alcohol is included, in spite of the important position its control occupied in the life and legislation of the whole period under review. It is omitted because, except for a few later papers by physicians and psychiatrists, the attitude of speakers at the Conference was moralistic and not scientific. This attitude persisted in spite of the extensive experimentation and research in the subject of alcohol conducted during this period. The Committee of Fifty to Investigate the Liquor Problem, under the late Henry W. Farnum, of Yale University, published significant findings during the period between 1898 and 1903 which had no echo in the Conference, although three Conference speakers made investigations for the Committee and published their results: John Koren, of Boston, on the *Economic Aspects of the Liquor Problem* (1899); Frederick H. Wines and John Koren collaborated on *The Liquor Problem in Its Legislative Aspects* (1898); and Raymond Calkins wrote *Substitutes for the Saloon* (1901). The hysteria on the matter of inebriety was too strong for the findings of these dispassionate researches to be heard at the Conference. Calkins read a paper at the Conference in 1919, in which he practically repudiated his book. Wines, whose investigations among states having prohibition laws predicted the dismal failure of national prohibition, prudently kept silence on the matter in all his many utterances before the Conference; and John Koren's life was

[2] Shelby M. Harrison and Frank E. Andrews, *American Foundations for Social Welfare* (New York: Russell Sage Foundation, 1946).

eventually shortened by the ostracism he met on account of his opposition to prohibition and his pacifist attitude in the first World War.

The Committee of Fifty attempted to stem the tide of hysteria when it published *Physiological Aspects of Liquor,* in 1903, by buttressing the work with the names of eminent physicians and pathologists, such as John S. Billings, of Johns Hopkins University; Harry P. Bowditch, Dean of the Harvard Medical School; Russell H. Chittenden, of Yale University; and William H. Welch, of Johns Hopkins University, who certified the findings of its author, Wilbur O. Atwater, of Wesleyan University. The book detailed the results of experiments on the effect of alcohol on animals, and could have been used effectively to promote the temperate use of alcohol, and even abstinence from its use. Nevertheless, because it demonstrated that alcohol is a food and has certain limited beneficial physiological functions, its findings were ignored, not only by the Conference, but by the great majority of men of good will. Now, after the disastrous experiment in a strong-arm method of control of the use of alcohol, the whole field has to be worked over anew, with the handicap of previous failure.

The Conference—and the social workers whom it represents—contributed nothing to a careful understanding of the physiological or the social function of alcohol. Moreover, the contemporary movement of Alcoholics Anonymous came into existence quite spontaneously from the victims of alcohol themselves, although the form of treatment used by that organization is a perfect example of democratically initiated and maintained social group work.

The National Conference of Social Work can fittingly be called the mother of conferences in the field of social welfare. As early as 1880, the *Proceedings* noted the affiliated meeting of the National Association for the Prevention of Insanity and the

Protection of the Insane. By 1908 the number of conferences meeting with the National Conference reached the point where formal recognition of their meetings, and some sort of integration with the parent organization, seemed necessary. By 1911 a new By Law was adopted, authorizing the coördination of the programs of affiliated conferences with the programs of the committees of the National Conference, and in 1925 specific methods of coördination were adopted, whereby each conference or association meeting at the time and place of the National Conference was required to become an institutional member of the parent body and have its program printed with that of the Conference. Later on, each one of the kindred group, as they were called, had a representative on the Program Committee, so that for the purpose of scheduling, all conferences were treated as one. Forty-five such kindred conferences were held at the time of the Buffalo meeting in 1946.

State conferences, in type very much like the National Conference, had been organized in forty-six states by 1946, the earliest one being formed in Wisconsin in 1881.³ The National Conference offers special advisory services to the state conferences, including, among other things, an annual meeting of secretaries of state conferences to exchange ideas and to promote a general increase of efficiency in the executive personnel of the local bodies.

International conferences on various aspects of charities and correction, such as the International Prison Congress and the International Congress of Charities, had been held before the National Conference was organized, and even simultaneously, as in Chicago in 1893, but quite independently. Dr. René Sand, secretary general of the League of Red Cross Societies, after attendance upon the fiftieth meeting of the Conference in 1923, received the inspiration which resulted in the establishment of

³ *Social Work Year Book, 1947* (New York: Russell Sage Foundation, 1947).

the International Conference of Social Work. The International Conference has held three meetings so far: in Paris in 1928; in Frankfort-on-the-Main, Germany, in 1932; and in London in 1936. The second World War prevented subsequent meetings, but it is planned to resume the International Conference in 1948, in connection with the Seventy-fifth meeting of the National Conference. In the promotion and guidance of the International Conference, the National Conference has played an important part, serving as the American committee for the international body.

During its nearly three quarters of a century, the Conference has had two unusually gifted general secretaries: Alexander Johnson (1905–13) and Howard R. Knight (1926–47). Alexander Johnson had, to a supreme degree, a genius for friendship. Conference members would stay to the close of the long general sessions just in order to enjoy his genial humor as he gave the announcements. He found the Conference an aggregation of programs and people; he left it a living organization.

Howard R. Knight, coming to the Conference after an outstanding record with the Ohio State Conference, found in the rapidly growing interest and size of the national body a challenge to his unusual capacity for organization and leadership. Never assuming responsibility for the duties of the elected officers or committees, he provided the setting within which they can function. To a large extent, the framework and the smoothness of operation of the unwieldy thing the Conference has become are the work of Howard R. Knight.

In the early years, secretarial and editorial work were performed as additional duties by members of the Conference. Franklin B. Sanborn carried most of the responsibility for them for ten years. Then Hastings H. Hart took up the task until 1901, when Joseph P. Byers, of the Ohio State Board of Charities, added it to his regular duties until Alexander Johnson took over as general secretary of the Conference in 1905. In addition, for "about a quarter of a century" before 1905, Isabel C. Barrows was the official reporter and editor of the *Proceedings;* from 1913 to 1933, Mrs. Bertha Freeman Hooper served in the same capacity. William T. Cross, who had served a successful apprenticeship as secretary of the Missouri State Conference, succeeded Alexander Johnson in 1914, and was in turn followed by William H. Parker, who served to 1925.

If "an institution is the lengthened shadow of one man," the Conference through its decades of discussions has created a philosophy and a way of life that would have warmed the heart of that "subversive thinker" Franklin B. Sanborn; for the choice men and women who have contributed to its vitality have established a heritage of liberal democracy of which America may well be proud.

Fourth Period · 1946-1956

By LOUIS TOWLEY

THE RICHES of the Proceedings of the National Conference of Social Work cannot be reflected in a short discussion. They are interwoven in a context too long for quotation or for adequate summary. Significant material that cries for inclusion would bulk to ten times the allowed length of this appendage to Frank Bruno's work. The Conference is an extraordinarily valuable body; and social work, dedicated, habitually conscientious, courageous in its effort to advance the cause of Man, is a profession that deserves well of the society it serves. Clearly, this supplement quite fails to do justice to these ten sobering years.

The appraisal here undertaken is meant to convey some of the impact the *Proceedings* had on one reader. Therefore, if this appraisal or profile has any virtues, they derive from the *Proceedings* and the writers therein. The defects, however, are mine, since they derive from my bias or lack of understanding.

The main source material for this supplement has been the *Official Proceedings* of the Annual Meeting (from 1954, the Annual Forum). A reference to *Proceedings*, followed by a date, is to one of these volumes, the title of which has been *The Social Welfare Forum* since 1949. In 1949 the Conference decided to publish additional volumes of selected papers in specialized subject areas. Thus in 1949 and 1950, one additional volume (*Social Work in the Current Scene*) supplemented the more general *Proceedings;* since 1951, but not in 1953, there has been a volume of casework papers and one on group work and community organization; and there have been volumes of papers on subjects of special interest in recent years: in 1952, on the aging; in 1953, on Social Security; in 1954, on administration, supervision, and consultation; and in 1955, on minority groups.

I owe much to the critical counsel of Benjamin E. Youngdahl and the late W. W. Burke, who read the manuscript, and to Mrs. Dorothy M. Swart, for her invaluable editing.

LOUIS TOWLEY

Washington University, St. Louis
February, 1957

37 · A NOTE ON THE CONFERENCE ITSELF

*T*HE *NATIONAL CONFERENCE OF SOCIAL WORK* (NCSW) is too manifold and many-sided to be briefly or easily described. It even changes its own name from time to time, not because it does not know its own mind but to recognize a change in the concept of the broad field whose spokesman it is. The NCSW is not what is called an "action" group, though it is made up of some of the most active community servants.

As one of the hundreds who every year attend the Annual Forum for the first time recently said, "Nothing seems to happen, nothing goes on, except the most exciting, rarest thing of all: ideas take shape, are presented, strike fire, and get turned into resolve to help bring the ideas alive." "Annual Forum" is a fitting name for the Annual Meeting (as it was called before 1954) that gathers in cities carefully selected according to a pattern devised to bring the sessions periodically to different parts of the country. The Conference is essentially the continuing machinery that makes possible this yearly discussion of questions of public or professional interest in the field of social welfare. It is both a marshaling-yard and a take-off point for ideas presented in a full week's program of three hundred or more papers, of which only a few can be included in the yearly *Proceedings*.

The choice of topics and of the speakers to present or discuss them is a function of the Program Committee, a widely representative group which includes the chairmen of the section and other committees and is elected by the membership. The membership is further heard: suggestions on program are yearly solicited from a liberal sample of members; and what the Conference calls "attendees" are asked to evaluate the Annual Forum in a questionnaire whose analysis gives useful guidance to the program-makers.

There is significance in the fact that an organization weighted toward one profession and its interests hears regularly from many members of other professions, and from people who refer to themselves as volunteers. The Annual Forum gains much vitality from these contributions and from the participation, as members, of non-social workers. The Lindeman Lectures given by eminent social scientists (a memorial to Edward C. Lindeman, renowned social work philosopher) have promoted more effective collaboration between social work and the social sciences.

In the past thirty years, the Conference has had only two General Secretaries. Howard R. Knight died of a heart attack October 7, 1947, in his twenty-second year of service as General Secretary of the Conference. In his building for the organization "he knew that what we achieve in terms of broader regard for human benefits, we achieve only by growth in human understanding and good will." [1]

Jane Chandler, Knight's assistant, carried the administration responsibility as acting Executive Secretary through the 1948 Annual Meeting and until September of that year when the vacant post of General Secretary was filled by appointment of Joe R. Hoffer. In the years since, the Conference board and membership have achieved a considerable reorganization that

[1] Dorothy C. Kahn, "Howard R. Knight and the International Conference of Social Work" (1948), p. 15.

modified and integrated the structure of both administration and program.

The suitability of its name has periodically concerned the Conference, not because its mind is changeable but because of an implicit need to have its name reflect the current concept of the whole field within its purview. The influence of the growing profession of social work caused the first change, in 1917, when the National Conference of Charities and Correction became the National Conference of Social Work. In 1956, on vote of the members, it became the National Conference on Social Welfare. The reasons in favor of the change had an incidental public relations aspect, but mainly they reflected the wide range of interests of the Conference, the wide membership among non-social workers, and—perhaps most significant —recognition that social welfare is greater than social work. A wishful interpretation of the change would be that social work was sufficiently secure to forego identification by name with matters that have become the warm concern of all citizens. It is somehow a tribute to social work that the new name rings true.

38 · THE BROAD FUNCTION AND SOME OF ITS CONCERNS

*T*HE NATIONAL CONFERENCE met a yearly test as a steward of its old legacy. This legacy is not unlike the legacy of an impoverished family of long lineage; it consists mostly of duties, obligations, responsibilities, a tradition of pulling its weight. These obligations, or at least the performance of them, must be the reality that gives substance to a philosophy and permits the social worker to be one professional person who is comfortable and unself-conscious in using the word "philosophy" with personal knowledge of how it translates into action.

SOCIAL POLICY

Almost any social worker—and some non-social workers—who presents papers at an Annual Forum articulates this philosophy. A succinct statement, an approach to illustrate the need to put the matter into "simple words for the public" ("for the social worker," would have been equally justified), was incorporated into his presidential address by Leonard W. Mayo at the 75th Anniversary Meeting in 1948:

Prominent in any expression of our philosophy and purpose must be a simple declaration of our articles of faith set forth in language of unmistakable clarity: our concern for people; our respect for the dignity, integrity, and rights of individuals; our abhorrence of injustice as one of the greatest foes of freedom; our responsibility to speak and act with respect to the causes as well as the results of social maladjustment; and our major concern, not only for prevention, restoration, and rehabilitation, but for helping to create relationships, homes, neighborhoods, and nations in which human beings may live out their lives and develop their full potentialities as free people. Let all this be positive rather than negative in approach, add the scientific bases of our sources of knowledge and methods, and we shall in due course develop a statement of philosophy around which we can rally, that scientists can respect, and the public can understand.[1]

As Mayo made explicit, *every* social worker needs to work at definition of his professional philosophy. This often repeated demand reflects the nonregimented, nonstatic nature of the profession, whose literature is liberally, almost annually, highlighted with articles and papers titled "New Horizons for Social Work," "The Future of Social Work," "A Reevaluation of Professional Goals," "The Challenge of Change." Social work gives every appearance of questioning what it does and looking for something different to do. So it does, but this is less self-doubt than a wish to improve what it does, a determination not to waste limited personnel and energy on less urgent tasks, an eager willingness to take on a new, harder job, an anxiety that no job it can do be left undone. The breadth of that job is truly social, holding to declared values. Benjamin E. Youngdahl stated their main tenor in 1952:

We have had a consistent interest in society as a whole and we have refused to limit our interests even to our own national boundaries. We believe that the form of society that gives the greatest effective hope and promise for happiness and abundant lives is the one that will survive. We have complete faith in the democratic process and we should like to apply it to all aspects of living.[2]

One of the continuing functions of social work, repeatedly frustrating, eventually rewarding, is that of goad and prodder

[1] Leonard W. Mayo, "Basic Issues in Social Work" (1948), p. 24.
[2] Benjamin E. Youngdahl, "What We Believe" (1952), p. 45.

of society, which likes the comfort of current status however onerous the status might be to the forgotten few. Social work in this function has been called the "conscience of the community." The phrase has a stern-daughter-of-the-voice-of-God tone to it, as of society's superego; but such an attitude is prevented by the profession's saving graces: its understanding, its steady grasp of reality and the possible, its sympathy and compassion, and above all its ethics. Social work is a profession in a society, is authorized and sponsored by the society, and it shares responsibility. It has the heart-warming habit of analyzing and correcting itself first, and it is never afraid of a new cluster of choices so long as the democratic process makes the choices, or "as long as the mechanism of review of their constitutionality is still available, as long as there is the power of public opinion to affect action," to use Leon Henderson's words (1947).

Social work papers routinely base social policy analysis or proposals on professional experience and principles. As brief a summary of such a yardstick as could be phrased was the close of Arthur J. Altmeyer's paper in 1948:

Social workers must continue to emphasize and re-emphasize that success or failure of all political and economic institutions, whether local, national, or international, must be measured by their effect upon the well-being of human beings.[3]

As Arlien Johnson said in 1947, quoting Whitehead: "Successful organisms modify their environment. Those organisms are successful which modify their environment so as to assist each other." She saw social work bridging the gap between observed daily facts and social theory, using the methods of scientific thinking within integrity of practice.

This well-being is repeatedly affirmed by social workers in

[3] Arthur J. Altmeyer, "Social Work and Broad Social and Economic Measures" (1948), p. 112.

simple statements of the fact that "there are no substitutes for jobs, good health, decent housing, adequate education, and equal opportunities and protection for all people under the law." This affirmation is documented in the case records of every agency in the country. In 1947 Donald Howard set forth three assumptions as guides in helping to maintain optimum living standards:

1. People, in order to retain personally satisfying and socially useful lives, not only require a given quantity of goods and services but need also to live in a socially constituted milieu.

2. People should have the opportunity with reasonable effort and without harm to themselves or others to attain the optimum standard of living which . . . all people in this country may enjoy.

3. People must be assured that this optimum standard of living is continuously available.

To have several goals or guidelines is one thing; to be specific is another. But social work rarely shirks this task. Out of the wealth of its clinical experience and its gradually increasing use of research methods in analyzing the experience, the profession continued to expand its area of interest and put forth "challenges" with energy and insight. The profession's modern function, thought Altmeyer, was marshaling communities to meet needs; and he attributed a special value in this respect to social work because it is "essentially an integrating profession." The function is thus not coordinate with education and health, if only because social work must take advantage of resources in all fields. Social workers do not sufficiently recognize that this integrating character can be of incalculable value in a society whose sciences, professions, and specializations tend to be insular. This attribute catches the interest of some observers, usually from without the profession. In 1956 Agnes E. Meyer considered social work as "strategically situated . . .

to point the way toward new institutions and a new, more orderly society in which a free, stable, and efficacious individuality can come into being." The implication is that social work might become the wanted "science of society."

Because of a strong influence touching the Conference in the nineteenth century, the Annual Meeting rarely lost sight of the principle (put forward by Arnold Toynbee in England and by Simon N. Patten at the University of Pennsylvania) that the economic system will flourish only if labor gets a wage sufficient to purchase what it produces. During the last generation this idea has been widely recognized throughout society, but it still appears and reappears in the *Proceedings*. The Rev. George G. Higgins (1948), rephrasing the principle, cited Bureau of Labor Statistics for March, 1946, to show that when the city worker's family budget ranged from $2,573 to $2,985 in 34 cities, almost a third of all American families (including farm families) had a total money income of less than $2,000. This common deficit in the economy is a steady concern of the Annual Forum, as is the failure of real income to rise equally with inflation; and it was welcome news to discover that increases in income in the years 1935–46 were "greatest for the lower 40 percent of the income scale"—68 percent—and 59 percent for those in the next two tenths of the income scale. It is inescapable that this redressed distribution of income took place during an unparalleled rise in gross national product.

The matter was of interest in at least two ways: the more adequate the wage, the less likely the family would be to fall afoul of difficulties that poverty invites; and the better the economic health of the nation, the more adequately will the necessary social services do their vital work—but only if the services get a needed share of the increased wealth.

Welfare in our economy.—The notion that welfare needs are increasingly a Federal cost, with resultant rise in the Federal tax burden, is true absolutely but not relatively. In the mid-thirties "Federal contributions accounted for $3.16 billion of $7.77 billion of welfare outlays, or 40 percent; but in 1950–51, the $9.6 billion provided was still but 40 percent; and excluding contributory insurance, but 37 percent." Seymour E. Harris, who made this observation (*Proceedings*, 1953), went on to say that in the same period the Federal share of total taxes rose from 38 percent to 70 percent. He suggested that "the Federal Government has in fact thrust the burden of welfare outlays primarily on the state and local governments." [4]

The proportion of the increased wealth devoted to welfare purposes was examined by Eveline M. Burns in 1949. She found that for the $1,250 of goods and services (share of net national product for domestic consumption) available per capita, about $50 went for social welfare goods and services. "The question is not one of affording, but of choice," Miss Burns believed; and choice still remains open, not only to cut down these expenditures, but to increase them, since there is still leeway. But with the trend of national income upward, the problem is "how to capture some of this new wealth for the social services," and to persuade the citizenry that social welfare "be given a high-priority claim on the instruments of production."

In any event, the public will not demand a social welfare service until that public is satisfied the service is worth the cost. Proving this fact has been social work's undone job, the failure that sympathetic businessmen have difficulty understanding.

Miss Burns was quite sure that financing would never be as adequate as social work wished, but she urged that the profes-

[4] It should be pointed out that Harris included education as one of the programs (Federal contribution only 2 percent); but to offset most of this, he included veterans' benefits also (Federal contribution 98 percent).

sion look to its administration of the funds in order to make performance as efficient as possible. She questioned such sacrosanct characteristics as lengthy records, supervision of the trained professional worker, committee and conference time, among other characteristics of social work. With the house in order, the profession might, with renewed confidence, urge the spending of what is needed to maintain social well-being.

But progress could not wait on such professional change. Miss Burns was one of the first to point out (*Proceedings*, 1951) that the far-reaching 1950 amendments to the Social Security Act "represent a major shift away from the principles of private, commercial insurance toward those of social insurance" by (1) liberalizing eligibility; (2) changing the benefit formula, to increase the yield to the insured; (3) increasing benefits to then-present beneficiaries; and (4) eliminating the one percent increment for years of coverage. The eligibility and benefits of workers who could not gain fully insured status with forty quarters of covered employment were considerably liberalized. Every change away from basing eligibility on the standard period of covered employment, every step away from basing the value of the benefit on the amounts contributed, was recognition of the social function of the insurance.

Unemployment insurance, she thought, was a relatively inefficient instrument for meeting human needs because of its way of financing: the tax is on employers only; experience rating results in rebates; and formulas are poorly adapted to the objective of stabilizing employment. All of this mitigates against "the social purpose of the program."

The main fault of the Amending Act of 1950 was "failure to enact permanent disability insurance" fully integrated with Old-Age and Survivors Insurance and enacting the "miserable substitute," the new permanent and total disability assistance program. The "unfinished business," the remedy for substantial lacks in social security in this country, Miss Burns believed to be some application of social insurance "to help meet the cost of rearing children and of medical care," both common in other countries and both dealing with causes of poverty, and thus proper subjects of public action.

Of these two types of insurance, the more debated—possibly not the more debatable—is medical care insurance; and one can hazard the guess that it is likely to come before the other. Children are considered a blessing whatever the cost, while illness is almost universally called a curse. Without putting health needs second, it is curious that social workers have given so little attention to some form of child allowances since the profession has always thought of itself as a kind of guardian with or without portfolio in the protection of children.

Welfare of children.—Every decade, more or less, since 1909, a concern for children has received the national attention of a White House Conference. The Midcentury White House Conference on Children and Youth, held in the fall of 1950, assembled authoritative facts and responsible views on children. This material had been gathered and analyzed over the preceding year by a distinguished fact-finding committee and its staff (both including social workers). It was discussed by friends of children from every state, and the recommendations charted the course of work for children and youth for far longer than the next decade.

There was need for concern: 8 million children move in one year; 2.5 million live in homes broken by death or divorce; 58 percent of divorces granted are to couples with no children; an increasing number of children are born outside marriage; Negro or non-white family income is not quite equal to half the white family income; a third of the Negro children are born without medical attendance.

Mulling over such facts, and volumes of others, plus the complex of difficulties in a world unlike the world in which today's adults grew up, the White House Conference soberly expressed the needs of children in a way to recommend measures and action. Ira de A. Reid, sociologist from Haverford College, summarized these needs in six categories at the 1951 Annual Meeting:

1. *The need to be understood as a personality.*—Although the White House Conference took a traditional position as to child rearing, a subgroup found that "we have not yet developed a science of child rearing." The hope is that "we may change such patterns as may cause [children] to be ill-equipped for the highly charged social experience they are going to face."

2. *The need for remodeled nurturing situations.*—The home, school, and church are preparing the child to face a world not even the adults quite grasp. These institutions tend to emphasize a position and a function they once held. The teacher who witnessed the advent of radio must communicate, "cope with children who have never known a world without television"; teachers from the buttonhook era deal with "a child enclosed in zippers." In the home, the child's own developing within the family situation must be regarded as the chief goal. "Every society desperately needs morality in the sense of common standards, and religion in the sense of orientation" toward various ultimate value-attitudes, but "we have tempered our affirmations [of these] and harnessed our negations." The White House Conference could not, however, say how in this culture "faith to promote social solidarity and individual security by affirming and symbolically enacting a system of common purposes" could be achieved. Ironically, the nature of the problem was thus illustrated.

3. *Freedom from the market.*—It is necessary to protect

children from the present "social and economic exploitation," not only child labor but box-top, give-away advertising, the "child-centered appeals of the mass media of comics, radio, and television . . ."

4. *Extended and remodeled public and private services.*— One of the greatest needs is the extension of services in the field of education, physical and mental health, and preventive and corrective welfare.

5. *The need for community reconstruction.*—We must do something to "alter the general social and economic climate." Concern was voiced over "the survival of low economic standards, urban and rural slums, continuous migration in search of economic competence, excessive morbidity and mortality, inadequate hospitalization . . . inability to acquire an education, discrimination . . ."

6. *The need for the benefits of our development of pertinent knowledge.*—We must overcome what Dr. Benjamin Spock calls "the immense inertia of our institutions and customs."

As Reid concluded, this White House Conference contrived a script, and "we need no longer 'ad lib' the needs of American children for surviving in a world they never made." The Midcentury White House Conference on Children and Youth served the country well, and the published works [5] that resulted will remain standard must reading for many years.

International.—The *Proceedings* of the National Conference during the post Second World War decade carry a number of topics of international concern. It was to be expected, in view of the way social work reflects the problems of the times. Social work's interest in the world situation, however, took the form of its usual effort to understand the way in

[5] A major example of these publications is the fact-finding report *Personality in the Making*, edited by Helen Leland Witmer and Ruth Kotinsky (New York: Harper, 1952).

which people relate to people, in the hope of improving relationships.

The way social work looked upon the international scene
and the way the Conference discussed it reflected a response to
current ideas. Undoubtedly, the profession was drawn spontaneously and with relief to the one-world concept, the economic indivisibility of the world, and the hope that common
cause in the interest of peace and well-being, economic and social, could be achieved with understanding. But no speaker
hailed the postwar era as an uncomplicated victory. For one
thing, the profession was already involved in problems of
deprivation, displacement, orphanage, rehabilitation at home
and abroad. The social work idea had been used as a part of
foreign policy in the United Nations Relief and Rehabilitation
Administration, in the Marshall Plan, and in the Point IV Program, later in the Technical Assistance phase of this general
instrument of foreign policy.

Coupled with this familiar area, there were the long-time
professional convictions that: (1) lack of necessities aroused
yearnings that are ripe ground for the dictator's appeal and
make a breeding ground for feelings of hostility and for overt
hostile behavior; and (2) national self-respect and good relationships are based on self-determination and freedom (the
indivisibility of human rights) whether in the United States of
America or in an undeveloped country.

René Sand, Isador Lubin, Chester Bowles, Ralph Bunche,
Joe Hoffer, Donald Howard, Dorothy Lally—these are some
of the speakers who talked on the professional idea as applied
to international social welfare. This stimulated the profession
to apply social work concepts and principles in thinking about
the development of a world security, psychologically balanced,
economically stable, and politically ethical. By these and other
means the profession was able to improve its cooperation with

State Department programs, with United Nations programs, and with various voluntary undertakings.

AUTOMATION

The recent attention to automation is anticipation of what has not yet arisen: the loss of human meaning and dignity that might result from automation, the inevitable replacement of manpower by automatic procedures.

The automation phase of technological advance threatens or takes over manpower's function in a new way: automation enables a machine to check itself, even correct itself, all but repair itself. A machine that senses and feels to unbelievably close tolerances is the threshold of a machine that thinks logically, and not too far from the unthinkable machine that thinks creatively.

Automation's place on a social welfare program is made clear by an examination of the effects predicted by John B. Shallenberger, of the Stanford Research Institute (Palo Alto), in 1955. Like the majority of benefits from the still continuing Industrial Revolution, automation carries problems in its wake. The expected results are self-revealing to social workers who are experienced in detecting the recoil of progress: increased leisure, which everyone wants and few people can properly use; upgrading of skills and need for a new kind of work force, with less demand for the unskilled, the untrainable; demand for more knowledgeable managers; more women in the work force; dispersion of plants; a larger, highly skilled middle class; decreased price of goods, increased cost of services; rising standard of living; and material abundance. Each of these expected results is a social good but risks dislocation of the present balance. Whether the final result will be boon or burden will depend on how soon forethought is given to the nonmaterial social values that suffer temporary neglect in a surge of material advance.

The solution is within the capacity of the country to find, and social work, with its professional sense of social problems, will almost surely make its contribution.

SOCIAL WELFARE PLANNING

Although democratic community action is indigenous to America (de Tocqueville made a point of it), social welfare planning has been somewhat institutionalized in the agency-council-chest structure. The road blocks to successful planning, as social work rates success, are equally indigenous to, or inherent in, the method of the planning. The slow, cumbersome, necessary process of fact-finding, analysis, deliberation, compromise, and personality conflict or conflict of issues is the inevitable small price for the democratic process. Other major blocks are beyond control, such as those listed by Leonard W. Mayo (1952): (1) power structures whose "backing [is] a 'must,'" not only business, labor, government, industry, but segments of health and welfare agencies when they attempt to control welfare or health policy; (2) vesting of the planning function in groups whose motivation may be good but whose interest is elsewhere; (3) immediate pressure—like depression, defense, war—leading to emergency, waste, stop-gap planning.

In the face of this, the social welfare field (it includes more than social work) has made solid gains. They can be noted in the *Proceedings*. Need is now commonly recognized as a fact, even when other individuals suffer it; and it is better defined than it was. Deprivation is recognized as contagious, at least in its side effects. Planning is on a more fundamental, continuing basis, more sophisticated in the sense that, for example, population shifts now rarely catch the planners unaware. Services have a better chance than before to keep within sight of changing needs; indeed, some needs are anticipated and programs to meet them have a better basis for wider community support. Advance along these lines has been possible because of greater knowledge (or at least more understanding) of behavior; there is some appreciation that need must govern what is done, even when the actions to meet the needs run counter to the policies of vested interests that control the usual means; and techniques and method are becoming recognized and communicable.

Despite the gains, the *Proceedings* seldom reflect complacency; shortcomings are still too many for comfort. Goals are too limited. Problems are solved for the day, not always for the future. Even present goals are not clearly defined: to instance, the public is not clear whether social work is interested in preventing family life breakdown or only in being around and able to pick up the pieces. And research is only beginning to demonstrate what it can do in the whole social welfare enterprise.

The *Proceedings* reflect the need to direct research toward a study of the whole present mechanism for social planning, and social work's role in the planning. Such research would have to be of the highest standard, the study itself impeccable, since community planning is a line of country in which the sound of grinding axes may be heard from time to time. (This fact has caused the Annual Meeting to be cautioned against research that has the task of validating predetermined conclusions.)

Social work seems to feel with Terence that, being human, it is indifferent to nothing involving humanity, and indeed, its center of concern is human needs and behavior. The profession does not hesitate to speak to human needs in a wide array of human activity. There is repeated opinion in the *Proceedings* that knowledge, insight, know-how, justify any contribution the responsible social worker is impelled to offer on questions or solutions involving human problems. This is the view of broad social work function that has given social work a useful voice on questions over a wide range: from efficiency at a top-secret atomic plant to the citizen-building function of sand-lot baseball; from consultation with clergymen to recreation for lifers; from geriatrics to prenatal care; from disaster relief to psychosomatic syndromes associated with assembly-line speed-up; from adjustment of primitive immigrants to Israeli life to the problem of plantation peonage in Hawaii. It would seem that Terence—and social work—is right. This is the assumption of what is occasionally called "social statesmanship." (Agnes Meyer's phrase is "social diplomacy.") Under whatever name, it is *leadership* to which the profession owes a good part of its rather vague, unrewarded, but not unfounded prestige. Leadership fulfills the professional criterion of contributing to social policy in a broad way. And it transcends the institutional limitations inherent in agency-centered practice.

Within the whole field of agency-sponsored practice, however, there lies a major group of questions requiring community answers. The questions touch vitally on community social welfare planning, and one of the questions is "What agency is to do what?"

Public or private?—Agency-sponsored social work divides into many types of agency, properly defined by function or activity. But one old, useful, and current division was between publicly sponsored and privately sponsored agencies. The line of division between public and private fields no longer rested on types of function; it no longer necessarily implied a difference in competence; and it hardly justified the implication of "mass" whenever a public agency was mentioned. Practice in clinics, Veteran Administration hospitals, and diagnostic services for children (among other settings) testified to the public agency's possible standards.

Unless one could evaluate a given agency by criteria of competence, the only safe differentiation was to say "public welfare agency" when it was authorized by specific statute and administered funds appropriated by a legislative body. Both public and private fields had large as well as small agencies; each could and did pioneer, experiment; both could be bureaucratic; and neither was necessarily exempt from political finagling.

The defining conditions, however, have changed somewhat with respect to the public nature of the funds spent. By 1952, Donald Howard was moved to point out that some Congressional acts provided that funds appropriated for a program were to be "available to private as well as to public agencies." He cited the Hospital Act of 1950 and the freedom of the public child welfare agency of a state to use private facilities, this latter being usually by contractual agreement. (Public funds were not appropriated to private agencies, however.) A move was apparent to lessen the scope of the public agencies and to increase that of the private, Howard thought.

There is no precise indication that this effort grew out of the profession of social work. It is probable that it came from groups less interested in social welfare than in economy, and possibly it was associated with protections against any further growth in "the power of government," this latter being seen as inimical to the economic health of the nation and to the maintenance of free democratic institutions. Opponents of social welfare openly use clichés for weapons and brandish them vigorously in the name of logic; but their secret weapon is the purse. It is likely that the private purse is more subject to the veto of social welfare opponents than is the public treasury. The public programs move in response to democracy's unique lever, the majority.

The oversimplification of the foregoing must be complicated by recognition of a more beguiling way in which the opponents put their opposition: the move to shift the balance of "control" to the states. This is more popular and more effective than any shift of programs from public to private auspices.

Although no mass program except OASI was wholly under Federal administration, Federal leadership, standard-setting, and the necessary audit of performance vested a very substantial authority in the central government to maintain the purpose and integrity of the grant-in-aid programs. This was a constant irritation to a few states, in some ways to all states; and states' rights sentiment, as old as the Republic, was challenged rather than subdued. Gains were being made in behalf of "state control" toward the end of the decade here discussed, but they were of a minor sort reflected less in legislation than in a shift of administrative-supervisory viewpoint that allowed the states more latitude.

A pessimist viewing the situation could hardly say that nothing had been learned in the twenty years since the Federal Emergency Relief Administration. It is more likely that time always goes forward despite the slight drag of friction from the occasional efforts to turn the clock back.

Howard spoke for many social workers in all types of agencies when he wished the private agency to move forward, but not at the cost of the needed gains of the public programs. There was unfinished work for both, and work not even started. The private agency could find much to incorporate into itself from the public agency character: services as a "right," not as a gratuity; integration of like functions in a geographic unit; assessment and reporting of unmet needs; and responsiveness to the wishes of the total community in setting policy. (The "regressive" base of contributions is probably beyond reform.)

The belief that the larger contributors have a considerable weight in community social welfare planning gave pertinence to some of the basic facts brought out by E. Emerson Andrews (*Proceedings,* 1952) when he spelled out the meaning behind the eightfold dollar increase in corporate giving in the preceding decade. A corporation executive estimated that corporate giving supported one eighth of all welfare services. A random sample in 1950 showed that 36 percent of the corporate gift dollar went to community chests. The small corporations gave at the rate of 1.3 cents per profit dollar; the intermediate corporations, at the rate of 0.8 cents per profit dollar; the largest gave at the rate of 0.3 cents on the profit dollar. All but the very smallest corporations (with net income under $25,000) were able to save in taxes from 52 to 82 percent of the charitable gift if the gift did not exceed 5 percent of the profit.

The motives for giving are varied, as they are for any group of givers: 30 percent, "benefit to the company" (half the large corporations said this); 28 percent, "public relations or customer pressure"; 9 percent, "benefit to employees"; 42 percent, "duty to community"; 16 percent, "moral obligations"; and others included "wish to limit government expansion," "profit position and tax consideration," and "example of other companies." (Many respondents gave more than one reason.)

The conclusions to be drawn from these findings are properly debatable. Corporations are giving sums that are at once handsome as dollars and Scrooge-like as a percentage or millage of the profit dollar. No responsible person suggests that corporations should give at the 5 percent tax deductible rate. (Andrews says "Congress might regard the reduction in revenue so seriously . . . that it would rescind the 5 percent provision.") A small fraction of the stock in a widely held corporation is often controlling, but this operating principle applied to a modern city's social welfare operation (an enterprise also "widely held") raises problems of democratic principle. The purpose of the business corporation is to make a profit for its owners by giving a service; the service is the means to an end. The purpose of a social welfare corporation is to render a service; the service *is* the end sought, unless it also be to make the service unnecessary. No one alleges that the chest-council-agencies method as now known has ever been ideally democratic, but the effort to be so, within the limits of a modest efficiency, has been nearly consistent. If the present slight tendency toward greater control by the articulate large corporate givers becomes a trend and a realized reality, private social welfare in our urban centers will undoubtedly be more efficient, by the givers' standards. Whether it will also be more effective in doing its full job as the community wishes, is another matter.

CIVIL LIBERTIES AND CIVIL RIGHTS

Speaking to the 1956 Annual Forum, Marion B. Folsom, Secretary of the Department of Health, Education, and Welfare, said that social work "has helped strengthen in America the voice of compassion, of duty, of social justice, of vision."

Even a well-disposed person may wonder why social workers are professionally and personally devoted to civil liberties and civil rights in a degree that brings the subject into Annual Forum focus almost every year. The personal devotion is no puzzle, since the social worker is a citizen of these United States and devoted to that "standard to which the wise and honest can repair." Although "the event is in the hands of God," the good citizen knows that the standard needs his steady support. But professional devotion to civil liberties is a slightly different matter. Possibly this devotion is implicit in professional principles that strive always to protect the client's self-determination and to strengthen his ability to choose or determine wisely. Whatever detracts from such American characteristics detracts from the professional enterprise. Thus, civil liberties and civil rights are matters of professional self-interest.

But such a simple functional explanation may be too simple.

It is inevitable that human rights should be uppermost in the consciousness of a profession that is the advocate of the disadvantaged, the deprived, the handicapped. There is no greater social deprivation in our Western society than loss or denial of rights. Absence of some rights may deprive the victim of the chance to make a decent living, to get a good education, to bring up his children in a good neighborhood.

The precious inheritance of man's rights came to the front of the country's attention at mid-century. Totalitarian principles and practices had furnished a massive example of what could happen to human dignity when civil liberties were denied. People in the United States, some of whom had known nothing but the passive enjoyment of their rights, began to learn their lessons by observing what happened in Italy, in Germany, and in Russia—though facts about the latter nation were slow to emerge and until the postwar years were difficult to evaluate because of the courtesy granted to a nominal and rather precarious military ally.

The American public, a decent and warm-hearted people, were concerned over the state of civilization. But generally there was a comforting, unrealistic conviction that "it couldn't happen here," even while the Negro was expected to be content with a second-class education, was barred from most hotels and restaurants in most states, and Jim Crow was accepted as a cultural tradition; when immigration quotas were established by the descendants of immigrants in such a way as to classify immigrants as of first and second-class desirability; and while some God-fearing citizens said, among themselves, "I don't for a moment condone what Hitler did to the Jews. He went entirely too far." It was to take a threat to all people's rights to arouse public concern.

No one, the social worker least of all, deserves credit for a firm, knowledgeable stand in behalf of civil rights and civil liberties. One might just as well deserve credit and expect praise for being honest. Just the same, the profession is among the groups who deserve the gratitude of the country for a sensitive and quick support of civil liberties when deterioration threatened to set in after the Second World War. In fact, it began to look as if it could happen here, owing to a common misjudging of the problem.

As Patrick Murphy Malin, Executive Director of the American Civil Liberties Union, said to the 1953 Annual Meeting:

. . . as long as we live, and as long as our children and our grandchildren live, in all probability, there will be enough tension and conflict between this country and the Soviet Union that we shall never be free of this problem [of national security and its protection against espionage and sabotage and infiltration]. . . . All of us . . . have as far ahead as I can see the most difficult job ever faced by believers in liberty.

Civil liberties interpose no obstruction to the prevention or punishment of actual subversive acts, any more than to the prevention or punishment of other illegal acts. Civil liberties do not constitute a charter of anarchy. Civil liberties in a time of national insecurity are exactly what they are in every other time—no more, and no less. Civil liberties mean three things: equal protection of the law for those who abide by the law; due process and fair trial even for those who are charged with violating the law; and freedom of speech and association this side of the line of clear and present danger of illegal action.[6]

[6] Patrick Murphy Malin, "Civil Liberties and Social Work" (1956), p. 35.

Civil liberties thus could continue, and continue to have citizen devotion, because citizens did not have to abridge civil liberties in order to combat the dangers to national security. "To prevent or to punish subversive attempts . . . is a police job, which needs to be done by experts—and is being done by experts, as effectively as fallible human beings can do any job." [7]

As to the civil liberties with which social work has been concerned from its beginning, Malin said "if you want to preserve your free speech, you speak freely." It is doubtful that social workers needed the advice they had been following for years—but it might have heartened the profession, which could not have remained wholly unaffected by the threatening atmosphere of hysteria and fearful suspicion. Long before 1954, when hysteria began to give way to the normal American state of courage, dignity, and self-respect, social work was speaking. In its speech it succeeded quite well in keeping the "delicate balance [between conformity and nonconformity] that must be jealously safeguarded," described by Telford Taylor in 1956.

The special field of social work's effort in behalf of rights was the rights of society as distinguished from those of individuals, as Donald Howard pointed out, citing compulsory school attendance laws, child labor laws, labor laws. Owing to their broad social interest, such laws have come to be regarded as worth the curtailment of individual rights and liberties. The professional principle seemed to be that "civil rights are indivisible: there is no middle ground. We have them or we do not have them," as Benjamin E. Youngdahl said at the 1949 Annual Meeting. His fears were that partial abridgment of civil rights, or the effort to reduce such rights would be accepted, possibly because of fear-induced silence in which, in Mac-Leish's eighteenth-century turn of phrase, "honest men, by

[7] *Ibid.*

scandals turned about/See honor murdered and will not speak out." The second-class citizenship churlishly allowed citizens with skin of darker pigment, and any erosion of civil liberties and democracy, prevents the nation from going with clean hands before the world, which is mostly darker skinned. The application made by Youngdahl, and by other Conference speakers, was that civil rights strengthen democracy and also, incidentally, are a requirement for good foreign relations. Thus the cause of civil rights was seen as an instrument of democracy in behalf of domestic justice and tranquillity, and also as the prerequisite for a good world opinion of the democracies.

Social work itself did not have clean hands, Youngdahl said, touching on a sore problem; and he cited cases to show that the profession must put its house in order if it was to speak with grace and a clear conscience in behalf of civil rights. The point was strongly made by Savilla Millis Simons (1956), in connection with desegregation in social agencies, that "clear-cut assumption of leadership by councils and chests in enunciating desirable policies is very important in freeing agencies to move, and in providing a favorable climate for action."

This is part of the problem that has troubled many social workers, and it has puzzled many sympathetic citizens who share social work's convictions without the time to indulge or implement them. The puzzle is how social work remains comfortable, level, balanced, in the midst of its great responsibility; in the face of its inability to carry it out because of society's lack of agreement or means; and despite the profession's own lack of knowledge, skill, time, or energy. How does social work avoid immobilizing itself from sheer excess of sense of guilt? The possible explanation is embodied in T. V. Smith's suggestion (1955): the way to absolve oneself from failure to perform an impossible task is to cultivate a philosophy of life in which there is a "very robust sense of humor" (possibly irony would do) and " 'piety' . . . identity with the world . . . in such fashion that one has perspective upon the world and does not feel himself to be alone." In this way, he suggests, we may solve what we can, resolve compromised predicaments, and absolve ourselves. Thus we "may achieve sanity at home and be prepared to spread its healing ointment in the wider world."

Employment of the Negro, meaning his lack of jobs as well as the type of work to which he was largely restricted, was a widespread example of deprivation of the human right to work. His gains in employment status and in the lines of endeavor open to him came about slowly, spottily, sporadically over the years as a result of "investment in good will" by many agents of fairness. Labor union seniority agreements got rid of discriminating lay-off practices in some urban communities; Urban League programs helped correct misunderstanding and added to a growing good will on an interracial basis. But the national state of Negro affairs continued under a burden of job discrimination until the Second World War and its unprecedented industrial, manpower effort. Then, if ever, there was a chance for equal employment—as a result of labor shortage if not as a response to the imperative ethics involved.

As Harold A. Lett said to the 1950 Conference, a generation of education in quite enlightened Northern states "had done little to alter the climate of human relations within which the freedoms of one large racial minority were being seriously limited." In the decline of any type of discrimination there is a significant point when it is no longer considered good public behavior to exhibit one's prejudices openly. The war-born Fair Employment Practices Committee quite possibly was this over-the-hump point for Negro job rights.

Opposition to the FEPC did not evaporate, especially in areas favorable to the dank atmosphere of racial prejudice and fear of economic competition. Added to this factor may be the conditioning bias in small provincial culture pockets, and where culture-pretense allows the act or attitude of intolerance to be cherished as a claim to status. With the expiration of the FEPC, not many states enacted their own equivalent. The advance has nevertheless been considerable, beyond the rather vague point noted above: the Negro worker has proved himself, and he was not fired en masse when his employer could do so with impunity; the Negro is gaining employment previously barred to him—in insurance companies, department stores, big league baseball, secretarial careers, nursing, among others; and a sign of the continuing progress is the way Negro students are increasingly counseled into trades, callings, professions for which they are fitted, without regard for color. Progress! It is a reproach to a great and good country that so eminently sane, commonsense, and just a course should be called progress under way.

The right to an education is a right so peculiarly of value accruing to an orderly society (if it is a democratically organized society) that up to a point one's enjoyment of the right is made mandatory through state compulsory school attendance laws. But some states, and thus the whole nation, were deprived of the potential value of education through the evil omissions of a system of segregated education in states "beyond the corn pone curtain" (to borrow George S. Mitchell's phrase). A segregated system of education, taking advantage of a Supreme Court decision, meant that Negro citizens were restricted under state law to a school "equal but separate" from the school for white citizens. Two school systems were thus the rule in these states. The equality of the systems was a fiction, but their separateness was a harsh reality steadily verified by the vigilant eyes of those citizens to whom the system reflected civic security and virtue. The Southern states had a substantial minority of citizens who deplored the system, either because it outraged their sense of justice, because it did not make sense, or because it was costly. The full price, however, was levied on the state as a whole and on the whole nation. The Negro schools were generally below the standard of the white schools, even when the teaching was on a par or superior. Housing and equipment were substandard, pay of teachers was not always equal throughout the two systems, and overcrowding was common. Even in counties with a population 80 percent Negro, the Negro schools came off with the short end.

Then in May, 1954, the United States Supreme Court "in a thunderclap of decision" said that Negroes are not to be barred from institutions of learning simply because they are Negroes. Segregated education was thus at one stroke made illegal, though a reasonable and proper amount of time was allowed to states to achieve compliance.

George S. Mitchell, talking to the 1955 Annual Forum, noted how well favored this nation was in the procedure that brought the court decision:

As it has proceeded elsewhere, this same conflict, this same surge of repressed peoples for equality for status, has been accompanied by violence, bitterness, sabotage, rebellion, Communism, war. In this country a battery of brilliant Negro lawyers, headed by a man named Thurgood Marshall, stands before nine justices and pleads for the full enforcement of the Constitution of the United States. That is legal, that is orderly, that is loyal, that is American. And it deserves the whole country's loyal, uncontentious, and American response in putting the decision into effect.[8]

In some Southern and border states integration of schools got under way quickly and with a relative smoothness suggesting that many of their citizens heaved an involuntary sigh of relief, as if they welcomed the voice of constitutional

[8] George S. Mitchell, "Segregation" (1955), p. 113.

authority calling them out of an anomaly. But other states continued intransigent, though their resistance cannot last long. In fact, there was some indication that what was now wanted in one or more of these states was a face-saving formula that would allow authority to act in accord with their second, more compliant, thought. The handwriting on the wall was large and indelible. "Respect for equal human dignity" has entered public education in these United States.

The issue, of course, is not fully settled at this writing. The issue remains for a time even after integration has been achieved in a school system, since prejudice is a wound in the body politic that does not heal quickly and must heal with a minimum of scar tissue if social serenity is to become a fact. No one who has "respect for equal human dignity" may safely rest on the achievement. Everyone needs to work at integration and make it work, and the best way is to "open the whole process of government to Negro citizens." The fruits could go far; in Carl T. Rowan's words (1956), "Boldness and courage in the town you live in is fuel for the torches of freedom in the many dark corners of the world."

HEALTH AND MEDICAL CARE

The Annual Meeting and the Annual Forum have always been interested in the health of people and the human-social price paid for the absence of medical care. Other matters might have the spotlight, and the interest in health needs might sound perfunctory, but the attention was rarely absent. Mostly social workers did the talking; they spoke of health as the end result of a complex of contributing factors; in fact, they thought of good health as something more positive than the absence of illness. Physicians also spoke, and they were usually men who were in favor of good health even for people who could not pay for it.

For a long time this economic group was the concern of Annual Meeting discussion, and the focus of interest was less frequently the patients who could qualify for free or low-pay out-patient services than it was the "medically indigent," a term that does indeed mean lack of medical care but more precisely means the person who can pay his own way except for medical care. Other problems were not of a public policy nature but of a professional policy-or-procedure order: the co-operative or team approach to the patient's needs; the inter-professional separation of functions; the social aspect of illness, treatment, and recovery; and the like.

The postwar decade saw the nation's health become a national issue of urgent but frustrated importance.

Medical societies themselves had become aware of a problem even more serious than medical indigency as early as the mid-thirties when studies showed large rural areas sparsely served by physicians and more meagerly by hospitals. As brought out in the *Proceedings* this situation seemed to be—and still seems—the result of several tendencies beyond the normal shift from country to city: medicine increased its dependence on laboratory facilities and costly equipment; the general practitioner was being replaced by the specialist, and frequently only a clinic, or an array of specialized consultants, could give the patient the best that medicine afforded; care more frequently required hospital facilities, and with Blue Cross and other private prepaid plans, hospitalization was modestly within financial reach of more people who once thought hospitalization the equivalent of grave crisis or terminal illness; and the urban practitioner reputedly earned a higher income. Medical care was not unavailable to the rural citizen, but many paid more for it because they went greater distances from home to get it, and often they got less than the best that modern medicine had to offer. The medically indigent included a higher income group under such circumstances, but it was the rural factor that made the care less than acceptable to the profession. It is worth bearing in mind that the medical profession took the lead in defining this problem.

Social workers were daily conscious of the medical needs of their client group; but to live with a problem that seems insoluble is to accept it as a reality. The magnitude of this reality was brought home to the profession and a good part of the country by the large percentage of selective service rejections for reasons that could be traced to inadequate medical or dental care, to malnutrition, or to various preventable if not remediable defects. Such conditions constitute a national deficit, especially when they are found in young men who are in what is called the "flower of their manhood," and in a nation as wealthy as any on earth, lacking no material good, and served by the most advanced medical science.

The medical care situation led to a good deal of pamphleteering, various reports assembling available data, and proposals for a national health insurance scheme. But public health insurance was strongly attacked by the medical profession on grounds that such insurance would limit the patient's right to choose his physician and endanger the professional practice of medicine. An impasse was the main outcome.

The situation led to a new and definitive study by the President's Commission on the Health Needs of the Nation, a group who worked throughout 1952 and whose report was published in 1953. The report was a mid-century achievement.

The findings were similar to those found in 1932 by the Committee on the Cost of Medical Care, in 1935 by the National Health Survey, and in 1948 by the National Health

Conference (part of the National Health Assembly). The Commission's findings had a ready audience. The Commission's make-up, its lack of special pleading, its sober, almost somber data, and the mass of its nonpartisan evidence could not be ignored.

The five volumes of the Commission's report [9] can hardly be summarized, but the overriding findings as discussed in the Annual Meeting are quickly listed. First, and most surprising, is that little is known about the health of people, since there is no system for reporting most of the diseases. People get these illnesses, among them the great killers like heart disease, the great cripplers like arthritis, the great nuisances like the common cold; but who, how many, and how serious—these facts are not known. The Commission found a first-class medical profession, equally superior hospitals and various ancillary health facilities, but, paradoxically, there were a large number of people unable to get medical service. The inability was most marked in relation to the preventive services, since few really serious or urgent illnesses went untended, especially if they were far advanced. Hardest put to obtain service were those of low income, rural dwellers, Negroes and other minority members, and migratory workers. Treatment rather than prevention absorbed most of medicine's attention, even to the neglect of early diagnosis and treatment, the latter being considered essentially preventive of more serious difficulty or disability. A major finding, in addition to the urban concentration of available resources, was a serious dearth of physicians, dentists, nurses, hospitals, and of all other means required if health care were to reach people uniformly all over the nation.

The Commission found that medical services were ill-

[9] The President's Commission on the Health Needs of the Nation, *Building America's Health;* 5 vols. (Washington, D.C., 1953).

organized, if at all, with little relation to volume, type, or place of need. Associated with all these findings was the basic economic fact that it is difficult to pay for medical care. Even existing prepayment plans were inadequate. This last statement seems dubious in view of the declared figures on the more than eighty million people with some form of prepaid insurance plan for care, but the sticking point is that all but four or five million of these have nothing but hospitalization insurance, and lack provision for physicians' fees and for care in the home or at the doctor's office. The Commission, however, came quite factually and unemotionally to the conclusion that thinking on the thorny problem of medical care must shift its emphasis from how to pay for it to how to bring it where it is needed. Payment is important, of course, but it is incidental to the effective presence of medical services to prevent or treat illness.

Dean A. Clark, M.D., General Director of Massachusetts General Hospital, who reported on these matters in 1953, made a special point of the Commission's philosophy that "in a country with an economy like ours, and with a technical level like ours, every person should have the opportunity for complete health service at the time when it would be to his best advantage to have it," in illness or to prevent illness. Not only was this possible economically, said the report, it would be uneconomical not to provide such service. The shortage of trained personnel was and is the main stumbling block; but the Commission did not consider it insuperable. Their recommendations sketched the general line of solution.

Federal funds were needed; but health services "are local in character and must be locally administered and locally controlled." A "small" expenditure of Federal moneys would give leadership and momentum resulting in an increasing proportion of state and local funds devoted to the purpose. But first,

the facts of health status must be found and then found continuously on a regular reporting basis. With this must come
provision of personnel, facilities for their proper training, development of suitable public health services, increased hospital
construction under a broadened Hill-Burton Act (or its like),
and continued research. For all of this, Federal funds were
needed.

Organization of medical services must be improved so that
every area of the country is eventually covered with a suitable
nucleus of facilities for each region through hospitals, clinics,
group practice, and various other devices to bring modern
medicine to patients who need it. The recommended distribution of services, Dr. Clark pointed out, closely followed the
plan set forth by the National Health Congress of 1935 and put
into a Congressional bill the next year by Senator Wagner.
The essential point involved Federal standards, implemented
by Federal funds to the states—the grant-in-aid plan that has
been refined into an effective instrument during this half-
century. The funds would not wholly represent a net increase
of appropriation, as seen by the Commission, since it was envisaged that some allocations could be made for the purpose
out of funds now available for specific groups such as veterans,
public assistance recipients, and possibly others.

The Commission went further to suggest a grant-in-aid to
states to encourage them to devise some plan of prepaid insurance for a wide distribution of medical or health services. So
mild a recommendation—far short of a national health insurance system—left social work only tepidly enthusiastic,
though applauding the report as a whole.

The impasse in which every proposal for national health insurance found itself was sufficient basis for the Commission's
caution, or wisdom, in stopping short of such a recommendation. Its way of approach to the problem—state systems—has

at least kept its report from being ignored out of hand. Citizens who fear Federal authority as an assertion of dominating control enjoy a comforting fiction that state control or authority, though not benign, is somehow not governmental control. As the *Proceedings* indicate, social workers do not generally hold this view, but they could look into the history of the public welfare programs they helped build and find a practical testimony to the Commission's common sense: public assistance programs were offered to the states, not imposed on them. And so with other aids and services. In just such fashion, near-universal health insurance might come to be.

In any event, it has not yet come to pass. No bill embodying significant components of the Commission's recommendation has had any serious chance of passage. Isolated items in partial harmony with the report have been incorporated into various legislation: medical services to public assistance recipients can now be paid for more expeditiously; traineeships for professional education financed by Federal funds have increased; Federally financed medical research has greatly expanded; maternal and child health services have at least been maintained; and rehabilitative services have finally been recognized as a major field of Federal concern, acting through state and private means. But the integrated approach to the whole problem of the nation's health as contemplated by the Commission is still lacking. Legislators and administrators step gingerly and warily around the question, which still remains viable and challenging. Partial solutions are debated, big solutions are proposed and fail, a presidential solution (to subsidize a modest reinsurance approach by voluntary groups) comes to nothing.

It is not that good health is in disfavor. In fact, it stands high on the list of noncontroversial matters like motherhood, religion, and patriotism; and illness is deplored as much as sin, though carrying less culpability. It is news to almost no one that the medical profession has been the main critic of large-scale health insurance plans and of many related measures. Time usually erodes the opposition or purifies the proposal if it involves research, hospital construction, or public health provisions; but the profession of medicine deeply fears the encroachment of government on its ancient right of practice under professionally supervised licensure. It is unavailing to say that the fears are based on misunderstanding of goal and method proposed, that decisions will still be the physician's right and duty, that the only purpose is to increase the availability and standards of medical services. Beyond the objections that stem directly out of professional concerns, there possibly lies a financial concern more appropriate to an entrepreneur than to a professional practitioner. Also, the mill-run physician now gives a splendid, and touching, amount of free service. It is not his fault that it is insufficient to the need and essentially benevolent because it is charity. The individual physician carries out his responsibility nobly; and it is ironic that no one but physicians and their bitterest critics think he would not do so if his work were compensated by fees set and prepaid through insurance. On a far higher plane than his economic success and social prestige, the physician is a dedicated person who would be the first to say that he was not called to the upper income brackets but to the practice of his professed competence.

The nation's health and how to build it and maintain it is still a live issue, and opinion is growing that it will remain a thorny, unforgotten problem until it is solved. The solution will probably be a form of prepayment or insurance, since the method is accepted by all concerned, as Odin W. Anderson, of the Health Information Foundation, declared in 1954. But whether voluntary or involuntary prepayment is the unsolved problem.

As Anderson pointed out, families with health insurance, "in contrast to those without insurance, were more likely to live in cities, had more money, and family heads were younger." (Illness, of course, is not so selective or urbanized.) The insurance itself concentrates on in-hospital costs; only 3 percent of the population enjoyed protection that pays completely for physicians' services. Of the $10.2 billion yearly medical costs (1952–53), insurance covered 15 percent.

These total costs of $10.2 billion included physicians' charges, 37 percent; hospital, 20 percent; medicine, 15 percent; and dental care, 16 percent. The average family incurred a $207 charge annually for personal health services, and the insured family "incurred a total median cost more than twice as great as those without insurance." Averages like these look manageable for most self-sufficient families, but Anderson showed what a difference lies between the average and the individual; one half of the families paid out 4.1 percent or more of their incomes for medical costs; about "a million paid out half or more of their incomes; and a half-million families paid out amounts equal to or exceeding 100 percent of their incomes." The inescapable conclusion is that illness may be a financial catastrophe, a fact that people have lived with so long that it has ceased to be a nightmare until it becomes a reality.

Insurance seemingly enables people so covered to get more care than those who do not have insurance, a difference especially striking when surgical procedures are involved—7 percent among the insured as against 4 percent among the uninsured. "See your dentist twice a year" must be one of the least followed of all good maxims: 34 percent of all individuals sought dentists' services during the year; but people with incomes above $7,500 were three times more likely to follow the advice than those with incomes under $2,000.

Medical debts came to $1.1 billion, largely among people

with greater medical costs. Although 60 percent of the population had some kind of voluntary health insurance, the insurance paid only 15 percent of all charges for personal health services. Both facts were well-nigh beyond prediction before the 1940s, but remarkable as the 60 percent is, the 15 percent goes far to explain the sentiment building up for a national solution to a national problem through a governmental insurance system. The 15 percent figure is not a fair reflection of the effectiveness or scope of voluntary insurance, however, since it is a percentage of *all* costs. Considered against its own risks, voluntary insurance shows a less hopeless, barely hopeful, aspect: it paid 50 percent of all general hospital charges, 13 percent of all physicians' services, and 38 percent of all surgery—a combined average of 26 percent.

The study from which all these figures—not necessarily this interpretation—are drawn, was made at the University of Chicago for the Health Information Foundation, and it brought out three additional findings of major significance: insured families incurred higher medical costs than the uninsured, partly, it could be inferred, because diagnostic service outside the hospital is rarely "in the policy"; costs not insured may be as great as those that are covered, i.e., house or office calls, out-patient diagnosis; and family health costs above $500 a year can hardly be cushioned by the typical health insurance program as it exists today.

On data of this nature, people divide into two camps, both in favor of building and maintaining the nation's health. One view holds that the phenomenal success of the voluntary prepayment plans holds a clear potential and even a promise for extension and improvement that will fill the glaring gaps and meet the problem. The other view holds that the voluntary system has been tried, found wanting, and has the inherent defect of being voluntary; and that the time has come to use

the knowledge available to devise a system of governmental
health insurance that will protect the low-income citizen as
well as his wealthier neighbor, reach into rural areas, emphasize
preventive services, and cushion catastrophe. It is hardly necessary to say that the feeling between the holders of the two
opposing views is not warm, except in the sense of "heated."

The issue of the nation's health will continue until that health
is built to, and maintained at, a level consistent with the best
standard made possible by medical skill. The tone of the *Proceedings* seems to be that this end will be reached only through
compulsory health insurance under governmental auspices, authorized by a law that strengthens the birthright of good health
through a legal right to services that will encourage such health
as a man is enabled to achieve.

There were many major developments in social welfare
during the postwar decade that are not found in this brief appraisal. Most of them represent advances from a beginning
already made. For example:

Mental health.—The establishment of the National Institute
of Mental Health (adjunct of the U. S. Public Health Service)
in 1947 testified to a new Federal policy of responsibility.
Under this policy, funds were appropriated and granted to
states for community services; there were grants for research
and for training of professional personnel, these latter grants
going both to states and to private institutions. The majority
of states strengthened their existing programs, and many of
them, in cooperation with local communities, sponsored
various types of preventive services and treatment clinics. At
the same time, the Veterans Administration was building its
extraordinary program of care of the ex-serviceman, with cen-

ters dotted around the country. A good part of that program was occupied with mental illness and mental health. Social workers were an important part of the total staff.

The *Proceedings* show a firm conviction that prevention must get urgent attention if mental illness is not to outstrip every potential means of treatment or custodial care. The broadest view was taken in a resolution by the Group for the Advancement of Psychiatry as quoted in a paper by Julius Schreiber, M.D. (1948). The group members were convinced that:

The social conditions necessary to insure mental health require the full protection for *all* citizens of . . . :
   "The right to the safety and security of person;
   "The right to citizenship and its privileges;
   "The right to freedom of conscience and expression;
   "The right to equality of opportunity." [10]

As Schreiber saw it, mental health means that an individual has found a reasonable measure of peace with himself and his environment.

Delinquency.—A postwar period is usually accompanied by some breakdown of restraint or a loosening of standards. One of the most troubling phases has been juvenile delinquency, which in this postwar period continues unabated. The subject was not new to the Annual Meeting, but the programs reflected the aroused concern of the country as a whole. This concern was not only over the higher incidence (seemingly associated with international tension, a "cold war" by-product) but because young people were committing more serious crimes. Social work had no more answer to the problem than anyone else, but its effort to see the problem avoided the pitfall of simplicity. Treatment and prevention were seen as complex

[10] Julius Schreiber, M.D., "Political Implications of Mental Health" (1948), p. 193.

and of wide ramification, expressing the conviction that whatever would givè young people a sense of real security and a chance to develop without unbearable pressure would reduce delinquent behavior. The U.S. Children's Bureau took leadership in studying the matter; attention was given to the probation services of juvenile courts; and accurate information was made readily available through the cooperation of many voluntary organizations and official bodies.

Various fields of interaction, relationship.—The Annual Forum is hospitable to speakers who are knowledgeable in areas touching social work's function. This has been illustrated conspicuously by the number of physicians, lawyers, and social scientists whose contributions appear in the *Proceedings*. There is a further protection against parochialism, however, in the increasing wish of the Annual Forum to consider the views of people who speak for industry or industrial management, for organized labor, for elementary and secondary schools, for religion. If a tendency may be read into this interest, it would be that social work is moved to better understand and define its place, function, and relationship in and with the forces that produce our material goods, educate our society, and mold our declared values.

39 · THE CONDITION OF SOCIAL WORK

INCLINED to be self-critical, social work around the beginning of its second half-century as a profession seemed to have turned a corner of its own devising and was especially self-evaluative. In 1952 the Council on Social Work Education was formed out of the American Association of Schools of Social Work and the National Association of Schools of Social Administration. In 1955 a single professional membership organization, the National Association of Social Workers, was formed out of no less than seven "specialized" membership bodies. A major study of social work education was completed. A study of 50,000 social workers was completed—who they were, where, what they did, what they earned, whom they worked for, what training they had, and more.

Little of these developments can find a place here, except the study that opens several points of concern: social work's effort to define itself more precisely.

SOCIAL WORK EDUCATION

Harriett M. Bartlett, chairman of the Study Committee of the Council on Social Work Education, in 1951, oriented the Annual Meeting to the "Hollis-Taylor report," [1] as it was commonly called. She thought the report put the profession

---

[1] Ernest V. Hollis and Alice L. Taylor, *Social Work Education in the United States* (New York: Columbia University Press, 1951).

clearly in focus, defined a long-range program in which education was seen as the business of the whole profession, and stated the basic principles on which all could join in building for the future. Beyond this she did not attempt evaluation other than to say it could have "an enormously stimulating effect."

The study saw the generic curriculum as a two-year Master's course, with specialization offered later. Moreover, the specialized fields suggested were supervision, consultation, administration, teaching, and research. A dubious view was taken of the strongly apprentice tone of the training and of the propriety of including material that could be offered in the undergraduate schools.

The report was stimulating even though it has not been used as a preceptor. Social work, the Great Modifier, modified the report it had authorized and proceeded on somewhat similar, slightly divergent lines to stress the integration of essential material into areas roughly equivalent to: (1) the social scene; (2) human growth and development; and (3) methods, three of the latter being widely agreed upon for some years past: casework, social group work, and community (or social welfare) organization. Many social workers believe that the Hollis-Taylor report, at present rarely cited, has not ceased to be a fact of social work's life; and that as practitioners get accustomed to its analysis and farsight, it will carry weight for a long time to come.

Ordinarily, the Annual Meeting left other social work associations to deal with matters in their area of interest; and so the formal training questions were seen as the responsibility of the Council on Social Work Education, except as items of broad interest arose. The Conference membership could not fail to be interested, for example, in the question of generic versus specialized content in the training curriculum, an issue that had exercised the schools' people all through the 1940s if not before—and continues to do so at this writing.

The question was not whether content basic to all practice should preempt all, or most, of the two-year curriculum; or whether a field of specialized practice required that the student training for such practice receive a component of special content applicable and peculiar to the field. (Perhaps "peculiar" is as wrong a word as "unique" would have been; it is difficult to define the issue sharply. The "special" is *usable* in any field, but perhaps not *essential* except in one field.) Extreme advocates of the generic refer off the record to specialized course material as "settings" courses, the connotation being that of an apprenticeship. This kind of labeling is a substantial error, but a grain of truth in it hurts. The extreme supporters of specialized content have some difficulty in avoiding the impression that the specialized product is a social worker of a higher order, that the specialized courses initiate the student into arcana beyond the garden (or generic) variety. Between these extremes, here exaggerated out of lifelike and polite proportions, the typical social worker could not be less interested and wished only that the job at hand could be got on with.

There are refreshing signs that this is happening: the effort to conceptualize more and more of social work knowledge, principles, method; the increasingly common clinical data; the research-oriented disposition to question, sift, discard, test, and validate emerging theory. There is a wider recognition that content needed by every social worker would fill a two-year curriculum unless room were released by consolidating and integrating like material or by putting other content into the undergraduate years. The solution, it should be noted, is not to abolish specialized practice (as if this could be done!) but to reconcile generic education with specialized practice. "I believe we can," Ruth E. Smalley said (1953), and "furthermore,

I believe that only as we can and do, do we have a profession at all. Otherwise, we are a composite of vocational schools preparing for the specifics of practice in a bewildering variety of jobs."

Many a practitioner, and not a few schools people, would agree with Miss Smalley that it is "the generic quality of social work education that makes it usable . . . essential, as preparation for practice in any social work field"; and that a school has the:

Responsibility to develop, and certify to in its graduates: (1) commitment to social work purpose; (2) discipline of the self in offering service so that the social work helper may be depended on to be always and truly at the service of the other person; (3) identification of place in the historical and contemporary pattern of social services within the context of the political and economic scene; and (4) possession of a reliable and tested, even though beginning, skill for making social services available in a way that gives them the best possible chance of being used for the individual and the social good.[2]

It is worth note that the social, political, or economic scene is here a base-point, as it is in most defining statements in social work practice, and in the Hollis-Taylor curriculum recommendations.

STUDY OF PERSONNEL

Social Workers in 1950[3] is the report of a study undertaken by the Bureau of Labor Statistics, using replies to a questionnaire from 50,000 of the 75,000 social workers in the country

[2] Ruth E. Smalley, "Can We Reconcile Generic Education and Specialized Practice?" (1953), pp. 314–15.
[3] *Social Workers in 1950—a Report on the Study of Salaries and Working Conditions in Social Work—Spring 1950* (New York: American Association of Social Workers, 1952).

—"a remarkably high coverage of so large a group of professional workers," said Ewan Clague in 1951, the year of publication. The most comprehensive study of the matter yet made (it included personnel in positions considered social work positions, whether professionally educated or not), it revealed conditions generally known for one or another segment of the total field. It showed a sad lack of professionally trained staff; most salaries established for an untrained level, generally without regard for competence; high mobility, especially of the trained people; and rather rapid upgrading of the qualified practitioner to jobs of responsibility and better salary, relative to the range. The study did not attempt to show the great and increasing demand for social workers in both new and customary settings. The demand cannot be met, and there is now no prospect that it can be met in the next generation.

A NEW PROFESSIONAL SELF-CONSCIOUSNESS?

There is an overtone in the *Proceedings* of a new orientation between the professional staff service and its social auspice, a relationship whose vitality must derive equally from the sponsoring groups and from the profession that implements the wish of the community in ways that meet the criteria of professional integrity. This is no claim that social work is a supercommunity whose function is to amend or veto the sponsoring community's will. This would be absurd, although there are critics who say "the community proposes, social work disposes." Rather, the professional staff function more as professional people, less like employees; in agency deliberations, staff apparently are looked to as experts to the degree that they can support such a role. And to the extent that staff can feel themselves to be a professional part of the community they increasingly play the role of citizens.

Nothing in such a development can diminish the agency in its essential function as an agent of society; but the agency is losing a substantial portion of its old cloak as a carrier of community charity. It consciously becomes the sponsor of a professional service, responsive to the profession's principles in slightly greater measure than may be apparent. The agency's role is increasingly that of the steward of community or social policy, a policy to which the agency contributes significantly. This view of the agency, rather wistful and rarely blunt, is implied in many *Proceedings* pages.

The testimony is indirect but mounting. The social function of the agency is not confined to its intramural enterprise. Increasingly, board and staff are contributing pertinent knowledge gained in practice to other community activity of a social welfare policy nature: to an understanding of delinquency and its prevention—though this has not been conspicuously successful to date; to problems of unsegregated housing and how to minimize them; to the effective planning of recreational areas; to the functions of various agencies; and to other aspects of community planning. Under this view, at no time does the social worker *as social worker* take over the rights and prerogatives of the citizen. He must remain a social servant. But as citizen, when this status is the basis of his community activity, he acts with all the rights and privileges thereof and not as a professional, however much his equipment must accompany him.

The contribution of the social worker to community councils is potentially substantial, always various. As great as any one item is an optimism, the simple knowledge of what human stuff is capable of becoming, given some slightly altered set of circumstances. This knowledge is not a faith as such—though it might be warmed and enlivened by faith. It is rather a partial understanding of what brings about a given behavior, what lies behind self-defeating qualities; and it is a developing theory of behavior that might facilitate a greater realization of the socially desirable potential in people; it is a reasoned conviction that society working in behalf of its individual members and those members working as responsible parts of society can find solutions to seemingly insoluble problems. In this way the potential may be released and realized.

The diminishing influence of the traditional agency on practice has undoubtedly been hastened by a greatly broadened use of the social caseworker—and of any kind of social worker. The setting is still predominantly the customary type with function recognizable as family, children's, psychiatric, medical, etc.; but increasingly the social worker is in a multidisciplinary atmosphere in which the institutional character is not wholly that of social work, if at all. The appropriate role on a multidisciplinary stage is not played by the same book as the role in a strictly social work agency. There is not an understudy or even a prompter—continuing the figure—who knows the part. Social casework in such circumstances must be articulate, self-defining, clinically responsible, and appropriately assertive within the function and the competence that support this function. Even where the social work service is large enough to be a substaff or department within the larger multidisciplinary setting (as in some hospitals), the demands of daily practice impose a substantial expectation on the worker as a professional practitioner vis-à-vis the practitioner of another profession. The result must necessarily be a growth of a self-conscious professional self that transcends, even as it serves, "agency." Possibly this fact—the necessities of work in a multidisciplinary setting—has sharpened the self-consciousness of branches of casework whose typical practice is with particular professions. Certainly these caseworkers have been spurred to an extraordinary amount of definitive work, mostly exploring

and fencing the boundaries of function, it is true, but also producing a goodly body of conceptualization and communicable know-how that is the admiration of other social workers. It also earns the respect of other professions, usually ungrudging.

The achievement of social work in pulling its weight on a team of several disciplines is added proof that social work can be practiced (with its social component) outside the traditional agency. This is so much a matter of course that the statement is a truism; but it is doubtful that the full import of the fact is generally grasped.

SOCIAL WORK is a helping or facilitating service to an individual, to a group, or to a community. An appropriate primary process (or method) is used, depending on the "object of the service": typically, social casework is used in working with an individual, social group work with a group, and social welfare organization with a community.

SOCIAL CASEWORK

To understand an individual's social problems and his difficulty, to assess his potential ability to deal with them, and to enable him to use this ability have been a goal of social work's activity from the beginnings of the profession. Variously defined with a degree of precision appreciated only by like-minded social workers, one approach to problems and the helping process is called "social casework." The term is not well understood by non-social workers, but as Bruno pointed out, social casework was the first process of social work to be defined in an educationally communicable technique. It became the dominant field and core of the profession.

Social casework has continued to advance in theory and concept structure, scientifically oriented, clinically tested and documented, clinically corrected, and possessing a uniformity of nomenclature not discernible in social group work or community organization. But the development has not been without its price. It has been necessary to recall casework to its social component in theory and in practice. The importance of the environment and of the client's response to its dynamics was brought out precisely or implicitly by a considerable array of speakers during the mid-century decade: Grace Marcus, Lucille Austin, Charlotte Towle, Eleanor Cockerill, Val Keating, Callman Rawley, among others.

"Periodically, we ask one another 'What is "social" about social casework?' as if to reassure ourselves of our identity," said Helen Harris Perlman in 1953, because of "our absorbed interest in the inner world of the personality and some loss of perspective about the outer world in which that personality lives. . . ." She saw the social components of casework practice implicit in the agency structure and equally in the complex within which the client lived with his problem. The fact of agency auspices is a necessary factor that prescribes the service to be offered, and possibly as a limit within which the social worker must operate, inasmuch as the agency stands for the social reality. Thus "it is not our methodology but the constructive, organized social purposes for which our methods are used which identify us both to ourselves and to others as caseworkers and as social workers too."

There are two polarities in the institutional structure of social casework in the agency. One is the caseworker's expectation that the community, having authorized the service through the agency, shall in other ways contribute to the individual citizen's welfare. (This might well underlie the caseworker's motive for social action.) The other is that the client shall be able, or be enabled, to find his solutions within the social standards or sanctions of his community. Clearly, the caseworker is not a professional buttress of status quo, or the apologist or advocate of a client's free-wheeling self-realization. A nice balance is required to help society recognize and provide for the satisfying of its citizens' normative needs, development, fulfillment; and at the same time to bring to the client a realistic, nonthreatening, self-motivating understanding of social expectations laid upon all community members.

This view considerably modifies the inept phrase, "the non-judgmental attitude of the social caseworker." There must be a constant estimate (or judgment) of what the community must do or is not doing in behalf of individual welfare; of what the client must do or must achieve in order to attain his best well-being. The saving point that makes this "nonjudgmental" is that the worker attempts to keep *personal* standards and views out of the equation. The yardstick is the community's, it is *social*. Many social caseworkers feel some discomfort over this, Mrs. Perlman said, after developing the view more clearly and at greater length than is here possible. The discomfort springs from several causes: "We have a burning conviction that the rights of the individual must vigilantly be guarded. . . . But the reality is that we cannot pit a man against his society nor lead him to isolation from it, because he is a societal creature." The values to which social caseworkers and most other people respond are so ingrained that their origin in the society and its conditioning are forgotten.

The social philosophy that underlies casework, the social auspice which sponsors it, the social aims it preserves, and the social focus it maintains "give casework its special character." Many papers in the *Proceedings* reflect this point of view. For example, Grace F. Marcus in 1955:

The distinctive purpose of social casework is to help the individual to find himself in his special relationships, to derive more benefit in his social living from the institutions existing to serve his social welfare, and to meet the shocks of social change without loss in himself or in direction in his life. The interaction between the human being and a dynamic industrial society is an essential part of the problem with which social casework is specifically engaged.[1]

Miss Marcus was speaking on the "advance of social casework": a realization that client problems are not peculiar to a class distinguished as financial, social, religious, racial, but are found throughout a society. Thus the clientele is not an inferior group that is to be molded to "the alleged interest of a superior one. Social casework has thus been purged of a bias which had justified the suspicion that its fundamental mission was blindly to preserve a status quo." From "helping the client to help himself," casework is now frequently realized "by means of a process in which the individual becomes the agent of change with support from the caseworker." Because casework faces weaknesses in the society, there is a new realism in facing needs and their causes. "Cultural lag" is identified as a factor, and social change is seen as a possibly dislocating impact on family living. Biology, anthropology, psychiatry, are part of a cluster of disciplines whose knowledge has combined to reinforce social casework in its belief that "invidious differences may no longer be regarded as innate in fixed classes, nations, or so-called 'races.' " New knowledge can now root the profession's convictions "implicit in our ethical and religious heritage, that hate and fear are the human being's most insidious inner enemies . . ."

Social work was open not only to new knowledge but to new tasks. It adapted itself to the demands of the military setting in the Second World War, to services to veterans, to education, industry, and to a greater partnership with other professions, who began to recognize a special contribution inherent particularly in the social casework equipment.

But the professional character continues. The literature of

[1] Grace F. Marcus, "The Advance of Social Casework" (1955), p. 22.

the mid-century decade quite consistently reflects a sober re-minder to casework that, in its traffic with problems of the individual in whatever setting, it is dealing with the individual in society; that the professional reason for being lies in the social component, sensitive, rounded, equable.

It might well be that multidisciplinary settings brought home the point that the caseworker's prime field lies in dis-covery, assessment, and use of the pertinent social data clinging to any client. The freedom of medical and psychiatric workers (and recently, of social group workers) to inquire into and define their peculiar function in the multidisciplinary setting had much to do with restoring the social component to prac-tice, even though some practitioners found the most highly skilled practice of their profession only in a deeper, inner therapy, frequently spoken of as if it had a reality apart from the society.

Granting this contribution from specialized casework prac-tice, it is equally likely that social work's typical self-evalua-tion and continuing analysis of its work led it constantly to the social phase of any problem whose solution must be in har-mony with the society. Social casework has seemingly demon-strated once again that its power should never be underesti-mated. It is able to resist anything except its own logic; and as a result it has modulated purposefully back into the dominant key of the profession. Clearly, it bids fair to continue to be *social* casework.

SOCIAL GROUP WORK

Social work's secret tool is the infinite untapped, unused, un-suspected capacity for growth in the sovereign individual per-sonality. As one speaker quoted, "Every sinner has the right to a future, just as every saint has a past." Of all types and breeds of social worker, the social group worker most consciously accepts this democratic premise in his work.

This specialized field is rich in democratic concepts; it has a wealth of examples; but in professionally unique concepts, "method theory," it has been curiously poor. Of all social work, social group work most commonly works with the least disadvantaged, at least to the extent that its clientele does not feel conspicuously deprived. It is possible that no social or economic class in a community is beyond profiting from what goes under the name of a "group experience." But it is difficult for a social group worker to communicate how and why this near-miracle happens, except to another group worker.

Social group work, in fact, produces a most versatile, able type of professional person; and an unusual number of social work leaders, valuable citizens, prove on inquiry to have a group work background. The slight tone of astonishment that can be read into this statement must not be misunderstood: it means that group workers tend to talk social work rather than social group work.

It dawns on an observer, after a bit, that social group work is essentially good citizenship, good human relationships, consciously practiced, exemplified, and communicated in an enabling way. In a casual gathering or in a committee room, for example, where every social worker is a guest and no one is a host, it is usually a group worker who inconspicuously and as a matter of course puts out and arranges chairs, empties ash trays, turns off the lights, closes windows that he has earlier opened. These services are not group work, obviously; they merely reflect its general thoughtfulness and responsibility. Above this white-collar janitorial level, it is the group worker who is the most sensitive to the other members of the group. He sees that the unpopular view gets heard. He believes in speaking up, taking issue, and in compromise to the end of agreement and action.

Social group work wants to face up to things, it is clear from the *Proceedings*. In 1955, to instance, Clara A. Kaiser called for a reexamination of practice in terms of "fundamental philosophical and scientific premises" because of the changes that were taking place. She clarified her meaning by quoting the hammer-blow eloquence of Dr. Robert Oppenheimer in his address given in honor of the Columbia University Bicentennial:

What is new in the world is the massive character of the dissolution and corruption of authority, in belief, in ritual, and in temporal order. Yet this is the world that we have come to live in. The very difficulties which it presents derive from growth in understanding, in skill, in power. . . . We need to recognize the change and learn what resources we have.[2]

The comment was pertinent to the social group work purpose of "enabling groups to achieve personally enriching and socially productive goals."

Reexamination of practice was seen in three parts: (1) a clearer definition of social group work's point of view and competence in furthering the social health of individual and community; (2) a review of the forms of group life for which social group work concepts and methods have meaning and what the practitioner needs to be effective in such context; (3) an appraisal of professional techniques in the light of new knowledge available. It was apparent that some groups (like teen-agers) tend to ignore or reject group work facilities at a time when these facilities are in demand in non-group work

[2] Robert J. Oppenheimer, "Prospect in the Arts and Sciences," in *Man's Right to Knowledge*, Second Series, "Present Knowledge and New Directions" (New York: Herbert Muschel, 1954; copyright Columbia University Press, 1955), pp. 111–12; quoted by Clara A. Kaiser, "The Advance of Social Group Work" (1955), pp. 34–35.

settings. In 1956 Gladys Ryland said that social group work in the medical setting has recently gone far beyond the earlier emphasis on recreational activities and now is used to strengthen the patient's ability to meet social conditions outside the hospital.

This growing demand for the social group worker as member of a treatment team was one factor that led Miss Kaiser to a far-reaching question: Is social group work still a specialized field or is it becoming, as she thought, "a full-fledged and recognized discipline basic to social work practice in many kinds of social services"? Not many social workers would agree with her, but many more would willingly say her question is foresighted, even prescient.

Gertrude Wilson's statement of a few selected concepts underlying the principles of work with groups (*Proceedings,* 1956) incidentally gives weight to Miss Kaiser's suggestion. The concepts implement basic assumptions that center on "a sense of belonging": that this sense is necessary to happiness; that it may be handicapped; that people may be helped to achieve it; that the skill in helping may be learned; and that social welfare depends on the interacting of its many small groups. A few of the ten concepts illustrate their nature: a group is the interaction of a collection of human beings; all groups are alike and all are different; all groups have a purpose, not necessarily conscious, which is expressed in the substance of the interaction; all groups originate either as "psycho" or "socio" groups—the first drawn together for the purpose of personal satisfaction, and the second, because of an external educational interest or common task; all groups experience conflict and exercise controls—the equilibrium or homeostasis of the group.

The concepts become operational through such principles as the following:

The enabler:

1. Respects all human beings and their social organizations through respecting their right to manage their own lives.

2. Accepts each individual and group as unique and the right of each to be different from every other.

3. Feels with individuals and groups without necessarily feeling like them.

4. Adjusts his behavior to his understanding of the behavior of the group.

6. Diagnoses where the group is and helps it to move on from there.

10. Recognizes the structure of interpersonal relations as an influential factor in group decisions.[3]

These principles dictate the use of various techniques, such as giving sociometric tests; discussing matters of interest to the members in their daily lives, not just the affairs of the group; using visual aids, arranging chairs in circle, and so on. The concepts and principles, at least, would seem acceptable to all social workers and might be used by them in appropriate situations.

Social group work has channeled the reemphasis on the sociological component in the professional equipment. Group workers more than others always have one eye on the social fact, the social norm. A social group worker, said Grace Coyle in 1949, "must be functioning in relation to some social objectives; however implicit or obscure they may be." At the same time Miss Wilson pointed to the social value: "No human being develops faith in isolation from others," and no one can contribute his share to the building of the road to a cooperative society unless he has had a group experience. Social work's "specialized knowledge of human needs and professional skill in helping people meet them place an additional obligation upon social workers."

[3] Gertrude Wilson, "Social Group Work Theory and Practice" (1956), pp. 151–52.

These comments suggest that the social group work agency has been a laboratory for democratic living, as Nathan E. Cohen said in 1949; but at mid-century the agency must include "working with the citizen of today if tomorrow is to become a certainty." (The extraordinary achievements in work with the aged underline the statement: with a growing proportion of aged in the population, it behooves a nation to see that they have a personally satisfying life and continue to be socially productive, on however small the scale, as age advances.)

Fast as social change was working in 1949, another six years brought further challenge: change at both ends of the population curve; an increase in size of the average family; mobility, urban to suburban; with suburban slums developing; shifts in racial and religious concentration, and resulting intergroup tensions; automation; mental health and juvenile delinquency problems; a greater interest in intergroup relations (owing to the Supreme Court decision on integration); and a general "groping for a more meaningful philosophy of life." Social group work was already responding to most of these events in constructive ways, but in volume and effectiveness these ways were inadequate even to that portion of the problem that could rightfully be considered suitable to social group work's solution.

Social group work has found a comfortable professional family in social work during the past thirty years—though who adopted whom is occasionally a question. The way has not been smooth. The younger member of the profession relied on social casework for many of its concepts. But the psychoanalytic view of the individual adapts poorly to the group, and its explanations by no means always consort with observed group facts. Then came a dynamic kind of sociology-anthropology: the concept of status, role, caste, and pattern, and the influence of the situation on conduct. Social group work responded to these sympathetic, explanatory, group-rooted ideas. Many workers share Cohen's belief that the social group work field is closer to these developments than is case-work and therefore should bring the ideas to social work as a whole. Social group work must take care, however, that its "scientific" preoccupation, its method, its process, do not leave behind a sense of moral values and a concern for the democratic social climate. The field has served this climate of democracy and democratic values very well indeed; and it owes more to this environment of goals and ethical premises than may be consciously apparent. The caveat here abridged from Cohen's paper (and with possible shift in emphasis) is not against science but against the use of science without the ethical measure of the common good.

SOCIAL WELFARE ORGANIZATION

The social worker is not the only community organizer. Organizers are all over the place, and very effective people they are. A chamber of commerce is one example; farm organizations are often another; each of course works from different viewpoints, motives and for different purposes. The social worker is typically in the health and welfare field of community concern; he attempts to increase and sharpen this concern and to establish democratic channels for its expression in effective action that improves community well-being. The means, techniques, process of achieving this, include data collection (facts surrounding an observed problem), analysis, discussion, recommendation, and public education.

Community organization as such is not plentifully reported in the *Proceedings*, partly because Community Chests and

Councils, Inc., through whose members most of the urban work is done, meets as an affiliated group and typically publishes its papers elsewhere; but partly because community organization activity is woven into the fabric of most of what social work does and thus appears in many of the papers that have another primary focus. The community organizers, however, formed an association for the study of their work, and there began to emerge a coherent body of fair consensus on the process and its nature.

Kenneth L. M. Pray said in 1947 that community organization is social work practice, and that practitioners can share in the development of a single profession of social work on three conditions: (1) if the focus is on guidance of a process that helps people find satisfying and fruitful social relationships, "not to the attainment of specific preconceived products of forms of relationship; (2) if a democratic philosophy permeates the process; (3) and if the worker directs himself to a helping, not a controlling relationship.

The community organization worker must begin to learn more ways of carrying out the basic principles of social work in the process of his job; for example, the scientific group process method is ethically congenial to the social worker, whereas the manipulation of groups (as a method) is an indefensible alternative. This view, held by Donald Van Valen (in 1949), is a fair gauge of the conceptual state of community organization and of progress in study of the nature of its process—a program of the Association for the Study of Community Organization. This special field of practice was in the familiar situation of achieving great things in a highly skilled manner before it knew quite how it was done, at least before knowing how to communicate its know-how. It is possible that the operating concepts of relationships carried over from the general social work viewpoint were the right concepts and not merely in default of better ones. Certainly the guiding principles seem indispensable.

The social worker helping a community to organize its social welfare is guided by the same principles stated and developed by Gordon Hamilton (1952) in discussing the role of social casework in social action: "Professional knowledge in use; ethical goals in methods (in human events means and end must equally be justified); and acceptance of the individual's right to be different . . ." [4] These principles gain point in the light of community organization function. The action is ultimately or residually citizens' action. The enablers who facilitate the action are not thereby "professional" citizens. (There is no such professional, since as a citizen everyone is a layman.) But the social worker may professionally assist and facilitate the citizen representatives with the utmost of his skill and knowledge, so long as decision is not his alone.

There is some ground for believing that community organization for social welfare suffers from the fact that its practice is task-oriented. A common road to a job in a community organization agency like a council of social agencies is practice in an agency offering services to clients. There have been exceptions, of course, and the exceptions increase as training facilities grow. But the great achievements of fund-raising, planning, community leadership, evaluation of resources, reorganization of welfare facilities—these are frequently accomplished by social workers who have a flair for, but no specialized training in, community organization. (Violet Sieder [1956] believed that the focus on the generic has put a heartier emphasis on group and community process.) It seems that every variety of social work practice involves a component of

[4] Miss Hamilton's paper, "The Role of Social Casework in Social Policy," was published in *Social Casework*, XXXIII (1952), 315–24; it was quoted by Patricia Sacks, "The Contribution of Mary Richmond to Current Casework Practice" (1953), p. 311.

social welfare organizing. Thus every social worker has *some* experience in it, consciously or not. The possibility that it may be unconscious is revealing.

Social welfare organization functions are carried on locally, state-wide, and nationally—more recently, internationally. But in a democracy the most important area is the local scene where service meets the need. In this respect it is regrettable that specialized community organization for social welfare is typically urban. The possibilities in the rural area are explored and the work done mostly by public welfare personnel and it is not always recognized as community organization, especially when it is well done. As to the rural community, a refreshing view was taken in 1953 by Charles E. Hendry, on the basis of a Canadian experience and some study of the Tennessee Valley Authority. His several assumptions: community organization (1) is not a monopoly of social work; (2) cannot be confined to any one narrow area of human need; (3) cannot be limited by arbitrary or artificial political or geographic boundaries; and (4) cannot rely chiefly on specialists who are only specialists. He quoted an Australian report at a Madras conference to the effect that there is a need for a multipurpose and multi-skilled social worker. And not only in Australia: Mrs. Agnes E. Meyer (1956) said that "the trend toward specialization in social work has led to such an emphasis on individual treatment and to the expansion of so many professional groups working independently of each other, that nobody is responsible for the family as a unit"; and on the Federal level there is no department to serve the family. "Yet we prate about the sacredness of the home . . ."

RESEARCH

Social work owes its growth and development as much to intuitive insight modified by evaluated clinical experience as to the findings of controlled experiments. It has sharpened itself as a profession quite as much by means of clinical observation sifted and shared as by *a priori* theorizing clinically tested.

To the extent that such an approach can be research or subject to research's discipline, the profession was hospitable to research; but it cannot be said that professionals were research-minded. The researchers in social work were conspicuous for their distinction and their rarity—in fact, ill-disposed social workers have said unfairly that the distinction came from the rarity. Philip Klein (1951) illustrated the fact that, bitter as critics of the profession may be, social workers are the readiest and often the sharpest in criticism of the field. Concerning research, he said that studies are rarely initiated by social workers; they rarely cooperate with research; and generally they adopt an attitude of "let the other fellow do it"—usually someone from another discipline. Klein thought the profession thus accumulated "safe and uncontroversial studies in neighboring and relevant fields," which in turn allowed "a curious aloofness from the findings." But the paper as a whole was optimistic.

The results of such studies as Klein mentions were valuable and laid the groundwork for major contributions to useful change in the social scene; but they supplied little guidance for the refinement of technique or method.

Schools of social work maintained a research component in the curriculum, and most of them demanded a thesis as a requirement for the degree; the larger agencies maintained a researcher on the staff; and research carried considerable prestige and respect wherever it went. Here and there it was even met with some understanding. But the basic defect was a different point; it is doubtful that many social workers felt any strong kinship with the whole process. Their lot as "researchers" in thesis writing was commonly dogged and painful, with a minute yield. Social work had not devised its own sovereign research approach; instead, as Klein said, it tended to borrow researchers from other disciplines; and frequently it aspersed their findings on this ground. More pertinently, social workers were skeptical of research's power to deal fruitfully with qualitative data of a subtle nature when the quality consisted of a fluid configuration of shifting variables observable only in an ever changing ("dynamic" was the usual word), interacting situation. The professional devotion to "the whole person" in his situation was repelled by the conventional research step of partializing. In the midst of such easy, sometimes shallow, criticism, few social workers realized that the difficulty would get no better until each of them took responsibility to use what research had to offer and adapted these useful tools to social work needs.

This need, the steps to take, and the generating motive to take them began to be apparent in the 1940s, more commonly in the later years of the decade. Characteristically, the profession was most troubled by one of its weaknesses: the lack of validation of its method, of its assumptions or concepts. The time was ripe: there was a growing tendency to conceptualize that multiplied available training time, increased applicability of ideas by allowing new contexts, and promised feasible testing of theories.

A major study along this line was carried out (1950) by J. McVicker Hunt and Leonard S. Kogan for the Community Service Society of New York on the development of a "scale" or measurement of movement in cases receiving casework service. It was a major achievement. Within the broad assignment "to determine and express how casework is carried on, at what cost, and with what success," Hunt and associates conceived their study as primarily methodological; their work represents a milestone in the profession. It has been criticized (by Klein specifically in 1951) for its limited types of cases, its narrow view of casework, and its omission of casework oriented to the "functional" persuasion. But the study needs no defense for its field of inquiry. By rigorous scientific methods, it developed a measure by which workers of like training and competence found themselves in more than moderate agreement in their estimate of cases. This result has had more than a little to do with the increasing regard for social work research observable among casework practitioners.

Questions about the best use of casework skill were raised by a study of the unit cost of casework service in Family Service of Philadelphia during the fiscal year 1951–52; and John G. Hill and Ralph Ormsby, who directed the study, reported the findings and implications in 1953. This frank effort to cost-account services opened eyes to the possible importance of such information in agency planning and administration. Costs labeled "casework" were the overwhelming share of the total, but the "resources devoted to client interviewing, the place where casework has meaning for the client, seems to be small"—42 percent for interviewing, 32 percent for case recording. Ormsby reported a number of steps to redress the balance: reduction of case recording, oral supervisory presentation, release of caseworkers from detailed compilation of "much seldom-used data," relief from some time-consuming meetings, and other "time-hallowed" practices. Results, it seems, cannot be quick because "the conditioned reflexes of long-established methods and routines are not changed overnight." A goal of the agency is the establishment of various standards for distribution of resources and for "production" by the staff.

With this tendency to test practice by research criteria—whether new or accentuated is difficult or uncharitable to say—came a near consensus on "social work research" as the proper term to use. It was a creation of wishful thinking, but it indicated the intent and the hopeful direction of development. Usage is still not uniform. In 1951, when the *Proceedings* had a large section devoted to research, the title was "Research in Social Welfare," reflecting the community emphasis in the focus of the papers.

Even social work research was not exempt from the warning not to forget the "social" in its name. Ewan Clague, in 1951, made a special point of reminding social workers that natural scientists "felt the necessity for supplementing pure research with a consideration of value judgments and social objectives" and he urged that social scientists should do likewise. He might have been implying that the wish or the need of the social scientist to be a cold "thinking machine," following his data and his method aloof from or blind to social values, detracts from his maturity as a scientist, however mature he may be as a technician; but the effect was to reassure the social workers who cherish their professional value system and fear its disruption under a scientific scrutiny devoid of social values. Granted that social workers, as well as other citizens, use the phrase "value system" oftener than they define it, these fears were not groundless. Clague's comfort had point.

The social value dimension has never been absent in the writings of social work research leaders, but the effort to achieve scientific objectivity and the discussion of the need for this approach in social work have possibly alarmed some social workers who might have misunderstood the researchers. The profession as a whole, however, continues to dream of a future in which assumptions (some of them value premises) will yield to research's experiments and thereby acquire a less precarious standing; in which methods will lose their mystique and gain precision and economy; in which cause and result may be now and then predicted without an act of faith; and in which the profession can take its place in the community of the professions with a more communicable technique and an understandable nomenclature, both expressing a substantial body of scientific knowledge. Pending so fine a consummation, however devoutly to be wished, a social worker might say that a body must have something to tie to, and the values of the society are the best available.

INDEX

Health insurance (*Continued*)
403; voluntary, 403-5; governmental, 406
Health services, need for Federal funds for, 400-401
Healy, William, 172, 173, 189, 295
Henderson, Charles R., 73, 136, 258, 260, 261
Henderson, Leon, 228, 372
Hendry, Charles E., 277, 430
Henry Street Settlement, New York, district nursing a unique function of, 118-19
Heredity, Dugdale's concept of, 50, 51
Hester, Mary, 275
Higgins, George G., cited, 374
Hill, John G., 433
Hill-Burton Act, 401
Hoadley, George, 89
Hodson, William H., 171-72, 195, 196, 355; quoted, 319-20, 321
Hoey, Jane, 340
Hoffer, Joe R., 368, 380
Hoffman, Frederick L., 258, 259, 336
Hofstein, Saul, 286
Hollingsworth, H. H., 254
Hollis-Taylor report, 409-10, 412
Home, importance of, to children, 56; right of state to remove children from unsuitable, 63; White House Conference on Child Welfare (1909) recognized value of, 177
Hooper, Bertha Freeman, 364
Hoover, Herbert C., 165, 303; quoted, 298, 302
Hopkins, Harry, 305; quoted, 249
Hospital Act of 1950, 385
Hospitals, proposals for coöperative, 243-44; for mentally ill: lack of, until nineteenth century, 44; cost of buildings, 45, 46; claims of cures questioned, 48; mismanagement of, 91
Housing, interest of Conference in, 225-27; Conference discussions (1928-46), 349-51; social problems created by housing projects, 351
Housing Reform (Vailler), 227n

Howard, Donald, 380; cited, 373, 385-86, 391
"Howard R. Knight and the International Conference of Social Work" (Kahn), 368n
Howe, Samuel Gridley, 11, 17, 51
How the Other Half Lives (Riis), 72
Hull House, Chicago, opened by Jane Addams and Ellen Gates Starr, 112; its founding directly inspired by Toynbee Hull, 115; varied program and activities of, 115-16; residents of, 118
Hull House Maps and Papers (Addams), 113, 117
Human relationships, application of scientific principles in study of, 4; theory of evolution in study of, 25 ff.
Human rights, *see* Civil liberties and civil rights
Hungry Club, Pittsburgh, 146
Hunt, J. McVicker, 432
Huxley, Thomas H., applied theory of evolution to social phenomena, 25

Ihlder, John, 350
Illegitimacy, concern of Children's Bureau with problems of, 155-56
Illinois, cottage system for insane patients created at Kankakee, 15; Governor's message to legislature on creation of state board, 31, 33; credited with first juvenile court, 169; passed law entitled "Funds to Parents Act," 178, 179; adopted "cabinet" form of administration of public welfare, 299
Illinois State Board of Charities, F. H. Wines's long tenure as secretary of, 14
Illiteracy, correlation of agricultural child workers with, 167
Immigrants, handbook for guidance of, published by American Social Science Association, 5n; capitation tax on, 122-23; danger of becoming public charges, 123-24; second generation presents real problem of assimilation, 124

Smith, T. V., quoted, 392-93
Smith, Zilpha D., 146, 183, 184, 278; biography, 99-100; quoted, 108
Smith College, Training School for Social Workers, 284
Snow, William F., 250
Social action, defined, 352
Social agencies, belief that relief given by private agencies preferable to public relief, 73; Ohio and Iowa employed private agencies to investigate public agencies, 77; fund-raising task of, 192; evaluation by council of social agencies, 196; general domination in councils of social agencies by private, 196-97; coöperation between, when serving same person, 276; interexchange of experiences and records, 279; training of personnel by apprenticeship, 279; role of, 414-16; casework and structure of, 418-19
Social casework, *see* Casework
Social change, causes of, discovered by scientific method, 25 ff.
"Social Consequences of the Immigration Law" (Addams), 327
Social Control of the Mentally Deficient (Davies), 51n
Social Diagnosis (Richmond), 100, 143, 186
"Social Function of Case Work" (Lee), 184
Social group work, its aim: to realize social capacity of individual, 270; difficulty of defining, 272; influenced by progressive education, 272; accepted (1935) as one of major activities of Conference, 273; as defined by Grace Coyle, 274; often serves same person as casework, 275-76; therapeutic influence upon children with behavior problems, 276; influence of Freud on, 277; only professionally trained worker used in, for therapeutic purposes, 277; social group worker, definition of, 274; coöperation with volunteers, 274-75; role of, 421-27

"Social Group Work Theory and Practice" (Wilson), 425n
Social hygiene, its place in Western civilization, 252 ff.; proposals made for teaching matters of sex to children, 253, 254; attempts to individualize treatment of prostitute, 255
Social insurance, invented in Germany, 257; created wide interest in early part of twentieth century, 258 f.; must include compulsion to be effective, 260; opposition of private insurance to, 260; Brandeis' arguments for, 262-63; constitutionality of compulsory insurance law upheld by Supreme Court, 264; combination of varied interests opposed to, 265; for the aged, 266-67; unemployment insurance last project in, 267; complete coverage far from achieved, 268; New Zealand's comprehensive act (1944), 269
Social policy, 370-81
Social problems, leaders of Conference accepted scientific approach to, 26; since 1910 programs on, a regular part of every Conference, 221; as result of first World War, 237-38
Social reform, far-reaching influence of settlements on, 117-19; concern of the Conference with, 220-29
Social research, 117
Social sciences, areas of, defined by American Social Science Association, 4, 5; statistical interpretation as method of, 5; contributions to study of charity, 134; courses in, offered by colleges, 134
Social Security Act, 224, 306, 315-21; encouraged development of public service to children, 61; established right of dependent to assistance in three categories, 126; restored maternal and child health services in rural districts, 158; Aid to Dependent Children, 178; health excluded from insurance provisions of, 265; allows states to choose either

Urban League, 393

Vagrancy, *see* Tramps
Vaile, Gertrude, 211-13, 234, 299
Vanderlip, Frank A., quoted, 261
Van Valen, Donald, cited, 428
Veiller, Lawrence, 227
Venereal disease, concern of social work with, 249, 252-55
Verry, Ethel, 288
Veterans, disability compensations paid to, and death compensations to dependents of, 231; bonuses to, paid by Federal Government and states, 231-32; problems of, in returning to civilian life, 236; vocational reeducation for injured, 236; facilities for treating neuropsychiatric, after first World War, 236-37
Veterans Administration, employment of social workers by, 319; mental health program of, 406-7
Veterans' Bureau, 232; use of social casework, 286
Visiting teachers, 291, 296; *see also* School social worker
Vives, J. L., 97
Vladeck, B. Charney, 350
Volker, William, 209-10
Volunteers, in care of the insane, 49; auxiliary women's group in Massachusetts to aid girl delinquents, 62; their functions in Eastern charity societies, 103, 104, 105; in probation work, 174

Wagner, Robert F., 313, 315, 401
Wagner-Murray-Dingell bill, 313
Waite, Edward F., quoted, 171
Wald, Lillian D., quoted, 116; 118-19, 152
Wanamaker, Claudia, 275
Wards, Robert A., 237
Warner, Amos G., biography, 100-101
Warner, Beverly, 336
Washington, Booker T., 336
Washington, George, 333
Wassermann, August von, 250
Wayland, Francis, 72

Weismann, August, 52
Welch, William H., 243
Welfare, and national economy, 374-77
Welfare work, advanced by men exercising supervisory functions, 38; increasing participation of states in, 42, 43; changed from public relief to public welfare, 207-13; care of needy sick, 241; participation of Federal Government believed unconstitutional, 259; need to evaluate methods, 279; "cabinet" form of administration of public, 299; Federal-state relations in depression, 303-7; *see also* Social work
Weller, Charles F., 104
West, Walter, 312
"What Have We Learned about Unemployment?" (Billikopf), 301
"What Is Social Group Work?" (Newstetter), 273
"What We Believe" (Youngdahl), 371*n*
When Social Work Was Young (Devine), 250
White, Albert S., 63
White, Alfred T., quoted, 225-26
White, William Allen, 222; quoted, 313-14
White, William C., 249
Whitehead, A. N., quoted, 372
White House Conference on Children and Youth, Midcentury, 377-79
White House Conference on Child Welfare (1909), 152, 177
Whitton, Charlotte, 329
Widowed Mothers' Fund Association, 181
Wiggin, Frederick H., 241
Wilbur, Charles T., opened school for feeble-minded, 51, 52
Wilcox, Mary, *see* Glenn, Mrs. John M.
Wile, Ira S., 253-54
Williams, Aubrey W., 268
Williams, Edward M., 200, 203
Williamsburg, Va., hospital for insane, 44